FAMILY THERAPY

Basic Concepts and Terms

S. Richard Sauber, Ph.D.
Columbia University
Luciano L'Abate, Ph.D.
Georgia State University
Gerald R. Weeks, Ph.D.
Marriage Council of Philadelphia

with a Foreword by Murray Bowen, M.D.

AN ASPEN PUBLICATION®
Aspen Systems Corporation
Rockville, Maryland
Royal Tunbridge Wells
1985

Library of Congress Cataloging in Publication Data

Sauber, S. Richard.
Family Therapy.

"An Aspen publication."
1. Family psychotherapy—Dictionaries. I. L'Abate,
Luciano, 1928- . II. Weeks, Gerald R., 1948- .
III. Title.
RC488.5.S27   1985   616.89'156'0321   84-18589
ISBN: 0-89443-556-6

Publisher: John R. Marozsan
Associate Publisher: Jack W. Knowles, Jr.
Editorial Director: Margaret M. Quinlin
Executive Managing Editor: Margot G. Raphael
Managing Editor: M. Eileen Higgins
Editorial Services: Scott Ballotin
Printing and Manufacturing: Debbie Collins

Library of Congress Catalog Card Number: 84-18589
ISBN: 0-89443-556-6

Printed in the United States of America

1 2 3 4 5

Table of Contents

List of Figures

Foreword

Family Therapy: Basic Concepts and Terms is the first family therapy dictionary that goes beyond the scope of a glossary. The authors have struggled for years with the problem. The literature burgeons, the number of family therapists proliferates, and new practitioners want to know more and more about ideas that govern the field. The authors have responded to the demand with a dictionary, which represents the way people understand the terminology. Rather than survey all the involved originators, the authors have used the device of going back to the literature to define terms the way they were used by the originating writers.

I have written this foreword to compliment the effort of those who have done this book, without becoming involved in all the detail about me, or anyone else. The authors are serious people who have done their best, whether old-timers agree or disagree. They have made an attempt to get beyond the maze of polarized personal opinions and to report the field as it exists today. They have made a contribution to the literature. The book is the best of its kind, to date. A copy of the book should be available to the entire profession, to the increasing number of family therapists, and to the hordes of students who hope to become family therapists.

It is difficult for me to write without some idea about the chaos and explosion in the family therapy field. Psychoanalysis, which began in the late nineteenth century, was the first of the psychological theories about human behavior. Its difference from medicine brought up the issue of nonmedical analysts. Psychoanalysis focused on the principle of psychopathology within the patient, which was treated in the analytic relationship. Poorly defined family ideas sur-

faced from time to time. Group therapy evolved in the 1930s. One can only guess why formal family research was delayed until the late 1940s and early 1950s. The research revealed a number of phenomena never previously reported in the literature. It gave voice to some smoldering ideas about family therapy that had existed in isolation. The research led to discussion about family therapy at a national meeting in March 1957.

I have been active in psychiatry since the mid 1940s, and active in the family field since its beginning in the mid 1950s. The explosion of family therapy starting in 1957 began immediately after it became a recognized open subject. Ideas about therapy displaced previous ideas about history and more complex notions about theory. Dozens of new professional people from divergent theoretical backgrounds began performing "therapy." New therapists quickly became teachers. Each teacher taught succeeding groups of trainees, who in turn became practitioners and teachers. As concepts passed from one generation of students to the next, the ideas were amplified, simplified, and distorted to fit the prevailing orientation of the teacher.

The first professional journal, *Family Process*, appeared early in 1962. Societal facts played a part. Mental health legislation in the early 1960s was designed to make services available to the masses. Family therapists were employed in the increasing network of mental health centers. The idea of "systems" became a catchword that helped define family therapy as different. There was an increase in the number of family institutes, where groups of teachers worked together for teaching and professional exchange. During the 1960s, the institutes began admitting those who had masters degrees in a discipline that dealt with human behavior. Psychiatry gradually moved away from its psychoanalytic orientation toward a more biological drug orientation. A big change and new growth came in the late 1970s when the government agreed that family therapy was new and different, and qualified to be a discipline on its own, without responsibility to the other professions. This all stimulated a rapid growth in the number of family therapists, family journals, and family meetings of all kinds. At the present time the field is in a state of explosion that is without parallel in my professional experience. The rapid growth and the profusion of terminology have been a powerful force in the writing of this dictionary.

The authors have done a credible job in defining the multiple terms in use today. I believe the rapid growth of past decades will continue into the foreseeable future. At some time in future years we may even look back on the good old days of 1984 as they were defined by this unique book. I hope the authors will have the energy to publish successive volumes as new terms come into use.

My own interest is more theoretical than therapeutic. One can only wonder about what will be taking place a century from now. I believe there is a powerful theoretical potential in the basic family idea, and that verifiable facts from the human family may eventually merge with other verifiable facts from other accepted sciences. The big hurdle comes from feelings that are not verifiable, but are still important to human experience. When feelings and imagination can be viewed as functional facts, they can contribute rather than detract from a final view of that part of man that is scientific. Brain research may help to close the gap.

Murray Bowen, M.D.
The Family Center
Washington, D.C.

Preface

The current proliferation of books and viewpoints in the field of family therapy demands that the student as well as the professional have available a ready reference that contains many of the new terms that have been coined in the past decade and earlier. This dictionary attempts to satisfy this need; the book has been long in the making. At the beginning of the 1970s, Roberta Golden, Ph.D. (then a graduate student), at Dr. L'Abate's prompting, started a glossary of family sociology terms. This early glossary, which was stenciled, lay dormant but was made available to interested professionals. Among those who received it was Richard Sauber, who used it in his seminars at Brown University and found it helpful to students and professionals alike. Dr. Sauber eventually asked Dr. L'Abate to collaborate on a full-fledged dictionary. The project proved to be so massive that several years later Gerald Weeks was asked to join in the effort. After calls to our colleagues, we started to receive definitions and examples from friends, colleagues,

and students. Eventually, the number of terms grew beyond our expectations and our plans. Finally, however, the work was completed. We are very grateful to all those—far too many to name—who contributed.

There are three major needs for a dictionary in the family therapy field: (1) as already noted, the need for a ready reference; (2) the need for a bibliographical source, where the student or the professional can find the original source of a term and its theoretical or practical origin; and (3) the need for a summary of the many viewpoints and sources that have by now proliferated beyond the command of any one person. Original citations are listed under "*Source*" and recent references under "*Quoted*" to provide additional information about the definitions. One cannot find under one cover the contributions that have mushroomed in family therapy in the past two decades. This dictionary thus attempts to condense into one volume many of the terms in the field and also to indicate the pragmatic use of each.

Acknowledgments

Writing a dictionary is probably the most difficult and tedious academic project that we have undertaken. Our work began in 1978, and we would still be adding and revising terms to this day if our publisher had not informed us that there were limits on the number of pages and it was time to go to press.

During our initial years of referencing, there were three major glossaries in the family therapy literature that were available to us. These included the works of Robert A. Golden at the Family Study Center of Georgia State University and the articles by Jules Riskin and Elaine E. Faunce, and by Michael J. Gerson and Marilyn Barsky published in *Family Process* (1972) and the *American Journal of Family Therapy* (1979), respectively.

We also wish to acknowledge the following colleagues who personally contributed concepts to our dictionary: Daniel L. Araoz, Ben N. Ard, Jr., Joanna R. Baisden, Arthur M. Bodin, Murray Bowen, Albert Ellis, Edmond F. Erwin, S.I. Greensdan, Fortune V. Mannino, M. Livia Osborn, Daniel R. Panitz, Gerald R. Patterson, and Robert A. Ravich. Many others contributed definitions and are acknowledged with their contributed entries throughout the text.

Our secretaries deserve recognition for their endless retyping efforts and attentiveness to detail: Linda Benevides for S. Richard Sauber, Marie Morgan for Luciano L'Abate, and Martha Jo Clemmons for Gerald R. Weeks. Carolyn Windham freely offered hours of editorial assistance, reviewing the manuscript for its technical quality. Sheila Phillips and Richard Loren also spent many hours tracking down elusive references and terms.

Finally, we appreciate the contribution of the countless individuals, colleagues, friends, and students who helped us in this enormous task.

S. Richard Sauber
Luciano L'Abate
Gerald R. Weeks

A

abortive runaways: An attempt to run away from home that does not succeed. The child either returns home after a short period of time or else contrives a situation in which the child will be retrieved by parents or other authorities.
Source: Stierlin, H. (1974). *Separating parents and adolescents.* New York: Quadrangle.

absence of involvement: A family in which members show no interest in each other except to share their instrumental functions.
Example: A family may operate smoothly insofar as their daily activities are concerned but not share any personal thoughts or feelings.
Source: Epstein, N., Bishop, D., & Levin, S. (1978). The McMaster model of family functioning. *Journal of Marriage and Family Counseling,* 4, 19–31.
Quoted: Epstein, N., & Bishop, D. (1981). Problem-centered systems therapy of the family (pp. 444–482). In A.S. Gurman & D.P. Kniskern (Eds.), *Handbook of family therapy.* New York: Brunner/Mazel.

absent member maneuver: A major form of resistance in family therapy, believed to be an attempt on the part of the family to preserve its system and pattern of functioning. One member of the family is not present in the session(s) in order to preserve fixed paired relationship patterns in the family. The maneuver involves the cooperation of the entire family.
Example: A father is given an assignment that involves spending more time with his son. Normally, the father would not spend any time with him because the father worked long hours. Also, there is covert conflict in the marriage that is not recognized by the couple because of their focus on the son. The father is absent in the session following the assignment in order to keep the present system intact.
Source: Sonne, J., Speck, R., & Jungreis, J. (1962). The absent member maneuver as a resistance in family treatment of schizophrenics. *Family Process, 1*, 44–62.
Quoted: Gerson, M., & Barsley, M. (1979). For the new family therapist: A glossary of terms. *American Journal of Family Therapy, 7*, 15–30.

accelerated change: An immediate change in behavior in relation to one's spouse, produced through a planned strategy.
Example: The therapist gives a prescription aimed at reversing self/other defeating, repetitious, transactional patterns between the couple. The prescription stresses action, not interpretation.
Source: Papp, P. (1976). Brief therapy with couples groups. In P. Guerin (Ed.), *Family therapy: Theory and practice* (pp. 350–363). New York: Gardner Press.

accession process: The addition of unwanted arrivals to the family, such as newborns, adopted children, and elderly parents.
Source: Reiss, D. (1980). Pathways to assessing the family. In C. Hofling & J. Lewis (Eds.), *The family: Evaluation and treatment* (pp. 86–92). New York: Brunner/Mazel.

accommodation: A tactic in which the therapist makes personal adjustments in order to join with the family; a calculated move used to achieve a therapeutic alliance by appearing to be similar to the family. (See **mimesis** and **joining**.)
Example: The male therapist removes his coat and tie for a family that comes to the session in shirt sleeves.
Source: Minuchin, S. (1974). *Families and family therapy.* Cambridge: Harvard University Press.
Quoted: Gerson, M., & Barsky, M. (1979). For the new family therapist: A glossary of terms. *American Journal of Family Therapy, 7*, 15–30.

accordion family: A type of family in which one parent is away for extended periods of time. The other parent then assumes the responsibilities of the

1

missing parent—e.g., nurturing, organizing—until that parent returns.

Example: The husband works for an international corporation that requires him to reside for several months in foreign countries. His spouse works out expected behaviors and family routines during the absence of her husband.

Source: Minuchin, S., & Fishman, H. (1982). *Family therapy techniques.* Cambridge: Harvard University Press.

achievement-sensitive families: Families that work competitively to master problems and whose members are optimistic about their individual abilities. Such families have also been clinically described as having a nasty view of people, with the parents bitter and angry at the children.

Example: The youngest of three brothers becomes a race car driver. His older brothers' success in school and eventually becoming doctors has engendered resentment on his part. He begins racing cars in high school, despite his parents' objections, and even their disapproval, despite his winning in many contests. He now receives more public recognition and attention than his brothers.

Source: Reiss, D. (1981). *The family's construction of reality.* Cambridge: Harvard University Press.

acting "as if": An action-oriented intervention in which one or both partners are instructed to behave as they wish they could but believe they cannot at the present time.

Source: Baruth, L.G., & Huber, C.H. (1984). *An introduction to marital theory and therapy.* Monterey, Calif.: Brooks/Cole.

acting out: The enactment of unconscious tension in the form of disruptive behavior. The behavior is associated with poor frustration tolerance, poor reality testing, and a tendency toward repetition compulsion. Defined from a family systems perspective, acting out is symptom-activated when a family is undergoing stress; it reflects back to cyclical, sequential patterns that may be referred to as operating principles, e.g., boundary dysfunction, systemic void, systemic intensity, and systemic rocking. In many cases, several of these principles may operate at once; in fact, one may lead to another.

Source: Carter, E.A., and McGoldrick, M. (1980). The family life cycle and family therapy: An overview. In E.A. Carter and M. McGoldrick (Eds.), *The family life cycle* (pp. 3–20). New York: Gardner Press.

action learning: A type of psychotherapy in which emphasis is placed on nonverbal exchanges and direct observation. Often, in this form of therapy, what the therapist does is much more important than what the therapist says; the model the therapist provides is rapidly internalized and effective, in contrast to the slow process of change accompanying traditional psychotherapies.

Example: Rather than talk about assertiveness with a client, the therapist models and role plays with the client, forcing interaction.

Source: Skynner, A.C.R. (1976). *Systems of family and marital psychotherapy.* New York: Brunner/Mazel.

active listening: A technique of listening to, reflecting comments from, and questioning clients in order to assist them in focusing and clarifying thoughts and feelings.

Example:

Therapist:	What do you want to tell your husband?
Client:	I don't want to tell him anything.
Therapist:	You say you don't want to tell him anything, but the way you just said that sounded like you're angry.
Client:	Yes, I guess I didn't realize just how angry I was about it.

Here the therapist uses active listening to focus on the underlying feelings of anger. The therapist may reflect not only what is said but also how it is said.

Source: Gordon, T. (1982). *P.E.T. in action.* New York: Bantam.

activity catharsis: The therapeutic release of feelings through activity or the acting out of conflicts as opposed to the verbal catharsis of an analytic therapy.

Example: A man experiences both hostility and hate. He is allowed to claim a piece of wood he has cut to look like a spear. He walks around saying he will kill anyone who crosses his path. The effect of redirecting his feelings through activity toward family members as substitutes helps the man feel relieved.

Source: Slavson, S. (1943). *An introduction to group therapy.* New York: Commonwealth Fund.

activity group therapy: A type of therapy, primarily for children and adolescents, in which group activities are used for therapeutic purposes.

Example: A withdrawn adolescent female is given a nonverbal task to perform. The task may be as

simple as handing an object to another family member. A discussion follows to engender experience-based learning, utilizing the here and now.
Source: Slavson, S. (1943). *An introduction to group therapy.* New York: Commonwealth Fund.

activity-interview group psychotherapy: A therapy for children involving group-play psychotherapy and individual interviews within the context of the group. This approach was designed for seriously disturbed latency-aged children.
Example: A child is given an opportunity to engage in play with other children in order to provide observational data on social interactions and personal behavior.
Source: Slavson, S. (1943). *An introduction to group therapy.* New York: Commonwealth Fund.

actuality therapy: A type of family therapy concerned with happenings in the present family. Psychic traumas arising within and outside the family are dealt with in the present, even though the problem may stem from some past event. Treatment at this level is oriented to restoring the individual to the pretrauma period.
Example: A mother presents with depression that first occurred when her daughter married. The current depressive episode was triggered by a phone call from the daughter. The actuality therapist would be interested in the current family situation that produced the problem.
Source: Howells, J. (1975). *Principles of family psychotherapy.* New York: Brunner/Mazel.

actualizing tendency: An "inherent tendency of the organism to develop all its capacities in ways which serve to maintain or enhance the organism." The movement is toward more autonomy and away from control by others. The construct includes other concepts of motivation, such as need reduction, tension reduction, and drive reduction.
Example: A healthy functioning family allows its members to develop ways of fulfilling individual potentials *within and without* the family context.
Source: Rogers, C. (1959). A theory of therapy, personality and interpersonal relationships, as developed in the client-centered framework. In S. Koch (Ed.), *Psychology: A study of a science, Vol. III. Formulations of the person and the social context* (pp. 175–213). New York: McGraw-Hill.
Quoted: Horne, A.M., & Ohlson, M.M. (1982). *Family counseling and therapy.* Itasca, Ill.: F.F. Peacock Publishers.

adversary system: A system that purports to help individuals resolve their differences but is likely to prolong and intensify hostilities and cause psychopathological behavior.
Example: In divorce proceedings, litigants are often provided with weapons to use against one another that they may not have realized they possessed. A wife may be advised by her divorce attorney to request 90 percent of her husband's income and all of their marital property and to withhold visitation with the children's father unless he pays her desired alimony and child support. Thus, attorneys often contribute to an increasingly vicious cycle of vengeance. Disputes are unnecessarily prolonged, and the hardship on both parties is often greatly increased. The divorce proceedings may in this way cause greater psychological pain to the parties than the marriage that brought about the decision for divorce in the first place.
Source: Gardner, R.A. (1982). *Family evaluation in child custody litigation.* Cresskill, N.J.: Creative Therapeutics.
Quoted: Marlow, L., and Sauber, S.R. (in press). *Handbook on Divorce Mediation.* New York: Brunner/Mazel.

advisory attorney: An attorney used in family mediation disputes. While the role of impartial advisory attorney is relatively new, lawyers have demonstrated their ability to move from the role of advocate into impartial roles, such as that of judge or arbitrator, often serving with distinction in the impartial role.

The advisory attorney first appears when the mediator and the couple believe they have arrived at a working settlement. The advisory attorney must refine this tentative agreement, as explained by the parties and the mediator, into a clearly worded legal agreement in a relatively short time. The agreement must be one that can be understood and followed by the parties in their ongoing relationship after divorce.

The attorney's knowledge, experience, and sensitivity in addressing the needs of the family's post-divorce relationships (including support, custody, and visitation) must equal the attorney's professional skill in dealing with property, legal questions, and tax-saving options. The attorney's impartiality must be beyond question. With a thorough understanding of the settlement arrangements developed by the mediator and the parties, the attorney must then draft the settlement document as a legal entity and present it to the parties, making sure that it conforms with their agreement.

Source: Coogler, O.J. (1978). *Structured mediation in divorce settlement.* Lexington, Mass.: Lexington Books.

affect: The feelings, short- and long-term, expressed in the family. Affect comprises the expression of feelings, moods, and tones (the emotional statement of the family), the degree of irresolvable conflict in the family, and the judgment of the amount of empathy present.

Example: Family members who discharge their aggressive impulses toward one another and also toward outsiders can be characterized as a hostile family.

Source: Beavers, W.R. (1977). *Psychotherapy and growth: A family systems perspective.* New York: Brunner/Mazel.

affect bridge: A sex hypnotherapy technique by which the client is directed to experience unpleasant feelings connected with a sexual problem and then to intensify the feelings until they become a memory bridge to a previous event in the client's life.

Example: A man suffers from erectile dysfunction. When he experiences the affect bridge, he remembers losing an erection once during homosexual play as a child.

Source: Araoz, D. (1982). *Hypnosis and sex therapy.* New York: Brunner/Mazel.

affection phase: The last stage of ideal group psychotherapy in which the members experience equality with the therapist and feel affection toward one another, with free expression of positive and negative feelings. In this phase, dependency and aggressive feelings are normal.

Example: A family member expresses toward the therapist or another member how angry she felt when that person interrupted or how secure she felt when another family member came to her rescue when she was "attacked."

Source: Kaplan, S., & Roman, M. (1963). Phases of development in an adult therapy group. *International Journal of Group Psychotherapy, 13,* 10.

affective binding: The exploitation of dependency needs with emphasis on regressive gratification. This process results in a fostered dependency that binds the individual, usually a child, to the family system. (See also **id binding.**)

Example: A man visits his parents and begins to play games with them by hiding in different places in the house. The parents act out the game in a ritualistic manner, giving the man approval, affec-

tion, and love. Otherwise the parents are cold and stern.

Source: Stierlin, H. (1974). *Separating parents and adolescents: A perspective on running away, schizophrenia and waywardness.* New York: Quadrangle Books.

affective disorders: A disorder of mood characterized by feelings of pervasive meaninglessness and emptiness.

Example: A middle child suffers from alienation feelings, finding no special place in his family with male siblings one year older and one year younger than he.

Source: Singer, M., & Wynne, L. (1965). Thought disorders and family relations of schizophrenics, III. Methodology using projective techniques. *Archives of General Psychiatry, 12,* 127–200.

Quoted: Foley, V. (1974). *An introduction to family therapy.* New York: Grune & Stratton.

affective involvement: The degree to which a family shows interest in and values the activities of other family members. The degree of involvement may range from none to a fusion of feelings.

Example: A wife may be overinvolved with her husband to the extent that she cannot separate her feelings from his.

Source: Epstein, N., Bishop, D., & Levin, S. (1978). The McMaster model of family functioning. *Journal of Marriage and Family Counseling, 4,* 19–31.

Quoted: Barker, P. (1981). *Basic family therapy.* Baltimore: University Park Press.

See also **enmeshment, symbiosis.**

affectivity rationality: Delineation of couples who react primarily on an emotional basis, as compared with those who react primarily on a logical basis, in trying to resolve a conflict situation.

Example: A couple might approach a conflict rationally by talking about different alternatives. On the other hand, they could approach the conflict affectively by expressing their feelings.

Source: Ryder, R., & Goodrich, D. (1966). Married couples' responses to disagreement. *Family Process, 5,* 30–42.

Quoted: Gerson, M., & Barsky, M. (1979). For the new family therapist: A glossary of terms. *American Journal of Family Therapy, 7,* 15–30.

affective responsiveness: The ability of the family to respond to a range of stimuli with the appropriate quality and quantity of feelings. The affective responses include welfare feelings (e.g., love, tenderness, joy) and emergency feelings (e.g., fear, anger, depression).

Source: Epstein, N., Bishop, D., & Levin, S. (1978). The McMaster model of family functioning. *Journal of Marriage and Family Counseling,* *4*, 19–31.

affiliation: A psychological motive to be with other people or to belong to a group. Affiliation is one of the components of love.

Example: A woman may wish to get married in order to be accepted and belong to a group of women, all of whom are married.

Source: Rubin, Z. (1973). *Liking and loving: An invitation to social psychology.* New York: Holt, Rhinehart, & Winston.

Quoted: Berscheid, E., & Walster, E. (1978). *Interpersonal attraction* (2nd ed.). Reading, Mass.: Addison-Wesley.

affirmation of self: A coding category referring to all statements made by a family member that pertain to that person's attributes and characteristics of behavior or to those of another family member. Discrepancies between what the individual says about self and what others say about that person are recorded.

Example:

    Mother: You are the laziest kid I know.
    Son: I'm not lazy.

Source: Lennard, H., & Bernstein, A. (1969). *Patterns in human interaction.* San Francisco: Jossey-Bass.

Quoted: Gerson, M., & Barsky, M. (1979). For the new family therapist: A glossary of terms. *American Journal of Family Therapy,* *7*, 15–30.

aftersession: An informal session without a leader that is held immediately after a therapy session. The session may last for an extended period of time and involve the expression of sexual and hostile impulses.

Example: A family member may ask another member to go for coffee and then discuss that member's behavior in the family therapy.

Source: Fried, E. (1971). Basic concepts in group psychotherapy. In H.I. Kaplan & B. Sadock (Eds.), *Comprehensive group psychotherapy* (pp. 47–71). Baltimore: Williams & Wilkins.

aggression: Behavior that is intended to harm oneself or another. Aggressive tendencies may block the expression of love.

Example: Drinking is often used to release pent-up aggression. Observing one's prospective partner under the influence of alcohol may be useful in the development of the relationship. The observer would be prepared for the aggressive behavior or could terminate the relationship.

Source: Ard, B. (1969). Love and aggression: The perils of loving. In B. Ard & C. Ard (Eds.), *Handbook of marriage counseling* (2nd ed. pp. 50–60). Palo Alto, Calif.: Science and Behavior Books.

agreement: A coding category that applies to all statements that contain an explicit agreement with the preceding statement.

Example: If two statements are positively evaluated, they are classified as being in explicit agreement.

Source: Lennard, H., & Bernstein, A. (1969). *Patterns in human interaction.* San Francisco: Jossey-Bass.

Quoted: Gerson, M., & Barsky, M. (1979). For the new family therapist: A glossary of terms. *American Journal of Family Therapy,* *7*, 15–30.

alignment: The ways in which family members align with or split off from one another in efforts to maintain homeostasis. As an alignment in one part of the family develops, a split may emerge in another part.

Example: A father and son manifest empathic responses to each other. The mother, noting the "two drawing close," intervenes with a remark designed to split the father from the son by inducing conflict and disagreement.

    Father: Maybe we could let you have the car,
    (to Jim) say once a week. Will you be willing to
            buy your own gas?
    Jim: Yeah, if I could have it next Saturday, I
            could earn enough.
    Mother: But if you let Jim have the car, you'd
            have to let Susan (daughter) have it
            too—and you know she can't be
            trusted.

The mother's comment diverts the father's attention from Jim to a potential area of conflict between the mother and Susan. Now Susan and father or Susan and mother become involved in new patterns of alignment. The son, meanwhile, has been split off from the family. He may attempt an alliance with his sister against one or both parents. In schizophrenic families, patterns of alignment and splitting off shift rapidly. Moreover, the specific meaning of

the split or alignment is difficult to analyze. Overall, the process creates chaotic forms of relationships with confused and disassociated meanings.
Source: Wynne, L. (1961). The study of intrafamilial alignments and splits in exploring family therapy. In N. Ackerman et al. (Eds.), *Exploring the base for family therapy* (pp. 95–115). New York: Family Service Association of America.

alliance: A type of alignment in which two or more family members join together without regard for anyone else.
Example: A mother and older daughter may form an alliance in order to fulfill certain needs, such as discussing particular problems while leaving out other problems.
Source: Minuchin, S. (1974). *Families and family therapy.* Cambridge, Mass.: Harvard University Press.

allocative discrepancy: A failure in role complementarity; one person questions another person's right to a role that that person has assumed.
Example: A mother is angry over the favoritism and attention the father gives to his oldest daughter. The mother accuses him of being seductive and not a typical American daddy. He denies that his behavior is inappropriate. In this situation, the father attempts to validate his ascribed role as father and achieved role as husband, while his wife attempts to invalidate these roles.
Source: Spiegel, J. (1957). The resolution of role conflict within the family. *Psychiatry, 20,* 1–16.
Quoted: Foley, V. (1974). *An introduction to family therapy.* New York: Grune & Stratton.

alteration: A maneuver in which one person characterizes another person's behavior in terms of the effect that that behavior has on the feelings of the first person.
Example: A child does something a parent does not like. The parent avoids commenting on the behavior directly, but says, "You're breaking my heart."
Source: Framo, J. (1965). Systematic research on family dynamics. In I. Boszormenyi-Nagy & J. Framo (Eds.), *Intensive family therapy: Theoretical and practical aspects* (pp. 407–462). New York: Harper & Row.

amourant: An ongoing relationship between two people in which there is no intention of a serious emotional commitment and the contact is primarily or exclusively for sexual purposes. The man is referred to as amator and the woman as amatrix, based on the latin term for lover.

Source: Sauber, S.R., & Weinstein, C. (in press). *Terminology for male/female relationships for the 1980s. Family Review, 2,* (1).

amyl nitrite: A drug considered to be an aphrodisiac that affects the excitement phase of sexual response. The use of this drug may be extremely dangerous to an individual.
Source: Kaplan, H. (1979). *Disorders of sexual desire.* New York: Brunner/Mazel.

analogic: Encoded so that a message to some degree resembles the idea or meaning it represents (as opposed to digital in communication theory). Most nonverbal communication is held to be analogic, but there are also verbal examples, such as onomatopoeic words ("tick-tock"); stylistics, such as capitalizing important words; and possibly, at a more abstract level, the use of metaphor. Analogic communication lacks the syntactical and logical precision of digital communication; this may be especially problematic since it seems to be the preferred code for representing feelings and relationships.
Example: A child indicates its age by holding up three fingers; the quantity of fingers resembles the quantity of years being represented. Wrinkling the nose to indicate disgust, rejection, or disapproval resembles the act of smelling a disgusting odor. Embracing someone is an analogy to the idea of closeness or union that it conveys.
Sources: Bavelas, J.B. (1983). *Personal communication*; Watzlawick, P., Beavin, J., & Jackson, D.D. (1967). *Pragmatics of human communication.* New York: Norton.

analogic communication: A class of messages in which each statement has multiple referents, in that it deals with resemblances of some thing to another thing. In analogic communication each message refers to a context of other messages; the message can be expressed in a verbal statement, e.g., analogy or metaphor, or in action, e.g., by showing how something is by acting it out.
Example:

Wife: I called your hotel last night but you weren't in.
Husband: I had to go out for a while. Did I mention that I was taking you out to your favorite restaurant tonight?
Wife: Now I know something is wrong here.

The husband's offer to take his wife out could represent several intentions. However, the wife

interpreted his gesture within the context of their marital situation to mean that something was wrong.
Source: Bateson, G., & Jackson, D. (Eds.). (1968). *Some varieties of pathogenic organization in communication, family, and marriage.* Palo Alto, Calif.: Science and Behavior Books.
Quoted: Haley, J. (1976). *Problem solving therapy.* San Francisco: Jossey-Bass.

analysis of correlative meaning: A procedure used to interpret the Thematic Apperception Test (TATs) of families. Analysis of the stories to each card proceeds in three steps: first, reading all the individually told stories to a given card as a collective family product; second, looking at each story to the card as an individual product of the storyteller; third, examining pairs or grouping of stories to discern interpersonal relationships within the family. This method of analysis rests on the assumption that the meaning of an individual's stories is not exhausted by reference to the individual's own personality or stories. The assumption is rather that a part of the meaning of the individual's stories is discovered by reference to the stories of the other family members.
Source: Handel, G. (1967). Analysis of correlative meaning: The TAT in the study of whole families. In G. Handel (Ed.), *The psychosocial interior of the family: A sourcebook for the study of whole families* (pp. 104–124). Chicago: Aldine.

analytic group psychotherapy: Group psychotherapy in which the therapist's interventions follow psychoanalytic principles. The group processes are deemphasized so the client can be viewed as a separate entity with intrapsychic changes occurring. The group serves to catalyze the intrapsychic dynamics of the individual.
Example: To facilitate uncovering of her feelings and to help her understand why she felt unloved by her parents, a woman might describe how she was neglected as a child.
Source: Slavson, S. (1943). *An introduction to group therapy.* New York: Commonwealth Fund.

anarchistic family: Families that set high values on personal freedom. In such families, there are few rules, and little attention is paid to boundaries.
Example: The parents were raised in poor families and believe their children have to work for everything they want. Both parents are employed, and their two children are responsible for fixing their own food, cleaning their room, and earning spending money by baby sitting, washing cars, etc. One

child spends most of her time with her best friend's family, eating in their home and watching television after school. The other child hangs out on the corner or at the sports center with other boys.
Source: Kantor, D., & Lehr, W. (1975). *Inside the family.* San Francisco: Jossey-Bass.
Quoted: Hoffman, L. (1981). *Foundations of family therapy.* New York: Basic Books.

androgyny: A situation in which cohabiting or marital partners do not perform tasks based on traditional sex roles but rather share tasks on the basis of equality.
Example: A husband might take turns cooking the meals while his wife takes care of their car, because each possesses special skills in these respective areas.
Source: Bem, S. (1974). The measurements of psychological androgyny. *Journal of Consulting and Clinical Psychology, 42,* 155–162.
Quoted: Kaplan, A., & Sidney, M. (1980). *Psychology and sex roles: An Androgynous perspective.* Boston: Little, Brown & Co.

antagonism: A state of negative expressiveness involving such concepts as conflict, hostility, disaffiliation, and angry rebelliousness and noncompliance.
Example: A sister teases her brother in order to receive attention from her mother.
Source: Parsons, T., & Bales, R. (1955). *Family, socialization, and interaction process.* Glencoe, Ill.: Free Press.
Quoted: Riskin, M., & Faunce, E. (1972). An evaluative review of family interaction research. *Family Process, 11,* 365–455.

antecedental therapy: Therapy directed toward the resolution of events that occurred in the past. The therapy may be conducted with the family of origin in discussing the effect the previous family had on the etiology of the problem.
Example: A woman presents depression over her work and marital situation. The depression stemmed from the fact that, when her mother became more successful than her father, the father became angry and depressed, eventually finding a woman who would be dependent on him.
Source: Howells, J. (1975). *Principles of family psychiatry.* New York: Brunner/Mazel.

antiandrogen therapy: A controversial procedure using antiandrogen (c y proterone acetate) that is advocated by some clinicians for the treatment of sexual offenders. The technique involves a dose-dependent, temporary, and therefore reversible,

reduction in the target organ's (especially central nervous system's) sensitivity to circulating androgens. The result is diminution of erotic arousal, desire, libido, and activity.
Example: An antiandrogen drug is used in case management of a heterosexual married man with a history of transvestism and homosexual incestuous pedophilia.
Source: Laschet, U., & Laschet, L. (1975). Antiandrogen in the treatment of sexual deviation of men. *Journal of Steroid Biochemistry, 6*, 821–826.
Quoted: Barlow, D., & Wincze, J. (1980). Treatment of sexual deviations. In S. Leiblum & L. Pervin (Eds.), *Principles and practice of sex therapy* (pp. 347–376). New York: Guilford Press.

anticipatory therapy: Therapy concerned with the resolution of events that could occur in the future. Special attention is given to ensuring the health of the children who are the future of the family.
Example: A married woman becomes pregnant by accident. She stays in the marriage for the sake of the child, redirecting her hostility from her husband onto the child. Therapy could be useful to help the mother realize what she is doing so that she can be accepting of the child.
Source: Howells, J. (1975). *Principles of family psychiatry.* New York: Brunner/Mazel.

anxiety cohesion: A patient's state of emotional helplessness and despair produced by the whole family's effort to deal with a conflict between frustrated dependency needs and the family ideal of independence, respectability, and avoidance of selfishness. In this situation, the family is integrated in a way that requires each member to give testimony to the family ideal, while suppressing individual needs. Anxiety cohesion is believed to play a role in the etiology of ulcerative colitis.
Example: A young man who lives at home is covertly rejected by both parents, who experience frustrated needs. The mother desires family solidarity, respectability, and social success. The father, fearing poverty and lack of security, compensates by overworking. At one level the parents consider the son a burden, but they also want him to reflect the success of the family. This kind of family structure causes him to feel helpless and hopeless. He develops ulcerative colitis in trying to deal with the situation.
Source: Titchner, J., Risking, J., & Emerson, R. (1960). The family in psychosomatic medicine. *Psychosomatic Medicine, 22*, 127–142.

anxiety induction: A flow of anxiety between persons, especially when there preexists a relationship charged with emotional tension.
Example: A father and son are in constant conflict. The father arrives home and starts complaining about his day at the office. The son reacts defensively. The son believes his father is certain to attack him because of the father's emotional state.
Source: Sullivan, H. (1948). The meaning of anxiety in psychiatry and life. *Psychiatry, 11*, 1–13.
Quoted: Zuk, G., & Rubinstein, D. (1965). A review of concepts in the study and treatment of families of schizophrenics. In I. Boszormenyi-Nagy & J. Framo (Eds.), *Intensive family therapy: Theoretical and practical aspects* (pp. 1–32). New York: Harper & Row.

arbitration: A method involving a neutral third party to resolve a controversy. The arbitrator's role is unlike that of the mediator and conciliator. Arbitration is used to resolve an impasse reached in mediation. When parties submit a controversy to an arbitrator, they agree to be bound by the decision the arbitrator renders. There is no appeal from an arbitrator's decision, and in most states it will be enforced by the courts.

Arbitration is an adversarial process when the parties are represented by legal counsel. Lawyers must use every lawful means of asserting their clients' interests. The parties may also present their own cases to the arbitrator without an attorney. It is considerably easier to do this in arbitration than it is in court. Even so, it is still an adversarial process because the parties, acting as advocates for themselves, compete with each other for a favorable decision by the arbitrator.

Arbitration offers the following advantages:

- It is private; only the parties, arbitrator, witnesses, and legal counsel (if any) may attend.
- Hearings are scheduled to meet the convenience of the arbitrator, parties, witnesses, and legal counsel.
- Hearings may be recessed when circumstances dictate and continued at another agreed-upon time.
- Hearings actually take place when scheduled.
- Only the issues submitted are considered by the arbitrator.
- The hearing takes place within a few days or weeks after the issues are submitted.
- The arbitrator has only one case to consider at a time.

- The arbitrator is selected by the parties.
- The outcomes are less dependent on the skill of legal counsel and technicalities.

Source: Coogler, O.J. (1978). *Structured mediation in divorce settlement.* Lexington, Mass.: Lexington Books.

areta: The qualities a person should ideally possess according to the values of that person's community. The qualities are not necessarily good for the person, nor what that person likes, gets, or does. They are what the person ought to be and do, were it not for human frailty, weakness, or accidents of fate. They constitute the moral imperative of a spiritually unified person.
Example: A husband should not get angry with his wife, neither in front of friends nor in the privacy of their own home.
Source: Goldschmidt, W. (1971). Areta-motivation and models for behavior. In I. Galdston (Ed.), *The interface between psychiatry and anthropology* (pp. 55–87). New York: Brunner/ Mazel.

argument: A communicative interchange in which there is an expression of ideas and feelings, but in which the partial or total conscious or unconscious purpose is to hurt the partner.
Example:

> *Husband:* I wish you could find some nice things to say about your job for a change.
>
> *Wife:* What! If it weren't for you, we wouldn't be stuck in this town and I would have a better job.

In this interchange, both partners are angry and make statements that hurt the other. The husband's hurtful remark is less direct. He negates his wife's feelings. The wife blames her husband for her situation.
Source: Wahlroos, S. (1974). *Family communication: A guide to emotional health.* New York: MacMillan.

arm levitation: A sex hypnotherapy technique used to treat male vasocongestive dysfunctions. The levitation of the arm (e.g., moving up in the air) is associated with penile erection.
Source: Araoz, D. (1982). *Hypnosis and sex therapy.* New York: Brunner/Mazel.

ascribing noble intention: A strategy in which the therapist attributes noble motivations to even the most destructive behavior shown by individuals in the family.
Example: Every time the parents of an alcoholic son start talking about divorce, the son goes on a binge. The therapist may start by saying to the parents, "You're lucky to have a son willing to sacrifice himself for your sake."
Source: Stanton, M., & Todd, T. (1979). Structural family therapy with drug addicts. In E. Kaufman & P. Kaufman (Eds.), *The family therapy of drug and alcohol abuse.* New York: Gardner Press.
Quoted: Stanton, M. (1981). Strategic approaches to family therapy. In A.S. Gurman & D.P. Kniskern (Eds.), *Handbook of family therapy* (pp. 361–402). New York: Brunner/Mazel.

asexuality: A state in which sexual appetites fall on the low side of the normal distribution. Asexual persons are not bothered by the infrequency of their need for sex unless external circumstances exert pressure.
Source: Kaplan, H. (1979). *Disorders of sexual desire.* New York: Brunner/Mazel.

assertiveness training: The training to develop the ability to be effectively assertive. The rights of self and others are emphasized. This training usually involves use of behavior therapy techniques, such as covert rehearsal, modeling, and role playing.
Example: A wife says in role-playing what she wants to tell her husband: "I resent your favoritism towards your daughter. You immediately take her side and avoid listening to our other children."
Source: Alberti, R., & Emmons, M. (1974). *Your perfect right: A guide to assertive behavior.* San Luis Obispo, Calif.: Impact Publishers.

assessment: The act of defining, observing, and recording behavioral and stimulus events occurring in the family. Objectives and quantitative data are derived from behavioral observations.
Example: A husband records how many times he and his wife have expressed loving statements to one another by incident, date, time of occurrence and who initiated the statements.
Source: Patterson, G. (1971). *Families: Applications of social learning to family life.* Champaign, Ill.: Research Press.

attention control strategies: An interactional domain defined operationally by participation rate, who speaks to whom, and statement length.
Example: The father talks the most. He is in control while he is talking. The wife and children defer to him as the head of the house.

Source: Mishler, E., & Waxler, N. (1968). *Interaction in families: An experimental study of family process and schizophrenia.* New York: John Wiley & Sons.

attraction: The tendency or predisposition to evaluate another person or a symbol of that person in a positive or negative way.
Example: A wife looks up to her husband and gives him special attention when he is dressed in a three-piece suit ready for work.
Source: Berscheid, E., & Walster, E. (1978). *Interpersonal attention.* Reading, Mass.: Addison-Wesley.

attributions: A "hypnotic" method of coercion and control of behavior—and ultimately identity—in which a family member is encouraged to be what is desired by telling the person that he or she has achieved this already.
Example: Parents may tell their son how he feels, or even tell a third party in front of him what he feels. Such attributions are thought to be more powerful than orders.
Source: Laing, R.D. (1960). *The divided self.* London: Travestock Publications.

autism: A tendency to be overly regulated by personal desires or needs in one's thinking or perceiving, at the expense of regulation by objective reality; a tendency to view the world as closer to one's wishes than it is objectively. The term also indicates the withdrawal from reality into a private world of thoughts and emotions that are not related to other individuals.
Example: An individual's daydreams may be self-centered and pure fantasy. In extreme cases, the schizophrenic's thinking is cut off from reality and represents the person's internal world.
Source: Knopf, I. (1979). *Childhood psychopathology: A developmental approach* (pp. 236–246). Englewood Cliffs, N.J.: Prentice-Hall.
Quoted: English, H., & English, A. (1958). *A comprehensive dictionary of psychological and psychoanalytic terms.* New York: David McKay.

autonomous otherness: Disregard for the discrete individuality of family members. Other family members are not allowed to be independent others.
Example: A mother might say, "You're feeling cold, aren't you?" The overprotective mother may supersede the child's feelings by completing sentences for the child or trying to express the child's innermost feelings.

Source: Boszormenyi-Nagy, I. (1965). A theory of relationships: Experience and transaction. In I. Boszormenyi & J. Framo (Eds.), *Intensive family therapy* (pp. 33–42). New York: Harper & Row.

autonomy: A condition of maximal independence and minimal restraint on one's actions. Autonomy seems to be essential to the development of a satisfactory ego identity, since one must be permitted to consider oneself a separate person, and to experience oneself as such, in order to find an identity. Without such autonomy, it is likely that a child will be unable to solve the basic problems of separation from the child's family of orientation and will remain overdependent.
Example: A teenager says to his father, "Thank you for offering to call your friends to get me a summer job, but I would rather try to get my own work, doing what I prefer."
Source: Westley, W., & Epstein, N. (1969). *The silent majority.* San Francisco: Jossey-Bass.
Quoted: Lewis, J.M., Beavers, W.R., & Gossett, J.T. (1976). *No single thread: Psychological health in the family system.* New York: Brunner/Mazel.
See also **interdependency.**

auxiliary ego: In psychodrama, a therapist or assistant therapist who acts or speaks roles that are representative of an important figure in a patient's life. The therapist recreates the patient's delusions, hallucinations, pleasurable wishes, or guilty feelings in order to concretize and intensify the patient's mental processes.
Example: During psychodrama, a therapist might role play the patient's deceased wife in order to further the grieving process.
Source: Moreno, J. (1971). *Psychodrama.* In H. Kaplan & B. Sadock (Eds.), *Comprehensive group psychotherapy* (pp. 460–500). Baltimore: Williams & Wilkins.

aversive stimulation: A punishment procedure in which a painful or unpleasant event is presented contingent on the emission of a behavior. Its major effect is to decelerate the behavior it follows.
Example: A four-year-old child reaches towards an electrical outlet. The mother makes a painfully loud remark to keep the child's hands away. The probability that the child will reach for the outlet again has been reduced.
Source: LeBow, M. (1972). Behavior modification for the family. In G.D. Erickson & T. Hogan (Eds.), *Family therapy: An introduction to theory and technique* (pp. 347–376). Belmont, Calif.: Wadsworth Publishing.

awareness: The "symbolic representation (not necessarily in verbal terms) of some portion of our experience." The term is synonymous with symbolization and consciousness.

- Availability to Awareness. "When an experience can be symbolized freely, without defensive denial and distortion, then it is available to awareness."
- Accurate symbolization. The "hypotheses implicit in awareness can be borne out if tested by acting on them."
- Perception. A perception is "a hypothesis or prognosis for action which comes into being in awareness when stimuli impinge on the organism." Perception and awareness are synonymous terms; however, perception emphasizes the stimulus in the process, while awareness is the "symbolizations and meanings which arise from such purely internal stimuli as memory traces, visceral changes, and the like, as well as from external stimuli."

Source: Rogers, C.P. (1959). A theory of therapy, personality and interpersonal relationships, as developed in the client-centered framework. In S. Koch (Ed.), *Psychology: A study of a science Vol. III, Formulations of the person and the social context* (pp. 184–256). New York: McGraw-Hill. *Quoted:* Thayer, L. (1982). A person-centered approach to family therapy. In A.M. Horne & M.M. Ohlsen, *Family counseling and therapy* (pp. 175–213). Itasca, Ill.: F.F. Peacock Publishers.

B

babes-in-the-wood marriage: Marriage in which the participants have not successfully mastered a particular developmental level.
Source: Skynner, A. (1976). *Systems of family and marital psychotherapy.* New York: Brunner/Mazel.

balanced ledger: A concept of health in a multiperson relationship or family (minimum two persons) as the balance of a long-range ethical ledger. The main dimensions include obligation, repayment, concern, and merit. Satisfactions for one member cannot be viewed without regard to the impact (justice) for others. Chronic imbalance is a pathological system.
Source: Boszormenyi-Nagy, I. & Spark, G.L. (1973). *Invisible loyalties: Reciprocity in intergenerational family therapy.* New York: Harper & Row.

bargaining: The step-by-step process that enables a couple freely and clearly to communicate with one another. The process produces "quid pro quos" that permit each to satisfy unconscious needs and expectations of equality within the relationship. The term also applies to the third stage of the dying process in which the dying patient attempts to "make a deal" with God, the doctors, nurses, hospital staff, etc. In exchange for getting better or living until some event has occurred, the patient promises to do something specific (e.g., "live a good life").
Sources: Jackson, D., & Lederer, W. (1968). *The mirages of marriage.* New York: Norton; Kubler-Ross, E. (1969). *On death and dying.* New York: MacMillan.
Quoted: Okun, B.F., & Rappaport, L.J. (1980). *Working with families: An introduction to family therapy.* Belmont, Calif.: Brooks/Cole.

basic assumption group: A group whose existence is based on basic needs, fears, or fantasies. Groups are said to function at two levels. At the manifest level, the group acts in ways that are conscious, rational, and constructive. However, when a leader is absent or the group has no further purpose, irrational fears and fantasies may rise to the surface. The reasons for the group's existence may include dependency needs, the need to find a sexual partner, or the need for security. Depending on the state of these basic reasons or assumptions, a leader must emerge to help fulfill the group's needs.
Example: A singles group may be formed without the overt intent of providing activities for its members. However, the hidden or latent needs of the group are to find sexual partners.
Source: Bion, W. (1960). *Experience in groups.* New York: Basic Books.

battle for initiative: The process of determining who controls a client's life, thereby enabling family members to take initiatives for new ways of relating.
Example: The father tells his mother in front of his wife that from now on the mother is excluded from discussions about disciplining the children.

Source: Bernard, C., & Corrales, R. (1979). *The theory and technique of family therapy*. Springfield, Ill.: Charles C Thomas.

battle for structure: In the early stages of therapy, the conflict over who controls the context of therapy. The therapist should win this battle as soon as possible.
Example: The therapist rearranges the seating arrangements, telling the father to sit next to his wife and the pampered teenager to sit on his mother's lap during the session.
Source: Bernard, C., & Corrales, R. (1979). *The theory and techniques of family therapy*. Springfield, Ill.: Charles C Thomas.

becoming alive: A sex hypnotherapy technique used to treat inadequate feelings of pleasure. The client is guided through a detailed process of awareness of bodily sensations, especially genital sensations.
Source: Araoz, D. (1982). *Hypnosis and sex therapy*. New York: Brunner/Mazel.

behavior control dimension: The pattern that a family adopts to handle behavior in physically dangerous situations—those that involve the expression of psychological desires or interpersonal socializing behavior in and outside the family. In meeting these needs, any of four style patterns may be used: rigid, flexible, laissez-faire, and chaotic.
Example. Regarding curfew:

1. Rigid: The child must be home at the prescribed time; no exceptions.
2. Flexible: The child is allowed to come home at different times depending upon the situation.
3. Laissez-faire: The child can come home whenever the child likes.
4. Chaotic: The parents set an arbitrary different curfew each night the child goes out.

Source: Epstein, N., & Bishop, D. (1981). Problem-centered systems therapy of the family. In A. Gurman and D. Kniskern (Eds.), *Handbook of family therapy* (pp. 444–482). New York: Brunner/Mazel.

behavior disorder: A disorder in which the sufferer has emotional pain, has no chronic psychotic symptoms, but experiences continuing difficulty in following the rules of behavior expected in the world beyond the family.
Example: A child who misbehaves in school may be manifesting a conduct disorder.

Source: Beavers, W.R. (1977). *Psychotherapy and growth: A family systems perspective.* New York: Brunner/Mazel.

behavior modification: A therapeutic approach for ameliorating the socially relevant problems of people. The technique deals basically with objectively defined and observable behavior occurring as a function of antecedent and consequent environmental events. These events are the crucial independent variables that must be manipulated in order to produce critical changes in behavior. Behavior modification occurs in three stages: assessment, intervention, and evaluation.
Example: A father disconnects the TV when the children argue about what show they prefer to view.
Source: LeBow, M. (1972). Behavior modification for the family. In G. Erickson & T. Hogan (Eds.), *Family therapy* (pp. 347–376). Belmont, Calif.: Wadsworth Publishers.

behavior reversal: A technique in which the patient is instructed to express personal feelings to the therapist, who assumes the role of an individual toward whom the patient has strong inhibited feelings.
Example: A woman may have difficulty asserting herself with her husband. The therapist may assume the role of the husband in order to give the client practice in saying "no."
Source: Wolpe, J. (1969). *The practice of behavior therapy*. New York: Pergamon Press.
Quoted: LeBow, M. (1972). Behavior modification in the family. In G. Erickson and T. Hogan (Eds.), *Family therapy* (pp. 347–376). Belmont, Calif.: Wadsworth Publishers.

behavioral approaches: Approaches that deal with the means of learning, reinforcing, or extinguishing certain behaviors, irrespective of their original causes. Even relatively minor changes in the behavior of a family member, or a dyad, may bring about a significant alteration in the behavior and feelings of the other family members. Techniques of behavioral therapy include assertiveness training, operant conditioning, relaxation and desensitization, contingency reinforcement, and cognitive behavior modification. Family members can be utilized as cotherapists in various behavior modification exercises that are rehearsed initially in the therapist's office and are assigned for practice at home.
Source: Hansen, T., & L'Abate, L. (1982). *Approaches to family therapy*. New York: Macmillan.

behavioral group therapy: Group therapy in which overt, observable behavior, especially symptomatic behavior, is emphasized rather than thoughts and feelings. The objectives are changes in behavior leading to the elimination of suffering and maladjustment. Conditioning and teaching techniques are used predominantly.
Source: Lazarus, A. (1968). Behavior therapy in groups. In G. Gazda (Ed.), *Basic approaches to group psychotherapy and group counseling* (pp. 149–175). Springfield, Ill.: Charles C Thomas.

behavioral marital therapy: Therapy that involves the training of couples in communication skills, contingency contracting, and the application of reinforcement principles to increase positive relationship behavior. A functional analysis of the client's presenting problem behaviors is conducted by continuous assessment of the identified target behaviors.
Example: The presenting complaint of the husband is secondary impotence. Data collected at home reveal that unsuccessful intercourse generally follows discussions "about the relationship." Husband and wife are taught communication skills and problem-solving techniques to be used at times that are not in close proximity to expressions of affection and intimacy. The result is that the husband is able to maintain erections when prior association are not negative and tension producing, as their previous interactions had been.
Sources: Jacobson, N. (1978). A review of the research on the effectiveness of marital therapy. In T.J. Paolino & B.S. McCrady (Eds.), *Marriage and marital therapy* (pp. 395–444). New York: Brunner/Mazel; Weiss, R. (1978). The conceptualization of marriage from a behavioral perspective. In T.J. Paolino & B.S. McCrady (Eds.), *Marriage and marital therapy* (pp. 165–239). New York: Brunner/Mazel.

behavioral units: Standard units in which behavior appears. In all cultures, individuals learn to perform and shape their behavior into molds or units that make the behavior mutually recognizable and predictable. These units have also been called structural units or behavioremes.
Example: The acts of bathing a baby or attending a church service.
Source: Pike, K. (1954). *Language, Part I*. Glendale, Calif.: Summer Institute of Linguistics.
Quoted: Scheflen, A. (1972). Human communication: Behavioral programs and their integration in interaction. In G.D. Erickson and T.P. Hogan (Eds.), *Family therapy* (pp. 86–102). Belmont, Calif.: Wadsworth Publishers.

behind-the-back technique: A technique used in encounter groups that requires that a patient sit with his back to the group after talking about himself to the group. Members of the group then discuss him as if he were not present. Subsequently, the patient turns around and participates in the group discussion.
Source: Spotnitz, H. (1971). Comparison of different types of group psychotherapy. In H. Kaplan and B. Sadock (Eds.), *Comprehensive group psychotherapy* (pp. 72–103). Baltimore: Williams & Wilkins.

belongingness: The basic human need for affirmation and acceptance by significant others.
Example: A student during school graduation exercises looks toward his parents and experiences a sense of belongingness.
Source: Maslow, A. (1954). *Motivation and personality*. New York: Harper & Row.

beneficial relationship: A relationship based upon an egalitarian, copartner type of relatedness ideology, emphasizing success through personal accomplishment, personal growth, and humanistic concern.
Example: The wife is a college graduate and the husband is a high-school dropout, but both are successful in their own endeavors and respect each other's accomplishments, and they volunteer together to support a foundation for victims of trauma.
Source: Weiss, R. (1978). The conceptualization of marriage from a behavioral perspective. In T. Paolino and B. McCrady (Eds.), *Marriage and marital therapy* (pp. 165–239). New York: Brunner/Mazel.

benexperiential psychotherapy: A type of psychotherapy in which the treatment consists of the use of a new beneficial experience. The beneficial experience is, in effect, the therapy. Psychosis, in an individual or in a family, is the result of malexperience—adverse experience in the past, adverse experience in the present, or the interaction of both. In contrast to the adverse neurotic process, benexperiential psychotherapy utilizes an experience that is to the advantage of the individual or family psyche.
Example: The therapist emphasizes activities that the family enjoys doing together (e.g., picnics, field trips).

Source: Howells, J. (1975). Principles of family psychiatry. New York: Brunner/Mazel.

best interests of the child: A term that emphasizes the rights of children in custody cases. In awarding custody, parental rights have traditionally dominated decision making. For many years, the child, as property, belonged to the father. Then the mother was deemed the natural parent. Gradually, however, it was recognized that society's best interests were promoted when children were reared in a manner that best ensured their effectiveness as adult citizens. The "best interests of the child" became a dominant concern in awarding custody. In 1963, the Family Law Section of the American Bar Association stated that "custody shall be awarded . . . according to the best interests of the child." The Revised Uniform Marriage and Divorce Act, enacted as a model for state legislation, stipulates that the court "shall determine custody in accordance with the best interests of the child." As laws change and place more emphasis on the child's well-being, it will be increasingly difficult for courts to award custody on the basis of parental sex.
Source: Little, M. (1982). *Family break-up.* San Francisco: Jossey-Bass.

bilateral identity delineation: In a dialectical model of the person, a postulated need for a bilateral identity delineation, one that is directed simultaneously toward both good and bad objects. The basic assumption is a transactional, ego-structural theory of ambivalence. The ultimate motivation for seeing others as good and bad stems from primitive archetypes of good versus bad, life versus death, etc.
Source: Boszormenyi-Nagy, I. (1965). A theory of relationships: Experience and transaction. In I. Boszormenyi-Nagy & J. Framo (Eds.), *Intensive family therapy: Theoretical and practical aspects* (pp. 33–86). New York: Harper & Row.

bilateral transference: Adaptation of some of the language, accents, or rhythm of the family and their use by the therapist as a metaphorical set.
Example: A wife found she did not have enough experience to get the job she wanted. She felt she did have the experience, but the employer wanted someone with much more. The husband developed the metaphor of major versus minor league jobs. He said she still needed to play in the minor league before moving up. The therapist used this metaphor to help the wife see that both leagues were acceptable and that she should really be ready before moving up.

Source: Whitaker, C., & Keith, D. (1981). Symbolic-experiential family therapy. In A. Gurman & D. Kniskern (Eds.), *Handbook of family therapy* (pp. 187–225). New York: Brunner/Mazel.

bilaterality: In family therapy, a sense of growth and change in both therapist and client.
Example: The therapist cites an illustration from the therapist's own family that is helpful both to the therapist and to the patient in treatment.
Source: Whitaker, C. (1970). *Marital and family therapy* (cassette audiotapes). Chicago: Instructional Dynamics.
Quoted: Barnard, C., & Corrales, R. (1979). *The theory and technique of family therapy.* Springfield, Ill.: Charles C Thomas.

bilocal residence: A rule of residence that allows a married couple the choice of living with either of the two parental families.
Example: A couple chooses to live with the wife's mother in order to have her assist with child care.
Source: Zelditch, M. (1964). Cross-cultural analyses of family structure. In H. Christensen (Ed.), *Handbook of marriage and the family* (pp. 462–500). Chicago: Rand McNally.

binding: A mode in which the family is gripped by centripetal forces. The family's unspoken rule is that satisfactions and securities can be obtained only within the family, while the outside world looks hostile and forbidding. The parents must delay their own developmental crises by keeping their children from leaving home.
Source: Stierlin, H. (1974). *Separating parents and adolescents.* New York: Quadrangle.

bioenergetic group psychotherapy: A therapeutic approach that directly involves the body through physical activity and contact with others. The approach is based on the assumption that personality change is incomplete unless accompanied by improved bodily form, motility, and functioning.
Source: Lowen, A. (1975). *Bioenergetics.* New York: Penguin Books.

black box concept: The idea that no ultimately verifiable intrapsychic hypotheses need to be invoked in order to study communication. The observer limits observations to input-output relations. This concept has been extended to viewing symptoms as one kind of input into the family system rather than as an expression of intrapsychic conflict. This term originally was used by B.F. Skinner and was then adapted by the communication school of family therapy.

Sources: Skinner, B.F. (1953). *Science and human behavior*. New York: Macmillan; Watzlawick, P., Beavin, J., & Jackson, D. (1967). *Pragmatics of human communication*. New York: W.W. Norton.

blame technique: A method for generating family interaction that is part of the structured family interview. The interviewer and the family are seated around a table with the father to the left of the interviewer, the mother to the father's left, and then the children in order of age. Each family member is handed a 3 × 5 index card and asked to write down "the main fault of the person to the left of you." After doing this, they hand the cards back to the interviewer, who mixes them up and inserts two cards that say "too good" and "too weak." Then the interviewer reads the cards in random sequence and asks each family member in turn to whom the fault applies.
Source: Watzlawick, P. (1966). A structured family interview. *Family Process, 5,* 256–271.

blamer: One who looks outside of self to explain a tension situation. The blamer's perceptual system is attuned to finding the causes in the other or in the environment and is incapable of looking inside of self.
Example: A classic blaming statement is "You made me do it." The individual does not accept personal responsibility but rather projects it outside of self.
Source: Satir, V. (1972). *Peoplemaking*. Palo Alto, Calif.: Science and Behavior Books.

blended families: Separate families united by marriage, stepfamilies.
Source: Nichols, N. (1984). *Family therapy: Concepts and methods*. New York: Gardner Press.

blended orgasm: A combination of the vulval orgasm and the uterine orgasm, one of three types of orgasm postulated by J. Singer and I. Singer. It is characterized by contractions of the orgasmic platform and is regarded as deeper than a vulval orgasm.
Source: Singer, J., & Singer, I. (1978). Types of female orgasm. In J. LoPiccolo & L. LoPiccolo (Eds.), *Handbook of sex therapy* (pp. 175–186). New York: Plenum Press.

blind walk: A technique that involves having one person take another on a walk while the second person keeps eyes closed. Particularly useful for couples with serious trust and dependence problems in their relationship.
Source: Satir, V. (1967). *Conjoint family therapy: A guide to theory and technique* (rev. ed.). Palo Alto, Calif.: Science and Behavior Books.

blocking and soothing: A technique by which, when a conflict escalates to the point where milder strategies are unsuccessful, the mediator or therapist can disrupt the situation by interrupting assertively and blocking the ongoing dialogue, taking charge of the discussion and converting the dialogue into a monologue, and slowing down the pace and turning the volume down to a calmer level. If this is done skillfully, the mediator or therapist can continue to maintain sole control by using an almost trance-like monotonal monologue about anything that will keep the conflict quelled. This gives the couple time to cool off and relax, and it also creates an opportunity for later discussions to be more productive. Obviously, the more the mediator or therapist talks, the less opportunity the spouses have to talk. For some couples, this means less opportunity for conflict. In such cases, the mediator or therapist can allow the spouses to talk only insofar as the talk is productive. Periodically, the mediator or therapist can again block the discussion and slow the spouses down until they are ready to continue their discussion in a calmer way.
Source: Saposnek, D.T. (1983). Strategies in child custody mediation: A family systems approach, *Mediation Quarterly, 1*(2), 29–54.

body contact maneuver: Any technique that involves group members' touching one another, then speaking of the feelings aroused. This maneuver is utilized mainly by encounter groups, but could be used with families where taboos about body contact may be present.
Quoted: Gottschalk, L., & Davidson, R. (1971). Sensitivity groups, encounter groups, training groups, marathon groups, and the laboratory movement. In H. Kaplan & B. Sadock (Eds.), *Comprehensive group psychotherapy* (pp. 422–459). Baltimore: Williams & Wilkins.

body language: The way in which a person's physical appearance, mannerisms, and gestures express that person's thinking. A person's body language may affirm a statement, or it may communicate a different kind of idea.
Example: A wife says she wants to go out, but she says it in a hostile tone, while turning her head away from her partner. Her verbal and nonverbal behavior are incongruent.

Source: Satir, V. (1972). *Peoplemaking*. Palo Alto, Calif.: Science and Behavior Books.

body trip: A sex hypnotherapy technique used to treat preorgasmia. The woman takes an imaginary trip through her genital area in order to find those special places that produce the most pleasurable sensations.
Source: Araoz, D. (1982). *Hypnosis and sex therapy*. New York: Brunner/Mazel.

bonding: The linking of two or more persons in intimacy and love; usually refers to marriage or parent-child relationships.
Source: Harlow, H. (1958). The nature of love. *American Psychologist, 13,* 673–685.
Quoted: Gleitman, H. (1981). *Psychology*. New York: W.W. Norton.

boundaries: The defining parameters of both individuals and systems. Boundaries between family members or subsystems may vary in permeability. They must be clearly drawn in order to attain psychological distance between the members or subsystems. At times, boundaries should be expanded to include family members into specific subsystems to make the individual and/or the system more effective.

Boundaries are invisible lines drawn within and among family members, e.g., the lines within the individual self and between the marital coalition and the children. Part of the therapeutic task is to help the family define, redefine, or change the boundaries within the family. The therapist also helps the family to either strengthen or loosen boundaries, depending upon the family's situation, e.g., when children are entering too much into the parents' domain. The therapist may help establish boundaries through either spatial or verbal techniques.
Example: A family living in a trailer does not have any inside doors except for the bathroom. In order to help define the parents' boundaries vis-à-vis the child's, doors are placed on the bedrooms.
Source: Minuchin, S. (1974). *Families and family therapy*. Cambridge, Mass.: Harvard University Press.

boundary function/dysfunction: Badly drawn or diffuse boundary lines among family subsystems. Boundaries are the invisible dividers that serve to define and structure the various generational and environmental subsystems within the overall family system, e.g., child, marital, family of origin, and environmental subsystems. Each subsystem has its own set of tasks, responsibilities, and roles, which can be performed only when boundary formation allows for subsystemic autonomy and appropriate degrees of interdependence. Boundaries must therefore be clearly defined to prevent undue interference in meeting subsystemic demands and also be permeable and sufficiently fluid to allow access and communication between subsystems and adaptability to developmental change. Diffusion leads to subsystemic "overload," whereby allocated positions and tasks are free-floating or inappropriately assigned. Structural therapy specific to boundary dysfunction involves the enactment and recreation of healthier transactional patterns, through altering communication patterns and marking boundaries vis-à-vis tasks that encourage a specific transaction.
Example: Acting-out results when a child is more powerful than a parent or when a member of another subsystem (e.g., grandparent) usurps a parent's power.
Source: Minuchin, S. (1974). *Families and family therapy*. Cambridge, Mass.: Harvard University Press.

boundary maintenance: A homeostatic mechanism within a system that functions to restrict the input of matter/energy/information to an amount the system can cope with and acts to restore equilibrium when the system has been disturbed.
Example: A family in the midst of a crisis attempts to protect itself from any new stresses or from dealing with input that would be even more disturbing.
Source: Skynner, A. (1976). *Systems of family and marital psychotherapy*. New York: Brunner/Mazel.

bounding: A mechanism by which families establish and maintain their territory with the larger community space by regulating both incoming and outgoing traffic. Members of the family decide what kinds of things are allowed to enter the family space and under what conditions, and what kinds of things are simply not permitted admission. Inevitably, bounding issues are issues of safety, of providing an enclosure for the protection of family members against external danger. A family demarcates a perimeter and defends its territory: "This is ours. We are safe here."
Example: A ten-year-old girl is told she may invite some of her friends over to the house, but not others. Similarly, she is encouraged to go to ballet practice, but warned against ice skating on a local pond.
Source: Kantor, D., & Lehr, W. (1976). *Inside the family*. San Francisco: Jossey-Bass.

break-away-guilt: Guilt over running away from home. The adolescent suffers from mainly unconscious guilt, which gives rise to either massive self-destruction or heroic atonement.
Example: Even though he hated his father for beating him, abusing his mother, and criticizing his baby sister, the runaway adolescent son feels that he should have stayed at home to help protect his mother and his younger sister. Because of this guilt, the son begins to use drugs.
Source: Stierlin, H. (1974). *Separating parents and adolescents*. New York: Quadrangle.

brief therapy: A therapy whose goal is to accomplish as much as possible in as short a time as possible, for example, in ten one-hour sessions. The therapist focuses on the main complaint, utilizes active techniques for promoting change, and searches for the minimal change required to resolve the problem.
Source: Fisch, R., Weakland, J., & Segal, L. (1982). *Doing therapy briefly*. San Francisco: Jossey-Bass.

bug-in-the-ear technique: A supervision strategy in which the trainee and the supervisor are linked by a microphone, while the supervisor observes the therapy session through a one-way mirror. The supervisor is able to communicate suggestions and criticisms to the trainee at all times.
Source: Okun, B.F., & Rappaport, L.J. (1980). *Working with families: An introduction to family therapy*. Belmont, Calif.: Brooks/Cole.

bull session: A leaderless group session in a social setting. While not ostensibly therapeutic, bull sessions can have anxiety-relieving and insight-producing effects.
Example: A family meets before, during, or after dinner, and the members discuss their feelings about what is going on in the home.
Source: Amaranto, E. (1971). Glossary. In H. Kaplan and B. Sadock (Eds.), *Comprehensive group psychotherapy*. Baltimore: Williams & Wilkins.

C

calibration: Setting a system to operate within a defined range. For the family, calibration is the rule that governs limits of behavior.

Example: A family may develop a rule that their adolescent daughter should be home between 10:30 and 11:00 P.M. If the daughter were to come in later, she would disrupt the system's calibration.
Source: Watzlawick, J., Beavin, J., & Jackson, D. (1967). *Pragmatics of human communication*. New York: W.W. Norton.
Quoted: Foley, V. (1974). *An introduction to family therapy*. New York: Grune & Stratton.

call system: The technique of calling on patients in a family in order to disclose a specific issue.
Example: The therapist asks the older brother to tell his younger sister how he managed his curfew when his friends stayed out later during school nights.
Source: Slavson, S. (1943). *An introduction to group therapy*. New York: Commonwealth Fund.

can't live with, can't live without syndrome: A syndrome typifying marriages in which the mates use each other or the children as bad internal object representations. The real personalities of the family members become extinct. The mates respond to each other as a parent or a child. Children may be ignored, punished, or used to express marital hostility.
Example: A wife exclaims to her husband: "You are your father's son, in whatever you do, say, and think. You are a child who just wants me to mother you."
Source: Dicks, H. (1964). Concepts of marital diagnosis and therapy as developed at the Tavistock Family Psychiatric Units, London, England. In E. Nash et al. (Eds.), *Marriage counseling in medical practice*. Chapel Hill: University of North Carolina Press.
Quoted: Framo, J. (1965). Rationale and techniques of intensive family therapy. In I. Boszormenyi-Nagy & J. Framo (Eds.), *Intensive family therapy: Theoretical and practical aspects* (pp. 143–212). New York: Harper & Row.

casual runaways: Runaways who experience little difficulty when they separate from their families. They appear tough and casual and are easily absorbed into the runaway culture. Their object relations are typically transient, shallow, and exploitive.
Example: Having reached her 17th birthday, a girl ran away with her girlfriend who had already joined a teenage prostitution group. The runaway never got along with her mother or with her father, who worked the evening shift. She was the only and unplanned child of a marriage later in life.

Source: Stierlin, H. (1974). *Separating parents and adolescents.* New York: Quadrangle.

catalytic: An agent, process, or context that accelerates or facilitates changes in others. In chemistry, a catalytic agent is itself unaffected by the process. In the clinical training process, the agents are people affected in discrete, continuing, and important ways by the new information, ideas, and processes that are developed.

Source: Duhl, B.S. (1983). *From the inside out and other metaphors.* New York: Brunner/Mazel.

catalytic agents: A group member who stimulates others in the group to engage in verbal and nonverbal social activities.

Example: A group member keeps asking for each person's opinion as therapeutic issues are raised.

Source: Slavson, S. (1943). *An introduction to group therapy.* New York: Commonwealth Fund.

category method: A technique used in structured interactional group psychotherapy in which group members are requested to rate other group members as to their intelligence, appearance, etc.

Example: Members might be asked to rate one another on their ability to be assertive.

Source: Kaplan, H., & Sadock, B. (Eds.). (1971). *Comprehensive group psychotherapy.* Baltimore: Williams & Wilkins.

catharsis: The reduction of tension by telling one's troubles to someone else. Catharsis helps to reduce purposeless vindictiveness and limit conflict by breaking the vicious cycle of attack and retaliation.

Example: A wife who tells her therapist about an affair her husband is having will feel less need covertly or overtly to attack and punish her husband.

Source: Blood, R. (1969). Resolving family conflicts. In B. Ard and C. Ard (Eds.), *Handbook of marriage counseling* (pp. 329–341). Palo Alto, Calif.: Science and Behavior Books.

celebrant role: A role in which the therapist joins in a celebration with the family regarding what they have accomplished. Rather than having termination of therapy perceived as rejection, it is important to identify the termination process as a commencement or graduation.

Example: During the session, the mother may serve a cake she baked in order to celebrate the accomplishments that have taken place as a result of family therapy.

Source: Zuk, G. (1971). *Family therapy: A triadic-based approach.* New York: Behavioral Publications.

Quoted: Bernard, C., & Corrales, R. (1979). *The theory and technique of family therapy.* Springfield, Ill.: Charles C Thomas.

centering: A mechanism for developing, maintaining, and transmitting spatial guidelines to determine how traffic should flow within and across a family's borders. Every family generates such guidelines to organize the total space in which it lives. Centering includes the assessment of whether traffic flows in accordance with the guidelines or whether the guidelines should be modified to accommodate the traffic.

Example: A black family, anxious to safeguard its identity after moving into a white neighborhood, turns its dinner hour into an occasion for pinpointing the racial demands of its new community.

Source: Kantor, D., & Lehr, W. (1976). *Inside the family.* San Francisco: Jossey-Bass.

central shared family group preoccupation: The sense of identity of the family group when the family is based on the binding around a shared preoccupation rather than the sharing of life tasks.

Example: A family may be bound together around the avoidance of mourning a death or impending separation or they may focus all their attention on the upcoming birthday of a child.

Source: Cooklin, A. (1974). *Family preoccupation and role in conjoint therapy.* Paper presented to the Royal College of Psychiatrists, London.

Quoted: Skynner, A. (1976). *Systems of family and marital psychotherapy.* New York: Brunner/Mazel.

central switchboard: A family member who acts as the official router of all discussions in a family session. Rather than allowing members to speak for themselves, the central-switchboard member speaks for them. Another name for this member is family spokesman. The term central switchboard has its origin in communications theory.

Source: Minuchin, S. (1974). *Families and family therapy.* Cambridge, Mass.: Harvard University Press.

Quoted: Gerson, M., & Barsky, M. (1979). For the new family therapist: A glossary of terms. *American Journal of Family Therapy, 7,* 15–30.

centrality: A situation in which the therapist directs all communications among family members toward the therapist.

Source: Minuchin, S., & Fisherman, H. (1981). *Family therapy techniques.* Cambridge, Mass.: Harvard University Press.

centralizing engagement: A situation in which the therapist discourages intrafamilial interaction by promoting transactions directly between the family as a whole or the members of the family and the therapist.
Example: A therapist may discuss good study habits with an adolescent apart from family issues. The discussion could take place in the context of the family or in an individual session.
Source: Aponte, H., & Van Deusen, J. (1981). Structural family therapy. In A.S. Gurman & D.P. Kniskern (Eds)., *Handbook of family therapy.* (pp. 310–360). New York: Brunner/Mazel.

centrifugal conflict solution: An approach to conflict resolution used by couples who openly admit their problems and look for satisfaction outside the marriage in such activities as careers, affairs, etc.
Example: Jim & Sally openly admit to having numerous marital problems. However, they stay together for the sake of their children. Jim spends his evenings and weekends in his gun shop in the basement, and Sally devotes her time to selling real estate.
Source: Steirlin, H. (1974). *Separating parents and adolescents.* New York: Quadrangle.

centrifugal family: A family in which sources of gratification are viewed as existing essentially outside, not inside, the family. The parents and children look beyond the family orbit when frustrated; they feel considerable pressure to distance themselves and to seek peers as solace when family conflict is great. In this type of family, children are expelled from the family in such a way that premature separation frequently occurs, as in the case of sociopathic behavior by the children.
Example: Kathy finds greater comfort outside her home than inside it. She enjoys the shallow relationships that frequently end as quickly as they began. She gets in trouble with the juvenile justice authorities for sexually acting out and stealing.
Source: Beavers, W.R. (1977). *Psychotherapy and growth: A family perspective.* New York: Brunner/Mazel.

centrifugal forces: Forces in the family that push the members apart.
Source: Stierlin, H. (1974). *Separating parents and adolescents.* New York: Quadrangle.

centripetal conflict solution: An approach used by couples to resolve conflicts. The couple deny they have any problems, presenting the facade of a happy couple to others.
Example: Although a couple argue continuously, they prefer to go everywhere together.
Source: Stierlin, H. (1974). *Separating parents and adolescents.* New York: Quadrangle.

centripetal family: A family that feels that family members hold greater promise for the fulfillment of crucial relationship needs than does the outside world. The world outside the family boundaries is perceived only dimly and appears frightening and threatening. Separation in such a family is therefore quite difficult. Characteristically, the children lag behind their peers in their investment in people and institutions in the larger world. This style binds children to the family.
Example: Efforts to have children "close by" promote guilt, the acceptance of the status quo in parental coalitions usually involves dominant/submissive patterns.
Source: Stierlin, H. (1974). *Separating parents and adolescents.* New York: Quadrangle.

centripetal forces: Forces in the family that keep the members together.
Source: Stierlin, H. (1974). *Separating parents and adolescents.* New York: Quadrangle.

changing the subject: A strategy used as a diversionary tactic when there is something to hide.
Example: The wife asks her daughter if she has been completing her homework assignments for school at a time the therapist is addressing the complaint of the daughter about feeling nagged, pressured, and harassed by her mother.
Source: Zuk, G. (1971). *Family therapy: A triadic-based approach.* New York: Behavioral Publications.

channels of communication: A mechanism that defines "who speaks to whom." When channels of communication are blocked, needs cannot be fulfilled, problems cannot be solved, and goals cannot be achieved. Channels of communication normally exist between and among all family members.
Source: Lennard, H., & Bernstein, A. (1969). *Patterns in human interaction.* San Francisco: Jossey-Bass.
Quoted: Riskin, M., & Faunce, E. (1972). An evaluative review of family interaction research. *Family Process, 11,* 365–455.

chaotic family: A family characterized by disintegration, lack of structure, chronic psychosis and delinquency, and low commitment to the family unit.
Source: Cuber, J., & Harroff, P. (1966). *Sex and the significant Americans.* Baltimore: Penguin.

Quoted: Glick, I., & Kessler, D. (1980). *Marital and family therapy* (2nd ed.). New York: Grune & Stratton.

charting: Keeping an accurate record of a problem behavior.
Example: In a case of a paranoid jealous wife, the woman is asked to keep a record of her irrational accusations.
Source: Katkins, S. (1978). Charting as a multipurpose treatment intervention in family therapy. *Family Process, 17,* 465–468.

child abuse: In a cognitive-behavioral context, a process that consists of four stages involving behavioral deficits and cognitive dysfunctions. The four stages are:

1. Parents have inappropriate expectations for their child. Maltreating parents have deficits leading them to have unrealistic expectations about the appropriateness of their child's behavior. Such unrealistic expectations may lead the parent to discipline the child for behaviors that the child is incapable of modifying and in a manner that the child is incapable of understanding. Abusing parents often disregard their child's needs, limited abilities, and general helplessness. Instead, they frequently perceive the essence of the child's role as providing for their own emotional needs.

   Example: After a difficult day at work, a father returns home expecting his newborn infant to give him love and nurturance.

2. The child disconfirms the parental expectations. Obviously, a child cannot meet expectations that are inappropriate to the child's age and behavioral capacity. Furthermore, many abused children have a history of risk factors, such as prematurity, which further limit their ability to meet even minimally their parent's expectations.

   Example: The newborn infant cries because of hunger.

3. Parents make idiosyncratic interpretations of their child's behavior. The parents interpret the child's inability to meet expectations as a willful act of disobedience and parental disrespect. The abusing parents may interpret their child's disobedience as negative feedback; for example, "He didn't obey me, therefore he thinks I'm a bad mother." Such parents may also negatively misperceive their child's innocuous behaviors. Thus, when an infant wets his diaper, a parent may suspect that "he wet his diaper because he's mad at me."

   Example: The father believes that the infant hates him and wants to annoy him.

4. The parents respond aggressively toward the child. Abusing mothers aggress more frequently against their children than do either neglectful or comparison mothers. Parental aggression is reinforced because it stops the child's negative behaviors (instrumental aggression) or because it serves as a release of frustration.

   Example: The mother repeatedly hits the infant to produce obedience and compliance.

Source: Twentyman, C.T., Rohrbeck, C.A., and Amish, P.L. (1984). A cognitive-behavioral approach to child abuse: Implications for treatment. In S. Saunders, A.M. Anderson, C.A. Hart, G.M. Rubenstein (Eds.), *Violent individual and families* (pp. 87–111). Springfield, Ill.: Charles C Thomas.

child and family psychiatry: The psychiatric discipline in which, having accepted the child as the referred family member, the psychiatrist thereafter gives the rest of the family equal attention in assessments and moves to treating the family as a whole. The family itself is the focus of endeavor. The child initially referred, though not given any more attention than the rest of the family, is given full attention, and of course benefits from the harmonizing of the child's milieu. The practitioner is limited to an introduction to the family through the referred child.
Example: "Johnny," says the therapist, "who else in your family uses bad language? . . . How about your mother and father?"
Source: Howells, J. (1975). *Principles of family psychiatry.* New York: Brunner/Mazel.

child-centered family: A family in which the parents give primary importance to the child's developmental needs and welfare. While child-centeredness may be functional at times, it is usually an expression of deviant family development. It often leads to deviant symptoms in the child and averts the resolution of marital difficulties.
Example: The wife states to her husband that she prefers to take her three children with her on their spring vacation rather than accept her mother's

offer to baby sit for the kids while the parents go away alone.

Source: Barragan, M. (1976). The child-centered family. In P. Guerin (Ed.), *Family therapy* (pp. 232–248). New York: Gardner Press.

child custody: Legal responsibility for child support and development. In the adversary legal system, controversies over custody are common and are frequently used by parents as a tactic to gain financial leverage. But in marital mediation, controversies over custody are rare, and the major contentions center on visitation arrangements for the noncustodial parent. This experience tends to support what matrimonial lawyers have been saying—that most custody fights are really financial squabbles. The current trend toward shared support responsibility, as well as shared parenting, offers the hope that both parents can cooperate to provide a better and more supportive environment for the development of their children, even though the parents lead separate lives.

Example: In reaching agreement regarding custodial arrangements that reflect the best interests of the child, the parties shall, according to current child custody guidelines, consider all relevant factors, including:

- the wishes of each parent as to the custody of the child
- the wishes of the child as to custodial arrangements
- the interaction and interrelationship with the child's parent or parents, siblings, and any other person who may significantly affect the child's best interests
- the child's adjustment to home, school, and community
- the mental and physical health of all individuals involved

The conduct of a parent that does not demonstrably affect that parent's relationship with the child, or in some other way can be shown to be contrary to the best interests of the child, shall not be considered. *Rights of the noncustodial parent.* Child custody guidelines further stipulate that the noncustodial parent of the child shall be entitled to reasonable visitation rights insofar as they do not adversely affect the child's education or physical health or significantly impair the child's emotional development. The noncustodial parent shall carry out visitation arrangements as a privilege and obligation of parenthood and must share parenting responsibility with the custodial parent. The noncustodial parent is entitled to participate in the child's development to the extent that that parent contributes meaningfully to the child's welfare and development.

Rights of the custodial parent. The custodial parent may determine the child's upbringing, including education, health care, and religious training, except as otherwise agreed by the parties. The custodial parent shall have the right to require that the noncustodial parent follow agreed-upon visitation rights with the children on a consistent and dependable basis.

Source: Coogler, O.J. (1978). *Structured mediation in divorce settlement.* Lexington, Mass.: Lexington Books.

child support: A legal responsibility requiring that either parent or both parents, according to their ability to do so, accept the duty of support for a child of the marriage and contribute an amount reasonably necessary after considering all relevant factors. These factors include:

- The financial resources of the child. For example, the child may have received an inheritance from a grandparent, uncle, or aunt that may contribute substantially toward the child's support.
- The financial resources and needs of the custodial parent. It is likely that both parents will have to use not only their income but other resources to provide support for their minor children.
- The financial resources and needs of the noncustodial parent. Obviously, both parents must be able to meet their reasonable financial and emotional needs if they are to provide financial and other support for their children.
- The standard of living established by the family prior to the dissolution of the marriage. Both parties must decide whether the maintenance of two households rather than one calls for a reduction in lifestyle.
- The physical and emotional condition and the educational needs of the child. Certain children have unusual physical or emotional disabilities that call for medical or psychological treatment and perhaps special education.

Source: Coogler, O.J. (1978). *Structured mediation in divorce settlement.* Lexington, Mass.: Lexington Books.

childlike family: A family characterized by spouses who have remained dependent on their own families or on the community, based on either inadequacy or immaturity.
Example: Whenever the wife has to make a decision, she asks her mother. Her husband objects, but she accuses him of not respecting her parent's wisdom.
Source: Cuber, J., & Harroff, P. (1966). *Sex and the significant Americans.* Baltimore: Penguin.
Quoted: Glick, I., & Kessler, D. (1982). *Marital and family therapy* (2nd ed.). New York: Grune & Stratton.

choreography: A technique that treats the physical arrangement of people in relation to one another while engaged in a transaction. This technique is usually used in families to project alliances, triangles, and emotional patterns outward, as in a silent motion picture.
Example: A family presented for treatment vaguely describes several problems. The family is asked to visualize what happens when a specific problem occurs. They are asked to play this scene out silently. The process of acting it out helps reveal their emotions, as shown on their faces, and clarifies some of the patterns of transaction within the family.
Source: Papp, P. (1976). Family choreography. In P. Guerin (Ed.), *Family therapy* (pp. 465–479). New York: Gardner Press.

circular causality: Thinking that involves the feedback model of causality in which a circular process is involved. The so-called cause is really an effect of a prior cause. What is initially defined as an effect becomes the cause of yet a later event. In essence, the concept involves the notion of a vital interrelationship of system members. The pattern can be viewed as a perpetuation of family dysfunction.
Example: An adolescent boy steals money from his mother and informs his father that his younger brother bought a new cassette tape, which he is hiding.
Source: Watzlawick, P., Beavin, J., & Jackson, D. (1967). *Pragmatics of human communication.* New York: W.W. Norton.

circular epistemology: A view of reality that one event does not directly cause another as in linear epistemology. This model of causality is multicausal, multidetermined, and reciprocal.
Example: A child says, "They never let me leave the house." The parents reply, "We tried, but he always gets lost." The circle of events spirals as each accuses the other.
Source: Hoffman, L. (1981). *Foundations of family therapy.* New York: Basic Books.

circular questioning: A technique for asking questions that address a difference or define a relationship.
Example: A child is asked to rank the family members on who has been most upset by a problem.
Source: Selvini-Palazzoli, M. et al. (1980). Hypothesizing-circularity-neutrality: Three guidelines for the conductor of the session. *Family Process, 19,* 3–12.

clarity: A quality of speech in which the words and the affective tone of voice match each other, i.e., are congruent and make sense to the observer.
Example: A mother screams at her daughter, "I am angry when you disobey me by going into the medicine cabinet."
Source: Riskin, M., & Faunce, E. (1972). An evaluative review of family interaction research. *Family Process, 11,* 365–455.

classification of bonds: A system developed by Dicks that groups bonds at three levels: the public level, the personal norm level, and the unconscious forces level. Each level is based on the Freudian structural model—superego, ego, id.
Source: Dicks, H.V. (1967). *Marital tensions.* London: Routledge and Kegan Paul.
Quoted: Skynner, A. (1976). *Systems of family and marital psychotherapy.* New York: Brunner/Mazel.

clear boundaries: A definitive separation of subsystems within a system, allowing a subsystem to close ranks in order to deal with an issue requiring a minimum of interference from other subsystems. The subsystems in a family constitute a hierarchy going from grandparents to parents and children. The absence of clear boundaries is associated with family pathology.
Example: In a family, the boundaries between mother and daughter become blurred. The daughter acts as a coequal with the mother. She does not accept any limit setting appropriate to her status. A clear boundary is necessary in order for the mother and daughter to assume their roles.
Source: Minuchin, S. (1974). *Families and family therapy.* Cambridge, Mass.: Harvard University Press.

clitoral adhesions: Adhesions that prevent the preorgastic rotation and retraction of the clitoris. The cure is a simple physical "freeing" procedure.

Source: Kaplan, H. (1981). *The new sex therapy.* New York: Brunner/Mazel.

closed family system: A family system in which all participating members must be very cautious about what they say. The principal rule seems to be that everyone is supposed to have the same opinions, feelings, and desires—whether or not this is true. Honest self-expression is viewed as deviant, and differences are treated as dangerous.
Example: A mother tells her son, "Don't invite your friends over to the house. We have our own way of being together."
Source: Satir, V. (1967). *Conjoint family therapy.* Palo Alto, Calif.: Science and Behavior Books.

closed system: A system that does not have the property of equifinality and whose final state is determined by initial conditions. When a therapist thinks of a family as a closed system, specific topics might be focused on, rather than patterns of behavior and interactions. Closed systems are usually nonliving systems, i.e., physical phenomena.
Source: Watzlawick, D., Beavin, J., & Jackson, D. (1967). *Pragmatics of human communication.* New York: W.W. Norton.

closure: The family's tendency to suspend or apply order and connected concepts to raw sensory experience. Closure encompasses the notion of continuity of experience over short time spans. Reiss's "environment-sensitive" families tend to manifest a considerable amount of delayed or suspended closure; the problem is experienced as "out there." In contrast, "distance-sensitive" and "consensus-sensitive" families tend to desire early closure. In consensus-sensitive families, early or premature closure is used as a barricade against the outside world, whereas distance-sensitive families employ early closure to maintain isolated continuity and solidarity over time.
Source: Reiss, D. (1981). The family's construction of the laboratory. In *The family's construction of reality* (pp. 13–77). Cambridge, Mass.: Harvard University Press.

closure problems: Problems that arise from responses in the form of questions, from disqualifying responses, or from contradicting a response in the same speech.
Example: A wife responds to her husband's question by saying, "What do you want me to do now?"
Source: Singer, M., & Wynne, L. (1965). Thought disorders and family relations of schizophrenics, III. Methodology using projective techniques. *Archives of General Psychiatry, 12,* 187–200.
Quoted: Riskin, M., & Faunce, E. (1972). An evaluative review of family interaction research. *Family Process, 11,* 365–455.

clue: An intervention designed to make the family aware that some behavior is likely to continue. Cluing is intended to build mutual support and momentum for carrying out later interventions.
Example: A therapist says to a family, "We want each of you to observe what happens when Jimmy is with you and misbehaves. Notice when this happens and exactly what he does."
Source: de Shazer, S. (1982). *Patterns of brief family therapy.* New York: Guilford Press.

coaching: A technique in which the therapist acts as an active, supportive agent in encouraging the client to make changes in the family. A therapist might use such coaching to help him delve into his own family system.
Example: The therapist suggests to the stepfather that there are several things he could practice saying and then say to his wife's son when he misbehaves.
Source: Bowen, M. (1971). The use of family theory in clinical practice. In J. Haley (Ed.), *Changing families* (pp. 159–192). New York: Grune & Stratton.

coalition: An alliance between specific members of a family. The following types of coalitions have been described by systems theorists:

- Functional coalition: A coalition in which the marital channel is the strongest pathway in the family, with all other channels open and about equal to each other in importance
- Schismatic coalition: A coalition in which either (1) there is a relatively weak or absent marital coalition but strong alliances across the generations and sexes (between father and daughter or mother and son) or (2) the cross-generational ties are between father and son, mother and daughter, with a relative absence of other effective channels.
- Skewed family coalition: A coalition in which one family member is relatively isolated from the others, who form the coalition or fairly cohesive unit.
- Generation-gap coalition: A coalition in which the marital unit and the offspring each form a fairly cohesive unit, with little or no interaction across generational lines.

- Pseudodemocratic coalition: A coalition in which all channels in the family seem to be of about equal importance, with the marital coalition and the parental role not particularly well differentiated.
- Disengaged family (no coalition at all): A family in which each member is cut off from every other member and expects very little sense of positive interaction or feeling of belonging to a family unit.
- Enmeshed family (total coalition): A family in which the coalition is tight between all members; and the actions, feelings, and thoughts of any member sends shock waves through the whole family.

Source: Glick, I., & Kessler, D. (1980). *Marital and family therapy* (2nd ed.). New York: Grune & Stratton.

coalition game: A situation in which there is switching of a two-party alliance with a third party on the outside; i.e., two people, A and B, talk about a third, C, then A talks with C about B, then B talks about A with C. A common coalition game is one in which there is a rigid, impenetrable boundary in the relationship of two people, as in a folie à deux, that does not allow others to come into it.
Example: A mother and child have a coalition that keeps father out, i.e., the mother and child talk about the father. When the father and mother get together, they talk about the child. Then, the father talks with the child about the mother.
Source: Minuchin, S. (1974). *Families and family therapy.* Cambridge, Mass.: Harvard University Press.

coercion: The general process of control by pain. The individual uses aversive behaviors as stimulus events in punishment and/or negative reinforcement arrangements.
Example: A child attempts to coerce his mother into buying him a candy bar in a store by having a temper tantrum or threatening to have one. The mother buys him some candy in order to turn off his tantrum, which reinforces his behavior.
Source: Patterson, G., & Reid, J. (1970). Reciprocity and coercion: Two facets of social systems. In C. Neuringer and J. Micheal (Eds.), *Behavior modification in clinical psychology* (pp. 133–177). New York: Appleton-Century-Crofts.
Quoted: Patterson, G. (1976). The aggressive child: Victim and architect of a coercive system. In E. Mash, L. Hamerlynck, & L. Handy (Eds.),

Behavior modification and families (pp. 267–316). New York: Brunner/Mazel.

coercive binder: A person who coerces others yet depicts self as well-meaning and caring. The more dependent and immature the bindee, the more fateful the violence of the binder.
Example: A father is hypercritical of his son in order to inure him to the perils of later life. The father depicts himself as being his son's savior.
Source: Stierlin, H. (1974). *Separating parents and adolescents.* New York: Quadrangle.

cognitive binding: A situation in which a parent interferes with the child's differentiated self-awareness and self-determination. The ability of the child to perceive and articulate personal feelings, needs, motives, and goals—as against those that others attribute to the child—is crucial in order for the child to cope without conflicts when separated.
Example: A mother who rejects her child misdefines her behavior to the child as loving. For example, she may tell her child that the child can't go to a dance because there would be undesirable people there.
Source: Stierlin, H. (1974). *Separating parents and adolescents.* New York: Quadrangle.

cognitive constructs: Verbal messages that are used to encourage clients to experience things in a different way.
Example: A sister frequently answers questions the therapist directs to her brother. The therapist says to her, "You're helpful, aren't you? You take his memory." This cognitive construct indicates a need for separation and nonintrusion.
Source: Minuchin, S., & Fishman, H. (1981). *Family therapy techniques.* Cambridge, Mass.: Harvard University Press.

cognitive discrepancy: A situation in which one member of a dyad does not know what is wanted or required by the other.
Example: A husband tells the travel agent that he and his wife want to go to Italy on a trip to visit his family. His wife is silent as she looks down at the floor in a depressed, repressed manner.
Source: Spiegel, J. (1952). The resolution of role conflict within the family. *Psychiatry, 20,* 1–16.
Quoted: Foley, V. (1974). *An introduction to family therapy.* New York: Grune & Stratton.

cognitive involvement: The degree to which a family system allows a topic to be discussed, e.g., death.

Example: A mother tells her children not to talk about their father's drinking.
Source: Lewis, J., Beavers, W.R., & Gossett, J.T. (1976). *No single thread.* New York: Brunner/Mazel.

cognitive style: The characteristic way a person selects information, processes it, and communicates the outcome to others. When spouses have different cognitive styles, they arrive at different conclusions, making it difficult to resolve their differences through direct argumentation.
Example: A father thinks his wife should take care of the children when he comes home from work tired, and the wife feels the children need time with their father and time away from her.
Source: Sager, C. (1981). Couples therapy and marriage contracts. In A.S. Gurman and D.P. Kniskern (Eds.), *Handbook of family therapy* (pp. 25–132). New York: Brunner/Mazel.

cohabitation: A living-together-arrangement (LTA) in which two adult persons, usually of different sex, reside under marriage-like conditions in the same household without having confirmed their relationship through the rituals of marriage. The relationship is defined as involving the sharing of a bedroom at least four nights a week for at least three consecutive months in order to differentiate it from a relationship involving merely a sexual partner's visitations.
Source: Macklin, E. (1972). Heterosexual cohabitation among unmarried college students. *Family Coordinator, 21,* 463–472.

coherence factor: The relative consistency and continuity of a system's identity and relationship to the ecosystem as the system's structure evolves and modifies.
Example: A family loses a member through death. The family may continue as a unit and define itself in the same way as before the death. On the other hand, the family may become incoherent. It could dissolve, and its members could acquire a new identity.
Source: Aponte, H., & Van Deusen, J. (1981). In A.S. Gurman & D.P. Kniskern (Eds.), *Handbook of family therapy* (pp. 310–360). New York: Brunner/Mazel.

cohesion. Those forces, whether positive or negative, that hold together a relationship. Cohesion is often expressed in terms of commitment and the degree of intimacy in the interpersonal dimension.
Example: The husband's attitude toward sexual exclusivity helps to enhance his wife's feelings of love for the husband and to help her resist a temptation to become involved in an extramarital affair.
Source: Waring, E.M., & Russell, L. (1982). Cognitive family therapy. In F.W. Kaslow (Ed.), *The international handbook of family therapy* (pp. 186–195). New York: Brunner/Mazel.

coital anxiety: Anxiety experienced by males during coitus that can be traced to feelings of inadequacy, apprehension, or possibly a childhood fear.
Source: Cooper, A. (1969). A clinical study of "coital anxiety" in male potency disorders. *Journal of Psychosomatic Research, 13,* 143.
Quoted: Reckless, J., & Geigger, N. (1978). Impotence as a practical problem. In J. LoPiccolo & L. LoPiccolo (Eds.), *Handbook of sex therapy* (pp. 295–322). New York: Plenum Press.

collaborative marital therapy: A therapeutic technique wherein each spouse is seen individually by separate therapists, who then collaborate. This therapy may be helpful in aiding a passive and withdrawn spouse to self-disclose. With this technique, clinicians may recognize distortions of reality and omission of facts, which often aids in the recognition of patients' ego defenses.
Source: Martin, P.A., & Bird, H.W. (1953). An approach to the psychotherapy of marriage partners: The stereoscopic technique. *Psychiatry, 16,* 123–127.

collaborative parent-child therapy: A form of therapy in which the parent and the child are seen individually by different therapists, who then collaborate. This therapy is particularly beneficial to adolescent patients, who are often reluctant to self-disclose while under the parents' scrutiny. With this technique, the clinician need not rely entirely on information provided by one patient—information that is often distorted.
Source: Johnson, A.M., & Fishback, D. (1944). Analysis of a disturbed adolescent girl and the collaborative psychiatric treatment of the mother. *American Journal of Orthopsychiatry, 14,* 195–203.

collaborative therapy: The use of two therapists, each seeing a spouse separately and then consulting together.
Example: The husband is in the process of terminating an affair and the wife is severely depressed. The spouses see separate therapists for their individual problems. The therapists consult with each other in order to obtain more complete pictures of their individual clients.

Source: Greene, B., & Solomon, A. (1963). Marital disharmony: Concurrent psychoanalytic therapy of husband and wife by the same psychiatrist. *American Journal of Psychiatry, 17,* 443–450.

Quoted: Prochaska, J., & Prochaska, J. (1978). Twentieth century trends in marriage and marital therapy. In T. Paolino & B. McCrady (Eds.), *Marriage and marital therapy* (pp. 1–24). New York: Brunner/Mazel.

collective cognitive chaos: Bizarre, disruptive intrusions of so-called primary process thinking. Individual statements may appear sufficiently normal so that one would not ordinarily question the isolated statements. However, the overall transactional sequence may be utterly disjoined and fragmented.

Example: A husband appears to be talking with his wife about how he feels about her attitude toward his going hunting on the weekend. She responds to him by talking about his attitude toward the children. Each continues a separate dialogue. While each person makes sense, their interaction is disjointed.

Source: Singer, M., & Wynne, L. (1963). Thought disorder and family relations of schizophrenics. I. A research strategy. *Archives of General Psychiatry, 9,* 191–198.

Quoted: Wynne, L. (1965). Some indications and contraindications for exploratory family therapy. In I. Boszormenyi-Nagy & J. Framo (Eds.), *Intensive family therapy: Theoretical and practical aspects* (pp. 289–322). New York: Harper & Row.

collective pleasure principle: The assumption that, if two or more people join forces to help each other avoid the pain of emotional growth, their escape from reality amounts to a shared venture, as though their regressive mental economy was guided by a collective pleasure principle. This principle requires the coordinated role playing of its adherents. The symbiotic goal of the relationship is usually unconscious.

Example: Two individuals marry in order to form a childlike relationship that is based on mutual dependency and the sharing of good times.

Source: Boszormenyi-Nagy, I. (1965). A theory of relationships: Experiences and transaction. In I. Boszormenyi-Nagy & J. Framo (Eds.), *Intensive family therapy: Theoretical and practical aspects* (pp. 26–32). New York: Harper & Row.

collusion: A form of defective communication that allows parts of a family system to exploit the whole system. Such a system operates according to private rules of morality. There may be competition between parents or siblings and hostility toward others, which can be talked about only with certain people; and two or more members of the family may collude to discuss these secrets. The end result may be the appearance of deviant symptomatic behavior.

Example: A father uses his adolescent daughter to express his dissatisfaction with his wife. The father and daughter share the secret of his covert hostilities toward his wife. The daughter then begins to act out in order to divert some of the hostility toward the mother.

Source: MacGregor, R., Ritchie, A., Serrano, A., & Schuster, F. (1964). *Multiple impact therapy with families.* New York: McGraw-Hill.

color matching test: A technique used to generate interaction. The test is designed to see how couples cope with differences through built-in deception. A husband and wife are seated opposite each other with an easel between them so that they are blocked from each other's view. Each spouse looks at a series of numbered colored cards and is instructed to come up with the best possible match with a card that the tester holds up in view of both of them. A series of 20 trials is administered; for half of them, the correctly matched card is numbered differently for each spouse so that they must come to some agreement between themselves as to the best possible match.

Source: Goodrich, D., & Boomer, D. (1963). Experimental assessment of modes of conflict resolution. *Family Process, 2,* 15–24.

comarital relationship: An intimate involvement, probably but not necessarily including sexual intimacy, that is an adjunct to an established dyadic marriage. Comarital relations are distinguished from extramarital relations in that they are open and shared rather than covert and unshared, and they are based upon prior agreement within the dyadic relationship.

Source: Constantine, L.L., Constantine, J.M., & Edelman, S.K. (1975). Counseling implications of alternative marriage styles. In A.S. Gurman & D.G. Rice (Eds.), *Couples in conflict* (pp. 124–134). New York: Jason Aronson.

combination: The similarity or identity of response elements given individually and together in the Wechsler-Bellevue Intelligence Test.

Source: Bauman, G., & Roman, M. (1966). Interaction testing in the study of marital dominance. *Family Process, 5,* 230–242.

Quoted: Riskin, M., & Faunce, E. (1972). An evaluative review of family interaction research. *Family Process, 11*, 365–455.

combined marital therapy: A mix of conjoint (seeing both spouses together) and concurrent (seeing spouses separately) sessions that responds to changing needs and promotes adaptation to variable marital patterns.
Example: The husband feels inadequate and needs help in viewing himself as more capable; he accepts individual therapy and practices being more assertive to his wife in conjoint sessions. The wife is extremely critical of others, especially of her husband. She needs individual therapy to understand her inferiority complex and how she strives to be superior by making others feel less competent; conjoint sessions help her learn how to allow and encourage her husband to be successful and do something right.
Source: Greene, B., & Solomon, A. (1963). Marital disharmony: Concurrent psychoanalytic therapy of husband and wife by the same psychiatrist. *American Journal of Psychiatry, 17*, 433–450.
Quoted: Prochaska, J., & Prochaska, J. (1978). Twentieth century trends in marriage and marital therapy. In T. Paolino & B. McCrady (Eds.), *Marriage and marital therapy* (pp. 1–24). New York: Brunner/Mazel.

commitment: A standard that measures whether or not the family members take clear, definite stands, i.e., commit themselves to ideas, suggestions, and issues, and how they are asked to take such stands.
Example: Parents enforce bedtime schedules with their children regardless of their children's efforts to make excuses and manipulate the parents so that they can stay up later in the evening.
Source: Riskin, J., & Faunce, E. (1968). *Family interaction sides scoring manual.* (Available from the authors).
Quoted: Riskin, M., & Faunce, E. (1972). An evaluative review of family interaction research. *Family Process, 11*, 365–455.

communal marriage: A marriage in which there is theoretically sexual access by all members of a community to all persons (or a large specified subset) of the opposite sex in the community.
Source: Constantine, L.L., & Constantine, J.M. (1971). Group and multilateral marriage: Definitional notes, glossary and annotated bibliography. *Family Process, 10*, 157–176.

communication: Nonverbal and verbal behavior in a social context. Communication includes all those symbols and clues used by persons in giving and receiving meaning. The communication techniques people use can be seen as reliable indicators of interpersonal functioning. A study of communication can help close the gap between inference and observation, as well as help document the relationship between patterns of communication and symptomatic behavior.
Source: Satir, V. (1967). *Conjoint family therapy.* Palo Alto, Calif.: Science and Behavior Books.

communication games: A series of interactional techniques used to teach people to communicate more effectively and congruently, using eye and skin contact. It is very difficult to argue or deliver an incongruent message when one is talking to, touching, and looking at the listener.
Example: A couple are first asked to talk to one another while standing back to back at a distance. Then they are asked to eyeball each other and hold hands while trying to argue. The therapist helps the couple process what they learn from these exercises—e.g., not looking at each other is a setup for miscommunication.
Source: Satir, V. (1967). *Conjoint family therapy.* Palo Alto, Calif.: Science and Behavior Books.

communication therapy: An approach started by J.J. Jackson, fostered by the theoretical writing of J. Bateson, and developed more fully at the Palo Alto Mental Health Institute by Watzlawick and his associates (Levant, 1984). This approach has been elaborated and applied more directly by the Milano group (Hansen & L'Abate, 1982). Family communication processes have been incorporated into the basic theory underlying family therapy (Nichols, 1984). From studies of communication patterns in schizophrenic families, the following observations have been made:

- The family members do not affirm what they say; instead, they disqualify their own statements (e.g., smiling while saying something hurtful).
- Members do not confirm statements made by other family members; instead, they challenge the right of the other members to express themselves.
- Members do not assume the initiative, or leadership, in communication.
- Members do not permit overt alliances between other members.
- The mother is blamed for a communication breakdown but in ways that enable her to avoid accepting blame.

Because of ineffective communication, a family may be in a constant state of chaos and unreality. The confused, often contradictory, patterns of communication obscure, or mask, family problems rather than facilitate their resolution.

Studies of schizophrenic families have yielded important information about communication on two levels: (1) denotative (literal or overt content of message) and (2) metacommunicative (a covert message about the overt message). Example: The denotative message may say, "I hate you"; but the metacommunicative message says, "I wish I could love you" or "You hurt me."

Sources: Hansen, J., & L'Abate, L. (1982). *Approaches to family therapy.* New York: Macmillan; Levant, R.F. (1984). *Family therapy: A comprehensive overview.* Englewood Cliffs, N.J.: Prentice-Hall; Nichols, M.P. (1984). *Family therapy: Concepts and methods.* New York: Gardner Press.

commuter marriages: A marriage of professional spouses who maintain separate residences in the service of dual careers. A commuter marriage distinguishes between household and family, the latter term denoting a kinship or relational concept. Since two-residence marriages are a financial drain, commuters tend to be highly committed professionals who view their work as "a central life interest."

Source: Gerstel, N., & Gross, H.E. (1983). Commuter marriage: Couples who live apart. In E. Macklin & R. Rubin (Eds.), *Contemporary families and alternate lifestyles* (180–193). Beverly Hills: Sage.

competition: A concept used in multiple family therapy to describe mechanisms of change. Competition between systems (families) or subsystems (individuals) produces change in the internal power distribution of the system faster than work with a single family could do. A threat to the status of a family or an individual stimulates competition, which leads in turn to productive interaction of the family members at an earlier stage in treatment.

Example: A young boy scratches sores produced by a skin condition. He is given several behavioral alternatives to reduce the scratching behavior. The family members are instructed to keep a record of his scratching so that the therapist can tell which family is most helpful to the boy.

Source: Laqueur, H. (1972). Mechanisms of change in multiple family therapy. In C. Sager & H. Kaplan (Eds.), *Progress in group and family therapy* (pp. 400–415). New York: Brunner/Mazel.

Quoted: Laquer, H. (1976). Multiple family therapy. In P. Guerin (Ed.), *Family therapy* (pp. 405–417). New York: Gardner Press.

competitive marriage: A marriage in which each partner tries to inflict the most harm on the other in order to gain the most for self.

Example: Mark constantly criticizes his wife Mary for her lack of attention and affection. Consequently, he feels justified in not acting in a loving way toward her and frequently goes out partying with his single friends.

Source: Ravich, R., & Wyden, B. (1974). *Predictable pairing.* New York: Wyden.

complementarity: (1) serving to fill out, complete, or make perfect; and (2) mutually supplying each other's lack. Complementarity refers to the degree to which the needs and abilities of both spouses dovetail effectively, to the specific patterns of family role relations that provide satisfactions, avenues of solution of conflict, support for a needed self-image, and means of buttressing crucial forms of defenses against anxiety. Complementarity in family role relations may be further differentiated as being either positive or negative. *Positive complementarity* exists when the members of family pairs and triads experience mutual fulfillment of a need in a way that promotes positive emotional growth of the relationships and of the interacting individuals. *Negative complementarity* in family relations signifies a buttressing of defenses against pathogenic anxiety but does not significantly foster positive emotional growth. Negative complementarity mainly neutralizes the destructive effects of conflict and anxiety and barricades family relationships and vulnerable family members against trends toward disorganization.

Example: Positive complementarity: A wife and husband who are faced with a long automobile trip that neither wishes to make alone decide to go together, to make it a pleasure trip instead of an anxiety-producing duty, and to cooperatively share the driving. *Negative complementarity:* A husband believes he must have financial responsibility to avoid becoming anxious, while his wife fears financial responsibility and becomes anxious and depressed if forced to assume control of fiscal matters; here the partners complement each other negatively: one wants control, the other eschews it.

Source: Ackerman, N.W. (1968). *The psychodynamics of family life.* New York: Basic Books. *Quoted:* Sager, C.J. (1976). *Marriage contracts and couple therapy.* New York: Brunner/Mazel.

complementarity of roles: A relationship in which each person automatically acts in conformity with the role that that person is expected to assume by the partner. When these expectations are violated, the result is tension, anxiety, and frustration.
Example: A husband acts passively to comply with the requests of his domineering wife.
Source: Goodwin, H.M., & Mudd, E.H. (1969). Marriage counseling: Methods and goals. In B. Ard & C. Ard (Eds.), *Handbook of marriage counseling* (pp. 93–105). Palo Alto, Calif.: Science and Behavior Books.

complementary schismogenesis: A tendency toward progressive change between individuals or groups of individuals. A cycle is established in which a change in one leads to a change in the others.
Example: In a marital relationship, one partner is more assertive than the other. The more the assertive the first partner, the more the other submits, thereby forcing the assertive partner to be even more assertive.
Source: Bateson, G. (1958). *Naven* (2nd ed.). Stanford, Calif.: Stanford University Press.
Quoted: Bodin, A. (1981). The interactional view: Family therapy approaches of the Mental Research Institute. In A.S. Gurman & D.P. Kniskern (Eds.), *Handbook of family therapy* (pp. 267–309). New York: Brunner/Mazel.

compliance-based paradox: An intervention in which the client tries to obey a paradoxical prescription, designed to bring an involuntary behavior under voluntary control by creating an ordeal for the patient.
Example: A woman who is a perfectionist at housecleaning is told to do more. The increased work makes her problem so aversive that she decides to give it up.
Source: Rohrbaugh, M., et al. (1981). Compliance, defiance, and therapeutic paradox. *American Journal of Orthopsychiatry, 51,* 454–467.
Quoted: Weeks, G., & L'Abate, L. (1982). *Paradoxical psychotherapy.* New York: Brunner/Mazel.

compliment: An intervention designed to build a yes set for a family. A compliment consists of some positive statement with which all members of the family can agree.
Example: The therapist says to the parents, "I am impressed with all the fine details you've given me. It's clear you are loving parents who have tried to find ways to solve the problem."

Source: de Shazer, S. (1982). *Patterns of brief family therapy.* New York: Guilford Press.

components in marital interaction: Four areas of interaction between spouses: (1) the things you know about yourself and those your mate knows about you; (2) the things your mate knows about you that you do not know about yourself; (3) the things you know about yourself that your mate does not know; and (4) the things about yourself that neither you nor your mate know. These components can be depicted graphically (see Figure 1).
Example: The marriage therapist knows that, at the beginning of the counseling, the "open" area is usually very small, otherwise the couple would be getting along better. As counseling proceeds successfully, Area 1 gets much larger as you and your partner really get to know each other. At the same time, the "hidden" area gets much smaller. You do not feel you have to be as defensive. Later in counseling, Area 2, "blindness," gets smaller as you grow more honest with yourself. Gradually, you gain the courage to face yourself, and you finally decrease the size of Area 4, the "unknown." You come to understand some of your unconscious motives and improve your ways of communicating. Permanent change in the marital relationship can occur at this stage.
Source: Sauber, S.R. (1972). *An honest guide to marriage counseling.* W. Palm Beach, Fla.: Mental Health Association Press.

compression theory: The theory that dysfunctional families continually oscillate from intense fusion with the nuclear family to intense fusion with the family of origin.
Example: A young couple are normally inseparable until they have an argument. Then they split and return to their respective families for support.

Figure 1 Components in Marital Interaction

	known to you	unknown to you
known to spouse	**1** OPEN AREA *freedom*	**2** BLIND AREA *caution*
unknown to spouse	**3** HIDDEN AREA *defensiveness*	**4** UNKNOWN AREA *fear*

Source: Stanton, M. (1981). Strategic approaches to family therapy. In A.S. Gurman & D.P. Kniskern (Eds), *Handbook of family therapy* (pp. 361–402). New York: Brunner/Mazel.

compulsory relationship: A relationship in which two family members feel that an association is not voluntary, so neither can accept as valid any indication from the other about wanting to be together. Affectionate gestures are disqualified as requests that the person doing the gesturing not be turned out or left alone; the gestures are rather regarded as a kind of bribery.
Example: A mother indicates with some contempt that her husband is afraid to leave her because he cannot stand being alone. She suggests he is cruel to her because he is angry at being tied to her. She also rejects his affectionate overtures because she considers them to be only a kind of bribery to ensure his staying with her. She herself is unable to leave him even for a night, though he is drunk several nights a week and beats her regularly.
Source: Haley, J. (1959). The family of the schizophrenic: A model system. *Journal of Nervous and Mental Disease. 129,* 357–374.
Quoted: Haley, J. (1972). The family of the schizophrenic. In G.D. Erickson & T.P. Hogan (Eds.), *Family Therapy: An introduction to theory and technique* (pp. 51–75). Belmont, Calif.: Wadsworth.

conation: The ability to choose goals and to pursue them with energy, motivation, and drive.
Source: Beavers, W.R. (1977). *Psychotherapy and growth: A family systems perspective.* New York: Brunner/Mazel.

conciliation: A technique often used in connection with mediation. The conciliator (1) offers options for the parties to consider, (2) points out the advantages and disadvantages of various options, and (3) encourages the parties to adopt an available option rather than remain at an impasse. To some extent, the conciliator takes over the parties' responsibility for examining the issues and discovering options. Conciliation is thus a less desirable procedure than mediation and serves as an alternative to an impasse. It may be needed not because the parties are unwilling to take responsibility but because they are often inexperienced in dealing with much of the subject matter.
Source: Coogler, O.J. (1978). *Structured mediation in divorce settlement.* Lexington, Mass.: Lexington Books.

concordance: The ratio of agreements to disagreements for an individual or the whole family.
Source: Lennard, H., & Bernstein, A. (1969). *Patterns in human interaction.* San Francisco: Jossey-Bass.

concurrent marital therapy: Therapy in which both spouses are simultaneously treated either by the same therapist or by different therapists who communicate with each other.
Source: Mittleman, B. (1944). The concurrent analysis of marital couples. *Psychoanalytic Quarterly, 13,* 479–491.
Quoted: Prochaska, J., & Prochaska, J. (1978). Twentieth century trends in marriage and marital therapy. In T. Paolino & B. McCrady (Eds.), *Marriage and marital therapy* (pp. 1–24). New York: Brunner/Mazel.

concurrent processes: Interviews with different groupings of the family conducted separately by the therapist during the same period of treatment.
Example: A couple cannot sit together in the therapist's office without fighting. While continuing the sessions together, they are also seen for individual sessions to help reduce the level of anger.
Source: Aponte, H., & Van Deusen, J. (1981). Structural family therapy. In A. Gurman & D. Kniskern (Eds.), *Handbook of family therapy* (pp. 310–360). New York: Brunner/Mazel.

conductors: Therapists with aggressive, public, charismatic personalities, who have strong value systems that are imparted in the therapy session. Conductors exercise their active control in families in direct and obvious ways. They take the role of educators or "super-parents" and openly and directly confront the family's pathological functioning. They may intervene persuasively, seductively, or manipulatively.
Example: A father takes charge of a family meeting and sees to it that most family business is transacted in a democratic atmosphere.
Sources: Skynner, R. (1976). *Systems of family and marital psychotherapy.* New York: Brunner/Mazel; L'Abate, L. (1983). Styles in intimate relationships: The A-R-C model. *The Personal and Guidance Journal, 61,* 81–83.

configuration: One of three underlying dimensions utilized by Reiss to characterize the concept of "family constructs." Configuration refers to the degree of complexity allowable in the experiences of family members. The configuration dimension varies from subtle, detailed, and highly structured

to coarse, simple, or chaotic. Families who tend toward the former pole of the dimension reflect a sense of optimism and mastery when confronted with a novel or ambiguous social setting; events and people are construed as multifaceted, with relationships between family members conditional on many factors. Families who tend toward low configuration reflect a resistance to exploring novel or ambiguous environments; such families would be classed according to simple attributes, and the relationships between family members would be perceived as either incomprehensible or very stylized.
Source: Reiss, D. (1981). *The family's construction of reality.* Cambridge, Mass.: Harvard University Press.

confirming: A process in which the therapist validates the reality of the holons (the component parts of the system that) the therapist joins. The therapist acknowledges and rewards positive aspects and identifies stressful, difficult, or painful areas. In confirming the positive, the therapist becomes an important source of self-esteem. By acknowledging the negative, the therapist becomes a source of sensitivity and understanding. Confirming may also be a nonjudgmental appraisal of transactions between family members.
Source: Minuchin, S., & Fishman, H. (1981). *Family therapy techniques.* Cambridge, Mass.: Harvard University Press.

conflict: Disruptions that, in abstract terms, are viewed as power struggles and, in simple operational terms, are regarded as interruptions or disagreements.
Example: A son tells his natural father that he prefers to spend time with his new stepfather.
Quoted: Riskin, M., & Faunce, E. (1972). An evaluative review of family interaction research. *Family Process, 11,* 365–455.

conflict-habituated marriage: A marriage characterized by severe conflicts but in which, unpleasant as it is, the partners are held together by a fear of separation. The spouses quarrel habitually, acknowledge their incompatibility, and accept tension as normal. Arguments are often over trivial matters.
Example: A husband and wife in their later years acknowledge their incompatibility as they identify the wife's intellectual curiosity about life and social interests and the husband's lack of education and his preference to be alone and to exclude himself from knowledge-stimulating experiences. Their dissatisfaction is compounded by the wife's resent-

ment of the excessive number of working hours her husband spends in his business and her hostility when he returns home after work exhausted from his long day.
Source: Cuber, J., & Harroff, P. (1965). *The significant Americans.* New York: Random House.

conflict negotiation: A process in which thoughts, feelings, and a range of solutions are shared by family members in conflict, as the members alternate roles of sender and receiver.
Source: Miller, S., Nunnally, E., & Wackman, D. (1975). *Alive and aware: Improving communications in relationships.* Minneapolis, Minn.: Interpersonal Communications Program.
Quoted: Barnard, C., & Corrales, R. (1979). *The theory and technique of family therapy.* Springfield, Ill.: Charles C Thomas.

conflict resolution family therapy: Therapy that presents the usual interaction framed as interpersonal problems and suggests that these problems have concrete solutions in the interpersonal realm. The tasks are clearly structured, deal with family situations, are focused on the here and now, and compel family members to search for solutions through interaction among themselves.
Example: A family council is established to meet weekly to review family chores—how each member is completing household responsibilities that that member has selected as contributions to the management of the home, and the consequences to the individual and the family when a member is unreliable.
Source: Minuchin, S. (1965). Conflict-resolution family therapy. *Psychiatry, 28,* 278–286.
Quoted: Minuchin, S. (1972). Conflict-resolution family therapy. In G.D. Erickson & T.P. Hogan (Eds.), *Family therapy: An introduction to theory and technique* (pp. 293–305). Belmont, Calif.: Wadsworth.

confusion technique: A systemic technique used to help couples or families who cannot formulate clear treatment goals because of their confusion. The therapist adds more confusion to the system by using language filled with incongruities, ambiguities, fuzziness, ill-formed sentences, and unclear statements.
Source: de Shazer, S. (1982). *Patterns of brief family therapy.* New York: Guilford Press.

congruent communication: Communication in which two or more messages are sent via different levels but none of the messages seriously contradicts any of the others.

Example: A husband says, "The dog is on the couch," in an irritable tone and in a context that tells his wife that he is irritated and why he is irritated.
Source: Satir, V. (1967). *Conjoint family therapy.* Palo Alto, Calif.: Science and Behavior Books.

conjoint family therapy: A therapeutic approach devised by Jackson in which the whole family is the therapeutic unit for treatment and the family members meet as a group with the therapist in order to change family interaction.
Sources: Jackson, D., & Weakland, J. (1961). Conjoint family therapy. *Psychiatry, 24,* 30–45; Martin, P. (1976). *A marital therapy manual.* New York: Brunner/Mazel.

conjoint marital therapy: A therapeutic model in which both marital partners are seen together by the same therapist, or by co-therapists—one male and one female—and in which the problem is seen as an interactional problem.
Source: Jackson, D., & Weakland, J. (1961). Conjoint family therapy. *Psychiatry, 24,* 30–45.
Quoted: Martin, P. (1976). *A marital therapy manual.* New York: Brunner/Mazel.

conjoint parent-child therapy: A therapeutic technique in which the parent and the child are seen together by one therapist. Conjoint parent-child therapy allows the clinician to assess the parent's functioning, the child's functioning, and the parent-child relationship. Children of ages six to ten often react favorably to this technique.
Source: Wertheim, E.S. (1959). A joint interview technique with mother and child. *Children, 6,* 23–29.

consanguine family: A family that is joined on the basis of blood relationships, so that several generations of offspring are included within one family unit.
Source: Christensen, H. (1964). Development of the family field of study. In H. Christensen (Ed.), *Handbook of marriage and the family* (pp. 3–32). Chicago: Rand McNally.

consecration ceremonials: Interactional behavior patterns, usually engaged in by all family members, that are often formalized and repetitive in nature. These ritual patterns define the family's image, exemplify its past history, and objectify its beliefs about itself.
Example: Three sons arm-wrestle with their father each time he returns home after a long absence, with their mother cheering them on. This ritual

encompasses the family's sense of its tough past. The concern of the father not to hurt the boys, and, as they become men, their care not to hurt him, symbolizes the family's compassion for the weak.
Source: Reiss, D. (1981). *The family construction of reality.* Cambridge, Mass.: Harvard University Press.

consensual experience theory: A theory developed to explain, relate, and predict observations made simultaneously on both family interactions and the thinking and perception of individual members as these unfold together through time. Essentially, the theory states that each family develops its own shared and distinctive view or explanation of its environment and of the patterns or principles that govern its members and events.
Example: A family moves to a new neighborhood. All of the family members see themselves as outsiders. The members are suspicious of their neighbors, carefully protect their privacy, and make it a rule never to disclose personal information about themselves or the family.
Source: Reiss, D. (1971). Intimacy and problem solving: An automated procedure for testing a theory of consensual experience in families. *Archives of General Psychiatry, 25,* 442–455.

consensual validation: A method by which patients compare mental reactions to certain experiences while learning to understand, recognize, and feel more certain of their expressions of thought and feeling.
Example: A father who thinks he is socially inept learns from his family's reactions that he can handle interpersonal situations with skill, but his belief that he cannot prevents him from doing so.
Source: Sullivan, H.S. (1953). *The interpersonal theory of psychiatry.* New York: W.W. Norton.
Quoted: In Kaplan, H., & Sadock, B. (Eds.). (1971). *Comprehensive group psychotherapy.* Baltimore: Williams & Wilkins.

consensus-sensitive family: A family in which the primary characteristic is the press toward agreement. Family members discard accurate information in favor of data that is consistent with the views of others. Consequently, information is not evaluated based on objective standards but according to its congruence with family myths. The outside world is viewed as unpredictable, which promotes agreement in the family as a needed source of security. The family members maintain a rigid boundary with an outside world that is rarely trusted. The members display little tolerance for feedback that

contradicts their view of the world. As a result, verbal and nonverbal communications that are contrary to the family's consensus are rarely expressed. *Example:* A father who has been unemployed for over a year blames the union for his lack of work. Despite the evidence that his dismissal is due to repeated failure to perform his duties, no one in the family mentions this. They also fail to mention that he has lost jobs in the past, usually relating to his drinking problem. Instead, they nod agreement to his indictment of the union, even contributing their own examples of the injustices wrought upon them by union staffers.
Source: Reiss, D. (1981). *The family's construction of reality.* Cambridge, Mass.: Harvard University Press.

constricted family: A family characterized by excessive restriction of a major aspect of family emotional life, such as expression of anger, negative affect, or ambivalence. These emotions become internalized into anxiety, depression, and somatic complaints. The presenting patient is often a passive, depressed child or young adult.
Example: A domineering mother resents anyone arguing with her and sets up family rules of compliance. Her son's manner of resisting her is to become sick and get out of family obligations.
Source: Cuber, J., & Harroff, P. (1966). *Sex and the significant Americans.* Baltimore: Penguin.
Quoted: Glick, I., & Kessler, D. (1980). *Marital and family therapy* (2nd ed.). New York: Grune & Stratton.

consulting break: A method of working with families that involves the use of a team that observes the therapist(s) and family from behind a one-way mirror. The therapist periodically leaves the treatment room to consult with the team. This provides the team opportunities to design interventions.
Source: de Shazer, S. (1982). *Patterns of brief family therapy.* New York: Guilford Press.

content: In family systems theory, the particular themes and concretized attributes of life that, joined together through time, give thematic meaning to the daily activities of a family and its members. Content refers to the psychological phenomena that are the substance of systems concepts, such as information and energy. The hopes, dreams, envies, loves, memories, and aspirations of people's daily lives make up the content of individual phenomenal experience. One may select for study a content theme—such as personal identity images, family ideals, or parental power—or one may postulate

that human activity is about anything, such as the defense against forbidden impulses, the organization of mental operations into automatic response patterns, and so forth. But once the content theme has been selected, one needs to recognize that it, per se, is only of secondary importance, at least from a systems perspective.
Example: The mother speaks about how busy her day was and all of the activities that she had to accomplish.
Source: Umbarger, C.C. (1984). *Structural family therapy.* New York: Grune & Stratton.

content-context syndrome: A kind of marital relationship in which one partner pays attention to content only in verbal communications, both his own and others, and the other partner pays attention to nonverbal communications, both his own and others. The first partner is content-oriented, the second context-oriented. In such a situation, there are bound to be communication gaps between the two.
Example: The wife listens carefully to what her husband says as he does home repairs and evening business work and they discuss family matters. The husband ignores his wife's "babbling" and responds only when she approaches him with nonverbal strokes of affection leading to sex or when, in anger, she stamps her foot to demand his attention.
Source: Hogan, P. (1963). The content-context syndrome. *Newsletter, Society for Medical Psychoanalysts, 4,* pp. 1–6.
Quoted: Gerson, M., & Barsky, M. (1979). For the new family therapist: A glossary of terms. *American Journal of Family Therapy, 7,* 15–30.

context: The situation in which people are communicating, including both the physical situation and the stated premises about what sort of situation it is. The context in which a statement is made may disqualify the statement.
Example: A college student makes a sexual statement to her instructor in class, but the statement is disqualified due to the public nature of the situation.
Source: Haley, J. (1972). The family of the schizophrenic. In G. Erickson & T. Hogan (Eds.), *Family therapy: An introduction to theory and technique* (pp. 51–75). Belmont, Calif.: Wadsworth.

contextual family therapy: Therapy in which family members are guided toward working on their own relational commitments and balances of fairness. The aim is to loosen the chains of invisible loyalty and legacy so that each person can give up symptomatic behaviors and explore new options. All partners shift their intentions toward a rejunctive effort.

Example: A father has difficulty showing love to his son. The therapist asks him about how his own father showed affection toward him. He also asks the father to see his own father's side in order to help open up a multilateral perspective of fairness toward his son. Additionally, the therapist may have the father open up his relationship with his own father in order to balance the ledger.

Source: Boszormenyi-Nagy, I., & Ulrich, D. (1981). Contextual family therapy. In A. Gurman & D. Kniskern (Eds.), *Handbook of family therapy* (pp. 159–186). New York: Brunner/Mazel.

contingencies of reinforcement: Situations in which, instead of rewarding maladaptive behavior with attention and concern, family members learn to give each other recognition and approval for desired behavior.

Example: When Johnny completes his homework, Dad reinforces his study behavior by showing his interest and approval and by playing a game of Scrabble with him.

Source: Liberman, R. (1970). Behavioral approaches to family and couple therapy. *American Journal of Orthopsychiatry.* 40, 106–118.

Quoted: Liberman, R. (1972). Behavioral approaches to family and couple therapy. In G.D. Erickson & T.P. Hogan (Eds.), *Family therapy: An introduction to theory and technique* (pp. 120–134). Belmont, Calif.: Wadsworth.

contingency contracting: A specific, usually written schedule or contract describing the terms for the trading or exchange of behaviors and reinforcers between two or more individuals.

Example: A man's newly married wife joined him when he had weekend visitations with his children. The husband then agreed to spend more time with his in-laws.

Source: Stuart, R.B. (1976). An operant interpersonal program for couples. In D.H.L. Olson (Ed.), *Treating relationships.* Lake Mills, Iowa: Graphic Publishing.

contingency management: A technique that involves assessing the way in which contingencies are being mismanaged and instructing change agents about the necessary modifications.

Example: A young encopretic boy is being reinforced by his mother's attention. When this is pointed out to the mother, who is the change agent, and she is instructed to reward certain toileting behaviors, the problem is ameliorated.

Source: Homme, L., & Tosti, D. (1969). Contingency management and motivation. In D. Gelfand, (Ed.), *Social learning in childhood: Readings in theory and application.* Belmont, Calif.: Brooks/Cole.

Quoted: LeBow, M. (1972). Behavior modification for the family. In G. Erickson & T. Hogan (Eds.), *Family therapy: An introduction to theory and technique* (pp. 347–376). Belmont, Calif.: Wadsworth.

continuity: A coding category referring to messages that affect the continuation of communication in terms of facilitating or interfering responses, e.g., pauses, silences, repetitions, or restatements of previous messages.

Example: A wife is not sure what she heard her husband say. She repeats what she thought she heard, which helps to facilitate the communication.

Source: Sojit, C. (1969). Dyadic interaction in a doublebind situation. *Family Process, 8,* 235–260.

contract marriage: A marital union, either legal or paralegal, that is identified by explicit written or spoken agreement outlining duties and privileges of the union's members. The contract may specify such items as who is responsible for domestic services, child care, and financial support and how many children the couple wishes to have.

Source: Rolfe, D. (1977). Pre-marriage contracts: An aid to couples living with parents. *Family Coordinator, 26,* 281–285.

Quoted: Belkin, G., & Goodman, N. (1980). *Marriage, family, and intimate relationships.* Chicago: Rand McNally.

contradictory communication: A communication in which two or more messages are sent in a sequence via the same communication level but in opposition to each other.

Example: A person says, "Come here," followed by, "No, go away;" or a person pulls another closer and then pushes that person away again.

Source: Satir, V. (1967). *Conjoint family therapy.* Palo Alto, Calif.: Science and Behavior Books.

control group: The family group that is compared to an experimental family group. Many types of control groups are analyzed in family interaction research, e.g., "normal" controls, hospitalized psychiatric nonschizophrenic patients and their families, hospitalized nonpsychiatric patients and their families, nonhospitalized patients and their families, and families from differing social classes and structures.

Source: Mishler, E., & Waxler, N. (1968). *Interaction in families: An experimental study of family processes and schizophrenia.* New York: John Wiley & Sons.

controlling-domineering messages: Messages that order, command, or forbid; challenge another's assertion; refuse to do something; contradict, protest, or deny; compare or compete; or brag or persist in a topic.
Example: A wife says to her husband: "You must visit my parents with me whether you like it or not."
Source: McPherson, S. (1968). *A manual for multiple coding of family interaction.* Unpublished manuscript.
Quoted: Riskin, M., & Faunce, E. (1972). An evaluative review of family interaction research. *Family Process, 11,* 365–455.

cooperating: A means of accommodation in a relationship. Each individual, couple, or family has a unique way of attempting to cooperate. The therapist's job is, first, to identify that particular manner, then to cooperate with the family's way, thus promoting change. The concept of cooperating completely negates the traditional concept of resistance. Whatever the family does is an expression of how they cooperate with the therapist.
Source: de Shazer, S. (1982). *Patterns of brief family therapy.* New York: Guilford Press.

cooperative marriage: A marriage in which the partners take turns exercising power in a positive way.
Example: The husband makes decisions about money after consulting with his wife, and she makes social and domestic plans after asking her husband's opinion.
Source: Ravich, R., & Wyden, B. (1974). *Predictable pairing.* New York: Wyden.

coordination: Family members' ability and willingness to develop similar problem solutions. Coordination also refers to the experience by all family members that they are, for the moment, in the same experiential universe, whose principles and patterns are equally true and equally relevant for all members.
Example: All members of a family agree that the best way to deal with cleaning the house is for everyone to have assigned tasks that are to be fulfilled on a specified day of the week.
Source: Reiss, D. (1981). *The family's construction of reality.* Cambridge, Mass.: Harvard University Press.

coping devices: Expedients that meet or attenuate the effect of an attacking agent and repair its damage. Coping involves defense, adaptation, and reparation. It is the price the organism must pay in order to preserve its integrity. The devices may be primitive (verbal hostility, withdrawal, anxiety) or directed (fantasy, unrealistic thought, perceptual distortions).
Example: A man suspects his wife is having an affair. His mother is dying of cancer. Rather than deal with his suspicions regarding his wife while under such stress, he begins to distort his perceptions of himself and to tell himself that he is an overly jealous husband.
Source: Howells, J. (1975). *Principles of family psychiatry.* New York: Brunner/Mazel.

coping patterns: The patterns used to respond to different kinds of influences to change behavior.
Example: Every time a wife asks her husband to make a specific change, he agrees, but then acts as if nothing had been discussed.
Source: Goldstein, M., Judd, L., Rodnick, E., Alkire, A., & Gould, E. (1968). A method for studying social influence and coping patterns within families of disturbed adolescents. *Journal of Nervous and Mental Disorders, 148,* 233–251.
Quoted: Riskin, M., & Faunce, E. (1972). An evaluative review of family interaction research. *Family Process, 11,* 365–455.

cop-out: The use of excuses for not engaging in potentially desirable behavior.
Example: A wife states that, if she shows her husband any affection, he will only want to have sex with her.
Source: Wahlroos, S. (1974). *Family communication.* New York: Macmillan.

cotherapeutic modeling: A process in which two therapists, each taking the point of view of one of the spouses, argue on behalf of their clients in front of the couple.
Example: The husband's therapist argues that he is dissatisfied with the marriage because he continually experiences criticism, no matter what efforts he makes to improve the relationship and please his wife. The wife's therapist points out that she sees her husband trying only to placate her superficially to assuage his guilt in making a separation.
Source: Lazarus, A. (1968). Behavior therapy and marriage counseling. *Journal of the American Society of Psychosomatic Dentistry and Medicine, 15,* 49–56.

Quoted: LeBow, M. (1972). Behavior modification for the family. In G. Erickson & T. Hogan (Eds.), *Family therapy: An introduction to theory and technique* (pp. 347–376). Belmont, Calif.: Wadsworth.

cotherapy: Therapy in which a male and female therapist work with a couple concerning sexual and identity issues in the marriage in order to represent each sex's point of view and to serve as couple-relationship role models and potential transference figures.
Source: Gurman, A., & Kniskern, D. (1978). Research on marital and family therapy: Progress, perspective, and prospect. In S. Garfield & A. Bergin (Eds.), *Handbook of psychotherapy and behavior change* (pp. 817–901). New York: Wiley.

counteraccusation: A primitive way of avoiding personal responsibility for solving a problem and of hurting another person in return.
Example: A wife says to her husband, "How long are you going to postpone fixing that fence?" The husband replies, "Look who's talking! What about you and your ironing? I don't even get to wear a clean shirt to the office!"
Source: Wahlroos, S. (1974). *Family communication.* New York: MacMillan.

countertransference: A process in which the therapist begins to experience feelings toward a family member that are reminiscent of feelings experienced in relation to a person in the therapist's past. The therapist can report this to the family, and the family can then process any similar feelings on its part. The countertransference material can then become corrective feedback for the family.
Example: A hostile father in a family reminds the therapist of abuse that the therapist sustained as a child, causing the therapist to respond to the father with fear and hostility.
Source: Barnard, C., & Corrales, R. (1979). *The theory and technique of family therapy.* Springfield, Ill.: Charles C Thomas.

covenant contracting: An intervention to help couples negotiate emotional and behavioral components of their relationship. Individual contracts are trileveled: (1) conscious and verbalized, (2) conscious but unspoken, and (3) beyond awareness. Their categories of expectation are based on (1) expectations of a relationship, (2) each individual's psychological needs, and (3) external problems resulting from the preceding two areas. The actual contract focuses on four sets of needs within the marriage: self, marriage, spouse, and children.

Example: A wife lists the following needs in her contract.

- Self: (1) I want to be more self-confident. (2) I want to exercise more.
- Marriage: (1) I want to do more things with my husband. (2) I want to talk more about feelings.
- Mate: (1) I want my spouse to believe in me. (2) I want him to be proud of himself.
- Children: (1) I want my children to be responsible. (2) I want my children to enjoy learning.

Source: Sager, C. (1976). *Marriage contracts and couple therapy.* New York: Brunner/Mazel.
Quoted: L'Abate, L., & McHenry, S. (1983). *Handbook of marital interventions.* New York: Grune & Stratton.

covert sensitization: A conditioning technique in which deviant sexual behavior is paired with noxious stimuli or an aversive event.
Example: A rapist is asked to imagine approaching a woman to rape her. He then shifts his image to one that is highly aversive to him, such as vomiting or seeing maggots on his victim.
Source: Callahan, E., & Leitenberg, H. (1973). Aversion therapy for sexual deviation: Contingent shock and covert sensitization. *Journal of Abnormal Psychology, 21,* 60–73.
Quoted: Walen, S., Hauserman, N., & Lavin, P. (1977). *Clinical guide to behavior therapy.* Baltimore: Williams & Wilkins.

covert sexual examination: A diagnostic sex hypnotherapy technique in which the client is asked to stand naked in front of a full-sized, three-way mirror and to describe and evaluate every part of his or her body.
Source: Araoz, D. (1982). *Hypnosis and sex therapy.* New York: Brunner/Mazel.

crazy-making: A variety of techniques, all of which have one thing in common: to make one doubt one's sanity.
Example: A husband exercises complete control over his wife's behavior. When she points out his control, he says that he is only taking care of her. In effect, he says it is for her sake that he monitors her behavior.
Source: Bach, G., & Wyden, P. (1968). *The intimate enemy.* New York: William Morrow.

creating a crisis: A situation in which the therapist deliberately creates or provokes a crisis situation in order to upset the family balance or homeostasis and to force the family to change.

Example: A family with an anoretic child might be forced into a direct confrontation by having the parents force the child to eat.

Source: Jackson, D. (1968). The question of family homeostasis. In D. Jackson (Ed.), *Communication, family, and marriage* (pp. 1–11). Palo Alto, Calif.: Science and Behavior Books.

Quoted: Gerson, M., & Barsky, M. (1979). For the new family therapist: A glossary of terms. *American Journal of Family Therapy, 7,* 15–30.

crisis: Events or happenings outside or inside the family unit that upset the traditional ways of interacting, thus demanding change in the family system. In an adaptive approach to crises, any change is carefully regulated so that when the crises occur, a minimal upset and a rapid return to the status quo is facilitated. Past experiences or future goals are used to solve the crises. In a maladaptive approach, no process for family interaction in crisis resolution is experienced. A crisis is handled by means of superimposed structures or fixed rules. If these structures are ineffective, a secondary crisis develops out of the family dysfunction.

Example: A wife suddenly announces to her husband that she is incapable of returning to the marriage and does not deserve his love. She admits having been sexually abused as a child and says she no longer wishes to be married. The wife's decision creates disruption and confusion. It can create an opportunity for individual and/or couple growth if pursued therapeutically, or it can lead to harm if the wife withdraws from her relationships and the husband becomes depressed, believing himself to be a failure in meeting the needs of his wife.

Source: Dodson, L., & Kurpuis, D. (1977). *Family counseling: A systems approach.* Muncie, Ind.: Accelerated Development.

crisis runaways: Runaways that fall between unsuccessful nonrunaways and abortive runaways. Crisis runaways manage to leave home for a while but do not find refuge in the runaway culture. They either return home or allow their parents to rescue them.

Example: A young adolescent male is caught shoplifting, then humiliated by his peers at school and rejected by his parents. He runs away but returns after a week.

Source: Stierlin, H. (1974). *Separating parents and adolescents.* New York: Quadrangle.

critical identity images: The internal memory pictures that comprise one's preferred self and ideal family. The conceptions of ''ideal self'' and ''ideal context,'' which each partner attempts to implement within an intimate relationship, result in a family system whose structure may be functional or dysfunctional.

Source: Kantor, D., & Lehr, W. (1975). *Inside the family.* San Francisco: Jossey-Bass.

Quoted: Okun, B.F., & Rappaport, L.J. (1980). *Working with families: An introduction to family therapy.* Belmont, Calif.: Brooks/Cole.

cross-confrontation: The use of audio- and videotapes, letters, and poems containing unpleasant, emotionally-charged material that is derived from one set of client families as stressor stimuli for another set of client families. The rationale underlying cross-confrontation is the need to assist people to perceive and understand that all feeling states are normal and that there are no abnormal fantasies.

Example: A family experiences difficulty grieving over the loss of a child. The therapist plays a tape from another family in which a breakthrough was made in dealing with a delayed grief reaction.

Source: Paul, N. (1976). Cross-confrontation. In P. Guerin (Ed.), *Family therapy* (pp. 520–529). New York: Gardner Press.

cross-generation coalition: A triadic structure that causes distress in social systems. The presence of such a triangle is associated with violence, symptomatic behavior, and dissolution of the system. The triangle consists of:

- two persons of the same status (generations) and another from a different level
- two members on different levels uniting against the third person
- two persons who have united in secret with the third person excluded covertly

Example: A mother feels lonely and bored in her marriage. She becomes dependent on her teenage son and begins to be overly permissive with him. The son takes advantage of the situation by becoming demanding, aggressive, and slack in school. The father attempts to discipline the son, but finds his attempts are covertly undermined by his wife.

Source: Haley, J. (1977). Toward a theory of pathological systems. In P. Watzlawick & J. Weakland (Eds.), *The Interactional View.* New York: W.W. Norton.

Quoted: Hoffman, L. (1981). *Foundations of family therapy.* New York: Basic Books.

cross-generational conflict: An inappropriate alliance between a parent and a child, who side together against a third member of the family.
Example: A woman and her mother always resented the daughter's husband for not providing her with the better things in life to which she was accustomed.
Source: Bowen, N. (1960). A family concept of schizophrenia. In D.D. Jackson (Ed.), *The etiology of schizophrenia*. New York: Basic Books.

cross-monitoring: A therapeutic exchange in which the person who is being spoken about is present and probably listening. Consequently, the person can alter behavior because of the information.
Source: MacGregor, R. (1962). Multiple impact psychotherapy with families. *Family Process, 1,* 15–29.
Quoted: MacGregor, R. (1972). Multiple impact psychotherapy. In G.D. Erickson and T.P. Hogan (Eds.), *Family therapy: An introduction to theory and technique* (pp. 150–163). Belmont, Calif.: Wadsworth.

cross-transactions: Situations in which, when asked a question, the respondent becomes defensive, assumes a child's ego state, and responds as if accused by a parent, thereby breaking off congruent communication.
Example: A husband asks a question from the adult ego state: "Would you like to go out tonight?" His wife responds from a child ego state: "No, you must want to go out so you can be with your friends." This elicits a response from the husband's parent ego state: "You're being childish again."
Source: Berne, E. (1967). *Games people play.* New York: Grove Press.

cryptic paradoxes: Messages used to create a state of confusion through the use of vague or ambiguous terms, undefined referents, contradictions, double meanings, etc.
Example: The following statement is made to a couple: "Your relationship is very nicely complementary, but since you can only be what the other is not, you cannot really be yourself."
Source: Weeks, G., & L'Abate, L. (1982). *Paradoxical psychotherapy.* New York: Brunner/Mazel.

crystal ball syndrome: A situation in which a client believes she should know something but doesn't and cannot ask. Furthermore, she assumes that the therapist should be able to guess what she is thinking.

Example: A male patient has a sexual attraction toward his male therapist but denies his homosexual feelings. He is too uncomfortable to express his emotions but thinks the doctor will be able to "read his mind."
Source: Satir, V. (1967). *Conjoint family therapy.* Palo Alto, Calif.: Science and Behavior Books.

cybernetics: The study of common processes in systems, especially analysis of the flow of information in closed systems. The cybernetic model is important to family theorists because it introduces the idea of circular causality by way of the feedback loop.
Example: A husband may be convinced that his wife's nagging (cause) makes him withdrawn (effect). She is equally likely to believe that his withdrawal causes her to nag.
Source: Weiner, N. (1954). *The human use of human beings: Cybernetics and society.* New York: Doubleday.
Quoted: Nichols, M. (1984). *Family therapy: Concepts and methods.* New York: Gardner Press.

cyclothymiosis: The cyclical nature of the mood changes of elation and depression. The condition is regarded as organic and endogenous.
Source: Howells, J. (1975). *Principles of family psychiatry.* New York: Brunner/Mazel.

D

decision making: The process used to make selections among alternatives based on understanding of past experiences, the present situation, and future expectations. The components include: 1) identifying the problem, 2) obtaining information and formulating possible courses of actions, 3) considering the consequences of each alternative, and 4) selecting a course of action. The content of a decision, the situation, and the personality of decision makers influence the arrangement of and the emphases within the components. The uses of the components are affected by the attitudes of the family members, the composition and resources of the family, the physical setting, and the power structure of the family.

Egalitarian decision making refers to sharing among all family members, in contrast to autonomic decision making, which is the delegation of decisions to individual family members according to specialization of areas. Strategies for decision making accord each family member a consensually agreed upon measure of control over the form and content of the interaction.

Example: A man who appears quite dominant in decision making may take cues from his wife's conversations that lead him to select a given alternative. Although he is dominant, his wife influences the outcome of the decision.

Source: Nickell, P., Rice, A.S., & Tucker, S.P. (1976). *Management in family living* (5th ed.). New York: John Wiley & Sons.

defense: The behavioral response of the organism to threat. The goal of defense is the maintenance of the current structure of the self. This goal is achieved (1) by the perceptual distortion of the experience in awareness in such a way as to reduce the incongruity between the experience and the structure of the self or (2) by the denial to awareness of the experience, thus denying any threat to the self. Thus, ''it is an observed phenomenon that material which is significantly inconsistent with the concept of self cannot be directly and freely admitted to awareness . . . When an experience is dimly perceived (or subceived is perhaps the better term) as being incongruent with the self-structure, the organism appears to react with a distortion of the meaning of the experience.''

Source: Rogers, C.P. (1959). A theory of therapy, personality and interpersonal relationships, as developed in the client-centered framework. In S. Koch (Eds.), *Psychology: A study of a science, Vol. III. Formulations of the person and the social context* (pp. 124–256). New York: McGraw-Hill. *Quoted:* Horne, A.M., & Ohlsen, M.M. (1982). *Family counseling and therapy.* Itasca, Ill.: F.E. Peacock Publishers.

defiance-based paradoxes: Interventions based on the assumption that the client will defy or oppose the paradoxical directive, that by predicting something will happen the therapist helps to make it not happen.

Example: A couple begins to have a few arguments after a couple of sessions of therapy. The therapist predicts more fights. This challenges the couple to prove the therapist wrong.

Source: Rohrbaugh, M. et al. (1981). Compliance, defiance, and therapeutic paradox. *American Journal of Orthopsychiatry, 51*, 454–467. *Quoted:* Weeks, G., & L'Abate, L. (1982). *Para-*

doxical psychotherapy. New York: Brunner/Mazel.

deficiency needs: Needs that are based on having been deprived of something necessary for emotional satisfaction, such as a need for love, respect, belonging, or security. The individual is thus motivated to fill the deficit.

Example: A woman raised soley by her divorced mother seeks relationships with older men.

Source: Maslow, A. (1954). *Motivation and personality.* New York: Harper & Row.

degradation ceremonials: Interactional behavior patterns, engaged in by family members, whose primary function is to conceal aspects of the family's life that are considered frightening. Scapegoating is one form of degradation ceremonial. (See **scapegoating**.)

Example: A family dealing with the father's heart trouble begins to accuse one child of constantly damaging things belonging to the child or the family. This scapegoating allows the family to conceal their shared fears regarding the possible death of the father.

Source: Reiss, D. (1981). *The family construction of reality.* Cambridge, Mass.: Harvard University Press.

deindividuation: The sum total of transferences, misidentifications, generational reversals, and fusions resulting in implicit weakening of all family members' discrete ego boundaries and regression to an ego mass or ego fusion in the family. The members of the group do not notice the other group members as individuals.

Example: Mrs. S's ego boundaries shift back and forth among (1) identifying with her daughter's childish self, (2) identifying herself as her daughter Mary's extension, and (3) identifying herself as her own mother's extension.

Source: Boszormenyi-Nagy, I. (1965). Intensive family therapy or process. In I. Boszormenyi-Nagy & J. Framo (Eds.), *Intensive family therapy: Theoretical and practical aspects* (pp. 87–142). New York: Harper & Row.

delegated legacy obligation: An obligation that is paid only in the manner in which an individual has been taught.

Example: A beaten child becomes the child-beating parent.

Source: Stierlin, H. (1976). The dynamics of owning and disowning: Psychoanalytic and family perspectives. *Family Process, 15,* 277–288.

delegates: The parents' tendency to subject their children to centrifugal and centripetal pressures. By making their child into a delegate, they send him out while at the same time they hold on to him. The child becomes an extension of the parents' ambivalence.
Example: An adolescent daughter is encouraged to go out with her friends, but the parents restrict her social contacts to the ethnic neighborhood and request that she tell them where she has been and all about her friends' parents.
Source: Stierlin, H. (1974). *Separating parents and adolescents.* New York: Quadrangle.

demystification: A technique by which the therapist counters mystification, which involves attribution (of negative traits that denote either ''weakness'' or ''badness''), invalidation, and induction. To counter damaging attributions, i.e., attributions that such and such a person is weak or sick, the therapist must make sure that the family members learn to speak for their own feelings, needs, and interests.
Example: A mother who has constantly said, ''Louise (her adolescent daughter) is always so depressed,'' ''Louise is afraid of boyfriends,'' ''Louise hates her teachers,'' etc., learns that Louise can speak for her own feelings, experiences, and interests. At the same time, the mother learns to speak for herself and hence learns to communicate: ''I feel depressed,'' ''I need to be alone,'' ''I am annoyed when Louise wears dirty blue jeans,'' or even, ''I need Louise as a buffer between me and my husband.''
Source: Satir, V. (1964). *Conjoint family therapy.* Palo Alto, Calif.: Science and Behavior Books.

denial: The invalidation of a previous statement or the contradiction of previous statement's content (a subcategory of the disagreement code developed by Lennard and Bernstein).
Example:

Wife:	Remember, you promised you would be home at 5:00 P.M. tomorrow.
Husband:	I did not. I never used the word ''promise.''

Source: Lennard, H., & Bernstein, A. (1969). *Patterns in human interaction.* San Francisco: Jossey-Bass.

denial of sexuality: The repression of erotic impulses. Frequently sex is viewed as pornographic or dirty; the individual is taught as a youngster that sexual impulses are not acceptable and that sexuality is nasty, hostile, and immoral.

Example: A teenage girl refuses contraceptives because she denies herself as a sexual being; she has been told premarital sex is sinful and immoral.
Source: Kaplan, H.S. (1974). *The new sex therapy.* New York: Brunner/Mazel.

denotative level: The literal content of a message.
Source: Satir, V. (1967). *Conjoint family therapy.* Palo Alto, Calif.: Science and Behavior Books.

dependence: A type of family system in which boundaries between individuals or family roles are distorted. In some cases, however, the boundaries may still be clearly articulated, i.e., when one member is self-reliant and another is servile in an interdependent relationship. The first person may function in a problem-solving capacity, while the other person may continually focus on personal feelings and needs. This type of symbiotic relationship is seen dramatically in the hardworking wife and the alcoholic husband. There is often a shift of feelings and responsibility for behavior from one person to the other, exemplified by the statement, ''She made me do it.'' For such symbiotic families, the goal in therapy is to help each person function independently, consistent with that person's developmental level. The aim is for each person to take responsibility for that person's own thoughts, feelings, and behaviors.
Source: Erskine, R.G. (1982). Transactional analysis in family therapy. In A.M. Horne & M.M. Ohlsen. *Family counseling and therapy* (pp. 245–275). Itasca, Ill.: F.E. Peacock Publishers.

dependency: Behavior characterized by overly frequent or intense attachment to another person. The attachment can be emotional, physical, or financial, depending on what one person needs to survive. The family life-cycle can be characterized in terms of three major stages: (1) dependency; (2) independence, or denial of dependence, as in adolescence; and (3) interdependence—autonomous adulthood with the recognition that all of us need to rely on others just as others need to rely on us.
Example: The child needs to rely on a caretaker to survive. However, when the child grows into adulthood s/he learns to become freer financially, achieve greater physical distance, and separate emotionally from the care-taker.
Source: L'Abate, L. (in press). Distance, defeats, and dependency: Descriptive and explanatory concepts in family therapy. In L. L'Abate (Ed.),

Handbook of family psychology and psychotherapy. Homewood, Ill.: Dow Jones-Irwin.

depersonalization: The process of not responding to feelings and of reducing another person to a thing. Depersonalization is employed by an insecure person when the other person becomes too tiresome or disturbing. The insecure person feels that any kind of relationship will be self-impoverishing.
Example: A husband gives his wife his paycheck and expects that she will provide meals, have sex with him when he requests, and take care of all the needs and problems with the children. He, in turn, brings in the money, and he is entitled to go out socially to the neighborhood bar and to sports events with his male friends on weekends.
Source: Laing, R. (1969). *The divided self.* Baltimore: Penguin.

descent group: A larger type of family group based on parent-child genealogical relationships.
Source: Zeldtich, M. (1964). Cross-cultural analysis of family structure. In H. Christensen (Ed.), *Handbook of marriage and the family* (pp. 462–500). Chicago: Rand McNally.

designed experience: Exercises, simulations, and planned procedures that provide a common structure within which individuals interact. In the process, each person's creativity, meanings, reflections, etc., come into play. Such experiential structures, when coupled with cognitive generalizations and frameworks, aid people in learning "from the inside out." Abstract concepts can be drawn from commonly experienced simulations and explorations.
Example: The following exercise could be used in helping a large group of strangers get to know each other: Think of two nicknames or adjectives used to describe you as a child. One of these labels should be positive and the other negative. When you enter the conference room go around the room and introduce yourself, using these two labels. Don't explain them, just say something like, "Hi, I'm beautiful and prissy."
Source: Duhl, B.S. (1983). *From the inside out and other metaphors.* New York: Brunner/Mazel.

detouring: A process by which a conflict between parents is transformed into a conflict between either mother and child or father and child, in order to maintain the illusion of a harmonious relationship between the parents, even at the expense of the child. This is a rigid form of triad in which the marital coalition or spouse subsystem is expressed

by their unity to attack or protect, either way avoiding their own antagonisms.
Example: The father goes to work but often leaves work during the day. The wife discovers this behavior and reprimands him for it. The child senses the tension between the parents and begins to play hooky from school in order to redirect the parents' conflict.
Source: Minuchin, S. (1974). *Families and family therapy.* Cambridge, Mass.: Harvard University Press.

detouring-attacking coalition: A situation in which, although conflict exists, the parents handle it by uniting against the child, who is defined as "bad" or "the family problem." This pattern tends to produce behavior disorders, delinquency, and learning difficulties.
Example: Two parents have recently completed graduate school and do not know how they wish to spend their lives together. Their daughter suddenly develops a learning problem to redirect the parents' attention.
Source: Minuchin, S. (1974). *Families and family therapy.* Cambridge, Mass.: Harvard University Press.
Quoted: Barragan, M. (1976). The child-centered family. In P. Guerin (Ed.), *Family therapy* (pp. 232–248). New York: Gardner Press.

detouring conflict: A situation in which two family members preserve their relationship by detouring incipient conflict through a third person.
Example: A father and mother, both stressed at work, avoid attacking each other at home by uniting in an attack on their child, thereby detouring conflict between themselves. This detouring can be shown graphically as:

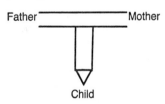

Source: Umbarger, C.C. (1984). *Structural family therapy.* New York: Grune & Stratton.

detouring-supporting coalition: A coalition in which the parents mask their relationship differences by focusing on their child. The parents get together in overprotecting, and being overly concerned with the child who they define as "weak" or "sick" rather than "bad." This pattern tends to produce shyness, insecurity, and psychosomatic disorders.

Example: Two parents have an implicit rule never to express conflict openly; this rule results in covert hostility. Their daughter refuses to eat, forcing them to redirect their attention to her anorexia. Or, when the husband becomes angry with his wife, she reminds him of their autistic child who must never see them argue. She fears her daughter would only withdraw further if subjected to parental disagreement and tension.

Source: Minuchin, S. (1974). *Families and family therapy.* Cambridge, Mass.: Harvard University Press.

detriangulation: The process of withdrawing from a role as buffer, go-between, or confounder in a disturbed family in which the members do not deal with each other on a one-to-one basis. Detriangulation reverses the process and permits the members to relate to one another on a person-to-person basis, responding rather than reacting.

Example: An older sister no longer finds it necessary to defend her effeminate younger brother when her father insists he play sports, stand up for himself when other kids in the school pick on him, and act like a man. He is now able to try to take care of himself.

Source: Bowen, M. (1971). The use of family theory in clinical practice. In J. Haley (Ed.), *Changing families* (pp. 159–192). New York: Grune & Stratton.

Quoted: Gerson, M., & Barsky, M. (1979). For the new family therapy: A glossary of terms. *American Journal of Family Therapy, 7,* 15–30.

deviation amplification: A process by which stress is increased in a system to a point of crisis, resulting in the need to organize a new set of relational patterns. This can be done by blocking the usual communication channels. The term is contrasted with deviation-counteracting. In deviation amplification, there may be a drift over time toward increasing differentiation, which at some point loses its advantageous nature and stability. All processes of mutual causal relationships that amplify an insignificant event build up deviation and impact from the initial state.

Example: Many young people start living together with the comfortable impression that they can always leave each other. Sooner or later, however, they find that time and habit have placed them in as binding a relationship as any marriage.

Source: Hoffman, L. (1981). *Foundations of family therapy.* New York: Basic Books.

devitalized marriage: A marriage that has lost its original zest, intimacy, and meaning. In this type of marriage the couple does not express dissatisfaction overtly. The spouses may conduct separate lives in many areas, but are joined together by legal and moral bonds and by children.

Example: The children have gone off to college, and the parents have little to share as husband and wife, since most of their relationship was child-oriented rather than couple-focused.

Source: Cuber, J., & Harroff, P. (1966). *Sex and the significant Americans.* Baltimore: Penguin.

Quoted: Glick, I., & Kessler, D. (1980). *Marital and family therapy* (2nd ed.). New York: Grune & Stratton.

differentiation: The degree of individuality one has vis-à-vis others, defined by a continuum of likeness (e.g., symbiosis, sameness, similarity, differentness, oppositeness, and autism).

Example: A son sees himself and acts in opposition to his father. He is not autonomous but is rather acting in terms of oppositeness.

Source: L'Abate, L. (1976). *Understanding and helping the individual in the family.* New York: Grune & Stratton.

differentiation and integration: A movement in open systems toward differentiation and elaboration, with specialized functions replacing diffuse global patterns. Human service organizations move in the direction of multiplication and elaboration of roles with increased specialization of functions. In this way, some parts of the open system come to cope with different parts of the external environment; other parts perform specialized tasks related to input, throughput, output, and other critical system processes. In order to maintain the unity of the parts as components of the whole, a reciprocal process of integration must occur. Without a sufficient degree of integration, the system breaks down into separate elements.

Example: A personality grows from crude, rather primitive organizations of mental functions into hierarchically structured and well-differentiated systems of beliefs and feelings. Thus, in this country today there are more medical specialists than general practitioners. Yet a new trend toward family practice and family medicine marks a revival of the generalist's attempt to integrate the parts into a whole.

Source: Sauber, S.R. (1983). *The human services delivery system.* New York: Columbia University Press.

differentiation of self: This concept is the cornerstone of Bowen's theory of psychotherapy. People are defined according to the degree of fusion, or differentiation, between emotional and intellectual functioning. This characteristic is so universal that all people can be classified somewhere along the continuum. People at the low end of the continuum are not able to distinguish between feeling and intellectual processes. These "fused" people are dominated by their automatic emotional system. Consequently, they are less flexible, less adaptable, and more emotionally dependent on those around them. These fused individuals are more easily stressed into dysfunction and have a difficult time recovering. People at the opposite end of the continuum are said to be differentiated. They are able to separate emotional and intellectual processes. They are more flexible, adaptable, and independent of others. The differentiated individual can cope effectively with the stresses of life which results in a relatively problem-free existence.
Example: An undifferentiated husband is not able to confront a marital problem rationally. He becomes upset and emotional as he expresses his perception of the problem.
Source: Bowen, M. (1976). Theory in the practice of psychotherapy. In P. Guerin (Ed.), *Family therapy* (pp. 42–90). New York: Gardner Press.

differentiation-of-self scale: A clinical scale developed to convey the idea that people have different gradations of differentiation of self. The scale is divided into four parts, each with an accompanying profile.
Example: At the low level of differentiation (0–25), individuals live in a feeling-dominated world in which it is impossible to distinguish fact from feeling. Individuals at this level are relationship-oriented and strive to win love and approval.
Source: Bowen, M. (1976). Theory in the practice of psychotherapy. In P. Guerin (Ed.), *Family therapy* (pp. 42–90). New York: Gardner Press.

differentness: How each person is innately different from every other person in the whole area of individuality. The concept relates to differences in physical appearance, personality, preferences, expectations, etc. These differences may unite a couple or create an irreconcilable division.
Example: A husband and wife have very different attitudes toward religion. The husband is areligious, while his wife stresses the importance of religious values and goes to church.

Source: Satir, V. (1967). *Conjoint family therapy.* Palo Alto, Calif.: Science and Behavior Books.

digital: The arbitrary encoding of a message so that it bears little or no resemblance to what it represents, as opposed to "analogic" in communication theory. Verbal language is primarily digital: it is abstract, efficient, and precise, yet may be less credible than analogical (nonverbal) communication in relationships. Whenever a word is used to represent something, the relationship between the noun and the thing is always arbitrary.
Example: The spoken words "I love you" represent a feeling. The words are arbitrary and they may not represent the way the person really feels. The person's actions (analogic communication) convey the true feelings.
Source: Watzlawick, P., Beavin, J., & Jackson, D. (1967). *Pragmatics of human communication.* New York: Norton.

directive: A therapeutic technique that is used to teach people how to behave differently while actively involving the therapist in the family system. The technique also provides the therapist with information regarding the functioning of the family system. The directive may consist of homework assignments, paradoxical or linear tasks, or specific prescriptions and specifications of roles and activities for various family members.
Source: Lange, A., & Van der Hart, O. (1983). *Directive family therapy.* New York: Brunner/Mazel.

disaffirmation: Contradictions contained in a message, including statements erroneously indicating that the other person misunderstood, thereby contradicting one's previous message, attributing one's own opinion to the other (although incongruent or contradictory with the previously stated opinion of the other), and reframing the previous message of the other incongruently or in contradiction with the other's previous message.
Example:

> *Husband:* I would like to go to the beach today.
> *Wife:* OK.
> *Husband:* I really have to work on the car today. It's not running right.
> *Wife:* Does this mean you're not going?
> *Husband:* I don't know.

Source: Sojit, C. (1969). Dyadic interaction in a double bind situation. *Family Process, 8,* 235–260.

disagreement: (1) denial of a previous statement, (2) negative evaluation of a previous statement, (3) qualification of the content of a previous statement, (4) dismissal of a previous statement as irrelevant, or (5) sarcasm in referring to a previous statement.
Example: The brother says to the child, "Put the paint back where you found it." The child responds, "This is where I found it."
Source: Lennard, H., & Bernstein, A. (1969). *Patterns in human interaction.* San Francisco: Jossey-Bass.
Quoted: Riskin, M., & Faunce, E. (1972). An evaluative review of family interaction research. *Family Process, 11*, 365–455.

discontinuity: A break in the sequence of interaction. In topic discontinuity, the previous statement is disregarded, or there is implicit disagreement.
Example: The husband says to the wife, "Did you get my clothes from the laundry?" The wife answers, "Mary called today. She wants us to go over to their place tonight."
Source: Lennard, H., & Bernstein, A. (1969). *Patterns in human interaction.* San Francisco: Jossey-Bass.
Quoted: Riskin, M., & Faunce, E. (1972). An evaluative review of family interaction research. *Family Process, 11*, 365–455.

discussion: A communicative interaction in which there is an exchange of ideas and feelings and in which the object is to reach greater understanding, to solve a problem, or simply to enjoy each other's company.
Example: The family members expect that at mealtime they will share their experiences and learn what is happening in the family.
Source: Wahlroos, S. (1974). *Family communication.* New York: Macmillan.

disengaged family: An extreme family type in which each family member is cut off from the other. There is little interaction, exchange of feelings, or sense of belongingness. There is a relative absence of connections, and relationships between family members are weak or nonexistent. The enmeshed family, by contrast, is characterized by a tight interlocking of its members.
Example: The father is involved with his work, the mother with church activities and various volunteer and charitable organizations. One child belongs to the Boy Scouts, working on an Eagle Scout badge, while another child skips school and acts out in predelinquent ways.

Source: Glick, I., & Kessler, D. (1980). *Marital and family therapy* (2nd ed.). New York: Grune & Stratton.

disengaged subsystem: A family subsystem that has developed overly rigid boundaries around itself. Members of disengaged subsystems function autonomously without interdependence and lack feelings of loyalty support and belonging; they have lost the ability to function interdependently or to request support when needed.
Example: Two siblings form an enmeshed relationship in delinquency that is separate and apart from parental influence.
Source: Minuchin, S. (1974). *Families and family therapy.* Cambridge, Mass.: Harvard University Press.

dismemberment crisis: The loss of an individual member from a family through divorce, separation, or death (as opposed to a crisis of accession, meaning an addition to the group, e.g., parenthood).
Source: Eliot, T.D. (1948). Handling family strains and shocks. In H. Becker & R. Hill (Eds.), *Family, marriage, and parenthood* (pp. 616–640). Boston: Heath & Company.
Quoted: Hoffman, L. (1981). *Foundations of family therapy.* New York: Basic Books.

disqualification: A method of denying a relationship by denying one or more of the four conceptual elements of communication: (1) "I (2) am saying something (3) to you (4) in this situation."
Example: A schizophrenic disqualifies a relationship with someone by saying he is someone else who is speaking (the "I" element).
Source: Haley, J. (1959). The family of the schizophrenic: A model system. *Journal of Nervous and Mental Disease, 129*, 357–374.

disruption in communication: A major interactional domain characterized operationally by tension release, laughter, pauses, repetitions, incomplete phrases, or incomplete sentences.
Example: A daughter is telling her father about her school work and test grades and then pauses suddenly, as she thinks about getting caught cheating and whether or not her teacher will notify her parents.
Source: Mishler, E., & Waxler, N. (1962). *Interaction in families: An experimental study of family process and schizophrenia.* New York: John Wiley & Sons.

disruptive behavior: Any disturbance that tends to interfere, detour, or distract from the flow and pattern of ongoing behavior.

Example: The husband gets angry when confronted by his wife about staying out late. The real issue is neither the confrontation nor his getting angry but rather the unsettled and unresolved distance between them. The wife is pursuing him to get closer. The husband's angry outburst, i.e., disruptive behavior, allows him to keep the distance unchanged and to take away attention from the real issue, that is the distance between them.
Source: Singer, M., & Wynne, L. (1966). Principles of scoring communication defects and deviances in parents of schizophrenics: Rorschach and TAT scoring manuals. *Psychiatry, 29,* 345–353.

dissipative stage: A stage of formation for a new system. In this stage, there is a high degree of information exchange between and within systems. There is also tension between the needs of the system and the needs of its individual members. This stage may be observed during couple formation and family formation, at the time children become school age, during adolescence, and when the children leave home.
Source: Minuchin, S., & Fishman, H. (1981). *Family therapy techniques.* Cambridge, Mass.: Harvard University Press.

distantiation: Discussion of experimental procedures or the expression of impersonal material, in referring to persons outside the family, talking about an absent family member, or discussing a family member in the third person as if that person were not present.
Example: A mother and father talk about their son's irresponsibility and what they should do about his interest in obtaining a driver's license and use of their car. The son is in their company, but he is not included in the discussion; they refer to him as "he-this" and "he-that" rather than as "you."
Source: McPherson, S. (1968). *A manual for multiple coding of family interaction.* Unpublished manuscript.
Quoted: Riskin, M., & Faunce, E. (1972). An evaluative review of family interaction research. *Family Process, 11,* 365–455.

distant-sensitive families: *See* **environment-sensitive families.**

distraction techniques: Techniques, subjective or objective, that are employed by a male partner to distract himself from his partner's demand for sexual fulfillment and to enhance ejaculatory control. These techniques are used frequently by premature ejaculators, although they are usually ineffective.
Example: Each time the husband is about to ejaculate before his wife is ready, he imagines sun bathing on the beach—feeling the heat of the sun, the sound of the waves, and the touch of the wind.
Source: Masters, W., & Johnson, V. (1970). *Human sexual adequacy.* Boston: Little, Brown.

disturbances in communication: (1) Communication deletions, i.e., removal of portions of an original experience; (2) communication distortions, i.e., change, exaggeration, or minimization of an experience; or (3) generalizations, e.g., "You never . . . ," or "You always. . . ." Deletions are equivalent to the psychoanalytic concept of repression, in most cases they involve the elimination of painful emotional experiences or the minimization of them by giving more emphasis to rational processes (distortions), which then result in a process of generalization. Other disturbances of communication take place through the process of externalization, in which external targets are made responsible for one's behavior.
Source: Bandler, R., and Grinder, J. (1975). *The structure of magic* (Vol. 1). Palo Alto, Calif.: Science and Behavior Books.

divided custody: A relatively unusual arrangement in which the children spend approximately half the time with one parent and half the time with the other. This arrangement is also called shared custody. Each parent generally has reciprocal visitation privileges. It is most workable when the two homes are in the same school district. Otherwise, it involves twice yearly upheavals from both school and neighborhood—a situation that most would consider educationally and psychologically detrimental.
Source: Gardner, R.A. (1982). *Family evaluation in child custody litigation.* Cresskill, N.J.: Creative Therapeutics.

divorce: A separation process that begins with the first serious thoughts and discussion a couple has about terminating the formal marriage contract and continues on to the moment of what seems to be a final decision. Divorce includes all the emotional, social, economic, and legal aspects related to the termination of a marital relationship.
Source: Barnard, C., & Corrales, R. (1979). *The theory and technique of family therapy.* Springfield, Ill.: Charles C Thomas.

divorce counseling or therapy: A process whereby the therapist helps those in the decision-making

phase of divorce to assess their needs, strengths and shortcomings and thus facilitates their arriving at a satisfactory decision (to stay married or to divorce). The therapist further helps couples and families that are facing divorce in the process of restructuring their individual lives, present and future relationships, problems with their children, financial difficulties, and general adjustment to singlehood.
Source: Kaslow, F. (1981). Divorce and divorce therapy. In A. Gurman & D. Kniskern (Eds.), *Handbook of family therapy* (pp. 662–698). New York: Brunner/Mazel.

divorce mediation: The process by which a couple meets together with a trained mental health professional or an attorney educated in mediation, and the psychology of the conflict resolution. The differences and issues for the couple are mediated in a task-oriented manner until a settlement is reached. In this process, each person assumes responsibility for his or her actions, respect for each other's concerns is expressed, and the integrity of the family unit is maintained. Although the husband and wife separate and obtain a divorce, the family continues and the agreement is discussed in terms of the relationships among mother, father, and children. The advisory attorney rewrites the mediated settlement in legal terms and relates impartially to the "family as the client," not to two parties in conflict. The settlement task for mediation includes division of marital property, possible spousal maintenance of rehabilitative alimony, required child support, shared parenting responsibilities, and custodial arrangements for the children.
Source: Sauber, S.R., & Panitz, D.R. (1982). Divorce counseling and mediation. In A. Gurman (Ed.). *Questions and answers in the practice of family therapy* (Vol. 2, pp. 207–213). New York: Brunner/Mazel.

doll's house marriage: Marriage in which a competent, powerful, but actually dependent, male is both mother and father to a helpless, childlike wife.
Source: Pittman, P.S. (1970). Treating the doll's house marriage. *Family Process, 9,* 143.
Quoted: Skynner, A. (1976). *Systems of family and marital psychotherapy.* New York: Brunner/Mazel.

domestic partners: Two individuals who reside together. For example, a partnership ordinance proposed in San Francisco in 1982 but not yet passed stipulates that the partners of city employees (heterosexual or homosexual) who are unmarried would be entitled to health and insurance benefits previously limited to the legally wed. The partners would file a sworn statement that they share in the "common necessities of life—as the principal domestic partner of the other and have been such for at least six months."
Source: Sauber, S.R., and Weinstein, C. (in press). Terminology for male/female relationships for the 1980s. *Family Review, 2(7).*

dominance: Variously defined operationally as the number of times one speaks, the percentage of time one speaks, the act of gaining attention, and speaking for a group.
Example: A wife tells her husband that he should not retire even though he has reached the age of 65 and no longer desires to work. She makes the decision for him about what is seemingly in his best interests to do. She overpowers his timid objections, and he complies with her requests by continuing to work.
Source: Riskin, M., & Faunce, E. (1972). An evaluative review of family interaction research. *Family Process, 11,* 365–455.

dominance-submission dimension: A dimension that reflects the status position that a speaker attempts to establish in relation to another.
Example: As they meet together as a family unit, the father tells his wife not to express her opinion until he decides what is best for the children.
Source: Gottman, M. (1979). *Marital interaction.* New York: Academic Press.

dominant-submissive marriage: A marriage in which one spouse habitually lets the other take charge.
Source: Ravich, R., & Wyden, B. (1974). *Predictable pairing.* New York: Wyden.

door knobbers: "Those very crucial comments dropped by family members when their hand is on the doorknob, ready for flight." Such comments prove particularly troublesome when one member "hangs behind the others to share an anecdote with the therapist."
Source: Luber, R.F., & Anderson, C.M. (1983). *Family intervention with psychiatric patients.* New York: Human Sciences Press.

double bind: An intense relationship in which a person feels that it is vitally important that she identify accurately the sort of message that is being communicated so that she can respond appropriately. The communicator is expressing two orders of messages, one of which denies the other. As a result, the recipient is unable to comment on the message being expressed in order to correct her discrimination of the order of message which she should respond to, i.e., she cannot make a metacommunicative statement. The conditions of a double bind situation are two or more persons; a repeated experience; a primary negative injunction; a secondary injunction that conflicts with the first at a more abstract level and, like the first, is enforced by punishments or signals that threaten survival; and a tertiary negative injunction prohibiting the victim from escaping from the field.

Example: Mother walks over to her husband and says to him, "Kiss me" (primary injunction). Then, if he attempts to do so, she moves away from him (secondary injunction) and berates him for not being a good husband (tertiary injunction). This interaction is repeated many times. The husband responds to a communication that has both overt and covert messages requiring mutually exclusive or incongruent responses.

Source: Bateson, G., Jackson, D., Haley, J., & Weakland, J. (1956). Toward a theory of schizophrenia. *Behavioral Science, 1,* 251–264.

double message: A message in which there is a contradiction between different aspects of the content or between the content level and the metacommunicative level.

Example: A person says to another, "You're really fun when you're stupid."

Source: Barnard, C., & Corrales, R. (1979). *The theory and technique of family therapy.* Springfield, Ill.: Charles C Thomas.

drama technique: A psychodramatic technique used in counseling to recreate a situation of conflict for the purpose of bringing painful experiences and affects of the past into the present situation. Once the real emotion is present in the context of the created situation, the problem and its dimensions can be more clearly seen than when merely talking about them, and an opportunity can be created for gaining understanding of the problem and for trying new behaviors.

Example: A family that has difficulty grieving the loss of a member recreates some aspect of the death, such as the funeral, in order to bring the feelings to the surface.

Source: Dodson, L., & Kurpius, D. (1977). *Family counseling: A system approach.* Muncie, Ind.: Accelerated Development.

drama triangle: In transactional analysis, a pathological triangle consisting of three interlocking roles: persecutor, rescuer, and victim. The per-

secutor blames the victim; the rescuer tries to save the victim; and the victim assumes the role of a helpless, sick, or bad person.

Source: Karpman, S. (1968). Script drama analysis. *Transactional Analysis Bulletin, 26,* 39–43.

dry ejaculation: Ejaculation in the absence of seminal fluid, possibly caused by the use of certain drugs that impair the adrenergic mechanism of the sympathetic nervous system that controls the emission phase of ejaculation.

Source: Kaplan, H. (1974). *The new sex therapy.* New York: Brunner/Mazel.

dual-career family: A family in which the husband and wife each engage in a career involving a high degree of emotional commitment and time, used synonymously with "dual paycheck family."

Source: Johnson, C., & Johnson, F. (1977). Attitudes toward parenting in dual-career families. *American Journal of Psychiatry, 134,* 391–394.

dyadic interview: An interview by a therapist with any dyad in the family. The kind of dyad can vary greatly, but the most common types are those that include the marital couple, a parent and child, or two siblings.

Source: Howells, J. (1975). *Principles of family psychiatry.* New York: Brunner/Mazel.

dyadic model: A model in which psychological problems are assumed to be the result of two-person interactions. Thus, the unit of treatment is the dyad. This concept more recently has been replaced with "triadic" concepts denoting a three-person interaction or coalition used in assessing family alliances.

Example: Johnny shoplifts to get his mother's attention. The treatment involves changing their interactional patterns.

Source: Nichols, M. (1984). *Family therapy: Concepts and methods.* New York: Gardner Press.

dynamic imagery: A hypnotherapy technique emphasizing ego-enhancing mental involvement through any or a combination of "the inner senses" (sight, hearing, etc.). It is usually combined with positive affirmations that become powerful self-suggestions.

Source: Araoz, D.L. (1981). Negative self-hypnosis. *Journal of Contemporary Psychotherapy, 12,* 45–51.

dysfunctional communication: A breakdown or impairment of communication in a family; its members neither give nor receive clear messages.

Example: One person says to a second person: (1) "You would like to see a movie, wouldn't

you?'' (2) "It would do you good to see a movie,'' or (3) "We might as well go to a movie.''
Source: Satir, V. (1967). *Conjoint family therapy.* Palo Alto, Calif.: Science and Behavior Books.

dysfunctional family: ''A family that cannot accommodate to and cope with stresses, such as those arising from changes in the life cycle of the family, usually involving addition or loss of a member. Boundaries between individual members are too loose, rigid, or distant, so that cooperation and support cannot occur. The family is not responsive to the developmental needs of its members. Homeostasis often (but not always) is sustained by one member being induced into being the identified patient, who overtly manifests symptoms.''
Example: An adolescent son avoids family meals and spends his time in the house alone in his room. He minimizes his conversations with family members, as he feels rejected because they do not understand him. His father is an alcoholic who is either absent from his home or intoxicated around the house. His mother is severely depressed.
Source: Pinney, E.L., & Glipp, S. (1982). *Glossary of group & family therapy.* New York: Brunner/Mazel.

dysfunctional marriage: A marriage marked by low self-esteem and trust. The partners attempt to use each other to ensure their self-esteem.
Example: Two persons marry solely on the basis of appearance. Each secretly feels unworthy of the other, but uses the other to bolster self-esteem.
Source: Satir, V. (1967). *Conjoint family therapy.* Palo Alto, Calif.: Science and Behavior Books.

dysfunctional pattern: A situation in which a family responds to stress situations with rigid, unyielding behavior rather than flexibility. A dysfunctional pattern is often the impetus that brings the family into therapy.
Example: A wife notices her husband has become less affectionate. She asks him to show her more attention. He maintains a rigid stance, communicating that, "if he gave an inch, she would take a mile.''
Source: Minuchin, S. (1974). *Families and family therapy.* Cambridge, Mass.: Harvard University Press.

dysorgasmia: Any kind of ejaculatory dysfunction: premature, retarded, absent, or retrograde.
Source: Araoz, D. (1982). *Hypnosis and sex therapy.* New York: Brunner/Mazel.

dyspareunia: Difficult or painful sexual intercourse.
Source: Masters, W., & Johnson, V. (1970). *Human sexual adequacy.* Boston: Little, Brown.

E

ecological approach: An approach to family therapy in which the total field of a problem is included, such as neighborhood professionals, extended family, community service providers, local citizens, institutional or governmental bureaucrats. In short, the therapist takes a holistic approach to the problem.
Example: The father is injured in an automobile accident and spends his time going to doctors for rehabilitation and to lawyers to seek revenge from the drunk driver that caused the accident and consequent disability. The family has to go on welfare for financial support, sell their home in the suburbs, and move to a less desirable neighborhood. The children feel upset about their father's injury, embarrassed about being on welfare, ashamed and fearful of living in a rundown house in a high-risk crime area, and depressed about going to a school with poor academic records and without their old school friends. The mother has to give up her full-time job to take care of her husband and to find part-time evening work when the children come home from school to be with their father.
Source: Auerswald, E. (1968). Interdisciplinary versus ecological approach. *Family Process, 7,* 205–215.
Quoted: Hoffman, L. (1981). *Foundations of family therapy.* New York: Basic Books.

ecological systems: Two or more coevolving, self-organizing systems. Coevolution is a necessary feature of the relationship between two or more self-organizing systems (e.g., living creatures and parts of their environment). It brings about the necessary reshaping of each and conserves and extends the systems' pattern match, upon which their continued growth and development crucially depends.
Source: Duhl, B.S. (1983). *From the inside out and other metaphors.* New York: Brunner/Mazel.

ecology: The science concerned with the nature of the interaction of organisms and populations with the embedding environment, which supports, influences, and determines the limits of the structures and functions of those organisms and populations. An ecological view of family intervention encompasses at least three different types of analyses:

1. An analysis of the community, social system, or organizational network through the interrelationship of the various kinds of human services provided within a defined geographic and population area. The principle underlying this type of analysis is that any change in operation of one service unit will affect the operation of all other service units. *Example:* An increase in admissions to one local human service agency is likely to be attributed either to a decrease in service opportunities at another facility or to a change in the social stress and tolerance patterns that may have produced more clients.
2. An ecological analysis that considers the relationship between the physical environment, the setting's physical characteristics, and the individual's behavior. *Example:* Research on population density, local community action groups' responses to public housing, or the effects of urban renewal on life styles.
3. An analysis of the interrelationships between individual behavior and the immediate social environment. Here, attention is directed to studying individuals in specific behavioral settings and redefining the concept of pathology in terms of behavior not viewed as sick or well but as transactional, i.e., an outcome of reciprocal interactions between specific social situations and the individual.

Example: A child complained to his mother of headaches shortly after he was placed in a new special education class.
Source: Sauber, S.R. (1983). *The human services delivery system.* New York: Columbia University Press.

ecomap: A diagrammatic assessment procedure that portrays the family's relationships to other systems, e.g., work, school, social welfare, church. The term relates to the concept of ecosystem in which the transactions between individuals, rather than the characteristics of each individual, are the primary data. Attention is focused on information and organization, with communication processes occurring within systems.
Source: Sluzki, C.E. (1978). Marital therapy from a systems theory perspective. In T.J. Paolino, & B.S. McCrady (Eds.), *Marriage and marital therapy* (pp. 366–394). New York: Brunner/Mazel.

ecostructural approach: The combination of an ecological approach with Minuchin's structural approach to family therapy. The ecostructural approach holds that the structure of the home situation is replicated in other settings.
Example: A boy who is misbehaving at home tends to replicate that situation at school.
Source: Aponte, H. (1976). The family-school interview: An ecostructural approach. *Family Process, 15,* 303–311.
Quoted: Hoffman, L. (1981). *Foundations of family therapy.* New York: Basic Books.

ecosystemic epistemology: An epistemological model that views symptomatic behavior or symptoms as the result of etiological factors. The symptom is seen as a metaphoric communication about the ecology of the patient's relationship systems.
Example: A child refuses to sleep in her bed at night. She sleeps by her mother's bedside because she is aware of the difficulties her mother has when her father arrives at home late at night.
Source: Keeney, B. (1979). Ecosystemic epistemology: An alternative paradigm for diagnosis. *Family Process, 18,* 117–129.

efficiency: An average or normal decision time for a family beyond which there is wastefulness in family functioning.
Source: Ferreira, A., & Winter, W. (1968). Decision-making in normal and abnormal two-child families. *Family Process, 7,* 17–36.
Quoted: Riskin, M., & Faunce, E. (1972). An evaluative review of family interaction research. *Family Process, 11,* 365–455.

ego fusion: A condition in which the intrapsychic systems of involved family members are so intimately fused that differentiation of one from the other is impossible. The fusion involves the entire range of ego functioning. One ego can function for that of another; i.e., one family member assumes she can accurately know the thoughts, fantasies, feelings, or dreams of another.
Example: In a psychotic family, one member becomes physically ill in response to the emotional stress of another.
Source: Bowen, M. (1976). Theory in the practice of psychotherapy. In P. Guerin (Ed.), *Family therapy* (pp. 42–90). New York: Gardner Press.

ejaculatory control: The ability consciously to control the ejaculatory reflex.
Source: Masters, W., & Johnson, V. (1970). *Human sexual adequacy.* Boston: Little, Brown.

ejaculatory incompetence: A male sexual disorder in which ejaculation is difficult, if not impossible, to achieve intravaginally. Retarded ejaculation is one form of ejaculatory incompetence.
Source: Masters, W., & Johnson, V. (1970). *Human sexual inadequacy.* Boston: Little, Brown.

ejaculatory inevitability: The point at which the male can no longer inhibit the ejaculatory reflex.
Source: Kaplan, H.S. (1974). *The new sex therapy.* New York: Brunner/Mazel.

ejaculatory pain: Pain due to muscle spasms that occur immediately after ejaculation. This syndrome may be treated by systematic in vivo desensitization.
Source: Kaplan, H.S. (1979). *Disorders of sexual desire.* New York: Brunner/Mazel.

elastic band syndrome: A syndrome in which families shift from disengagement to involvement.
Example: A child progressively increases acting up behavior in an attempt to elicit a response from a disengaged parent. At some point, the irritated parent responds, often violently, to the child. The syndrome is analogous to stretching a rubber band until it breaks, with the child being hit as the band snaps back.
Source: Minuchin, S., Montalvo, B., Guerney, B.G., Jr., Rosman, B.L., & Schumer, F. (1967). *Families of the slums: An exploration of their structure and treatment.* New York: Basic Books.
Quoted: Levant, R.F. (1984). *Family therapy: A comprehensive overview.* Englewood Cliffs, N.J.: Prentice-Hall.

emancipation of offspring: The separation of children from the parental family. Such emancipation is an evolutionary task in a nuclear family system and culture. The emancipation must occur physically and geographically as well as psychologically and socially. The separation is the culmination of many forms of increasing psychosocial separateness between parent and child.
Example: The son leaves the family, gets a job, and is able to live separately and support himself; he feels more confident in social relationships and becomes a mature adult, no longer dependent upon his parents.
Source: Fleck, S. (1972). An approach to family pathology. In G. Erickson & T. Hogan (Eds.), *Family therapy: An introduction to theory and technique* (pp. 103–119). Belmont, Calif.: Wadsworth.

embittered-chaotic parent: A parent in extreme and bitter opposition, such as in a divorce situation.

Every aspect becomes an opportunity for the expression and consolidation of rage, particularly when the children are present as an audience.
Example: A woman whose husband has deserted her goes into a rage over the lack of money, etc., whenever her husband visits the children. The maneuver is intended to produce guilt in the husband.
Source: Wallerstein, J., & Kelly, J. (1980). *Surviving the breakup: How children and parents cope with divorce.* New York: Basic Books.

emotional complementarity: A fused relationship in which each partner plays out the opposite side of each manifestation of togetherness. The end result often gives the appearance of one partner's being more independent or differentiated than the other, when in fact both have equivalent needs for togetherness and equivalent capacities to be a self.
Example: One partner appears independent, cool, and unemotional, while the other is dependent and desires closeness in the relationship. In fact, they both have the same emotional needs, but the needs are played out in mirror-opposite ways.
Source: Bowen, M. (1971). Family therapy and family group therapy. In H.T. Kaplan & B. Sadock (Eds.), *Comprehensive group psychotherapy* (pp. 384–421). Baltimore: Williams & Wilkins.
Quoted: Kerr, M. (1981). Family systems theory and therapy. In A. Gurman & D. Kniskern (Eds.), *Handbook of family therapy* (pp. 226–264). New York: Brunner/Mazel.

emotional cutoff: A method of dealing with unresolved fusion with families of origin by insulating or cutting oneself off emotionally from the parental family. This process can be accomplished by physical distance, keeping contacts with the parental family brief and infrequent, or through such internal mechanisms as withdrawal and avoidance of emotionally charged areas while in the presence of the family.
Example: A son who feels he must always defend his alcoholic mother from a persecuting father simply isolates himself from the family in order to escape the psychic pain of dealing with the issue.
Source: Bowen, M. (1978). *Family therapy in clinical practice.* New York: Jason Aronson.

emotional distance: Distance between two people that is based on their emotional reactivity to each other, causing them to focus their togetherness needs elsewhere. The distance is a compromise people make to reduce their anxiety or discomfort about too much closeness.

Example: A husband enjoys affection, hand holding, and tender expressions; and his wife prefers to sleep alone to avoid being touched. In a nonverbal exercise, a husband walks toward his wife and stops at whatever distance he feels comfortable. Then the wife walks toward the husband and does the same. The physical distance between the spouses correlates positively with their emotional distance and depicts the difference in their comfort level.
Source: Kerr, M. (1981). Family systems theory and therapy. In A. Gurman & K. Kniskern (Eds.), *Handbook of family therapy* (pp. 226–264). New York: Brunner/Mazel.

emotional divorce: A marked emotional distance and lack of any kind of bond between marital partners. Although the marriage appears to have the form and content of closeness, emotional divorce may arise in a relationship in which the marital partners seem to have few overt differences and live conforming lives but in which highly charged personal feelings are not shared; on the other hand, it may describe a marital relationship in which the partners appear congenial in ordinary social settings but cannot tolerate each other when alone together.
Example: The marriage partners are very polite and proper around others but when alone spend their time emotionally isolated and resentful of one another.
Source: Bowen, M. (1960). A family concept of schizophrenia. In D. Jackson (Ed.), *The etiology of schizophrenia* (pp. 346–372). New York: Basic Books.

emotional process: The process by which one family member emotionally responds automatically to the emotional state of another without being consciously aware of the process. This emotional process is deep and is related to the "being" of the person. It occurs silently, beneath the surface, between two people who have very close relationships.
Example: Schizophrenic families may have little or no conflict but the emotional process may be intimately involved in perpetuating the "silent" family.
Source: Bowen, M. (1960). A family concept of schizophrenia. In D.D. Jackson (Ed.), *The etiology of schizophrenia* (pp. 346–372). New York: Basic Books.

emotional room: A situation in which a family appears to be able to support only a certain amount of emotional disturbance among its members at any one time. Thus, following disaster, the family members may have to take turns being emotionally disturbed. When one finally improves, another may mysteriously fall ill.
Example: The mother undergoes brain surgery for a neurological condition. During her operation, her younger son wets his bed and her daughter develops a school phobia. Once the mother shows signs of recovery, the father becomes agitated and expresses somatic complaints of stomach cramps and dizziness. The oldest sibling soon thereafter gets caught at school for taking angel dust—a new occurrence since his mother's operation.
Source: Hill, R., & Hensen, D. (1962). Families in disaster. In G. Baker and D. Chapman (Eds.), *Man and society in disaster* (pp. 185–221). New York: Basic Books.

emotional shock wave: A network of underground aftershocks of serious life events that can occur anywhere in the extended family system in the months or years following serious emotional events in the family.
Example: Years after a family tragedy, members of the nuclear or extended family develop symptoms ranging from psychosomatic illness to phobias and psychotic conditions.
Source: Bowen, M. (1976). Family reaction to death. In P. Guerin (Ed.), *Family therapy* (pp. 335–348). New York: Gardner Press.

emotionality: (1) Expressive behavior, including laughter and verbal and nonverbal expressions of feeling; or (2) a tendency to use and rely on emotions and feelings rather than rationality or activity.
Sources: O'Connor, W., & Stachowiak, J. (1971). Patterns of interaction in families with high adjusted, low adjusted, and mentally retarded members. *Family Process, 10,* 229–241; L'Abate, L., & Frey, J. (1981). The E-R-A model. *Journal of Marital and Family Therapy, 9,* 143–150.

empathic involvement: Deep caring among family members about each other's thoughts and feelings. This is characteristic of healthy families.
Example: When his mother became ill, the son flew to his home town to provide emotional support to his father and to assist his mother. He was concerned about their welfare and understood their worries about growing older.
Source: Epstein, N. et al. (1978). The McMaster model of family functioning. *Journal of Marriage and Family Counseling, 4,* 19–31.
Quoted: Epstein, N., & Bishop, D. (1981). Problem-centered systems therapy of the family. In A.

Gurman & D. Kniskern (Eds.), *Handbook of family therapy* (pp. 444–482). New York: Brunner/Mazel.

empathy: The accurate perception of the internal frame of reference of another person, including the emotional components and meanings that pertain thereto, as if one were that other person, but without ever losing the "as if" condition. If the 'as if' quality is lost, the state is one of identification.
Source: Rogers, C.P. (1959). A theory of therapy, personality, and interpersonal relationships, as developed in the client-centered framework. In S. Koch (Ed.), *Psychology: A study of a science, Vol. III. Formulation of the person and the social context* (pp. 184–256). New York: McGraw-Hill.
Quoted: Thayer, L. (1982). A person-centered approach to family therapy. In A.M. Horne, & M.M. Ohlsen. *Family counseling and therapy* (pp. 175–213). Itasca, Ill.: F.E. Peacock Publishers.

empty chair technique: A technique in which the counselor sets up two chairs to illustrate the opposite pulls within the person, and then the counselor has that person perform a dialogue with the symbolized opposites as a means of reaching sufficient synthesis within the person to be able to communicate more clearly and increase awareness.
Example: The therapist sets up a situation in which a daughter is to play out two opposite feelings she has toward her mother (e.g., rejection versus acceptance).
Source: Perls, F.S. (1969). *Gestalt therapy verbatim*. Moab, Utah: Real People Press.

empty nest syndrome: A situation in which the parents cannot cope with the separation of their children from the home because of their fear of being alone as husband and wife and being no longer able to fulfill their children's parenting needs.
Example: A mother becomes an evening volunteer at a training center for retarded children when her last child gets married and leaves home.
Source: Glick, I., & Kessler, D. (1974). *Marital and family therapy*. New York: Grune & Stratton.

enactment: The actualization of transactional patterns under the control of the therapist. This technique allows the therapist to observe how family members mutually regulate their behavior and to determine the place of the problem behavior in the sequence of transactions. Enactment is also the vehicle through which the therapist introduces disruption in the existent patterns, probing the system's ability to accommodate to different rules and ultimately forcing the experimentation of alternative, more functional rules.
Example: The therapist asks the mother whether she feels comfortable with the situation as it is—the grownups trying to talk while two little girls run in circles screaming and demanding everybody's attention. When the mother replies that she feels tense, the therapist invites her to organize the situation in a way that will feel more comfortable and then asks her to "make it happen," which will be the motto for the following sequence. The purpose of this enactment is to facilitate an experience of success for the mother and the experience of a successful mother for the rest of the family. The therapist keeps the enactment going on until the mother eventually succeeds in organizing the girls to play by themselves in a corner of the room, so that the adults can resume their talk.
Source: Colapinto, J. (1982). Structural family therapy. In A.M. Horne, & M.M. Ohlsen (Eds.) *Family counseling and therapy* (pp. 112–140). Itasca, Ill.: F.E. Peacock Publishers.

enactment induction: The technique of encouraging family members to transact their habitual patterns of relating.
Example: The therapist raises a core issue in the family and then withdraws in order to allow the participants to demonstrate their usual way of relating.
Source: Aponte, H., & Van Deusen, J. (1981). Structural family therapy. In A. Gurman & D. Kniskern (Eds.), *Handbook of family therapy* (pp. 310–360). New York: Brunner/Mazel.

encouraging resistance: A situation in which the client's resistance is defined as cooperative behavior. This has a tendency to defuse or short-circuit the effect the client's behavior normally has on those in the client's environment.
Example: A client is not sure he is ready to find a job yet. The therapist encourages his resistance by agreeing that it may be several years before he is ready to return to work. This technique defuses the power struggle that could occur between the therapist and the client over the issue of work.
Source: Watzlawick, P., Weakland, J., & Fisch, R. (1974). *Change: Principles of problem formation and problem resolution*. New York: Norton.

enculturating tasks: Tasks that help to socialize the child, i.e., to transmit cultural values to the child.
Example: Teaching the child to obey parents transmits the value of respect for parents and elders.
Source: Fleck, S. (1972). An approach to family

pathology. In G. Erickson & T. Hogan (Eds.), *Family therapy: An introduction to theory and technique* (pp. 103–119). Belmont, Calif.: Wadsworth.

energized family: A healthy family endowed with a fluid internal organization, characterized by flexible role relationships and shared power; this type of organization promotes personal growth and member autonomy.
Example: When the father becomes ill, the ensuing family crisis is approached by the family members with a sense of unity and shared responsibility in order to perform the required tasks.
Source: Pratt, L. (1976). *Family structure and effective health behavior: The energized family.* Boston: Houghton-Mifflin.

energy: A family characteristic that is both static and kinetic: static in that family members have supplies of stored energy available to them, and kinetic in that members actually expend those supplies. Though each family's use, deployment, and restoration of its energies will vary, a general pattern of charging and discharging energy is common to all families. In general, the more energy that is involved in a sequence, the more intense the sequence. The energy sphere interfaces with the time sphere, enabling the therapist to gauge the amount and intensity of energy present in a family at the beginning, the middle, and the termination of events. Some families (and persons) have high impetus, but make little or no impact. They are forever starting, but they almost never finish things.
Source: Kantor, D., and Lehr, W. (1976). *Inside the family.* San Francisco: Jossey-Bass.

engulfment: A situation in which a person lacks a clear and strong sense of autonomy. Since a firm sense of one's own autonomous identity is needed to be able to relate as one human being to another, the person with vague or weak ego boundaries is constantly afraid of being swallowed up by the other, i.e., of being engulfed. There are only two options for this person: absorption in the other (engulfment) or complete aloneness (isolation).
Example: A woman isolates herself from others in order to preserve a fragile sense of self.
Source: Laing, R. (1965). *The divided self.* Baltimore: Penguin Books, Pelican edition.
Quoted: Foley, V. (1974). *An introduction to family therapy.* New York: Grune & Stratton.

enmeshment: A transactional style in which family relationships tend to be undifferentiated, closed, and diffuse. The behavior of one family member as a subsystem spreads contagiously to every other member in the family, rather than remaining confined in the subsystem where it began. There may be overprotectiveness or overinvolvement on the part of a parent with a child, which, in turn, affects both the parent's and the child's relationship with every other member of the family. The boundaries between members are blurred. A heightened sense of belonging is gained by sacrificing or discouraging autonomy. Enmeshment is at the opposite end of the continuum from disengagement.
Example: A mother is overinvolved with her child to the point where she does not allow the child to accept any responsibilities for himself or herself. This pattern excludes the father from assuming any parental responsibility and, by forcing him away, affects his relationship with his wife.
Source: Minuchin, S. (1974). *Families and family therapy.* Cambridge, Mass.: Harvard University Press.

entitlement: What one is due as a parent or child, or what one has come to merit.
Example: In return for giving loving support to a child, the parent is entitled to loyalty.
Source: Boszormenyi-Nagy, I., & Ulrich, D. (1981). Contextual family therapy. In A. Gurman & D. Kniskern (Eds.), *Handbook of family therapy* (pp. 159–186). New York: Brunner/Mazel.

entropic family: A family that maintains rigid unchanging patterns by being oblivious to input from other members.
Example: Parents who have a daughter late in life refuse to allow the daughter, as an adolescent, to behave as she claims her friends behave. They follow the rules and child-rearing practices as they were instructed by their parents.
Source: Beavers, W.R. (1977). *Psychotherapy and growth.* New York: Brunner/Mazel.

entropy: The tendency for a system to become degraded into less organized states. When entropy occurs unimpeded, maximum disorganization or disorder is the result. In order for open systems to survive, therefore, they must acquire a steady state of negentropy. Negative entropy counterbalances the process of entropy, which is a constant process and therefore needs to be checked constantly. Organization represents the presence of information, and disorganization the absence of information. Thus, the way to balance entropy is to introduce more organization. In this way, open systems restore their energy and repair breakdowns in their organization. There is a general trend in an open system, as long as it is alive, to maximize the ratio of imported to expended energy. Open systems typically seek to improve their survival position and to acquire in their reserves a comfortable level of organization.

Example: Some families have strict taboos on what information should be allowed into the house, limiting the introduction of news, music, visitors, or politics. By the same token, other families have practically no rules on what information enters the house.

Source: Sauber, S.R. (1983). *The human services delivery system.* New York: Columbia University Press.

environmental acclimation: The task of creating and maintaining a safe environment for change, one in which people can risk to be different, try new behaviors, and express those thoughts and feelings they once considered inexpressible. This task calls for the application of growth-enhancing rules during sessions.

Example: The therapist enhances the safety of the therapy session by making a rule that members may not bring up the past.

Source: Dodson, L., & Kurpuis, D. (1977). *Family counseling: A system approach.* Muncie, Ind.: Accelerated Development.

environment-sensitive families: Families characterized by clarity in communication and flexibility in perception. When confronted with a problem, the family members perceive the problem as separate and apart from the family. Thus, the problem has no symbolic value to the family, and the solution to the problem is generally governed by rules of logic. This logical approach to problem resolution requires a thorough consideration of all objective evidence. Information from other family members is evaluated on its own merit with little contamination related to the informant's role in the family. Members of environment-sensitive families continually undergo change in their world view, in order to adjust their perceptions to changing external realities.

Example: The oldest son in a family explores a number of colleges during his senior year in high school. Although he considers his father's alma mater, he does not feel pressured to go there. He is not certain about his occupational choice, so he talks with family, friends, counselors, and workers in various fields. As the deadline for application approaches, he decides that it is premature to decide on an occupational field. Therefore, he selects a school with a broad liberal education that includes his main areas of interest.

Source: Reiss, D. (1981). *The family's construction of reality.* Cambridge, Mass.: Harvard University Press.

episodic dyscontrol: Episodes of violent behavior in a family member. Others in the family have difficulty transmitting values regarding the control of aggression.

Example: The adolescent son becomes enraged when his parents deny him. He breaks things and threatens to injure them; his siblings and parents are fearfully paralyzed—not knowing what to do.

Source: Harbin, H. (1977). Episodic dyscontrol and family dynamics. *American Journal of Psychiatry, 134,* 1113–1116.

Quoted: Glick, I., & Kessler, D. (1980). *Marital and family therapy* (2nd ed.). New York: Grune & Stratton.

episodic therapy: Therapy in which sessions are held at irregular intervals as needed.

Example: A multiproblem family calls the psychologist for an appointment when a crisis occurs. The therapist is receptive to seeing the family— knowing they have limited coping skills, especially for the complex difficulties that seem to arise frequently in the family.

Source: Hoffman, L. (1981). *Foundations of family therapy.* New York: Basic Books.

epistemology: A branch of philosophy that investigates the origin, nature, methods, and limits of human knowledge. In the field of family therapy, the term has come to mean a formal world view, like a paradigm—a framework for thinking and conceptualizing (an adaptation derived from the contributions of Bateson, Auerswald, and MacLean).

Source: Duhl, B.S. (1983). *From the inside out and other metaphors.* New York: Brunner/Mazel.

equatability: A situation in which all are entitled to have their individual welfare interests considered in a way that is fair from a multilateral perspective. One who contributes to the balance by regarding and supporting the interests of another may be said to acquire merit. The term is basic to relational ethics.

Source: Boszormenyi-Nagy, I., & Ulrich, D. (1981). Contextual family therapy. In A. Gurman & D Kniskern (Eds.), *Handbook of family therapy* (pp. 159–186). New York: Brunner/Mazel.

equifinality: The concept that, no matter where one enters the system, the patterning in the family will be the same. As applied to systems-based therapy, the term means that the therapist studies patterns of behavior and interaction, not individual topics. This and related terms relate to causality: different causes can produce the same results. This is in opposition to equipotentiality, where the same cause can produce different results.

Example: A family exhibits a number of symptoms, but they all reflect an underlying dynamic. Wherever the therapist chooses to start, the interaction is basically the same; only the content differs.

Source: von Bertanlaffy, L. (1968). The meaning of general systems theory. In L. von Bertanlaffy (Ed.), *General systems theory*. New York: Braziller.

Quoted: Foley, V. (1974). *An introduction to family therapy*. New York: Grune & Stratton.

equilibrium model: A model that postulates that the family tries to maintain a steady state. This model is based on the second law of Thermodynamics, i.e., all entities in the universe tend toward entropy, a gray random sameness without movement or change.

Example: When the "rebel and troublemaker" in the family is behaving well, the "goodie-goodie" sibling begins to fail in her school work.

Source: Hoffman, L. (1981). *Foundations of family therapy*. New York: Basic Books.

equipotentiality: One cause may produce different results in general systems theory.

Example: Father-daughter incest may promote sexual promiscuity or sexual inhibition in the daughter later in life.

Source: Sauber, S.R. (1983). *The human services delivery system*. New York: Columbia University Press.

See also **equifinality.**

equivalent: Reciprocally and correspondingly differentiated and valued, not necessarily equal: people can be equivalently new to different situations. The concept is based on respect and differentiation of individual skills, attributes, meanings, and experiences.

Example: A soccer ball for the son and a leotard for the daughter are equivalent gifts, given each one's interests. Similarly, for the child, "play" is equivalent to adult "work."

Source: Duhl, B.S. (1983). *From the inside out and other metaphors*. New York: Brunner/Mazel.

erratic distancing: Highly unstable styles of relating to and establishing proper distance with other family members. At one moment, the members are

remote and emotionally detached; at the next, they are intrusive or engulfing. The cognitive focal distance appropriate for a given task or communication shifts bewilderingly.

Example: One moment, a wife is angry and distant from her spouse; at the next moment, she tries to engulf him emotionally by demanding his attention and affection.

Source: Singer, M., & Wynne, L. (1965). Thought disorder and family relations of schizophrenics, III. Methodology using projective techniques. *Archives of General Psychiatry, 12,* 187–200.

Quoted: Wynne, L. (1965). Some indications and contraindications for exploratory family therapy. In I. Boszormenyi-Nagy & J. Framo (Eds.), *Intensive family therapy: Theoretical and practical aspects* (pp. 289–322). New York: Harper & Row.

error-amplifying feedback: A systems process in which an attempted solution to a problem adds to the problem.

Example: Parents who have one child plan to have another child to reduce marital stress.

Source: Watzlawick, P., Weakland, J., & Fisch, R. (1974). *Change: Principles of problem formation and problem resolution*. New York: Norton.

Quoted: Gerson, M., & Barsky, M. (1979). For the new family therapist: A glossary of terms. *American Journal of Family Therapy, 7,* 15–30.

escalation: In a relationship of coercive interchange, a process in which one person escalates in intensity and the other follows suit. Given the reciprocal increases in intensity, one person eventually does not reciprocate the increase but rather terminates the exchange. In doing so, that person becomes the "victim." At this point, the mechanism of negative reinforcement operates to increase the likelihood that, in future exchanges, the winner will start at higher levels of intensity.

Example: A daughter begins a series of irritating behaviors. The parents deal with the problem by using punishment. However, the child responds by escalating her behavior, and the parents match her response by escalating their punishment.

Source: Patterson, G. (1976). The aggressive child: Victim or architect of a coercive system? In E. Mash, L. Hamerlynck, & L. Handy (Eds.), *Behavior modification and families* (pp. 267–316). New York: Brunner/Mazel.

ethnicity: A sense of commonality transmitted over generations by the family and reinforced by the surrounding community. Ethnicity is more than

race, religion, or national and geographic origin; it involves conscious and unconscious processes that fulfill a deep psychological need for identity and historical continuity. It plays a major role in determining what we eat, how we work, how we relax, how we celebrate holidays and rituals, and how we feel about life, death, and illness. An interest in families inevitably leads to an interest in ethnicity.
Example: The dominant American (WASP) focuses on the intact nuclear family; black families focus on a wide network of kin and community. Italians have strong, tightly knit, three- or four-generational families that include godparents and old friends. The Chinese go beyond this and include as family all their ancestors and all their descendants.
Source: McGoldrick, M. (1982). Ethnicity and family therapy: An overview. In M. McGoldrick, J.K. Pearce, and S. Giordano (Eds.), *Ethnicity and family therapy* (pp. 3–30). New York: Guilford Press.

ethos: (1) "The fundamental character or spirit of a culture; the underlying sentiment that informs the beliefs, customs or practices of a group or society; dominant assumptions of a people or period. (2) The moral element in dramatic literature that determines a person's action rather than his/her thought or emotion." Each family has its own feel, ambience, and ethos that create the bond of connection of each member to the whole.
Source: Duhl, B.S. (1983). *From the inside out and other metaphors.* New York: Brunner/Mazel.

evasiveness: A mechanism that effectively obscures its user's knowledge and, when pervasive and continuous, contributes to incoherence.
Example: An adolescent boy asks whether he can use the family car. His mother responds by talking about how much money his father has just spent on repairing the car.
Source: Beavers, W.R. (1977). *Psychotherapy and growth: A family systems perspective.* New York: Brunner/Mazel.

exchange theory: A theory based on an economic analysis of the interaction between two actors. The interaction is viewed in terms of the rewards and costs the actors mediate for each other; it focuses on the exchange aspect of the mutual dispensation of rewards and punishments or costs. The general assumption is that individuals behave in a manner that maximizes the differences between the rewards and costs they experience. Thus, A has power over B and can influence B's behavior to the extent that

A can determine or control the rewards and costs B experiences.
Sources: Cromwell, R.E., & Olson, D.H. (1975). *Power in families.* New York: Halstead; Thibant, J.W., & Kelley, H.H. (1959). *The social psychology of groups.* New York: John Wiley & Sons.

excitement phase: The first phase of the sexual response cycle. It is generally characterized by the appearance of the erection in the male and vaginal lubrication in the female.
Source: Masters, W., & Johnson, V. (1970). *Human sexual adequacy.* Boston: Little, Brown.

excuse: A statement that hides a reason or avoids stating a reason fully.
Example: A wife kept making excuses for not following through on those marital matters to which she agreed with her husband to do.
Source: Wahlroos, S. (1974). *Family communication.* New York: Macmillan.

expelling: A transactional mode consisting of enduring neglect and/or outright rejection of an individual. The individual is left with a sense of being a creditor, definitely not a debtor, in the framework of loyalties and obligations. As a result, the expelled individual's behavior toward others may be characterized by a "the-world-owes-me" attitude. This mode is activating and demonstrative of the centrifugal forces in the family.
Example: A mother who has an unwanted child treats the child with neglect and rejection. The child runs away from home with the idea that the world will give him what he never received at home.
Source: Stierlin, H. (1974). *Separating parents and adolescents.* New York: Quadrangle.

expelling mode: A transactional pattern in which the parents contribute to distorted separation. In trying to deal with their own crisis, the parents begin to see their children as hindrances. They do not want their children, which results in neglect, rejection, and withdrawal of love.
Example: A young professional couple are striving to become successful in their careers, and they get caught up in competition and striving for superiority. The demands of their children—e.g., time, caring when sick and lonely, etc.—are perceived as obstacles to their vocational goal attainments.
Source: Stierlin, H. (1974). *Separating parents and adolescents.* New York: Quadrangle.

experience: "All that is going on within the envelope of the organism at any given moment which is potentially available to awareness." In a psycho-

logical (not physiological) sense, experience "includes events of which the individual is unaware, as well as all the phenomena which are in consciousness. . . . To experience means simply to receive in the organism the impact of the sensory or physiological events which are happening at the moment. . . . To experience in awareness means to symbolize in some accurate form at the conscious level the above sensory or visceral events. . . . To experience a feeling means that one has "an emotionally tinged experience, together with its personal meaning." The "cognitive content of the meaning of that emotion in its experiential context" is included in the concept. An individual experiences a feeling fully when that individual is "congruent in his experience (of the feeling), his awareness (of it), and his expression (of it)" (197–198).
Source: Rogers, C.P. (1959). A theory of therapy, personality and interpersonal relationships, as developed in the client-centered framework. In S. Koch (Ed.), *Psychology: A study of a science, Vol. III. Formulations of the person and the social context* (pp. 184–256). New York: McGraw-Hill.
Quoted: Thayer, L. (1982). A person-centered approach to family therapy. In A.M. Horne & M.M. Ohlsen (Eds.), *Family counseling and therapy* (pp. 175–213). Itasca, Ill.: F.E. Peacock Publishers.

experiential family therapy: An approach to therapy that (1) gives attention to current emotionality of the family/therapist interaction as the pivotal point for all awareness and interventions and (2) requires the involvement of the therapist as a person. This approach was derived from gestalt family therapy.
Source: Kempler, W. (1981). *Experiential psychotherapy within families.* New York: Brunner/Mazel.

experiential psychopathology: Psychopathology arising from harmful experience, i.e., all the harmful events the organism has been subject to or undergone in life.
Source: Howells, J. (1975). *Principles of family psychiatry.* New York: Brunner/Mazel.

experimental isomorphism: A methodological assumption that a valid laboratory experiment with a family can be conducted as long as the experimentally produced variables are conceptually similar to those in the real world.
Source: Straus, M. (1970). Methodology of a laboratory experimental study of families in three

societies. In R. Hill & R. Konig (Eds.), *Families in east and west.* New York: Norton.
Quoted: Riskin, M., & Faunce, E. (1972). An evaluative review of family interaction research. *Family Process, 11,* 365–455.

exploitation: A process denoting a breakdown of trustworthiness in a relationship. Interactions become ethically stagnant or pathological, and there is no support for future acts of merit.
Example: A wife who shows her husband love and affection that is not reciprocated feels exploited.
Source: Boszormenyi-Nagy, I., & Ulrich, D. (1981). Contextual family therapy. In A. Gurman & D. Kniskern (Eds.), *Handbook of family therapy* (pp. 159–186). New York: Brunner/Mazel.

exploration: A process in which clients explore existing relationships or alternative ways of interacting within those relationships.
Source: Minuchin, S., & Fishman, H. (1981). *Family therapy techniques.* Cambridge, Mass.: Harvard University Press.

expressive family function: A family task involving the maintenance of solidarity and the management of tensions, with primary responsibility for care and emotional support of children.
Example: A family develops an internal conflict over the tasks of its children in the house. Traditionally, the mother has led in the resolution of this type of conflict and acts accordingly.
Source: Parsons, T. (1955). The American family: Its relation to personality and social structure. In T. Parsons & R. Bales (Eds.), *Family socialization and interaction process* (pp. 3–34). Glencoe, Ill.: Free Press.

expressive leader: The family member who is the mediator or conciliator of the family, the person who smoothes over disputes and resolves hostilities in the family. The expressive leader is solicitous, warm, affectionate, and emotional with the children—the comforter and consoler.
Source: Parsons, T. (1955). The American family: Its relation to personality and social structure. In T. Parsons & R. Bales (Eds.), *Family, socialization and interaction process* (pp. 3–34). Glencoe, Ill.: Free Press.

expressiveness: Marked manifestations of feelings, affect, and emotion that can be either positive or negative in tone.
Source: Mishler, E., & Waxler, N. (1968). *Interaction in families: An experimental study of family processes and schizophrenia.* New York: John Wiley & Sons.

Quoted: Riskin, M., & Faunce, E. (1972). An evaluative review of family interaction research. *Family Process, 11,* 365–455.

extended family: "A group of individuals consisting of the nuclear family (husband, wife, and children), as well as individuals related by ties of consanguinity. Extension of ties exists among parents and their children, grandchildren, and between siblings. In America, the extended family has been common among rural and frontier societies, immigrants, as well as the very wealthy. Anthropologically, the term is restricted to two or more nuclear families affiliated by blood ties over at least three generations."
Source: Murdock, G. (1949). *Social structure.* New York: Macmillan.

extended family systems therapy: Therapy that combines various strategies in a context involving all the significant people in a person's life.
Example: The husband wants to save his marriage after he has an argument with his wife and she impulsively moves out of the house. The therapist encourages the husband to communicate with his wife's family and friends to persuade her that he loves her and that he wants to try again to work out their marital differences. The husband asks his mother-in-law to persuade her daughter that she should get marital counseling or at least try one more time to maintain her marriage before she decides to seek divorce.
Source: Boszormenyi-Nagy, I., & Ulrich, D. (1981). Contextual family therapy. In A. Gurman & D. Kniskern (Eds.), *Handbook of family therapy* (pp. 159–186). New York: Brunner/Mazel.

extended kin network: The group of individuals relevant to a family's functioning, going beyond the nuclear family. The network includes grandparents, uncles, and aunts, as well as friends and neighbors.
Source: Speck, R., & Attneave, C. (1972). *Family networks.* New York: Pantheon.

external frame of reference: A mode of perception that lacks empathy with the perceived object. "To perceive solely from one's own subjective internal frame of reference without empathizing with the observed person or object, is to perceive from an external frame of reference" (Horne & Ohlsen, p. 211).
Example: A mother had her own idea of what was best for her son, regardless of his statements or actions.

Sources: Rogers, C.P. (1959). A theory of therapy, personality and interpersonal relationships, as developed in the client-centered framework. In S. Koch (Ed.), *Psychology: A study of a science, Vol. III. Formulations of the person and the social context* (pp. 184–256). New York: McGraw-Hill; Thayer, L. (1982). A person-centered approach to family therapy. In A.M. Horne and M.M. Ohlsen (Eds.), *Family counseling and therapy* (pp. 175–213). Itasca, Ill.: F.E. Peacock Publishers.

extinction: A process involving the discontinuation of the reinforcement that maintains the behavior in question, resulting in a decrease in the behavior as it returns to its operant level, i.e., the prereinforced rate of the behavior.
Example: The therapist advises the parent to ignore the child's symptomatic behavior until it becomes extinct.
Source: LeBow, M. (1972). Behavior modification for the family. In G. Erickson & T. Hogan (Eds.), *Family therapy: An introduction to theory and technique* (pp. 347–376). Belmont, Calif.: Wadsworth.

F

facilitating engagement: An involvement by the therapist that encourages the interaction of family members.
Example: A therapist encourages a discussion between father and son over the choice of a college. The therapist acts as observer, moderator, and facilitator.
Source: Aponte, H., & Van Deusen, J. (1981). Structural family therapy. In A. Gurman & D. Kniskern (Eds.), *Handbook of family therapy* (pp. 310–360). New York: Brunner/Mazel.

famcum: A family in which one member carries the symptoms and in individual terms could be described as schizophrenic or neurotic. This situation is referred to as a famcum neurosis, rather than as one in which one family member is "sick." In other words, the member carries the symptoms for the whole family.
Example: A family presents for therapy, requesting that their son be treated for depression. In fact, the whole family is depressed, but the son is the only member who exhibits the symptoms overtly.

Source: Bloch, D. (1975). Notes and comments. *Family Process, 1,* 109–110.

family: A basic unit of society, characterized as one whose members are economically and emotionally dependent on one another and are responsible for each other's development, stability and protection. The "nuclear" family includes two adults, one of each sex, who maintain a socially approved sexual relationship, with one or more children of their own or with adopted children. The family serves as the basic unit of socialization to teach cultural values and adaptation to society. Currently, in our society, the traditional definition of the family is undergoing transition because of the emerging prominence of alternative lifestyles. For example, there are now growing numbers of families without children, one-parent families, homosexual families, and extended families.
Source: Burr, W.R., Hill, R., Nye, F.I., & Reiss, I.L. (Eds.). (1979). *Contemporary theories about the family* (Vols. 1–2). New York: The Free Press.

family actualization: The enhancement of personal growth and that of other family members, and the pooling of knowledge, skill, feeling, intuition, and uniqueness to evolve a system of interaction that will facilitate and enrich each individual's process in a way that that individual could not accomplish alone. The system serves the individuals within the family unit.
Source: Dodson, L., & Kurpius, D. (1977). *Family counseling: A systems approach.* Muncie, Ind.: Accelerated Development.

family adaptability: The ability of a marital or family system to change its power structure, role relationships, and relationship rules in response to situational and developmental stress. Like cohesion, adaptability is a continuum on which the central levels of adaptability are hypothesized as more conducive to marital and family functioning than the extremes. In family theory, adaptability was originally presented as homeostasis or the ability of a system to maintain equilibrium. More recently, writers have stressed the dual concepts of morphogenesis (system altering or change) and morphostasis (system maintaining or stability) and the family's need for a dynamic balance between the two. Families very low on adaptability (rigid systems) are unable to change even when it appears necessary. On the other hand, families with too much adaptability (chaotic systems) also have problems dealing with stress. Thus, a balance of sta-bility and change appears most functional to individual and family development.
Source: Olson, D.H., Russell, C.S., & Sprenkle, D.H. (1980). Family therapy: A decade review. *Journal of Marriage and the Family. 42,* 973–993.

family art therapy: A form of therapy that employs art techniques conducted with the whole family to observe how the family unit operates. This can then provide material for further discussion of how the members function together.
Example: The family members each draw a picture of their home and then discuss their drawings.
Source: Kwiatkowska, H.Y. (1978). *Family therapy and evaluation through art.* Springfield, Ill.: Charles C Thomas.

family as a subsystem: A perspective of the family as a subsystem of society with a degree of internal organization and a certain level of self-regulatory functioning but without the ability to be self-sufficient and enduringly independent of the larger societal system of which it is a part.
Source: Parsons, T., & Bales, R. (1955). *Family, socialization, and interaction process.* Glencoe, Ill.: Free Press.
Quoted: Wynne, L. (1965). Some indications and contraindications for exploratory family therapy. In I. Boszormenyi-Nagy & J. Framo (Eds.), *Intensive family therapy: Theoretical and practical aspects* (pp. 289–322). New York: Harper & Row.

family boundaries: The limits of a family's world of experience. These boundaries are more or less constraining and also more or less permeable to relationships and experiences defined as extrafamilial. As each family maps its domain of acceptable and desirable experience, it raises signposts for goals and signals for danger. But these boundaries, which lie within persons as well as among them, are continually tested as new experiences occur, new feelings arise, and new actions are taken.
Example: Neighboring boys who are close in age know which toys and personal belongings they can use together in play and which ones they cannot share.
Source: Hess, R., & Handel, G. (1959). *Family worlds.* Chicago: University of Chicago Press.

family boundary market: A therapeutic device by which the therapist joins with one subsystem of the family and excludes others during sessions of the entire family in order to differentiate boundaries.
Example: A mother and son are overinvolved with one another. The therapist joins with the father and son, excluding the mother from the interaction.

Source: Minuchin, S. (1974). *Families and family therapy.* Cambridge, Mass.: Harvard University Press.

family choreography: A method of actively intervening in the nuclear and extended family by realigning family relationships. This realignment is done by exploring alternative transactional patterns in terms of physical movement and positioning. Family choreography is an outgrowth of family sculpture.

Example: A family with marital difficulties and conflicts between the parents and their two grown children is presented for therapy. Each person is asked to mold the family in order to visualize the problem. Next, the members are asked to mold the family as they would like it to be. The first set of sculptures indicates the type of problem the family is experiencing. During the second set of sculptures, members are asked to take responsibility for changing what is happening. Initially, the wife places her husband outside the room. She is later encouraged to find a way of bringing him back into the family. She does so by extending her hand to him while at the same time letting go of the children.

Source: Papp, P. (1976). Family choreography. In P. Guerin (Ed.), *Family therapy* (pp. 465–479). New York: Gardner Press.

family climate: The general emotional atmosphere or tone in a family. At times, the emotional climate may be difficult to perceive as it truly exists, because of a facade created for others. To determine the family climate, the focus is upon interpersonal relationships among family members, on the directions of personal growth emphasized in the family, and on the organization or structure of the family. The Family Environment Scale developed by Moos consists of ten subscales that measure dimensions in three domains of the family climate: relationship dimensions (cohesion, expressiveness, conflict), personal growth or goal-orientation dimensions (independence, achievement, moral-religious, intellectual-cultural, and active-recreational), and systems maintenance and change dimensions (organization and control).

Source: Fuhr, R., Moos, R., & Dishotsky, N. (1981). The use of family assessment and feedback in ongoing family therapy. *American Journal of Family Therapy, 9,* 24–36.

family coalition: A pattern of communicative, emotional, and physical interactions in a family. Graphic representations of some family coalitions are shown in Figure 2. A "typical" four-member family is taken as the unit, with the squares representing males and the circles females. The larger symbols stand for spouse/parent; the smaller symbols represent the offspring/siblings, respectively. The solid straight lines joining these symbols represent positive communicational, emotional, and activity bonds between the individuals involved; these bonds are semiquantitative indicated by the number of straight lines utilized. Dotted lines, on the other hand, are meant to represent the relative absence of such bonds or the relatively negatively tinged tone of the interactions.

Figure 2 Types of Family Coalitions

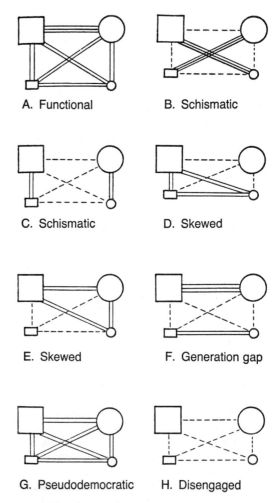

A. Functional   B. Schismatic

C. Schismatic   D. Skewed

E. Skewed   F. Generation gap

G. Pseudodemocratic   H. Disengaged

Source: From *Marital and Family Therapy* (p. 78) by I. Glick and D. Kessler, 1980, New York: Grune & Stratton. © 1978. Reprinted by permission.

Turning first to Example A, the functional family, the marital coalition here has the strongest pathway in the family, with all other channels open and about equal to each other in importance. In contrast, note the various types of dysfunctional families. In Example B, for example, the marital coalition is relatively weak or absent; instead there are strong alliances across the generations and sexes, between father and daughter and between mother and son. Other channels are relatively unavailable.

Source: Glick, I., & Kessler, D. (1980). *Marital and family therapy.* New York: Grune & Stratton.

family cohesion: The emotional bonding that family members have vis-à-vis one another. At the extreme high end of the cohesion dimension (enmeshed systems), there is an overidentification with the family, which results in extreme emotional, intellectual, and/or physical closeness. The low extreme of cohesion (disengaged systems) there is emotional, intellectual, and/or physical isolation from the family. It is hypothesized that the central area of this continuum is most viable for family functioning because the family members are able to experience and balance being independent from and being connected to their families. Adaptability is one of the two sides of Olson and his associates' complex model of family functioning.
Source: Olson, D.H., Russell, C.S., & Sprenkle D.H. (1980). Marital and family therapy: A decade review. *Journal of Marriage and the Family, 42,* 973–993.

family conference or council: A group of people who live together—whether or not they are related by blood or marriage—have regularly scheduled meetings, and operate under rules agreed upon in advance. The meetings are open forums at which all members can speak without interruption, with freedom of expression, without fear of consequences, and without regard for age or status. The group's deliberations result in decisions only when all members present agree, that is, come to a common understanding. The group must adhere to the following basic criteria:

- equality of all members
- mutual respect
- open communication
- regularity
- agreed rules
- joint deliberation
- reciprocal responsibility
- mutual decisions

Sources: L'Abate, L. (1981). The role of family conferences in family therapy. *Family Therapy, 8,* 33–38; Dreikurs, R., Gould, S., & Corsini, R.J. (1974). *Family council.* Chicago: Contemporary Books.

family consensual experience: The experience of perception held in common by family members concerning the family's environment and the family's relationship to the environment.
Example: All the members of a family believe that other families in their neighborhood cannot be trusted.
Source: Reiss, D. (1981). *The family's construction of reality.* Cambridge, Mass.: Harvard University Press.

family constellation: The sociopsychological configuration of a family group. The personality characteristics and emotional distance of each person, age differences, order of birth, the dominance or submission of each member, the sex of the siblings, and the size of the family are all factors in the family constellation and affect the development of the personality. The position of each child in the family constellation not only helps to determine that child's personality development but also enables the therapist to understand the particular client's personality dynamics. Certain behavior types can be characterized by examining the individual's place in the constellation. Thus, the first born, the second born, the third born, and the only child each have certain characteristics that render their personalities predictable in terms of attitudes, personality traits, and subsequent behavior.
Source: Shulman, B.H., & Nikelly, A.G. (1971). Family constellation. In A.G. Nikelly (Ed.), *Techniques for behavior change: Applications of Adlerian theory* (pp. 35–40). Springfield, Ill.: Charles C Thomas.

family construct: The family's subjective estimate of its environment; one of the primary theoretical concepts of a theory of consensual experience. The family construct serves to relate individual thinking to family interaction.
Example: The individuals in a family see the world as a dangerous and unpredictable place. Collectively, they see the world in the same way, which reinforces the family's construction of reality.
Source: Reiss, D. (1981). *The family's creation of reality.* Cambridge, Mass.: Harvard University Press.

family developmental tasks: Norms sanctioned by society which, at each stage in the life cycle of the family, stipulate certain role expectations of the family's members. Successful adherence to these norms leads to personal satisfaction, equilibrium of the family, and success with later tasks. Failure leads to distress in the family, disapproval and sanctions by society, and emotional problems with later developmental tasks.
Example: During infancy the mother seeks to fulfill her child's symbiotic needs for merging, but during adolescence the family needs to allow for individuation and separation.
Source: Duvall, E. (1977). *Marriage and family development* (5th ed.). Philadelphia: Lippincott.

family diagnosis: Diagnosis of a family's roles, relationships, communications, expectations, and conflicts, with a view to resolving the family's presented problem(s). The diagnosis encompasses the following:

1. The presented complaint, the specific reasons for referral as seen by family and the referral source. Specifically, the following children's functions are explored:
   - adjustment to school
   - adjustment to work
   - adjustment to the family
   - adjustment to the community and their peers
   - significant personality disorders
2. Role functioning. The following areas in relation to the parents, as husband and wife and as father and mother, are explored:
   - Disorders in functioning:
     (1) sexual functioning
     (2) capacity to give and receive affection
     (3) decision making
     (4) discipline and parental concern
     (5) economic and social functioning
     (6) basic patterns of interaction.
   - Nature of role expectations:
     (1) expectations of husband in own role
     (2) expectations of wife in own role
     (3) conflict or competition in role expectation
     (4) adaptation to role by each
     (5) breakdown in role performance
3. Family relationships:
   - alignments and splits
   - scapegoating
   - dynamics of relationships

4. Communication process:
   - use of silence
   - disqualifications (evidence that one or more family members attempt to disqualify self or another family member to give information or to participate in communication)
   - double-bind
   - digression (use of digression as a technique to obscure or avoid conflict, excessive attention to detail in recital of events, tendency toward "babbling," and reaction of family to babbling and disgression)
5. Resolution of conflict:
   - tolerance
   - unity (degree of solidity or rigidity imposed by the family when faced with conflict)
   - patterns of avoidance
   - patterns of resolution

Source: Thorman, G. (1965). *Family therapy: A handbook.* Beverly Hills, Calif.: Western Psychological Services.

family dynamics: The intrapsychic, interpersonal, and family-as-a-whole patterns operating in the family system, such as the thoughts, feelings, and behavior, conscious or unconscious, that two or more members of the family consistently employ, as well as the attitudes and emotional climates which the whole family maintains as the framework for its relationships.
Example: Sibling rivalry for the mother's negative attention (to compensate for her lack of positive attention) dominates the family members' interactions.
Source: Framo, J. (1965). Systematic research on family dynamics. In I. Boszormenyi-Nagy & J. Framo (Eds.), *Intensive family therapy: Theoretical and practical aspects* (pp. 407–462). New York: Harper & Row.

family ecology therapy: A therapeutic approach designed to place the correct interventions needed in order to help a client deal with a crisis. The approach deals with the converging forces that have come together to effect a condition of disorganization in the family system—a condition that shows up as a crisis in one part of the system. In family therapy, the approach defines the therapeutic tool and modality used to put into effect the planned interventions within the parameters of the actual contacts with the client in therapy sessions.

Example: The therapist invites the acting-out adolescent to bring the leader of his peer group to the session.
Source: Leonhard, E. (1977). Toward a new formulation of object relation-systems theory from analysis and family ecology theories. In T.J. Buckley, J.J. McCarthy, E. Norman, & M.A. Quaranta (Eds.), *New directions in family therapy* (pp. 42-56). Oceanside, N.Y.: Dabor Science Publications.

family ego mass: The whole constellation of attitudes, feelings, values and beliefs that constitute a family's emotional system.
Source: Bowen, M. (1976). Theory in the practice of psychotherapy. In P. Guerin (Ed.), *Family therapy.* New York: Gardner Press.
Quoted: Gerson, M., & Barsky, M. (1979). For the new family therapist: A glossary of terms. *American Journal of Family Therapy, 7,* 15-30.

family enrichment: One of the many fields of prevention (Kahn & Kamerman, 1982; L'Abate, in press) that have been spawned in the past decade, using a prearranged number of sessions on a specific topic for functional or semifunctional couples and families. Family enrichment covers approaches that vary in degree of structure, format, focus, length, and intensity (Hoopes, Fisher, & Barlow, 1984); for example: (1) marital enrichment, represented by, among many others, the Association of Couples in Marital Enrichment (Mace, 1983); (2) Bernard Guerney, Jr.'s relationship enhancement; (3) L'Abate's structured enrichment (L'Abate, 1984); and (4) Minnesota Couples Communication Program (L'Abate & McHenry, 1983).
Sources:
Hoopes, M.H., Fisher, B.L., & Barlow, S.H. (1984). *Structured family facilitation programs: Enrichment, education, and treatment.* Rockville, Md.: Aspen Systems Corp.
Kahn, A.H., & Kamerman, S.B. (1982). *Helping America's families.* Philadelphia: Temple University Press.
L'Abate, L. (in press). Structured enrichment with couples and families. *Family Relations.*
L'Abate, L. (in press). Prevention of marital and family problems. In B. Edelstein & L. Michelson (Eds.), *Handbook of prevention* New York: Plenum.
L'Abate, L., & McHenry, S. (1983). *Handbook of marital intervention.* New York: Grune & Stratton.

Mace, D. (Ed.). (1983). *Prevention in family services: Approaches to family wellness.* Beverly Hills, Calif.: Sage.
See also **family facilitation and family life education.**

family facilitation: An approach to mental health that is designed to strengthen individuals and families by utilizing the family context. Family facilitation covers a broad range of activities, from high-school family life classes to family therapy that customizes treatment for pathological families. The process is designed to enhance a family's ability to reach desired goals. Therefore, a structured family facilitation program may be defined as a formal plan with predetermined parameters that is designed to facilitate a family's achievement of goals. Structured family facilitation programs involve a group format, including several family units with one or more facilitators.

There are three basic approaches that facilitate family change and growth: family life education, family enrichment, and family treatment (see Table 1). Structured family life education programs include programs that are primarily instructional in focus, with the intent of imparting information and skills to family members outside of an educational setting (for example, in community-based parent education classes). Structured family enrichment programs are designed to enhance skills and health family interactions through instructional and experiential activities. Structured family treatment is designed to resolve problems encountered or developed by a functional or semi-functional family.
Source: Hoopes, M.H., Fisher, B.L., & Barlow, S.H. (1984). *Structured family facilitation programs: Enrichment, education, and treatment.* Rockville, Md.: Aspen Systems Corp.
See also **family enrichment.**

family functioning: The ability of a family to function in four critical areas: (1) *personal* functioning (e.g., satisfaction with self in the family), (2) *marital* functioning (e.g., giving and receiving attention or the gratification of sexual needs), (3) *parental* functioning (e.g., use of parental authority, socialization of children), and (4) *socioeconomic* functioning (e.g., family values or economic status).
Source: L'Abate, L. (1976). *Understanding and helping the individual in the family.* New York: Grune & Stratton.

Table 1 Comparison of Elements of Family Life Education, Family Enrichment and Family Treatment Approaches

	Family Life Education	Family Enrichment	Family Treatment
Function	Education/Prevention	Prevention/Enhancement	Remediation/Education/ Enrichment
Goal	To provide information about a relevant content area	To prevent dysfunction and increase relationship skill and satisfaction	To correct dysfunction or assist in coping with a stressful situation
Change process	Occurs through assimilation of information/knowledge; primarily a cognitive process	Occurs through exercises, activities, and practice of skill; primarily an experiential process	Occurs through discussion of issues; primary focus is on resolution of an area
Information flow and generation of energy	Moves from leader to participants	Moves within family, between families, leader to participant, participant to leader	Moves within family, between families, leader to participant, participant to leader
Participants	Usually includes individual members of a family wanting information	Usually includes whole families or couples wanting to enhance their relationships	Usually includes whole families or family subsystems experiencing specific problems
Facilitator role	To impart information and teach	To direct activities and discussions	To facilitate learning activities and discussions
Process	Uses lecture, discussion, question-answer activities	Uses family activities, discussion, homework assignments	Uses group and family activities and discussion

Source: From *Structured Family Facilitation Programs: Enrichment, Education, and Treatment* (p. 13) by M.H. Hoopes, B.L. Fisher, and S.H. Barlow, Rockville, Md.: Aspen Systems Corp., © 1984. Reprinted by permission.

family group diagnosis: A procedure by which all individuals who are meaningful in the family's situation at a particular time are interviewed together. This may involve two or three generations, and it may include others living in the family household at the time. The procedure aims to get a firsthand picture of the dynamics of the family.
Source: Howells, J. (1975). *Principles of family psychiatry.* New York: Brunner/Mazel.

family group therapy: Short-term therapy designed to facilitate change in the family in sessions with one or more family members. Its basic theoretical formulations are derived from conventional individual theory and the practice of group therapy. The method is determined more by who attends the sessions than by the method employed.
Source: Bowen, M. (1971). Family therapy and family group therapy. In H. Kaplan and B. Sadock (Eds.), *Comprehensive group therapy* (pp. 384–421). Baltimore: Williams & Wilkins.

family growth framework: A situation in which family members confront issues as they appear in the life process and deal with each incident without the need for precedents or established patterns for behavior. The family is involved in a process of interaction in which current data and feelings are considered in decision making.
Example: Susan does not receive the award in school that she expected to win and feels depressed over the situation. The family discusses Susan's expectations with her and how she feels about the situation. The family's unconditional love for her is reaffirmed and differentiated from conditional love. The former says "I love you regardless of how you perform"; the latter says, "I love you provided you perform according to my expectations," and Susan becomes aware of her unrealistic expectations.
Source: Dodson, L., & Kurpius, D. (1977). *Family counseling: A systems approach.* Muncie, Ind.: Accelerated Development.

family healer: The family member who takes on the role of peacemaker, protector, healer, or "family doctor" in order to rescue a "victim" from a punishing attack. To the degree to which the rescuing member holds the capacity to neutralize the destructive force of the prejudicial assault, that member offers to the victim some immunity against breakdown. At times, the member who starts out in the role of persecutor or destroyer may shift to the role of victim or even healer, and vice versa.

Example: When he drinks, an alcoholic father (persecutor) starts to belittle his son (victim). When this pattern begins, the oldest daughter (healer) steps in to placate the father and direct his attention elsewhere.

Source: Ackerman, N. (1966). *Treating the troubled family*. New York: Basic Books.

family homeostasis: A balance in family relationships. The family unit establishes an internal, ongoing, interactional process and rule structure that its members maintain overtly and covertly in relative balance and constancy. Repetitious, circular, and predictable communication patterns in the family provide evidence of the balance. When family homeostasis is precarious, the members exert much effort to maintain it.

Example: An alcoholic husband is trying to remain sober, but his wife, while saying she supports him in this effort, selects a restaurant in which he will see his old drinking buddies at the bar.

Source: Jackson, D. (1968). The question of family homeostasis. In D. Jackson (Ed.), *Communication, family and marriage* (pp. 1–11). Palo Alto, Calif.: Science and Behavior Books.

family interaction: The systems-based, psychodynamic ways by which members of a family communicate and relate to each other and play their roles vis-à-vis one another.

Source: Framo, J. (1965). Systematic research on family dynamics. In I. Boszormenyi-Nagy & J. Framo (Eds.), *Intensive family therapy: Theoretical and practical aspects* (pp. 407–462). New York: Harper & Row.

family interaction scales: Scales designed to assess whole family interaction. The scales cover the following family characteristics:

- clarity: whether family members speak clearly to each other
- topic continuity: whether family members stay on the same topic with each other and how they shift topics

- commitment: whether family members take direct stands on issues and feelings with one another
- agreement and disagreement: whether family members explicitly agree or disagree with one another
- affective intensity: whether family show variations in affect as they communicate with one another
- relationships: whether family members are friendly or attack one another

Source: Riskin, M., & Faunce, E. (1972). An evaluative review of family interaction research. *Family Process, 11*, 365–455.

family leader: A family member who assumes or is selected by the family to take on the role of peacemaker or protector in an attempt to rescue the victim from the scapegoating attack of the family or to turn the attack away from himself.

Source: Ackerman, N. (1958). *The psychodynamics of family life*. New York: Basic Books.

Quoted: Luber, R.F., & Anderson, C.M. (Eds.). (1983). *Family intervention with psychotic patients*. New York: Human Sciences Press.

family life cycle: A longitudinal view of family's development, comprising both expected and unexpected or traumatic phases. The development is cyclical in that the couple starts out as a single unit and then goes through a series of developmental stages until the family unit is again only the original couple. Stages of family life include separation from one's parents, marriage, having children, aging, retirement, and finally, death. See Figure 3.

Source: Carter, E.A., & McGoldrick, M. (Eds.). (1980). *The family life cycle: A framework for family therapy*. New York: Gardner Press.

Quoted: Glick, I., & Kessler, D. (1980). *Marital and family therapy* (2nd ed.). New York: Grune & Stratton.

family life education: A well-established and widely used educational process and method in teaching the community to inform the public about issues and acquire helpful family skills involving family life.

Example: Parent education programs, such as systematic training for effective parenting, are the most common types of courses in family life education.

Sources: Sauber, S.R. (1973). *Preventive educational intervention for mental health*. Cambridge, Mass.: Ballinger; L'Abate, L. (in press). The pre-

Figure 3 The Family Life Cycle

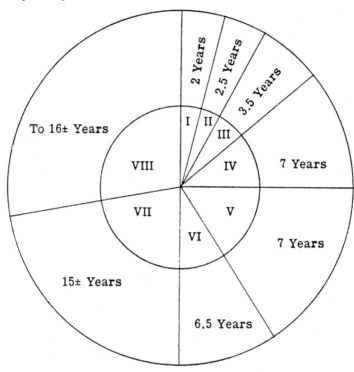

Phase	Family phase	Family description
I	Beginning family	Married couple without children
II	Childbearing family	Oldest child, up to 30 months
III	Families of preschool children	Oldest child, 30 months to 6 years
IV	Families with school children	Oldest child, 6-13 years
V	Families with teenagers	Oldest child, 13-20 years
VI	Families as launching centers	First child gone to last child leaving home
VII	Families in the middle years	Empty nest to retirement
VIII	Aging families	Retirement to death of both spouses

Source: From *Marital and Family Therapy* by I. Glick and D. Kessler, New York: Grune & Stratton. © 1980. Reprinted by permission.

vention of marital and family problems. In B. Edelstein & L. Michalson (Eds.), *Handbook of prevention*. New York: Plenum Publications.

family life style analysis: Analysis of the cognitive maps—styles of acting, thinking, and perceiving—from which family members select the specific operations that enable them to cope with life tasks. Study of the family constellation and the family members' basic orientations toward life provides brief individual portraits of the members' early social worlds, the influential forces to which they reacted, and the raw material they selected to create an apperceptive framework to assist their survival and progress through life. The factors most frequently discussed in the analysis are birth order, comparative sibling characteristics and interactions, the parental relationship (between the parents and with their children), adjustments to physical development, schooling, family values, socioeconomic status, achievements and deficiencies, and peer relationships.

The basic objectives of a family life style analysis is to extract the following central themes:

- The individual family member's *roles* within the family (either alone, or in comparison with the roles played by other members of the family)
- Major areas of success and failure
- Major influences that seem to have affected a member's decision to adopt a specific role
- Each member's apparent major goals and/or conceptions of self and others, of life in general, or of some particular aspect of life.

This analysis, when completed, provides a picture somewhat similar to that given by playwrights when introducing their characters: the family members have a clearer understanding of themselves and their interrelationships within the family.
Source: Dinkmeyer, D., Pew, W., & Dinkmeyer, D. (1979). *Adlerian counseling and psychotherapy.* Belmont, Calif.: Wadsworth.

family loyalty system: A system of positive affect and interaction in both normal and schizophrenic families. For all its constrictingly pathologic aspects, a family loyalty system provides a nucleus of genuinely positive feeling that is, for all family members, including the patient, a cherished possession.
Source: Searles, H. (1965). The contributions of family treatment to the psychotherapy of schizophrenia. In I. Boszormenyi-Nagy & J. Framo (Eds.), *Intensive family therapy: Theoretical and practical aspects* (pp. 463–496). New York: Harper & Row.

family map: A diagrammatic representation of the family in the therapeutic process. The family map can provide new insights into how the family functions. Including both a family history and a diagramming of the organizational schema, it can help the therapist understand the complex material gathered from the family. The family may take into account the development of each member of the nuclear family, the families of origin of each parent, the extended kin network, and the origins and transmissions of power across generations.
Example: The therapist's family map shows the positions of family members in their coalitions and

affiliations and in the way they group themselves in explicit and implicit conflict resolution.
Source: Bowen, M. (1971). The use of family theory in clinical practice. In J. Haley (Ed.), *Changing families* (pp. 159–192). New York: Grune & Stratton.

family myths: Well-integrated beliefs shared by all family members concerning each other and their relative positions in the family. These myths go unchallenged by everyone involved, in spite of the reality distortions they may conspicuously imply. Myths serve the homeostatic mechanisms in that their purpose is to maintain the "steady-state" of their family. The family myth is to the relationship what the defense is to the individual.
Examples: All members of a family believe that partners should be totally honest with each other: "Nothing bothers daddy," "I only want the best for you," "Mother is the sick one," and "Marriage should make one totally happy."
Source: Ferreira, A. (1963). Family myths and homeostasis. *Archives of General Psychiatry, 9,* 457–463.

family of origin: The family into which a person is born or adopted. In family therapy, at least one session is often conducted with each marriage partner or that partner's family of origin. This approach is based on the belief that current family problems are partial reenactments of previous or current problems with the families of origin.
Example: A woman was assigned the role of family healer in her family of origin. She continues to play this role in her marriage, which prevents her from getting her needs met in the marriage.
Source: Framo, J. (1981). The integration of marital therapy with sessions with family of origin. In A. Gurman & D. Kniskern (Eds.), *Handbook of family therapy* (pp. 133–158). New York: Brunner/ Mazel.

family of procreation: The family that an individual establishes through marriage and reproduction.
Source: Christensen, A. (1964). Development of the family field of study. In A. Christensen (Ed.), *Handbook of marriage and the family* (pp. 3–32). Chicago: Rand McNally.

family power structure: The structure that determines who wields power and what the hierarchy or "pecking order" is in a family.
Source: Beavers, W.R. (1976). Theoretical basis for family evaluation. In J.M. Lewis, W.R. Beavers, & J.T. Gossett (Eds.), *No single thread:*

Psychological health in the family system (pp. 46–82). New York: Brunner/Mazel.

family priorities: The allocation of commitments, attachments, and allegiances to the various components of the family (i.e., self, marriage, children, work, in-laws, friends, and leisure) and the various modalities of functioning (such as doing, having, and being).
Example: A father's overinvolvement with work produces a parallel overinvolvement with the children on the mother's part.
Source: L'Abate, L. (1983). *Family psychology: Theory, therapy, and training.* Washington, D.C.: University Press of America.

family problem-solving effectiveness: The family's ability to work as a group in solving an individual family member's problem.
Source: Reiss, D. (1981). *The family's construction of reality.* Cambridge, Mass.: Harvard University Press.

family process: The pattern of interaction between family members. The study of the family process as distinguished from "content," requires insightful perception of the family members and of the significance of their transactions within the family. *What* a family argues about is *content*; *how* the family argues is *process*. To identify these processes and the purposes they serve, the therapist may construct a model of family interactions that takes into account 1) alignments and splits (Is any member usually isolated from the others?), 2) pseudomutuality (Are strong efforts made to overcome divergences?), and 3) scapegoating (Is one person singled out as being at fault, as the "black sheep"?).
Example: The therapist asks the family members to imagine they are planning an outing or picnic and to discuss who will do what. As the family plans the activity, the therapist watches the various interactions unfold. The therapist observes that the father is uninvolved in the process, which suggests that he is also uninvolved in family activities at home.
Source: Thorman, G. (1965). *Family therapy: A handbook.* Beverly Hills, Calif.: Western Psychological Services.

family projection process: The transmission of a parental (husband and/or wife) problem to one or more of the children or a spouse. The transmission occurs when parents focus on their child instead of dealing with their own difficulties. Such a process helps maintain the illusion of a harmonious marital relationship, but at the expense of transmitting symptoms to the child. Thus, the child becomes the presenting patient.
Example: Two immature parents are not able to express their anger toward each other. Their child becomes hostile in response to the parents' supression of anger and begins to act out. The parents direct their anger toward the child rather than each other.
Source: Bowen, M. (1978). *Family therapy in clinical practice.* New York: Jason Aronson.
Quoted: Haley, J. (Ed.). (1971). *Changing families.* New York: Grune & Stratton.

family psychology: A specialization within psychology that is devoted to the study of the relationship between the individual and the family. As an academic specialization, family psychology is an offshoot of developmental child psychology, and on the borderline between social psychology and personality theory. As an applied field (i.e., clinical family psychology), it emphasizes research and evaluation of family therapy outcomes, theory testing, and prevention.

Family psychology, therefore includes, but is not limited to, family therapy. Thus far, only a few institutions (Georgia State University, whose program was the first to receive approval by the Commission on Accreditation of the American Association of Marriage and Family Therapy; Michigan State University; and the University of Rhode Island) grant degrees in clinical programs in this specialty. As a whole, family psychology has been ignored by the field of psychology, both as a science and as a profession.
Source: L'Abate, L. (1983). *Family psychology: Theory, therapy, and training.* Washington, D.C.: University Press of America.

family psychotherapy: Psychotherapy directed at the hypothesized emotional oneness within the family, i.e., the "family ego" as opposed to individuals in the family. The therapy is directed at the family unit rather than the individual, both conceptually and clinically. It deals with the "family" as a single organism, as a "unit of illness" or "unit of treatment." The goal is to help the family members differentiate themselves from the "undifferentiated family ego mass" by meeting with two or more of them together.
Source: Bowen, M. (1978). *Family therapy in clinical practice.* New York: Jason Aronson.

family reconstruction: In-depth exploration of a family background. In the process, all family participants explore their life histories and learn about

themselves and one another. Such techniques as role playing and psychodrama can be used to bring out significant past events in the lives of the members. A family map or genogram is used to diagram the family of origin.
Source: Glick, I., & Kessler, D. (1980). *Marital and family therapy* (2nd ed.). New York: Grune & Stratton.

family relations indicator: A picture projective technique designed to indicate relationships between individuals in the family. The subjects' responses are analyzed on a linguistic basis and thus may be interpreted by any school of psychopathology.
Example: A child is shown several pictures of family interactions. He is asked to tell a story about each picture. In one instance, the child is shown a picture of a family without a father. The boy remarks that this is like his family since his dad is rarely home.
Source: Howells, J. (1975). *Principles of family psychiatry.* New York: Brunner/Mazel.

family roles: A pattern of acts structured and learned in accordance with cultural values for the function a person has with his role partners in a social situation. Trouble can result from role conflicts that are not faced directly, negotiated, and modified but are avoided or distorted so that it seems as if one person is dysfunctional. Role theorists see "complementarity" as a goal.
Source: Kluckhohn, F.R., & Spiegel, J.P. (1954). *Integration and conflict in family behavior* (Report No. 27). Topeka, Kans.: Group for the Advancement of Psychiatry.
Quoted: Luben, R.F., & Anderson, C.M. (Eds.) (1983). *Family intervention with psychiatric patients.* New York: Human Sciences Press.

family rule systems: A system of rules that family members establish to respond to each other and to govern their behavior. The family is thus a self-correcting, error-activating system. Should one family member break a family rule, the others become activated until the member conforms to the rule again or until a new rule is successfully established.
Example: If a member breaks a family rule not to comment on certain behavior, all the other members may respond by disqualifying the message.
Source: Haley, J. (1972). The family of the schizophrenic. In G. Erickson & T. Hogan (Eds.), *Family therapy: An introduction to theory and technique* (pp. 51–75). Belmont, Calif.: Wadsworth.

family rules: The explicit and implicit agreements between members of a family. Some rules are totally unconscious. Such rules govern the transactional patterns of the family, including the mutual expectations that family members have developed about each other over a period of years. The concept was developed as an alternative to "family roles" to study family relationships for the purpose of detecting certain redundancies—typical and repetitive patterns of interaction which characterize the family as more than a collection of individuals.
Example: A family has an implicit rule that conflict is not openly acknowledged.
Source: Satir, V. (1967). *Conjoint family therapy.* Palo Alto, Calif: Science and Behavior Books.

family schizophrenia: Schizophrenia as a family process that requires three or more generations to develop.
Example: The paternal grandparents (first generation) were relatively mature and highly respected members of the farming community in which they lived. Their eight children were also relatively mature, except for a son (second generation), who was the father of the patient and who was much less mature than his siblings. As a child, he was very dependent on his mother and distant from his father. In adolescence, he suddenly became very successful in business but was uncomfortable in close personal relationships. There was a similar pattern on the mother's side of the family. Here were two people who had high levels of immaturity and loneliness and who were aloof in relationships with others. Once married, their relationship become covertly conflictual and one of "emotional divorce." Their child also has a high level of immaturity and develops schizophrenia in an attempt to adapt to the demands of growing up. Thus, the combined immaturity of the grandparents was acquired by a child who was strongly attached to his mother. When married to a similar spouse, their child in turn becomes the patient in the third generation.
Source: McFarlane, W.R. (1983). *Family therapy in schizophrenia.* New York: Guilford Press.

family sculpture: A nonverbal technique whereby each family member tries to create a physical representation of their relationships at one point in time by arranging their bodies in space. The goals are to reveal the way in which the person experiences the family in terms of space, attitudes, alliances, and underlying feelings and to recognize defenses, particularly of projection of blame and intellectualization.

Example: The daughter places herself in her mother's lap in a rocking position with her father by her side and requests her brother and sister to leave the room.

Source: Duhl, F., Kantor, D., & Duhl, B. (1973). Learning, space and action in family therapy: A primer of sculpture. In D. Bloch (Ed.), *Techniques of family psychotherapy* (pp. 47–63). New York: Grune & Stratton.

family sets: Patterned sequence of interaction among family members.

Example: A mother invariably interrupts her husband whenever he tries to discipline the child. The husband simply withdraws from the family, allowing the mother to dominate. This sequence repeats itself over and over, making it a habitual family set.

Source: Minuchin, S. (1974). *Families and family therapy.* Cambridge, Mass.: Harvard University Press.

family sociogram: The pattern that develops when family members are asked to locate themselves in the therapy room according to how they perceive themselves in relation to other family members. With this technique, the alliances, coalitions, triangles, boundaries, and other dimensions of the family become apparent.

Example: The youngest son places himself between his mother and father and then places his older brother, who picks on him, beside his father and his sister, with whom he relates well, behind him.

Source: Bernard, C., & Corrales, R. (1979). *The theory and technique of family therapy.* Springfield, Ill.: Charles C Thomas.

family status quo: A situation in which family variables are maintained as they have been in the past, i.e., the maintenance of sameness through avoidance of change and rejection of new and different ideas, values, and behaviors. *See also* **family homeostasis.**

Example: A family begins to work out a behavioral contract for their child's poor school performance and problems at home. In the past, the father treated these problems, using only punishment. Just as the contractual system is ready to begin, the father rejects the process and drops out of therapy.

Source: Zuk, G. (1971). *Family therapy: A triadic-based approach.* New York: Behavioral Publications.

family structure: The routinized characteristics of the family-as-a-whole that have become stabilized as properties of the family group. Family structure evolves with family development and serves to describe the family group at a given time. It is highly resistant to change. Therapeutic attempts to change it lead to overt calls for loyalties, covert fear, and guilt-inducing maneuvers.

Source: Minuchin, S. (1974). *Families and family therapy.* Cambridge, Mass.: Harvard University Press.

family style: A way of defining intimate relationships in a family. Three different styles can be distinguished (1) an apathetic-abusive-atrophied style, (2) a reactive-repetitive-retaliatory style, and (3) a conductive change-oriented commitment to improve the relationship. The first pattern is characterized by physical coercion, giving up, powerlessness, hopelessness, and inadequacy (both emotional and interpersonal), which may result in physical and/or pharmacological abuse. In the second style, verbal coercion (rather than physical coercion) is used; this defines one's behavior according to the behavior of the other (I did this because you did that!). Reactivity comes out of a context of apathy, while conductivity comes out of a context of self-knowledge and mature awareness of self.

Source: L'Abate, L. (1983). Styles in intimate relationships: the A-R-C model. *Personnel and Guidance Journal, 61,* 277–283.

family syntonic disorder: Bizarre or disturbed behavior that may appear as such to outside observers but is accepted by the family as being "normal" and therefore acceptable. In fact, the behavior could be considered to be an asset or a strength that represents the family's closeness and functionality.

Example: Some families accept nudity as "normal." Other families consider not touching each other as "normal." Still other families consider criminal behavior as acceptable. In each case, the bizarre behavior is incorporated as being representative of the family identity.

Source: Wynne, L. (1965). Some indications and contraindications for exploratory family therapy. In I. Boszormenyi-Nagy & J. Framo (Eds.), *Intensive family therapy: Theoretical and practical aspects* (pp. 289–322). New York: Harper & Row.

family system: The family viewed as a social system that operates through transactional patterns. The system consists of repeated interactions that establish patterns of how, when, and to whom to relate. Repeated operations build the patterns, and the patterns underpin the family system. The patterns that evolve become familiar and preferred. The system maintains itself in a preferred range; deviations that pass the system's threshold of tolerance usually elicit counterdeviation mechanisms that reestablish the accustomed range.

Source: Minuchin, S. (1984). *Families and family therapy.* Cambridge, Mass.: Harvard University Press.

family tasks: Therapists assigned tasks for the family to perform during the session and between sessions, focusing on behavioral change. The tasks usually ask people to stop doing something, to start doing something, or to do things in a different way. A family task may also be an activity for which a family member assumes responsibility according to self-interest, i.e., a family-initiated sharing in daily life duties or roles.

Example: The therapist directs the parents to set aside 15 minutes a day to discuss a new program or behavior assigned to their children.

Source: Haley, J. (1976). *Problem-solving therapy.* San Francisco: Jossey-Bass.

family theme: A pattern of feelings, motives, fantasies, and conventionalized understandings that are grouped about some particular locus of concern in the personalities of individual family members. The pattern comprises some fundamental view of reality and some way or ways of dealing with it. In family themes are found the family's implicit direction, its notion of "who we are" and "what we do about it."

Example: A member of the family stops going to church, and the family pulls together to assert to the member that they are a Christian family and to imply that certain social sanctions will follow if the member does not conform to the family theme.

Source: Hess, R., & Handel, G. (1959). *Family worlds.* Chicago: University of Chicago Press.

family therapy: Therapy in which the family is the unit of treatment and more than one member of the family is seen, individually or conjointly, during the course of the therapy. In this sense, when a therapist works with a mother and child, the parents and children, or any combination of family members, the treatment would be regarded as family therapy. Family therapy operates generally in the following way:

- Since the family is considered the unit of treatment, no individual member of the family is singled out as the patient. Rather, the individual family member whom the family identifies as the patient reflects the disturbances of the family itself.
- The family members are usually seen conjointly rather than individually.
- The diagnosis of an emotional or behavioral disorder is based upon observations of the family as a unit.
- New diagnostic concepts are used; traditional concepts and theories that describe personality functioning to explain individual behavior are usually inappropriate to the diagnosis and treatment of family pathology.
- The therapist relates to the family rather than to its individual members. If the therapist meets with the family as a unit but continues to relate to individual members, the therapist is not engaged in family therapy. The therapist must see the family as a unit emotionally as well as physically.
- Therapeutic goals and methods are family-centered. The therapist is concerned primarily with the outcome of treatment insofar as the total family's welfare is concerned.

Family therapy is more than a novel therapeutic technique; it is an entirely new approach to understanding human behavior. Prior to family therapy, behavior was considered to be a product of individual personalities as influenced by discrete events in the past. This "monadic" view based on "linear causality" was replaced by the idea that behavior is a product of "family systems" which operate according to "circular causality" (i.e., part of ongoing, circular causal loops).

Sources: Thorman, G. (1965). *Family therapy: A handbook.* Beverly Hills, Calif.: Western Psychological Services; Nichols, M.P. (1984). *Family therapy: Concepts and methods.* New York: Gardner Press.

family transference: The tendency of a hospital setting to evoke a family-like atmosphere for some patients.

Example: Hospitalized patients begin to respond to other patients as siblings, evoking the same type of hostility that is usually directed toward siblings at home.

Source: Boszormenyi-Nagy, I., & Framo, J. (1962). Family concept of hospital treatment of schizophrenia. In J. Masserman (Ed.), *Current psychiatric therapies* (Vol. 2, pp. 159–166). New York: Grune & Stratton.

Quoted: Zuk, G., & Rubinstein, D. (1965). A review of concepts in the study and treatment of families of schizophrenics. In I. Boszormenyi-Nagy & J. Framo (Eds.), *Intensive family therapy: Theoretical and practical aspects* (pp. 1–32). New York: Harper & Row.

family types: Structural and strategic patterns that distinguish families. The three basic family types are (1) the closed family system, which typically relies on stable structures (fixed space, regular time, and steady energy) as reference points for order and change; (2) the open family system, in which order and change are expected to result from the interaction of relatively stable, evolving, family structures (moveable space, variable time, and flexible energy); and (3) the random family system, in which unstable structures are experimented with as reference points for order and change (dispersed space, irregular time, and fluctuating energy).
Source: Kantor, D., & Lehr, W. (1976). *Inside the family*. San Francisco: Jossey-Bass.

family typology: A way of classifying the complexity of marital and family life styles. There are currently several ways of classifying families: by the rules for defining power, by parental stage, by level of intimacy, by personality style, or by a description of the family in treatment.
Source: Glick, I., & Kessler, D. (1980). *Marital and family therapy*. New York: Grune & Stratton.

family unit: A conceptualization of the family as though it were a single unit or organism. The focus is on "family oneness" rather than the individual. The family is both the unit of illness and the unit of treatment. The three major levels of therapist awareness are intellectual (conceptual understanding of the family unit), clinical (treatment of the family), and emotional (changing from emotional identification and involvement with the individual to an emotional awareness of the family unit).
Source: Bowen, M. (1978). *Family therapy in clinical practice*. New York: Jason Aronson.

family violence: Acts by family members that result in, or are likely to result in, physical injury. A family is defined as violent if at least one such act has occurred within the year. Violent acts include acts of minor violence with the potential for causing serious injury, for example, pushing, shoving, slapping, and throwing things. Minor violence is thus distinguished from severe violence—such as kicking, biting, punching, hitting with an object, "beating up," or attacking with a knife or gun—which has a high likelihood of causing serious injury.

Source: Straus, M. (1980). Victims and aggressors in marital violence. *American Behavioral Scientific, 23,* 681–704.
Quoted: Shapiro, R.J. (1984). Therapy with violent families. In S. Saunders, A.M. Anderson, C.A. Hart, and G.M. Rubenstein (Eds.), *Violent individuals and families* (pp. 112–136). Springfield, Ill.: Charles C Thomas.

family-centered family: A family in which there is a strong emphasis on the importance of the whole family as a unit and in which individuals are subordinated to the needs and functions of the family group.
Example: Meal planning and food selection are based upon the preferences of most of the family rather than on the particular favorites of individuals that may be disliked by the majority.
Source: Reiss, D. (1981). *The family's reconstruction of reality*. Cambridge, Mass.: Harvard University Press.

feedback: The process by which the input of each family member leads to a more complex, systems-oriented output. The output of the family system is thus no longer individually determined and analyzed. Rather, the whole becomes more than the sum of its parts. Therapeutic feedback to a family is geared not toward individuals but toward the system and its alteration. The concept of feedback assumes that the malfunction of any one person is caused not by a breakdown in the intrapsychic machinery but by the failure of the family system itself to operate properly. Treatment, therefore, consists of correcting, changing, or altering the feedback mechanism. There are two basic types of feedback in families:

1. *Negative:* Negative feedback attempts to correct a system in trouble and to reestablish its previous state of equilibrium. For example, a child is given the role of "acting sick" in order to reestablish harmony between her parents. Thus, negative feedback is used to keep the status quo or maintain family homeostasis.

2. *Positive:* Positive feedback forces a family into new ways of behaving by making old behavior patterns untenable. It is often used to counteract negative feedback, i.e., as a crisis-inducing mechanism to produce therapeutic movement and prevent the family from maintaining the status quo. For example, a maneuver on the part of the therapist may prevent the

family from using the identified patient to hide other family issues.

Source: Watzlawick, P., Beavins, J., & Jackson, D. (1967). *Pragmatics of human communication.* New York: Norton.

feedback loop: The relation of two objects or events in a circular fashion. Instead of assuming that the objects or events are related only in a straight-line cause-and-effect fashion, they can, in certain circumstances, be assumed to be related in a circular pattern, in either a positive or a negative feedback loop.
Example: A wife tells her husband that she wants him to be more emotionally intimate with her. He responds but she thinks he is doing it only to please her. Her response turns him away and he becomes distant again. They become ensnared in a feedback loop in which things stay the same.
Source: Weiner, N. (1962). *Cybernetics.* Cambridge, Mass.: MIT Press.
Quoted: Steinglass, P. (1978). Marriage from a systems theory perspective. In T. Paolino & B. McCrady (Eds.), *Marriage and marital therapy.* (pp. 298–365). New York: Brunner/Mazel.
See also **positive feedback loop.**

female sexual dysfunctions: Female sexual disorders comprising general sexual dysfunction, primary and secondary orgasmic dysfunction, dyspareunia, and vaginismus:

1. General sexual dysfunction consists of the inhibition of the vasocongestive/arousal stage of the sexual response, so that vaginal lubrication and swelling develop minimally or not at all.
2. Orgasmic dysfunction consists of the inhibition of the orgasm phase of the female sexual response. It is subdivided into primary orgasmic dysfunction, which exists when the patient has never experienced an orgasm in any way, and secondary orgasmic dysfunction, a disorder in which the client has had an orgasm at least once through some form of sexual stimulation but currently experiences coital orgasms rarely or not at all. (The term *frigidity* is often used in the literature on sexual dysfunctions as a catchall category for orgasmic dysfunction and general sexual dysfunction. The term has, however, little utility.)

3. Dyspareunia (painful intercourse) can range from postcoital vaginal irritation to severe pain during penile thrusting.
4. Vaginismus is a condition in which the vaginal introitus closes tightly when intercourse is attempted, thus preventing penetration. It is caused by an involuntary spastic contraction of the sphincter vaginae and the levator ani, the muscles surrounding the vagina.

Source: LoPiccolo, J., & LoPiccolo, L. (Eds.). (1978). *Handbook of sex therapy.* New York: Plenum.

filial therapy: A therapeutic technique by which parents are trained to conduct Rogerian client-centered therapy with their emotionally disturbed children. Filial therapy is usually done in groups of six to eight parents. There are three general stages in the therapy: (1) explanation of the benefits of Rogerian techniques to the parent-child relationship and instruction in the techniques; (2) play therapy sessions at home with the child; and (3) termination. Filial therapy allows the parent both to be helped and to be of help. Negative patterns of interaction may be weakened, and there may be increased awareness of destructive aspects of the relationship that may continue to be worked through after the play therapy itself is discontinued.
Source: Guerney, B. (1964). Filial therapy: Description and rationale. *Journal of Consulting Psychology, 28,* 304–310.

finger catalepsy: A condition induced by a sex hypnotherapy technique to treat male vasocongestive dysfunction. The technique consists of associating a rigid finger with penile erection.
Source: Araoz, D. (1982). *Hypnosis and sex therapy.* New York: Brunner/Mazel.

finger hypersensitivity: A condition induced by a sex hypnotherapy technique to treat retarded ejaculation. The technique consists of associating or transferring hypersensitivity in a finger to the penis.
Source: Araoz, D. (1982). *Hypnosis and sex therapy.* New York: Brunner/Mazel.

finger numbness: A condition induced by a sex hypnotherapy technique to treat premature ejaculations. The technique consists of associating or transferring numbness in the fingers to numbness in the penis.
Source: Araoz, D. (1982). *Hypnosis and sex therapy.* New York: Brunner/Mazel.

fixed distancing: A relentless, deadening fixity of distance in relationships and a rigid manner of organizing thoughts and perceptions. The family members are aware of the need for relatedness but feel blocked in their attempts to allow intimacy or affection.
Example: A son appears angry and restless in a session, as shown by his appearance and counting down to a shout of "blast off." The family distances itself from the boy's anger by referring only to his obsession with counting.
Source: Wynne, L. (1965). Some indications and contraindications of exploratory family therapy. In I. Boszormenyi-Nagy & J. Framo (Eds.), *Intensive family therapy: Theoretical and practical aspects* (pp. 209–322). New York: Harper & Row.

flexibility: A system's ability to shift its organization to achieve a goal and to create new structures for itself as required by circumstances.
Source: Aponte, H., & Van Deusen, J. (1981). Structural family therapy. In A. Gurman & D. Kniskern (Eds.), *Handbook of family therapy.* (pp. 310–360). New York: Brunner/Mazel.

fluctuating families: Families that change in either locational or familial composition. Locational fluctuations occur in military families in which one spouse is transferred many times, or in ghetto families that move from one place to another because of overdue rent, etc. Familial fluctuations occur most frequently when a single parent has serial love affairs.
Source: Minuchin, S., & Fishman, H. (1981). *Family therapy techniques.* Cambridge, Mass.: Harvard University Press.

focus: The subject of a family interaction, i.e., the content rather than style of its communications.
Source: Mishler, E., & Waxler, N. (1968). *Interaction in families: An experimental study of family processes and schizophrenia.* New York: John Wiley & Sons.

folie à deux: A mental disorder in two or more predisposed individuals who have been symbiotically associated. The disorder is characterized by delusional ideas of a persecutory nature that may be transferred from one to the other.
Example: A husband and wife both have delusions that the world is coming to an end and that aliens will come to rescue them.
Source: Tuke, D. (1982). *Dictionary of psychological medicine* (Vol. 1). Philadelphia: Blakiston and Company.

forbidding change: A paradoxical intervention in which the family is told that it should not attempt to change at the present time.
Example: A couple arrives for treatment with a sexual problem. The therapist asks them not to have intercourse. They respond to this request by doing just the opposite, and doing it successfully because their performance anxiety has been relieved.
Source: Weeks, G., & L'Abate, L. (1982). *Paradoxical psychotherapy.* New York: Brunner/Mazel.

force: In a therapeutic context, the relative influence strength, and intensity of each family member on the outcome of an activity. In an underorganized family, force is not distributed in an orderly way.
Example: A mother holds all the force in a family. Her children behave in her presence, but do whatever they like in her absence.
Source: Aponte, H. (1976). Underorganization in the poor family. In P.J. Guerin (Ed.), *Family therapy: Theory and practice* (pp. 432–448). New York: Gardner Press.

foster care placement and parenting: A substitute child-care arrangement for the child's natural parents that varies according to the length or time of placement (temporary vs. permanent), the development stage of the child (adolescent or infant home), the disability of the child (e.g., mental retardation, emotional disturbance, visual impairment), and the acceptance of siblings in the same home. Foster parenting is a nonnormative parenting arrangement. When a child enters foster care, parental authority is shared by the natural parents, the agency, and the foster parents.
Source: Eastman, K.S. (1982). Foster parenthood: A nonnormative parenting arrangement. In H.E. Gross & M.B. Sussman (Eds.), *Alternatives to traditional family living* (pp. 95–120). New York: Haworth Press.

fractured families: Families in which husbands avoid their wives and are verbally and perhaps physically abusive to them. The wives attempt to gain support for themselves through emotional appeals; but, as they increase their appeals, their husbands become more withdrawn and abusive. The women and children in such families eventually have problems requiring professional attention. Relationships in the home are fractured not by a divorce but by the destructive behaviors exhibited in daily living. The children generally perceive one parent as the loser. This noticeable imbalance in power in the husband/wife relationship impels the

child into a protective alignment with the "losing" parent. The split-parenting pattern is reflected in a split within the children, who love both parents but feel compelled to support one over the other.
Example: The son assumes the role of the caretaker for his mother, who is cast in the role of "loser" in the marital battle. In fact, she has historically set the stage to become the victim in order to secure her son's devotion.
Source: Little, M. (1982). *Family break-up.* San Francisco: Jossey-Bass.

fragile bond: A marital relationship in which the husband and wife both withdraw and move away from each other when they encounter problems. A deceptive tranquility is maintained by both avoiding confrontation on troublesome issues. Over the years, the two partners drift apart emotionally but cling to the shell of their marriage. One day, quite suddenly, the marriage ends when one partner simply walks away. The abrupt ending shocks the partner who is left in the home.
Example: A husband and wife emotionally and behaviorally separate themselves from each other and create two different worlds: male and female.
Source: Little, M. (1982). *Family break-up.* San Francisco: Jossey-Bass.

fragility syndrome: A situation in which the patient thinks, "If I ask, the other person will fall apart," or, "If I ask, I will get an answer that will make me fall apart."
Source: Satir, V. (1967). *Conjoint family therapy.* Palo Alto, Calif.: Science and Behavior Books.

fragmentation: Disruptions in communication that are operationally defined as incomplete sentences, repetitions, incomplete sentences or fragments, or laughter.
Example: A wife says, "How could you do that?" The husband says, "Well . . ." then laughs and the sequence is repeated.
Source: Mishler, E., & Waxler, N. (1968). *Interaction in families: An experimental study of family processes and schizophrenia.* New York: John Wiley & Sons.

frames: Principles of organization that govern events—at least, social ones—and people's subjective involvement in them. A frame can be compared with the rules of a game, or with a " 'code' as a device which informs and patterns all events that fall within the boundaries of its application." Frames, in short, operate as if they are the rules that define situations. The family thinks and operates as though it has a certain set of rules, or overlapping

sets of individual rules plus "unit rules," that define its situation. The rules may define what is serious versus what is not serious, what is good versus what is not good, and how to show love versus how not to show love. Identification of many other such rules (inferred by the observer) is necessary to have a full description of a family's frames.
Example: Two spouses' unspoken frames stipulate different rules about which behaviors can be included in "how to show love versus how not to show love."
Source: de Shazer, S. (1982). *Patterns of brief family therapy.* New York: Guilford.

fraternal polyandry: A family pattern in which several brothers are cohusbands.
Source: Christensen, H.T. (Ed.) (1964). *Handbook of marriage and the family* (pp. 462–500). Chicago: Rand McNally.

freeze frame: The result of arranging the bodies of the family members in terms of their positioning and posture (family sculpture), thus graphically portraying the hidden and poignant aspects of family life, i.e., those private perceptions or invisible structures that come to light only very slowly through verbal techniques.
Source: Simon, R.M. (1972). Sculpting the family. *Family process, 11,* 49–57.
Quoted: Levant, R.F. (1984). *Family therapy: A comprehensive overview.* Englewood Cliffs, N.J.: Prentice-Hall.

frustrated dependency needs: Unfulfilled needs resulting from the failure of a marital union to meet lifelong narcissistic yearnings for all-absorbing, unconditional love. Alcohol abuse is a common consequence of the frustration of dependency needs. Typically, a husband will struggle with unacceptable, unmet dependency yearnings, which are usually kept repressed because of the threat their recognition would constitute to his sense of masculinity but which are permitted expression through episodes of total alcoholic helplessness—a helplessness mercifully kept from clear representation in consciousness by the fact of his intoxication.
Source: Blinder, M., & Kirschenbaum, M. (1969). The technique of married couple group therapy. In B. Ard & C. Ard (Eds.), *Handbook of marriage counseling* (pp. 233–246). Palo Alto, Calif.: Science & Behavior Books.

functional action: Observable acts within a family, including the manifestation of purposes or motivations, evaluations, resolutions and decisions,

interpersonal adjustments, rehearsals, and other elements of total action processes.
Example: Communications are generated within a family to help the family reach a goal: how to plan finances for a vacation.
Source: Bell, J. (1976). A theoretical framework for family group therapy. In P. Guerin (Ed.), *Family therapy* (pp. 129–143). New York: Gardner Press.

functional analysis of behavior: The process in operant behavior therapy of determining what environmental and interpersonal contingencies are maintaining undesirable behavior or reducing the occurrence of desirable behavior.
Example: If a child is misbehaving, the therapist seeks a precise definition of the problem behavior and information about what happened before, during, and after the symptomatic behavior.
Source: Liberman, R. (1972). Behavioral approaches to family and couple therapy. In G. Erickson & T. Hogan (Eds.), *Family therapy: An introduction to theory and technique* (pp. 120–137). Belmont, Calif.: Wadsworth.

functional coalition: A coalition in which the marital relationship is the strongest dyad, the generation boundary is intact, and other channels are open and coequal.
Source: Glick, I., & Kessler, D. (1980). *Marital and family therapy* (2nd ed.). New York: Grune & Stratton.

functional family: A family characterized by:

- a flexible power structure with shared authority, a clear family rule system, a strong parental coalition, intact generational boundaries, and an affiliative style.
- individuation of family members, characterized by both separateness and closeness, comfort with disagreement and uncertainty, freedom and spontaneous communication, respect for and sensitivity to differentness and the subject world of others, and little scapegoating or blaming.
- strong marital and community relationships
- family myths attuned to reality
- humor, tenderness, caring, and hopefulness, with conflict out in the open and an absence of chronic resentments

Source: Glick, I., & Kessler, D. (1980). *Marital and family therapy* (2nd ed.). New York: Grune & Stratton.

functional family therapy: Therapy utilizing an interpersonally based model of behavior change combining both behavioral and systems-based interventions. The central concept of function guides the therapist to a set of step-by-step decision rules regarding goals, therapist behavior, and treatment technologies for each phase of family intervention. The model emphasizes operationalization of system theory concepts for assessing family interaction and planning intervention, applications of cognitive (attribution) change techniques prior to the application of behavior change technology, and the importance of therapist characteristics and nontechnical behaviors.
Source: Alexander, J., & Parsons, B.V. (1982). *Functional family therapy.* Monterey, Calif.: Brooks/Cole.

functional level of differentiation: The degree of fusion between intellectual and emotional systems, based on shifts in the level of anxiety a person experiences. A person acts more differentiated as a result of fusion with another; basic changes in personality do not result.
Example: A person enters therapy because of overriding anxiety. He fuses with the therapist and begins to act more appropriately, as long as the relationship with the therapist continues.
Source: Kerr, M. (1981). Family systems theory and therapy. In A. Gurman & D. Kniskern (Eds.), *Handbook of family therapy* (pp. 226–266). New York: Brunner/Mazel.

functionality: The suitability of behavior for achieving common goals while minimizing impasses and backlogs. Functionality is a component of stability/instability.
Source: Lederer, W., & Jackson, D. (1968). *The mirages of marriage.* New York: Norton.
Quoted: Bodin, A. (1981). The interactional view: Family therapy approaches of the Mental Research Institute. In A. Gurman & D. Kniskern (Eds.), *Handbook of family therapy* (pp. 267–309). New York: Brunner/Mazel.

funneling technique: An interviewing strategy in which the initial aspects of the interview focus on broad, general topics and gradually proceed toward more sensitive topics.
Source: Gelles, R. (1974). *The violent home: A study of physical aggression between husbands and wives.* Beverly Hills, Calif.: Sage.
Quoted: Okun, B.F., & Rappaport, L.J. (1980). *Working with families: An introduction to family therapy.* Belmont, Calif.: Brooks/Cole.

fusion: The merging of the intellectual and emotional aspects of a person, paralleling the degree to which that person fuses into or loses self in relationships. Fusion undermines the person's ability to maintain individuality in relationships. Fusion can be both a source of relief and a source of anxiety.
Example: A man fuses with his wife. He cannot think for himself. He consults her over the smallest decision. He also mirrors her feelings. His ability to function independently is overshadowed by what he thinks his wife thinks and feels.
Source: Bowen, M. (1976). Theory in the practice of psychotherapy. In P. Guerin (Ed.), *Family therapy* (pp. 42–90). New York: Gardner Press.
Quoted: Kerr, M. (1981). Family systems theory and therapy. In A. Gurman & D. Kniskern (Eds.), *Handbook of family therapy* (pp. 226–266). New York: Brunner/Mazel.

future pacing: The neurolinguistic process of ensuring that the changes accomplished during therapy become generalized and available in the appropriate outside contexts. Too often, changes that occur in therapy become anchored to the therapist's office or even to the therapist, rather than made available to the client in the specific situations that most need the new behaviors and responses. The primary method of future pacing new behaviors is to anchor the new behavior or response to a sensory stimulus that naturally occurs in the applicable context.
Example: The therapist asks the client, "What is the very first thing you will see, hear, or feel externally that will indicate that you need this resource?" When the specific experience is identified, the client is asked to generate it internally and then anchor it to the appropriate resource. When the stimulus later occurs in external experience, it naturally or unconsciously triggers the appropriate feelings/behavior.
Source: Dilts, R., & Green, J.D. (1982). Applications of neurolinguistic programming in family therapy. In A.M. Horne & M.M. Ohlsen (Eds.), *Family counseling and therapy.* (pp. 214–244). Itasca, Ill.: F.E. Peacock Publishers.

future tense: A diagnostic sex hypnotherapy technique, by which the client is asked to visualize a double scene in the mind's eye. The person is encouraged to see self now with the problem and also in the future when the problem no longer exists.
Source: Araoz, D. (1982). *Hypnosis and sex therapy.* New York: Brunner/Mazel.

G

general sexual dysfunction: A dysfunction that causes the female to derive little, if any, erotic pleasure from sexual stimulation.
Source: Kaplan, H. (1974). *The new sex therapy.* New York: Brunner/Mazel.

generation: "(1) a body of living beings constituting a single step in the line of descent from an ancestor; (2) a group of individuals born and living contemporaneously; (3) a group of individuals having contemporaneously a status (as that of students in a school) which each one holds only for a limited period; (4) the average span of time between the birth of parents and that of their offspring; (5) the action or process of producing offspring." In families, a different order in the power hierarchy, on the basis of age and years, such as parent and child.
Sources: Webster's New Collegiate Dictionary (1977 ed.). Springfield, Mass.: G & C Merriam; Haley, J. (1969). *Problem-solving therapy.* San Francisco: Jossey-Bass.

generation gap family: A family in which the marital unit and offspring form cohesive subsystems, with little interaction across generational lines. A coalition takes place in the generation gap when the marital unit and offspring each form a fairly cohesive duo, with little or no interaction across generational lines.
Example: The parents travel extensively and spend all their time in an adult world, while the children form a cohesive unit in order to ensure their emotional survival.
Source: Glick, I, & Kessler, D. (1980). *Marital and family therapy* (2nd ed.). New York: Grune & Stratton.

generational boundaries: Reorganized generational limits, on family member roles. In well-functioning families there are invisible lines between parents and children that are clearly demarcated and observed: children remain in child roles, and parents remain in parental roles. Children do not take over parent roles or become parental figures, nor do they usurp the traditional roles belonging to the parents. Thus, a child does not have to "mother" her own mother. The relationship of the parents, sometimes called the marital coalition or the spouse subsystem, is the unit within the family where the adults can meet their needs for sexual gratification and for companionship. This relationship is separate and private from their relationship with the children, yet enables them to provide support, limits, and privacy to the children.

Source: Minuchin, S. (1974). *Families and family therapy.* Cambridge, Mass.: Harvard University Press.

generational inversion: A family situation in which an elderly parent is dependent on the younger generation for emotional, financial, physical, or mental support. Generationally invented families are no longer unique. They are in fact increasing as a result of greater longevity and increasing numbers of physically and financially dependent elders. In these families, not only the roles are reversed, the entire set of generationally linked rights, responsibilities, and obligations are also reversed.

Thus, today it is not uncommon for one or two brothers or sisters to bear the responsibility for four or five family members over 75 years of age who are no longer able to live independently. The existence of multiple generations in generationally inverse families is a growing phenomenon, and the impact of "parent caring" on the middle-aged offspring is increasingly apparent. The question of who takes care of the caretakers when the caretakers need taking care of needs to be raised. In short, the problems created by increased longevity are not confined to the elderly, but encompass the whole family life cycle.

Example: The 34-year-old divorced mother of two children spends most of her time caring for her ill mother and attending to her father's postoperative recovery.

Source: Steinmets, S. (1983). Dependency, stress, and violence between middle-aged caregivers and their elderly parents. In J.I. Kosbers (Ed.), *Abuse and maltreatment of the elderly* (pp. 134–149). Littleton, Mass.: John-Wright, PSG.

genogram: "A schematic diagram of the family relationship system based on the genetic tree, usually involving two or three generations as developed by Bowen. Squares are used to represent men and circles to indicate women. These are tied together with a horizontal line to indicate marriage (the date of marriage may be entered here) and vertical lines drawn down from the horizontal, with the appropriate square or circle to indicate children and their sex. The ages of these individuals may be entered in the square or circle. The families of origin may then be drawn in with parents and siblings of each spouse. Death of a member is indicated by placing a

cross over the square or box. Other important events may be listed as well as indications of patterns of alliance and conflict; the former may be indicated by a straight line drawn between the members and the latter by a curvy line."

Example: See Figure 4.

Source: Guerin, P., & Pendergast, E. (1976). Evaluation of family system and genogram. In P. Guerin (Ed.), *Family therapy* (pp. 450–465). New York: Gardner Press.

Quoted: Pinney, E.L., & Slipp, S. (1982). *Glossary of group and family therapy.* New York: Brunner/Mazel.

Gestalt family therapy: An experientially oriented approach to marital and family therapy which is relational in nature, but uses the same techniques traditionally used in individual Gestalt therapy developed by Fritz Pearls. The assumption is that awareness and congruence of thoughts and feelings are the primary requirements for change.

The goal of treatment is to help the clients achieve self-awareness and increased self-direction. By focusing on here-and-now experiences, the therapist attempts to remove blocks and entrenched patterns in the relationship. The ultimate goal of therapy is to promote individual and systemic growth by facilitating spontaneity and the creation of new experiences.

Figure 4 A Genogram

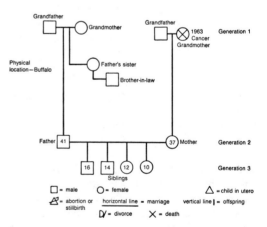

Source: Guerin, P., & Pendergast, E. (1976). Evaluation of family system and genogram. In P. Guerin (Ed.), *Family therapy* (p. 453). New York: Gardner Press. © 1976. Used with permission.

Source: Kempler, W. (1981). *Experiential psychotherapy with families.* New York: Brunner/Mazel.
Quoted: L'Abate, L., & McHenry, S. (1983). *Handbook of marital interventions.* New York: Grune & Stratton.

ghost families: A family that has lost a member, through either death or desertion, and is having difficulty coming to terms with the loss. Relegating the missing member's responsibilities and functions may be regarded as an act of disloyalty. Many times the family will feel that, if the missing person had lived, that person would have known what to do. Old mannerisms and restrictions may be enforced, as if the member were still there.
Source: Minuchin, S., & Fishman, H. (1981). *Family therapy techniques.* Cambridge, Mass.: Harvard University Press.

give-to-get principle: A therapeutic stipulation that one marital partner approach the other with the intention of giving sensate pleasures while the other partner focuses on receiving the pleasures. After a reasonable time, the marital partners exchange roles of pleasuring (giving) and being pleasured (getting).
Source: Masters, W., & Johnson, V. (1970). *Human sexual inadequacy.* Boston: Little, Brown.

giving in: A paradoxical approach to treatment in which the client is told to surrender to a symptom.
Example: A man believes it is bad to feel depressed. He constantly fights depressed feelings. The therapist instructs him to give in to his depression in order to find out just how bad it really would be. "Allow yourself to be depressed. You've been fighting it for so long and see what has happened. Stay with your depression."
Source: Weeks, G., & L'Abate, L. (1982). *Paradoxical psychotherapy.* New York: Brunner/Mazel.

goal discrepancy: A situation in which one partner in a dyad has goals that conflict with those of the other partner.
Example: A husband stresses the importance of making money and moving up socially, while his wife is oriented toward the internal emotional needs of the family.
Source: Spiegel, J. (1957). The resolution of role conflict within the family. *Psychiatry, 20,* 1–16.
Quoted: Foley, V. (1974). *An introduction to family therapy.* New York: Grune & Stratton.

go-between process: A process in which the therapist probes issues in the family, establishes the existence of conflict, encourages open expression of disagreement, exposes and resists the family's efforts to deny or disguise disagreement, encourages the expression of recent or current disagreement rather than rehashes of the old, and encourages expression of conflict between members who are present at the session. The four steps in the process are:

1. introduction of an issue on which there are at least two identifiable opponents
2. intensification of conflict and the beginning movement of a person into the role of go-between
3. attempts by the principals and go-between to define and delimit each other's roles or positions
4. a recession or cessation of conflict associated with a change in the principals' positions or redefinition of the conflict, or both.

The intent is to apply leverage against "pathogenic relating" in families in order to break it up. The therapist positions himself to take or trade the roles of mediator and side-taker during conflicts in family therapy.
Example: The therapist mediates between the narcissistic father and nuturant daughter who has taken on the mother-wife role. The father, in turn, is destructive to the real mother-wife.
Source: Zuk, G. (1971). *Family therapy: A triadic based approach.* New York: Behavioral Publications.

good faith contract: Contracts in which nonproblem behaviors are used as reinforcers; a reward (or penalty) is substituted for the behavior targeted for change. An agreement that, if a spouse engages in a desired behavior, she receives a positive reinforcer that is independent of the change in her partner's behavior. In such a contract there is no benefit in waiting for one's partner to change first. Each partner receives rewards for changing in the desired direction.
Example: Tom would like Sue to figure the household budget, and Sue would like Tom to play cards with her. A good faith contract between them might read: (1) If Tom plays cards with Sue for one hour, then he is entitled to choose the TV programming for that evening; or (2) if Sue figures the household budget, then she gets private time for an evening while Tom watches the children. In such a contract,

there is no benefit in waiting for one's partner to change first. Each spouse receives rewards—from the partner, the external environment, or the therapist—for changing in the desired direction.
Source: Weiss, R., Hops, H., & Patterson, G. (1973). A framework for conceptualizing marital conflict: A technique for altering it, some data for evaluating it. In L.A. Hamerlynck, L.C. Handy, & E.J. Marsh (Eds.), *Behavior change: Methodology, concepts and practice* (pp. 309–342). Champaign, Ill.: Research Press.

graded sexual assignments: A procedure for promoting sexual adequacy and responsiveness, in which the patient is instructed not to make any sexual responses that engender feelings of tension or anxiety but to proceed only to the point where pleasurable reactions predominate.
Source: Wolpe, J. (1958). *Psychotherapy by reciprocal inhibition.* Stanford, Calif.: Stanford University Press.

group analytic family therapy: A systems approach to family and marital therapy developed by A.C. Robin Skynner from the "group-as-a-whole" ideas of S.H. Foulkes (group-analysis) and the British object-relations school of psychoanalysis.
Source: Skynner, A.C.R. (1976). *Systems of family and marital psychotherapy.* New York: Brunner/Mazel.

group analytic technique: An analytic technique that necessitates the involvement of the therapist as a person who interacts with the family to facilitate a process of growth and development on both sides. The key requirement for the therapist is a deep awareness of self-identity, which is able to sustain in the face of overwhelming emotional arousal engendered by encounter with profoundly disturbed family systems seeking to externalize their pathology.
Source: Beels, C., & Ferber, A. (1969). Family therapy: A view. *Family Process, 8,* 280–318.
Quoted: Skynner, C. (1981). An open-systems, group analytic approach to family therapy. In A. Gurman & D. Kniskern (Eds.), *Handbook of family therapy* (pp. 39–84). New York: Brunner/Mazel.

group dynamics: Interactions among group members that emerge as a result of properties of the group rather than individual personalities.
Source: Slavson, S.R. (1943). *An introduction to group therapy.* New York: The Commonwealth Fund.

group marriage: A marriage involving multiple mates for both wife and husband.

Source: Christensen, H. (1964). Development of the family study field. In H. Christensen (Ed.), *Handbook of marriage and the family* (pp. 3–32). Chicago: Rand McNally.

group of meaning: A coding category used with the Relations Rorschach that measures the accuracy and sensitivity of others' communications, the level of differentiation, and imaginativeness.
Source: Loveland, N. (1967). The Relations Rorschach: A technique for studying interaction. *Journal of Nervous and Mental Disease, 142,* 93–105.
Quoted: Riskin, M., & Faunce, E. (1972). An evaluative review of family interaction research. *Family Process, 11,* 365–455.

growth orientation: An approach to therapy in which the goal of therapy is the expansion of the life of the human being, as opposed to solving specific problems. The therapist's task is to help enrich the person's life through experiential means.
Source: Haley, J. (1976). *Problem-solving therapy.* San Francisco: Jossey-Bass.

growth vitality games: Exercises in which each person includes self and others in interaction by expressing self and also permitting others to express themselves. This occurs on the content reality level rather than on the survival level (as is also the case in rescue, coalition, and lethal games). A growth vitality game allows one to agree or disagree with one's own self in accord with one's own experience of reality.
Source: Satir, V. (1967). *Conjoint family therapy.* Palo Alto, Calif.: Science and Behavior Books.

H

heterogamy: "(1) Sexual reproduction involving fusion of unlike gametes often differing in size, structure, and physiology; (2) the condition of reproducing by heterogamy." The predisposition of people to choose partners with traits different, if not opposite, from their own.
Example: A man who is shy marries a woman who is very outgoing.
Sources: Webster's New Collegiate Dictionary (1977 ed.). Springfield, Mass.: G. & C. Merriam Co. Ard, B. (1969). Love and aggression: The perils of loving. In B.N. Ard & C.C. Ard (Eds.),

Handbook of marriage counseling (pp. 50–60). Palo Alto, Calif.: Science and Behavior Books.

heuristic: Of, or relating to, exploratory problem-solving techniques that utilize self-educating techniques to improve performance.
Example: A therapist sets up a group experiment that allows family members to discover a principle of cooperation.
Source: Drever, J. (1952). *A dictionary of psychology*. Baltimore: Penguin.

hierarchical structure: family functioning based on clear generational boundaries with the parents maintaining control and authority.
Source: Nichols, M. (1984). *Family therapy: Concepts and methods*. New York: Gardner Press.

holism: The view that the whole structure of a family system determines the system's properties and functions. A clinician holding this view of family systems (1) examines the present context and structures within which a symptom manifests itself (e.g., an apparently socially disabled 27-year-old male still living at home is the last of three children to leave), (2) looks for the etiology and the sustaining dynamics of the particular problem within the present active functioning of the organism (the child's guilt about leaving and the parent's anxiety about having "no one" at home), and (3) diagnoses and treats the problem on the basis of these "holistic" observations.
Source: Okun, B.F., & Rappaport, L.J. (1980). *Work with families: An introduction to family therapy*. Belmont, Calif.: Brooks/Cole.

holistic principle: The theoretic principle that a person or group has a totality or gestalt that is distinct and unique and cannot be understood by merely studying the individual elements or "atoms" comprising the whole.
Example: A child's behavior appears unusual when the child is interviewed alone, but makes sense when viewed within the context of the family.
Source: Hinsie, L., & Campbell, B. (1970). *Psychiatric dictionary* (4th ed.). New York: Oxford University Press.

holons: The component parts of a system, each of which is considered to be a whole in its own right as well as a part of the larger system. (The term was coined by Arthur Koestler to indicate systems of people within society.) There are many types of holons—the individual, the nuclear family, the extended family, and the community. A holon exerts competitive energy for autonomy and for self-preservation as a whole in itself. It also carries integrative energy as a part of the larger whole. Thus, the nuclear family is a holon of the extended family, the extended family is a holon of the community, and so forth.
Example:

- *Parental holon*—The system of individuals whose responsibility is the care and management of a child or children. It may include grandmothers and aunts, a child who is given the responsibility for siblings, etc.
- *Sibling holon*—The system in which children first learn to interact, to support, give, take, and enjoy. In this holon, children establish patterns that continue into extrafamilial peer groups. The sibling holon is a subset of the family holon.
- *Family holon*—The system of individuals comprising the "family." Usually this means the nuclear family, but it may also include the extended family. The family holon comprises all family members who take an active part in maintaining the system.

Sources: Umbarger, C.C. (1984). *Structural family therapy*. New York: Grune & Stratton; Koestler, A. (1979). *Janus: A summing up*. New York: Vintage Books.
Quoted: Minuchin, S., & Fishman, H. (1981). *Family therapy techniques*. Cambridge, Mass.: Harvard University Press.

home observations: Procedures involving the observation of family members interacting together in their home.
Source: Hansen, C. (1969). An extended home visit with conjoint family therapy. *Family Process*, 7, 67–87.

home visits: The therapist's visits to the family's home to hold sessions. This procedure gives the therapist the opportunity to determine what effect the physical environment has on the interactions of family members.
Source: Bloch, D. (1973). The clinical home visit. In D. Block (Ed.), *Techniques of family therapy: A primer* (pp. 39–45). New York: Grune & Stratton.

homeodynamics: The dynamics of family interaction. A nearly constant condition, such as that resulting from the homeostatic control of temperature within the body, is impossible in the area of interpersonal relations. Homeodynamics functions not merely to restore a preexisting equilibrium but also to make room for accommodation to new experience, for learning, change, and growth.

Example: A teenage son receives his driver's license. New rules are developed to deal with his driving, staying out, and dating.

Source: Ackerman, N. (1966). *Treating the troubled family.* New York: Basic Books.

homeostasis: The tendency toward maintenance of a relatively stable internal environment through a series of interacting physiological processes. In psychodynamic theory, homeostasis is the maintenance of balances in the intrapsychic system. Family theorists use the term to mean the maintenance of balances within a family to keep a certain established equilibrium or to ensure a relatively stable family environment. Systematic attempts are made by the family to restore the equilibrium when it is threatened in any way. Usually, all members of the family are engaged in this process.

Example: A schizophrenic daughter attempts to leave home. The parents say she cannot leave because of her illness. The solidarity of the family is protected by her illness.

Source: Jackson, D. (1969). The question of family homeostasis. In D. Jackson (Ed.), *Communication, family, and marriage* (pp. 1–11). Palo Alto, Calif.: Science and Behavior Books.

Quoted: Gerson, M., & Barsky, M. (1979). For the new family therapist: A glossary of terms. *American Journal of Family Therapy, 7,* 15–30.

homogamy: A perceived tendency for husbands and wives in American families to resemble one another in various physical, psychological, and social characteristics. Endogamy and assortive mating are other terms used to indicate the process of choosing a partner similar to oneself.

Source: Burgess, E., & Wallin, P. (1953). *Engagement and marriage.* Philadelphia: Lippincott.

horizontal bookkeeping: In human relationships, the attempt to analyze and manifest one's behaviors with the view to balancing them against others in the same generation. In this orientation, behavior in relationships is understood in accordance with what individuals feel they owe to, or have coming to them from, these various relationships.

Example: A single-parent mother feels guilty about depriving her exhusband of his daughter; so she feels she owes him special favors, while he feels he deserves those favors.

Source: Boszormenyi-Nagy, I., & Spark, G.

(1973). *Invisible loyalties.* New York: Harper & Row.

hostility: Disapproving, acrimonious, or attacking relationships in the family.

Quoted: Riskin, M., & Faunce, E. (1972). An evaluative review of family interaction research. *Family Process, 11,* 365–455.

how rule: The assumption that the use of "how" to begin a question contributes to the development of a problem-solving orientation between partners. The corollary is that "why" questions create an accusatorial exchange.

Example: A couple fighting with each other might ask, "Why do we fight?" A more productive approach would be to ask, "How do our arguments begin?"

Source: Baruth, L.G., & Huber, C.H. (1984). *An introduction to marital theory and therapy.* Monterey, Calif.: Brooks/Cole.

human services: The provision of comprehensive and coordinated services to people in need. Service delivery requires integrative approaches by the major help-giving systems of mental health, social welfare, health, education, and criminal justice. Other related services are also frequently classified under the human services rubric, e.g., family planning, recreation, parole and probation, advocacy and legal services, industrial relations, protective and foster care services for children and the aged, employment counseling, vocational rehabilitation, youth services, education programs for formal training, alternative learning schools, and continuing education.

Example: An adolescent who has a drinking problem is likely to come to the attention of the traffic court for driving while intoxicated; of the school counselor for truancy and inability to concentrate; of his family physician for disturbed sugar metabolism with symptoms of dizziness, weakness, and blackouts; of the welfare worker for fighting and abuses in the home; and of the mental health center for alcoholism. Family treatment is indicated.

Source: Sauber, S.R. (1977). The human services delivery system. *International Journal of Mental Health. 5,* 121–140.

humor: A disposition or state of mind that allows one (1) to relabel a situation and thus gain control over a situation in which one had previously been caught or (2) to reduce tension and thus restore a sense of commonality that was cut off by bitterness. Thus, the therapist makes humorous comments to ease a tense moment or to make changes in the family.

Carrying a situation to the point of absurdity often helps people to gain perspective on their overly intense involvement in a rigid position and to reduce what was threatening and serious to triviality.

Example: A mother who says she can't get anything done and can't stay focused on one thing for very long is viewed as seriously disturbed by members of the family. Saying that she has a ''jumping bean'' mind lightens the mood. It implies that the problem may not be as serious as the family thinks it is.

Source: Carter, E.A., & McGoldrick-Orfanidis, M. (1976). Family therapy with one person and the family therapist's own family. In P.J. Guerin, Jr. (Ed.), *Family therapy* (pp. 193–219). New York: Gardner Press.

hypoactive sexual desire: A sexual dysfunction characterized by persistent and pervasive inhibition of sexual desire. The specific etiology of the low libido has not yet been determined. Primary causes are depression, stress, drugs, and hormone imbalances.

Source: Kaplan, H.S. (1979). *Disorders of sexual desire.* New York: Brunner/Mazel.

hysteric-compulsive family: A family in which the father is a caricature of maleness, strong and silent; the mother caricatures the female by being quite emotional and seemingly relatively powerless.

Source: Lewis, J., Beavers, W.R., Gossett, J., & Phillips, V.A. (1976). *No single thread: Psychological health in the family system.* New York: Brunner/Mazel.

I

"I" position: A position in which a family member is able to "differentiate" himself or herself by taking action and responsibility for happiness and well being and avoids defining self in terms of others.

Source: Bowen, M. (1966). The use of family theory in clinical practice. *Comprehensive Psychiatry, 7,* 345–374.

"I" rule: A rule of self-expression that holds that self-statements should begin with the pronoun I. I statements are expressions of self-responsibility.

They are clear, are based upon personal awareness, leave room for the awareness of others, and encourage the disclosure of differences.

Source: Miller, S., Nunnally, E.W., & Wackman, D.B. (1976). *Couple workbook: Increasing awareness and communication skills.* Minneapolis, Minn.: Interpersonal Communication Program.

Quoted: Barth, L.G., & Huber, C.H. (1984). *An introduction to marital theory and therapy.* Monterey, Calif.: Brooks/Cole.

id binding: Parents' exploitation of the dependency needs of their children, with an emphasis on regressive gratification. The result is infantilization of the adolescent.

Source: Stierlin, H. (1974). *Separating parents and adolescents.* New York: Quadrangle.

See also **affective binding.**

identification: Any of a number of ways by which a person or family can be characterized. Identification has been defined variously by a number of different writers, and there are several broad classes of phenomena to which the term has been applied, sometimes by the same theorist: For example, identification as behavior (emphasizing overt action), identification as motive (disposition to act), identification as process (a mechanism by which behaviors and motives are acquired), or identification as a set of beliefs or cognitions about the self. Freud usually treated identification as a process—the sequential interplay of forces, internal and external, that impel a child to take on the characteristics of the parent (e.g., anaclitic and aggressive identification). But on at least one occasion he used the term to describe the product or outcome of the process—the resultant similarity in the characteristics of the child and the model.

Identification is also used in reference to one person's similarity to another individual, to individuals belonging to a particular group, or to individuals falling within a single category. Finally, identification may be applied to a perceived similarity, a motive to become similar, a process of becoming similar, or a state of being similar.

Source: Hall, C., & Lindzey, G. (1970). *Theories of personality.* New York: John Wiley & Sons.

Quoted: L'Abate, L. (1976). *Understanding and helping the individual in the family.* New York: Grune & Stratton.

identified patient: The symptom bearer or official patient as identified by the family. For example, it may be the family member who is most obviously affected by a pained marital relationship or most

subjected to dysfunctional parenting. The identified parent's (IP) symptoms signal the parents' pain and family imbalance. They also distort the IP's growth as a result of trying to absorb and alleviate the parent's pain.
Source: Satir, V. (1967). *Conjoint family therapy.* Palo Alto, Calif.: Science and Behavior Books.

identity struggle: The manifest content of family verbal conflicts, often taking the form of an argument over what kind of person each of the participants is. Each party alternately plays the role of aggressor and defender, at times accusing the other of having an undesirable characteristic, at other times stoutly defending one's own character from criticism.
Example: A mother wants her daughter to be friendly and outgoing and to confide in her. She tries to force this behavior by accusing the daughter of being unfriendly. The daughter responds by accusing the mother of not being understanding.
Source: Wallace, A., & Fogelson, H. (1965). The identity struggle. In I. Boszormenyi-Nagy & J. Framo (Eds.), *Intensive family therapy: Theoretical and practical aspects* (pp. 365–406). New York: Harper & Row.

idiopanima: The perception of another's perception of one's self. Idiopanima is related to insight and empathy. While empathy refers to the understanding of another, idiopanima is one's understanding of another's concept of one's self.
Source: Corsini, R.J. (1966). *Roleplaying in psychotherapy: A manual.* Chicago: Aldine.

image relationship: A relationship in which the inner image of the other person takes precedence. The emphasis is on changing reality to fit with expectation rather than on changing expectation to fit reality.
Example: A husband is seen as cold and insensitive by his wife because of her history with men. In fact, he is quite warm and sensitive.
Source: Brodey, W. (1961). The family as the unit of study and treatment, workshop: 3, Image, object and narcissistic relationships. *American Journal of Orthopsychiatry, 31,* 69–73.
Quoted: Searles, H. (1965). The contributions of family treatment to the psychotherapy of schizophrenia. In I. Boszormenyi-Nagy & J. Framo (Eds.), *Intensive family therapy: Theoretical and practical aspects* (pp. 463–496). New York: Harper & Row.

image thinking: The development of imagination and the ability to think visually. As the therapist listens to family members talk, visualizations of what they are saying are created. The therapist can then "see" what is being discussed.
Source: Dodson, L., & Kurpius, D. (1977). *Family counseling: A systems approach.* Muncie, Ind.: Accelerated Development.

immovability: Inflexible family patterns that the therapist tries to modify, change, or eliminate. The relevant therapeutic technique may be either a joining technique or a maneuver to initiate change. With a joining technique, the therapist enters the therapeutic relationship, demanding that the members of the system accommodate the therapist. This relays the message that there is a possibility for change. With a technique for initiating change, the therapist forces the family to change patterns that have been inflexible. They must now be modified to accommodate the inflexible therapist.
Example: A young student who recently had a psychotic break returns to his parents' home with his wife. Upon beginning therapy, he agrees to a date for him and his wife to move out of his family's house into an apartment of their own. On that date, the son oversleeps, and they subsequently do not move out. In the next therapy session, the therapist deals with this issue intensively and confronts the son. The wife, backed by the therapist, decides to move alone. The son protests, but the wife and the therapist are adamant. Heretofore, the families modified their behavior to allow for the son's behavior. The therapist (and his wife) then became immovable to force the son to move.
Source: Minuchin, S., & Fishman, H. (1981). *Family therapy techniques.* Cambridge, Mass.: Harvard University Press.

impartial expert: Experts appointed by a court who make child custody recommendations based on impartial investigations. With the court's support (preferably via a signed court order), the impartial expert interviews the parents and children and invites (not requires) others—such as stepparents, live-in parental surrogates, prospective stepparents, etc.—to provide meaningful information regarding custody arrangements. The goal of these interviews is to decide who is the better parent for custody purposes. The impartial expert does this by determining each parent's assets and liabilities as a parent and then weighing each parent's assets against that parent's liabilities. A comparison is then made between the two parents with regard to the balance of assets and liabilities. Usually, the courts rely on mental health professionals, rather than advocates in custody conflicts, to serve as impartial experts.

Example: Mr. & Mrs. S. appear to be equally competent as parents. However, Mr. S's availability for parenting is compromised significantly by the fact that his work obligations allow him little flexibility with regard to taking care of the children after school, during school vacation periods, and at times of sickness. All of the other liabilities that each parent exhibits do not appear to be significant. Accordingly, the expert suggests that the court allow Mrs. S. to continue to have custody of the children.

Source: Gardner, R.A. (1982). *Family evaluation in child custody litigation*. Cresskill, N.J.: Creative Therapeutics.

implosion: The empty feeling experienced by the ontologically insecure person, a feeling similar to the terrible fear that the world will crash in on one's self and wipe out all identity, like gas rushing in to fill up a vacuum. Consequently, because reality is necessarily implosive by nature, any contact with it is dreaded.

Example: A schizophrenic man has the feeling that he is totally alone in the world. He dreads his day-to-day life, fearing that only harm will come to him.

Source: Laing, R. (1969). *The divided self*. Baltimore: Penguin.

Quoted: Foley, V. (1974). *An introduction to family therapy*. New York: Grune & Stratton.

implosive therapy: Therapy designed to eliminate avoidance behavior through the process of extinction. The therapist floods the patient with anxiety-provoking stimuli without allowing any harm to come.

Example: A boy suffering from a school phobia is asked to imagine anxiety-arousing stimuli in their extremes without being allowed to leave the situation or to experience harm.

Source: Stampl, T., & Lewis, D. (1967). Essentials of implosive therapy: A learning theory based on psychodynamic behavioral therapy. *Journal of Abnormal Psychology, 72*, 496–503.

impotence: A condition that prevents the male from obtaining and/or maintaining an erection long enough to accomplish intercourse. Primary impotence refers to a male who has never had a successful coital experience; secondary impotence refers to a male who has had at least one successful experience but can no longer function. Impotence is also termed an erectile dysfunction.

Source: Masters, W., & Johnson, V. (1970). *Human sexual inadequacy*. Boston: Little, Brown.

impulsive family: A family characterized by an adolescent or young adult acting out anger toward a parent onto the community or expressing the parents' difficulties in a socially unacceptable way.

Source: Cuber, J., & Harroff, P. (1966). *Sex and the significant Americans*. Baltimore: Penguin.

Quoted: Glick, I., & Kessler, D. (1980). *Marital and family therapy* (2nd ed.). New York: Grune & Stratton.

incompatibility: A marital situation in which two people, usually husband and wife, have nothing in common or are conflictful and cannot get along because of different personality makeups, interests, or values. The two partners may use attributed or real differences between them to justify separation and divorce, i.e., incompatibility is an excuse to avoid closeness. This is the process of "monsterizing" that some partners need to achieve what they cannot achieve otherwise, i.e., distance. By the same token, however, differences can be used to unite and enhance a relationship and make it more vital and interesting. Hence, the differences underlying incompatibility can justify breaking a relationship, even though the same differences could be used to sustain the relationship.

Example: The husband is warm, affectionate, and sexually oriented; the wife is cold, distant, and lacks sexual desire. He values human sharing and intimacy as most important, and she is interested in power through social recognition and career success.

Source: Ellis, A., & Harper, R. (1961). *Creative marriage*. New York: Lyle Stuart.

incongruent manifestation: Communication in which a person's words and expression are disparate; the person says one thing but seems to mean another by voice or gestures. The person thus presents an incongruent communication, and the person to whom the person is talking receives a double-level message.

Example: A man tells his wife that he wants to go to the beach with her; but, as he speaks, he frowns and clinches his teeth.

Source: Satir, V. (1967). *Conjoint family therapy*. Palo Alto, Calif.: Science and Behavior Books.

independence: The process of denial of dependence, of being able to be alone and self-sufficient. Inde-

pendence is a stage between the dependence of childhood and the autonomous interdependence of ideal adulthood. It is usually found most prominently in adolescence.
Source: Erskine, R.G. (1982). Transactional analysis and family therapy. In A.M. Horne & M.M. Ohlsen (Eds.), *Family counseling and therapy* (pp. 245–275). Itasca, Ill.: F.F. Peacock Publishers.

index patient: The individual family member whose behavior is labeled as problematic. Sometimes, the use of this label may lead to an incorrect labeling of the entire family, as in referring to "schizophrenic families" or "drug addiction families."
Source: Umbarger, C.C. (1984). *Structural family therapy.* New York: Grune & Stratton.

indicator therapy: Treatment of a symptom that is so life-threatening, inconvenient, or painful that it deserves therapy in its own right.
Example: A boy steals women's underclothes. This symptom has serious personal and social consequences. The initial treatment is aimed at stopping the stealing behavior.
Source: Howells, J. (1975). *Principles of family psychiatry.* New York: Brunner/Mazel.

individual therapy: Therapy in which the focus is on the individual patient and the cure of the individual is the treatment goal. Individual therapy can be contrasted with family therapy along the dimensions listed in Table 2.
Source: Carroll, J. (1964). Family therapy—Some observations and comparisons. *Family Process, 1,* 180–182.

induction: The unknowing compliance of the therapist to the transactional structures and communicational rules of the family system. Induction is unwitting accommodation to the family patterns and occurs frequently in the initial phases of therapy.
Example: Dr. S. joins the family by occasionally converting to its folkways.
Source: Umbarger, C.C. (1984). *Structural family therapy.* New York: Grune & Stratton.

I-ness: The ability of individual family members to express themselves clearly as feeling, thinking, acting, valuable, and separate individuals and to take responsibility for thoughts, feelings, and actions.
Example: The therapist asks the mother to restate herself in a dispute with her husband regarding the children, using the pronoun "I" rather than "we." Thus, "We should not get angry with each other if we really love each other," becomes "I should not get angry at you if I really love you." The therapist

thereby diverts the wife's statement toward her husband and away from the children. The mother experiences the impact of her irrational belief.
Source: Beavers, W.R. (1976). A theoretical basis for family evaluation. In J.M. Lewis, W.R. Beavers, J.T. Gossett, & V.A. Phillips (Eds.), *No single thread: Psychological health in the family system* (pp. 46–82). New York: Brunner/Mazel.

information: A type of energy that leads to a reduction in the level of uncertainty within a system.
Source: Rappaport, L. (1953). What is information? *Synthese, 9,* 157.
Quoted: Steinglass, P. (1978). The conceptualization of marriage from a systems theory perspective. In T. Paolino & B. McCrady (Eds.), *Marriage and marital therapy* (pp. 298–368). New York: Brunner/Mazel.

information exchange: In operational terms, the number of times a family member explicitly states a choice, approval, disapproval, preference, etc. among the number of alternatives the family is asked to select on the Unrevealed Differences Questionnaire.
Source: Ferreira, A., & Winter, W. (1968). Information exchange and science in normal and abnormal families. *Family Process, 7,* 251–276.
Quoted: Riskin, M., & Faunce, E. (1972). An evaluative review of family interaction research. *Family Process, 11,* 365–455.

information processing style: The individual approach to perceiving, giving meaning, organizing, storing and outputting data and experience that each person has. It includes thinking in images, kinesthetically, or by nonlinguistic sounds, as well as in verbal modes.
Source: Duhl, B.S. (1983). *From the inside out and other metaphors.* New York: Brunner/Mazel.

inhibition of developmental potential: A situation in which a person, because of family organization, cannot act in ways appropriate to that person's age within the family.
Example: An adolescent girl does not wear makeup and dress as her friends do because of sexual taboos and restrictions in the family.
Source: Aponte, H., & Van Deusen, J. (1981). Structural family therapy. In A. Gurman & D. Kniskern (Eds.), *Handbook of family therapy* (pp. 310–360). New York: Brunner/Mazel.

inner dials: The focus of a sex hypnotherapy technique in which the client imagines an inner dial of sexual desire. The client then adjusts the dial knob

Table 2 Individual Therapy Contrasted with Family Therapy

Individual Therapy	Family Therapy
1. Focus: Illness of the individual patient. The primary interest is in intrapsychic disturbances of the individual.	1. Focus: Illness of the family. The primary interest is in the processes that occur within the family as a group.
2. Responsibility: The therapist is responsible to the individual; the cure of the individual is the treatment goal.	2. Responsibility: The family is the patient. The therapist is responsible for the total family's welfare, rather than that of any one individual.
3. Process: The therapist studies the individual in depth, often apart from the individual's social environment and family relations.	3. Process: The therapist studies the individuals as members of the family group, relating behavior to interactions with other family members.
4. Content: <ul><li>The therapist relates present material to past experiences of the patient.</li><li>Fantasy, dream materials, and their meanings are used, more or less, as the content of treatment.</li><li>Fantasy and dream materials may be interpreted and related by the therapist to feelings, attitudes, and behavior.</li><li>Patient's identity often is clarified by examining the integrations the patient makes between conflicts of the superego and id.</li><li>Transference may be highly individualized, with distortion of the image of the therapist based on infantile emotional experiences.</li><li>Materials revealed by the patient are highly confidential.</li></ul>	4. Content: <ul><li>Emphasis is on the "here and now" and on ways the family can achieve healthy functioning.</li><li>Interactions between family members and their meanings form the focus of treatment.</li><li>Family interactions and processes are pointed out by the therapist; their meanings are explored as they occur.</li><li>Patient's identity evolves from a clarification of the role the patient plays in the family, the patient's self-image in this role, and the patient's role expectations.</li><li>Transference is diluted; the therapist is a reality figure.</li><li>Materials are openly shared by the family with the therapist.</li></ul>
5. Goals: <ul><li>Diagnosis, analysis and cure of the individual's illness or disorder.</li><li>Understanding oneself as a unique individual.</li><li>Exploring, developing insights, and gaining relief from inhibiting conflicts.</li></ul>	5. Goals: <ul><li>Attaining effective family functioning, regardless of individual pathology.</li><li>Understanding oneself and other family members in relation to each other.</li><li>Establishing healthy interactions between family members.</li></ul>

Source: From "Family therapy—Some observations and comparisons" by J. Carroll, *Family Process, 1,* pp. 180–182, © 1964. Reprinted by permission.

---

upward while imagining the good sexual feelings associated with it. This technique is used to treat sexual desire dysfunctions.
Source: Araoz, D. (1982). *Hypnosis and sex therapy.* New York: Brunner/Mazel.

input: A form of energy received by open systems from their external environments. The pattern of activities or energy exchange in an open system has a cyclic character. An open system receives input—some form of energy from the external environ-ment—then transforms or reorganizes it through the application of throughput processes. The outputs of the system then become available for use as inputs for another system. The conception of an open system as a cycle of input ⟶ conversion ⟶ output facilitates the analysis of living systems at a variety of levels, from cell to the society.
Example: The son gets caught stealing, and his parents tighten up the family rules for all members. The parents ask the school counselor to monitor their son's behavior

Source: Sauber, S.R. (1983). *The human services delivery system.* New York: Columbia University Press.

insight-awareness approach: A therapeutic approach in which observation, clarification, and interpretation are used to foster understanding, and presumably change.
Source: Glick, I., & Kessler, D. (1980). *Marital and family therapy* (2nd ed.). New York: Grune & Stratton.

instrumental activity: Behavior that is directed toward some goal and helps the behaving person adapt to that person's environment. In traditional families, it is the husband's role in decision-making and task functions.
Example: A husband finds that he has trouble standing up to his wife, so he enrolls in a course in assertiveness training.
Source: Parsons, T., & Bales, R. (1955). *Family, socialization and interaction process.* New York: Free Press.

instrumental discrepancy: A situation in which one partner has something, e.g., money, that gives that partner leverage that the other does not have.
Source: Spiegel, J. (1957). The resolution of role conflict within the family. *Psychiatry, 16,* 1–16.
Quoted: Foley, V. (1974). *An introduction to family therapy.* New York: Grune & Stratton.

instrumental expression axis: A continuum of differences in instrumental versus expressive functions of a system. Instrumental functions concern the system's relation to situations outside the system and aimed at maintaining equilibrium (i.e., material goods and money). Expressive functions concern the integrative relation between members and the regulation of the patterns and tension levels of system's component units (i.e., feelings and emotions).
Source: Parsons, T., & Bales, R. (1955). *Family, socialization and interaction process.* New York: Free Press.

instrumental family functions: The ways in which a family deals with the outside world in terms of attaining goals and maintaining its equilibrium.
Example: A father spends much of his time away from home, engaging in work activity, so that his family can maintain itself financially.
Source: Parsons, T., & Bales, R. (1955). *Family, socialization, and interaction process.* New York: Free Press.

instrumental influence: The sum of giving opinions and suggestions in Bales' coding system.
Source: Bales, R. (1950). *Interaction process analysis: A method for the study of small groups.* Cambridge, Mass.: Addison-Wesley.
Quoted: Riskin, M., & Faunce, E. (1972). An evaluative review of family interaction research. *Family Process, 11,* 365–455.

instrumental leader: The person who is the judge, the final court of appeals, and the executor of punishment, discipline, and control in the family.
Source: Bales, R. (1950). *Interaction process analysis: A method for the study of small groups.* Cambridge, Mass.: Addison-Wesley.

integrative family therapy: Therapy designed to integrate the awareness of the simultaneous existence of a variety of viewpoints or systems levels, such as nonverbal modes of communication, felt meanings, information processing styles, and core images of the past, present, and future. It is a broad-based approach to family therapy, based on the idea that the family has its subsystems and suprasystems in operation at the same time.
Source: Duhl, F., & Duhl, B. (1981). Integrative family therapy. In A. Gurman & D. Kniskern (Eds.), *Handbook of family therapy* (pp. 483–513). New York: Brunner/Mazel.

intense relationship: A relationship in which both the positive and negative responses of each person are exaggeratedly important.
Example: A mother attempts to deal with her child with a mixture of overaffection and exasperation.
Source: Haley, J. (1976). *Problem-solving therapy.* San Francisco: Jossey-Bass.

intensionality: Seeing "experience in absolute and unconditional terms, to overgeneralize, to be dominated by concept or belief, to fail to anchor his reactions in space and time, to confuse fact and evaluation, to rely upon abstractions rather than upon reality-testing." The term is derived from general semantics and includes the concept of rigidity.
Source: Rogers, C. (1959). A theory of therapy, personality and interpersonal relationships, as developed in the client-centered framework. In S. Koch (Ed.), *Psychology: A study of a science, Vol. III. Formulations of the person and the social context* (pp. 184–256). New York: McGraw-Hill.
Quoted: Horne, A.M., & Ohlsen, M.M. (1982). *Family counseling and therapy.* Itasca, Ill.: F.E. Peacock Publishers.

intensity: Changing maladaptive transactions by using story affect, repeated intervention, or prolonged pressure. A quality of the therapist's message, correlated to the level at which the family "hears" and assimilates the message. Families often have a highly selective sense of hearing, and therapists have to increase intensity in order to go above the family's threshold of deafness. This may be done in various ways—from soft intervention with great drama to high levels of involvement on everyone's part.
Source: Minuchin, S., & Fishman, H. (1981). *Family therapy techniques.* Cambridge, Mass.: Harvard University Press.

interaction: An interpersonal activity in which one person acts upon another; person is balanced against person in a causal interconnection.
Example: A person's behavior impacts another, causing the second person to react in some predictable way.
Source: Dewey, J., & Bentley, A. (1949). *Knowing and the known.* Boston: Beacon Hill Press.
Quoted: Framo, J. (1965). Systematic research on family dynamics. In I. Boszormenyi-Nagy & J. Framo (Eds.), *Intensive family therapy: Theoretical and practical aspects.* New York: Harper & Row.

interaction pattern: The rules, implied or explicit, concerning who does what, when, where, and to whom. The relevant interaction is virtually synonymous with communication. The term bridges abstract concepts of systems theory to specific behavior.
Source: Barnard, C., & Corrales, R. (1979). *The theory and technique of family therapy.* Springfield, Ill.: Charles C Thomas.

interaction process analysis: An analytical method, devised by Bales, to quantify face-to-face, group interactive data. Probably the most widely used system for categorizing social interaction, the method relies on the interpretation of manifest level of activity. Based on the theoretical idea that the basic nature of social interaction is problem-solving, the assumption is that groups are instrumentally task-oriented, which in turn creates strains leading to emotional-integrative problems; the groups then attempt to deal with the resulting expressively positive and negative tensions in order to reintegrate back to the task. The flow back and forth between instrumental and expressive activities constitutes the essence of the Bales method. The content of Bale's 12 categories, their sequential and symmetrical relationships, and their ordering with respect to each other are empirically and theoretically based. The categories are (1) shows solidarity, (2) shows tension release, (3) agrees, (4) disagrees, (5) shows tension, (6) shows antagonism, (7) gives suggestion, (8) gives opinion, (9) gives orientation, (10) asks for orientation, (11) asks for opinion, and (12) asks for suggestion.
Source: Bales, R. (1950). *Interaction process analysis.* Cambridge, Mass.: Addison-Wesley.

interaction testing technique: A procedure used to generate spouse or family interactions. First, each spouse (or family member) is asked to fill out separately a subtest form of the Wechsler-Bellevue Comprehension and Similarities Test. Second, the respondents are brought together and asked to fill out the same form together, then to discuss each answer as they make their joint decisions.
Source: Bauman, G., & Roman, M. (1966). Interaction testing in the study of marital dominance. *Family Process, 5,* 230–242.

interactional approach of the Mental Research Institute: A family interactional approach based on the theories of Harry Stack Sullivan, Franz Alexander, and Ludwig von Bertalanffy as derived from the philosophies of Russell, Whitehead, Wittgenstein, and others. The goal is to change transactions and communication patterns in the dysfunctional family that effect the identified patient. Attention is paid to verbal and nonverbal behaviors, their timing, and their congruence. The focus is on modification and change of behavior, not on cognitive insight or emotional catharsis.
Example: A patient is asked not to change (a paradoxical instruction) or is pressured to change, by making the change contingent on continuation of therapy.
Source: Pinney, E.L., & Slipp, S. (1982). *Glossary of group and family therapy.* New York: Brunner/Mazel.

interactional contract: The operational contract that describes how two mates try to achieve fulfillment of the terms of their separate contracts. It is the set of conventions and implicit rules of behaviors, maneuvers, strategies, and tactics that they have developed in their dealings with each other.
Example: A husband and wife contract for one night a week to be with their own set of friends. The contract dictates how they will fulfill certain needs but not necessarily what each will do.
Source: Sager, C. (1981). Couples therapy and marriage contracts. In A. Gurman & D. Kniskern

(Eds.), *Handbook of family therapy* (pp. 85–132). New York: Brunner/Mazel.

interactional sequences: Patterns of behavior within a family system that reflect the roles and hierarchical positions assigned to each family member.
Source: Haley, J. (1976). *Problem solving therapy*. San Francisco: Jossey-Bass.
Quoted: Levant, R.F. (1984). *Family therapy: A comprehensive overview*. Englewood Cliffs, N.J.: Prentice-Hall.

interdependency: The combination of autonomy of independence and acknowledgment of responsibility and dependency that each person experiences in relation to others with whom that person is living, directed at the satisfaction of some emotional or physical need. The basic areas of interdependency include (1) the exchanges between the system and its environment, (2) the processes within the system, and (3) the processes through which parts of the environment are related to each other. Each of these sets of interdependencies—transactional, internal, and interdependencies within the environment itself—must be considered.
Example: A recently married man bought his bride a car which she couldn't afford to buy herself. He wanted her to be more mobile and less dependent on the use of his car.
Source: Sauber, S.R. (1983). *The human services delivery system*. New York: Columbia University Press.

interdependent triad: The intense interdependence between father, mother, and patient in disturbed families. In such families, change among the members occurs slowly.
Example: Members of a family form intense dependencies on each other in order to avoid looking at their own unhappiness. Mother and father argue constantly but have such low self-esteem that they cannot split; the child believes he is no good to the outside world, so he stays tied to the parents' problems.
Source: Bowen, M. (1965). Family psychotherapy with schizophrenia in the hospital and private practice. In I. Boszormenyi-Nagy & J. Framo (Eds.), *Intensive family therapy: Theoretical and practical aspects* (pp. 213–245). New York: Harper & Row.

interexperience: The experiential relationship that goes on between people: "Your behavior and mine as I experience it, and your behavior and mine as you experience it"—a statement that indicates that self exists only in relation to others.
Source: Laing, R. (1967). *The politics of experience*. New York: Ballantine Books.
Quoted: Foley, V. (1974). *An introduction to family therapy*. New York: Grune & Stratton.

interface: The area of contact between one system and another. An organizational system engages in numerous transactions at the interface—including the transfer of matter, energy, information, and people. Drawing the boundaries of a system is the first step in defining its structure. The next step usually entails defining the relationship of the elements to each other. Most frequently, the elements are grouped together in a hierarchical arrangement so as to be either subordinate or superordinate to each other. Accordingly, groups of related elements may be classified as subsystems or suprasystems. Face-to-face interaction by family members across the family system interface can be conceptualized as interaction between the system and its environment.
Example: As a distinct systemic entity, a family service agency must maintain some discontinuity from its external environment in order to continue to exist as a separate system. Its boundaries may be rigid and closed, not permitting any interaction between the elements inside and outside the system; or they may be flexible and open, permitting interaction with elements outside of the system. In the case of the family, a boundary may be difficult to detect in terms of physical factors, but may be more readily observed in terms of the discontinuity in pattern clusterings of family interactions.
Source: Sauber, S.R. (1983). *The human services delivery system*. New York: Columbia University Press.

intergenerational family therapy: Therapy that attempts to rebind family loyalties and relationships between generations, using family conflict as a growth ingredient rather than as an obstacle with grandparents, parents, and children.
Source: Boszormenyi-Nagy, I., & Spark, G. (1973). *Invisible loyalties*. New York: Harper & Row.

interlocking jealousy patterns: A complex system of interlocking neurotic needs and attitudes that binds many pathological families. A system of mutual projection such as this is difficult to understand or treat in intrapsychic terms.
Example: A wife suspects her husband of being unfaithful. The husband feeds her suspicions by frequently going out without telling her where he is

going, because she, too, is fanning his jealous suspicions by making secret telephone calls.
Source: Boszormenyi-Nagy, I. (1965). A theory of relationships: Experience and transaction. In I. Boszormenyi-Nagy & J. Framo (Eds.), *Intensive family therapy: Theoretical and practical aspects* (pp. 33–86). New York: Harper & Row.

interlocking need template: A pattern of spouses locked into a tightly over-ritualized relationship in which each serves as the "monstrous" part of the other, i.e., substitutive victimization.
Example: A wife who complains that her husband is not intimate enough covertly frustrates his attempts to get closer, while her obsession with his distance allows her to disown her role in the problem.
Source: Boszormenyi-Nagy, I. (1962). The concept of schizophrenia from the point of view of family treatment. *Family Process, 1,* 103–113.
Quoted: Boszormenyi-Nagy, I., & Ulrich, D. (1981). Contextual family therapy. In A. Gurman & D. Kniskern (Eds.), *Handbook of family therapy* (pp. 159–186). New York: Brunner/Mazel.

interlocking pathology: A situation in which all members of the family are locked together psychologically, and one or more of its members are not individuating. In this type of family, there is no allowance for differentiations of self.
Example: A wife who acts hysterically marries a man with obsessive-compulsive features. The two form an interlocking system, in that one is undercontrolled emotionally while the other is overcontrolled emotionally.
Source: Ackerman, N. (1982). Interlocking pathologies. In D. Bloch & R. Simon (Eds.), The strength of family therapy: Selected papers of Nathan W. Ackerman (pp. 174–184). New York: Brunner/Mazel.
Quoted: Barnard, C., & Corrales, R. (1979). *The theory and technique of family therapy.* Springfield, Ill.: Charles C Thomas.

interlocking racket system: A dysfunctional family in which awareness of each person's needs and desires is avoided or concealed and family problems are met with rigidity and manipulation. The dynamics of an interlocking racket system are illustrated as various family members attempt to live out their scripts. Each person influences and is influenced by the behavior of others in the family, and the members provide reinforcing experiences that confirm their script beliefs. In family therapy, the therapist watches for the transactions (or lack of

appropriate transactions) that are script-reinforcing for someone in the family.
Example: A wife exhibits long periods of silence without initiating contact with her husband. The husband interprets his wife's avoidance behavior as "there is something wrong with me." The husband then angrily defends himself against his wife and son. The wife withdraws further.
Source: Erskine, R.G. (1982). Transactional analysis and family therapy. In A.M. Horne & M.M. Ohlsen (Eds.), *Family counseling and therapy* (pp. 245–275). Itasca, Ill.: F.E. Peacock Publishers.

internal frame of reference: "All of the realm of experience which is available to the awareness of the individual at a given moment." The subjective internal frame of reference includes the "full range of sensations, perceptions, meanings, and memories, which are available to consciousness."
Source: Rogers, C. (1959). A theory of therapy, personality and interpersonal relationships, as developed in the client-centered framework. In S. Koch (Ed.), *Psychology: A study of a science, Vol. III. Formulations of the person and the social context* (pp. 184–256). New York: McGraw-Hill.
Quoted: Thayer, L. (1982). A person-centered approach to family therapy. In A.M. Horne & M.M. Ohlsen (Eds.), *Family counseling and therapy* (pp. 175–213). Itasca, Ill.: F.E. Peacock Publishers.

internalized family: A family characterized by a fearful, pessimistic, hostile, threatening view of the world, leading to a constant state of vigilance. Such a family has a well-defined role structure, high family loyalty, and a pseudomutual bond between the parents. Also called an enmeshed family.
Source: Cuber, J., & Harroff, P. (1966). *Sex and the significant Americans.* Baltimore: Penguin.
Quoted: Glick, I., & Kessler, D. (1980). *Marital and family therapy* (2nd ed.). New York: Grune & Stratton.

interpersonal competence: Effectiveness in interpersonal relationships based on (1) self-acceptance, the degree to which the individual has self-confidence; (2) confirmation, the result of others experiencing the person as that person experiences self, thus leading to self-confidence; and (3) essentiality, the use of one's central abilities and the expression of one's central needs, leading to commitment. These conditions facilitate the behaviors of owning up or accepting responsibility for one's ideas and feelings; being open to the ideas and feelings of others and those from within one's self; experi-

menting with new ideas and feelings; and helping others to own up to, and be open and experiment with, their ideas or feelings. Facilitation of these behaviors leads to individuality (rather than conformity), concern, and trust.
Source: Argyris, C. (1970). *Intervention—Theory and method.* Reading, Mass.: Addison-Wesley.

interpersonal distance-sensitive family: A family characterized by extreme independence of each member. Because neither the outside world nor the family is trustworthy, each problem situation is viewed by each member as an individual challenge to be mastered alone. Feedback from others is considered to be either irrelevant information or unsolicited criticism. Therefore, decisions are usually reached in isolation from the other members. Some members maintain their isolation by making impulsive decisions based on insufficient information, while others remain steadfastly independent by collecting information indefinitely without taking a position.
Example: A family with three children ranging in age from 10 to 17 receives a cash windfall that allows them to plan their first vacation in two years. When presented with the prospect of planning a joint vacation which all would enjoy, they begin talking about how each would spend a proportion of the money. The subject thus shifts from selecting a family vacation to how to split the money equitably. The oldest child clings to her suggestion to split the money evenly among the five, while the parents consider a number of elaborate plans for dividing the money. Discussion of a family vacation is abandoned.
Source: Reiss, D. (1981). *The family's construction of reality.* Cambridge, Mass.: Harvard University Press.

interpersonal perceptivity: The ability of an individual to guess, nonverbally and more or less accurately, the mood, attitude, and behavior of another individual.
Example: A mother notices her daughter withdrawing in her behavior after school. She knows her daughter must be feeling depressed again over a boy she has been dating.
Source: Ferreira, A. (1964). Interpersonal perceptivity among family members. *American Journal of Orthopsychiatry, 34,* 64–70.
Quoted: Riskin, M., & Faunce, E. (1972). An evaluative review of family interresearch. *Family Process, 11,* 365–455.

interruption: Breaking into the speech of another so that the interrupted statement is left incomplete.
Source: Mishler, E., & Waxler, N. (1968). *Interaction in families: An experimental study of family processes and schizophrenia.* New York: John Wiley & Sons.
Quoted: Riskin, M., & Faunce, E. (1972). An evaluative review of family interaction research. *Family Process, 11,* 365–455.

intersubjective continuum: A dimension defined by extreme consensus and agreement among family members at one end and complete disagreement and inability to share one's viewpoint or perception of reality at the other end. At the first extreme, family agreement may rob the members of individual choices and freedom of choice. At the second extreme, individual perceptions are allowed as the only basis for a "right" choice for each individual. The first extreme tends to produce conformity, while the second tends to develop individuality.
Sources: Kantor, D., & Lehr, W. (1975). *Inside the family.* San Francisco, Calif.: Jossey-Bass; Reiss, D. (1981). *The family's construction of reality.* Cambridge, Mass.: Harvard University Press.

intervention: The process of entering into an ongoing system of relationships between or among persons, groups, or objects for the purpose of helping them. An important implicit assumption is that the system exists independently of the intervener. There are many reasons one might wish to intervene, ranging from helping the clients make their own decisions about the kind of help they need to coercing the clients to do what the intervener wishes them to do. Intervention acknowledges interdependencies between the intervener and the client system. It focuses on how to maintain or increase the client system's autonomy, how to differentiate more clearly the boundaries between the client system and the intervener, and how to conceptualize and define the client system's health independently of the intervener's. The client system is valued as an ongoing, self-responsible unit that has an obligation to be in control over its own destiny. An intervener, accordingly, assists the system to become more effective in problem solving, decision making, and decision implementation in such a way that it can be increasingly effective in such activities and have a decreasing need for the intervener.
Source: Argyris, C. (1970). *Intervention: Theory and method.* Reading, Mass.: Addison-Wesley.

Quoted: Sauber, S.R. (1973). *Preventive educational intervention for mental health.* Cambridge, Mass.: Ballinger.

intimacy: Physical, intellectual, and emotional closeness and self-disclosure with another person (Sloan & L'Abate, in press). Intimacy means sharing our hurts and our fears of being hurt, the expression of our vulnerabilities, fallibilities, frailties, and needs to the ones we love and who love us (L'Abate, 1977). From this definition derive three paradoxes: (1) we need to be separate as individuals before we can be close to another person; (2) we hurt mainly the ones we love, because hurt and love are intertwined (i.e., we love others to the extent that we hurt when they hurt); and (3) we need to receive comfort from and give comfort to those whom we have hurt and who have hurt us (L'Abate & L'Abate, 1979). Our inability, sometimes the unwillingness, to be intimate appears to be a basic cause of marital and family dysfunctionality (L'Abate, Weeks & Weeks, 1979). Jessee and L'Abate (1982, 1983) suggest that intimacy in a couple's relationship is an antidote for depression. The ability to be intimate requires a certain degree of self-hood (i.e., each of us must have a self before we can share it with another self).
Example: The wife cries and blames the husband for her hurt ("It's all your fault!"). Typically, the husband responds in anger or simply leaves the room. In this case, no intimacy can be achieved. In contrast, the wife cries, but says, "I feel very bad right now, and I need you to be close to me and comfort me." The husband hugs her and responds, "I cannot stand it when you cry and hurt, because when you hurt, I hurt, too." In this case, intimacy is achieved.
Sources:
Jessee, E., & L'Abate, L. (1982). The paradoxes of depression. *International Journal of Family Psychiatry, 3,* 175–187.
Jessee, E., & L'Abate, L. (1983). Intimacy and marital depression: Interactional partners. *International Journal of Family Therapy, 9,* 39–53.
L'Abate, L. (1977). Intimacy is sharing hurt feelings: A reply to David Mace. *Journal of Marriage and Family Counseling, 3,* 13–16.
L'Abate, L., & L'Abate, B. (1979). The paradoxes of intimacy. *Family Therapy, 6,* 175–184.
L'Abate, L., Weeks, G., & Weeks, K. (1979). Of scapegoats, strawmen, and scarecrows. *International Journal of Family Counseling, 1,* 86–96.
Sloan, S.Z., & L'Abate, L. (in press). Intimacy. In L. L'Abate (Ed.), *Handbook of psychology and therapy.* Homewood, Ill.: Dow Jones-Irwin.

intrafamilial alignment: A concept describing the perception by two or more people that they are joined together in a common interest or bond and in that experience they have positive feelings toward one another. This is used to describe shifts and sequences in a family.
Example: A father was the coach for his son's little league team.
Source: Wynne, L.C. (1961). The study of intrafamilial alignments and splits in exploratory family therapy. In N.W. Ackerman, F.L. Beatman, & S.N. Sherman (Eds.), *Exploring the base for family therapy.* New York: Family Services Association.

intrafamilial split: The perception by two or more people that they are in opposition to or have differences from each other with associated negative feelings. The alignments and splits within a social system define the emotional organization of the system.
Example: Sisters were one year apart in age but they made it clear to everyone that they were far apart in personality and preferences.
Source: Wynne, L.C. (1961). The study of intrafamilial alignments and splits in exploratory family therapy. In N.W. Ackerman, F.L. Beatman, & S.N. Sherman (Eds.), *Exploring the base for family therapy.* New York: Family Services Association.

introjection: A primitive form of identification taking in aspects of other people which then become part of self-image.
Example: A young girl admired her teacher and began to imitate her mannerisms.
Source: Nichols, M. (1984). *Family therapy.* New York: Gardner Press.

intrusion: The process by which a family member diffuses the boundaries of another family member and thereby incorporates the first member into the other's role and place in the family.
Example: Often in a family consisting of a mother and a child, the two rely heavily on one another. The child often spends a lot more time with adults than with peers, and often has an intense symbiotic relationship with the mother, in which the two respond as one. Another kind of intrusion may be observed in a dyad in which there is one "competent" member and one "helpless" one. The com-

petent member may be intrusive in order to "help," protect, and handle events for the "helpless" one.
Source: Minuchin, S., & Fishman, H. (1981). *Family therapy techniques.* Cambridge, Mass.: Harvard University Press.

intrusiveness: Any act or series of acts that perforates, or is allowed to perforate, the emotional boundaries defining the relationships among family members.
Example: In a single-parent family, the oldest child is required or reinforced to fulfill a parental role. This breaks down the necessary generational boundaries between parent and child. Incest is an extreme act of intrusion, physical or otherwise.
Source: Riskin, J., & Faunce, E. (1970). Family interaction order. I. Theoretical framework and method. *Archives of General Psychiatry, 22,* 504–512.

invalidation: A coercive disqualification of a dependent person's statements, as when parents ignore those views of their children that threaten their (the parents') authority and positive self-image.
Example: Laing refers to the first schizophrenic patient in psychiatric literature whose major "feature" was a hatred of his father. The psychiatrist, Dr. Morrel, acting as the father's agent, managed to invalidate the man's hatred by declaring it to be a symptom of mental illness.
Source: Laing, R.D. (1965). Mystification, confusion, and conflict. In I. Boszormenyi-Nagy & J.L. Framo (Eds.), *Intensive family therapy* (pp. 343–364). New York: Harper & Row.

invasiveness: The disqualification of another's experience; invading another's personal life space by speaking for that person.
Example: A child who is angry is told by the mother, "You don't really feel that way."
Source: Beavers, W.R. (1977). *Psychotherapy and growth.* New York: Brunner/Mazel.

inventory of marital conflict: The generation of marital interactions with an emphasis on differences and how they are handled. Each spouse is given a list of 18 short vignettes concerning various types of marital conflict, e.g., conflict concerning a wife's lateness for dinner engagements, conflict about sexual relationships, etc. For each vignette, there are two possible ways of resolving the conflict, which the spouses are asked to either accept or reject. They are also asked, "Who is primarily

responsible for the problem?" "Have you had a similar problem?" and "Have you known other couples who have similar problems?" After the spouses have individually filled in their answer sheets, they are brought together and asked to discuss each conflict and to decide jointly who is responsible for the problem.
Source: Olson, D., & Ryder, R. (1970). Inventory of Marital Conflicts (IMC): An experimental interaction procedure. *Journal of Marriage and the Family, 32,* 443–448.

invisible loyalty: The ethical base of expectations, the central motivating factor in families, the commitments to one's parents, spouse, children. Accountability with an action orientation. A child's belief that the debt to the parents is endless and that its payment takes priority over every other human concern. In order to be this type of loyal member, one has to internalize a spirit of expectation and have a set of specifiable attitudes to comply with the internalized injunctions.
Example: The son's area of study and occupational choice are the same as his father's, since the father was paying his college tuition.
Source: Boszormenyi-Nagy, I., & Spark, G. (1973). *Invisible loyalties.* New York: Harper & Row.

involvement: The process of having all family members involved in the therapy starting from the point of scheduling for the initial interview, e.g., family members discussing available times, continuing during the treatment and termination phases. Each family member needs to attend and participate in contributing their thoughts, feelings, and opinions. All members have some role in planning the action the family takes.
Example: The major focus for several sessions with a family may be for an adolescent boy and his parents to learn to communicate more effectively about household chores. The therapist might express appreciation of the younger sister's presence because she may have some ideas on how her brother and parents can get along better. She may want to communicate better with all three herself, and she will surely not want agreements negotiated in her absence about household chores that may affect her role.
Source: Nelsen, J.C. (1983). *Family therapy: An integrative approach.* Englewood Cliffs, N.J.: Prentice Hall.

involvement devoid of feeling: Intellectual interest among family members, but no emotional ties.

Example: A husband admires his wife's intellect but shows no interest in sharing an emotional life with her.
Source: Epstein, N., Bishop, D., & Levin, S. (1978). The McMaster model of family functioning. *Journal of Marriage and Family Counseling, 4,* 19–31.
Quoted: Epstein, N., & Bishop, D. (1981). Problem-centered systems therapy of the family. In A. Gurman & D. Kniskern (Eds.), *Handbook of family therapy* (pp. 444–482). New York: Brunner/Mazel.

isomorphic transactions: Messages, given by one subsystem of the family to another, that are not structurally but dynamically equivalent.
Example: A mother insists that her 18-year-old son not date and not learn to drive. She wants to effectively control his life. The sum of these messages is "Don't grow up." Although the messages are not structurally equal, they convey the same message.
Source: Minuchin, S., & Fishman, H. (1981). *Family therapy techniques.* Cambridge, Mass.: Harvard University Press.

isomorphism: The relationship of two complex structures when they are mapped onto each other in such a way that for each part of one structure there is a corresponding part in the other structure. ("Corresponding" means that the two parts play similar roles in their respective structures.) The term as used in family therapy is derived from a more precise notion in mathematics. It is the perceptions of isomorphism that create meanings in the minds of people. The meaning of the therapy situation can be described as "change." In general, the change process can be seen to start with an "idea" ("news of a difference") that is a "result" of reframing or changing the contextual meanings of a set of concrete "facts."

Thus, the concept of isomorphism as applied to family therapy is the ability of the treatment team to describe the family's patterns (A) in such a way that their reframed description (A$_1$) can serve as a guide for designing an intervention that can be mapped onto the pattern (A) the family has described and shown. The elements of the team's description must correspond with the elements of the family's description and the patterns it has shown the team in the therapy sessions. Furthermore, the team's description (A$_1$) must be from a different angle, so that the family (at least potentially) can receive the news of a difference, a perceptual shift, that promotes change in the family patterns. The resultant

behavior change creates a different subjective experience. This isomorphic description enables the therapy team to design isomorphic interventions, in particular the "compliment subset" of the intervention set of "compliment and clue."
Source: de Shazer, S. (1982). *Patterns of brief family therapy.* New York: Guilford Press.

J

joining: The process of "coupling" that occurs between the therapist and the family, leading to the development of the therapeutic system. It includes the myriad ways in which the therapeutic contact is embraced, resisted, and reciprocated by the family as a unit and by the individual family members. "The therapist's data and his diagnoses are achieved experientially in the process of joining the family . . . Diagnosis in family therapy is achieved through the interactional process of joining." The therapist joins primarily through contact with individual family members, not with some abstraction called the "system"; although some properties of the superordinate entity—such as mood, tempo, language—will soon emerge, and these will influence the therapist's joining style. The process of contact and response to contact is inevitable, since to join a family is of necessity to interfere with its life. Joining is an effort to cross the family-unit boundary, gaining a foothold wherever possible and seeking alliances with any subgroup willing to make one. Joining as a diagnostic strategy requires one to attempt an alteration of the family's rules and then to observe how the family reacts.
Example: Instead of contacting the mother directly, the therapist addresses all communications to the maternal grandmother. The therapist asks the grandmother to speak to the mother. If the therapist wants to restructure this arrangement, the therapist can challenge the communicational pathway and speak directly to the mother, perhaps asking her to give the history of a child's difficulty. The accommodation intervention would allow for one kind of joining, probably an alliance with the grandmother and a temporary estrangement from the mother. The restructuring intervention would promote an alliance with the mother. The examples in Figure 5 illustrate the use of the symbols of structural map-

Figure 5 Two Kinds of Therapeutic Joining with a Family

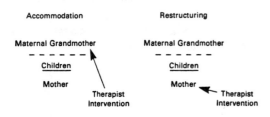

Source: From *Structural Family Therapy* (p. 49) by C.C. Umbarger, New York: Grune & Stratton. © 1984. Reprinted by permission.

ping and the assumption that the therapist's experience of joining the family offers diagnostic information.
Source: Minuchin, S. (1974). *Families and family therapy.* Cambridge, Mass.: Harvard University Press.
Quoted: Umbarger, C.C. (1984). *Structural family therapy.* New York: Grune & Stratton.

joint custodial parents: Divorced parents who agree to establish a cooperative relationship with each other regarding the exercise of their continuing responsibilities as parents of their children. They accept that each has an equal right to determine and share in the children's upbringing, including their education, health care, and religious training. They agree that the child's living arrangements between the two parents shall be such as are in the best interests of the child. Even though joint custody reflects a cooperative attitude on the part of both parents, specific living arrangements are included in the settlement agreement.
Source: Coogler, O.J. (1978). *Structured mediation in divorce settlement.* Lexington, Mass.: Lexington Books.

joint process: A therapeutic arrangement in which all those involved with the family problem are in the same room with the therapist in order to work on their relationships with mutual awareness, consent, and effort.
Source: Aponte, H., & VanDeusen, J. (1981). Structural family therapy. In A. Gurman & D. Kniskern (Eds.), *Handbook of family therapy* (pp. 310–360). New York: Brunner/Mazel.

Kegel's exercises: Exercises developed by Kegel to strengthen musculature. These exercises have been used effectively in treatment programs for inorgasmic women. They consist of tightening and relaxing the pubococcygeal muscle surrounding the vaginal outlet.
Source: Kegel, A. (1952). Sexual functions of the pubococcygeal muscle. *Western Journal of Surgery, Obstetrics, and Gynecology, 60,* 521–524.
Quoted: Kline-Graber, G., & Graber, B. (1978). Diagnosis and treatment procedures of pubococcygeal deficiencies in women. In J. LoPiccolo & L. LoPiccolo (Eds.), *Handbook of sex therapy* (pp. 227–240). New York: Plenum Press.

kinship rating scheme: A scoring system for determining whether or not family members ascribe relationships to figures depicted on TAT cards. The system includes the following six categories:

1. clearly defined nuclear family member
2. vaguely mentioned nuclear family member
3. extended family member
4. friend, business acquaintance, or social contact
5. identified figure but with no specific role determination
6. total avoidance of character; never mentioned

Source: Goldstein, M., Gould, E., Alkire, A., Rodrick, E., & Judd, L. (1970). Interpersonal themes in the Thematic Apperception Test stories of families of disturbed adolescents. *Journal of Nervous and Mental Disease, 100,* 354–365.
Quoted: Riskin, M., & Faunce, E. (1972). An evaluative review of family interaction research. *Family Process, 11,* 365–455.

labeling: Attaching a linguistic symbol to a person's behavior. The label influences how the client behaves, as well as other people's perceptions of and reactions to the label-bearer. Specific labels also have a way of generalizing to the whole person. In psychology, many labels are negative.

Example: A child who is blind is said to be a blind child. A person who has a bad habit is carelessly labeled a neurotic.
Source: Weeks, G., & L'Abate, L. (1982). *Paradoxical psychotherapy.* New York: Brunner/Mazel.

lack of functional power: A condition in which individuals are unable to exercise the force necessary to carry out the functions appropriate to themselves in the system in which they are operating.
Example: A mother is not able to carry out the executive function of directing her child's behavior. She fosters dependency by hindering the child from playing with friends, yet allows the child to stay up late with her.
Source: Aponte, H., & VanDeusen, J. (1981). Structural family therapy. In A. Gurman & D. Kniskern (Eds.), *Handbook of family therapy* (pp. 310–360). New York: Brunner/Mazel.

laughter: A spontaneous chuckle or explosive sound expressing a variety of emotions, e.g., joy, mirth, scorn. Laughter can be used to disguise such feelings as anger, love, hostility, and shame; or it may reflect some general tension or anxiety. It may be a socially acceptable cloak for feelings that are unacceptable, or a mechanism for disguise.
Source: Zuk, G. (1971). *Family therapy: A triadic-based approach.* New York: Behavioral Publications.

leaving the room: An unexpected strategic action by the therapist to reduce escalating conflict. It is aimed at keeping spouses off balance and startling them into realizing how nonproductive their behavior has become. The action conveys a potent message to the sparring spouses; at the same time it serves as a self-preservation tactic for the mediator or therapist who may welcome the short break from the argument.
Example: The therapist stands up and says to the couple: "I am not interested in hearing you two argue. That behavior is for the courtroom, not for mediation. Please continue your argument until you are finished. I will be in the waiting room. When you are done arguing and are ready to mediate, please let me know." The therapist then walks out of the room and closes the door. Usually, within five minutes or so, one of the spouses opens the door to announce that they have finished arguing and that they are ready to resume mediation.
Source: Saposnek, D.T. (1983). Strategies in child custody mediation: A family systems approach. *Mediation Quarterly, 1*(2), 29–54.

ledger of merit and indebtedness: An accumulation of the accounts of what has been given and what is owed in the family. The ledger has two ethical components. The first has to do with the debts and entitlements dictated by legacy. These may vary greatly, even between two siblings, e.g., it may be imperative for the son to become a success, for the daughter to become a failure. According to the legacy of this family, the son may be entitled to approval, the daughter only to shame. Thus, the legacy may fall with gross unfairness on the two. The second ethical component has to do with the accumulation of merit through contributions to the welfare of the other. Thus, "entitlement" may combine what is due as a parent or child and what one has come to merit. A natural mother who abandons her child may have earned no merit, yet the legacy of filial loyalty puts the child into a special ledger position vis-à-vis the mother, who still retains some entitlement.
Example: A woman took care of her sick mother during the latter's last few years. Now she expects her own daughter to take care of her whenever she is sick.
Source: Boszormenyi-Nagy, I., & Urich, D. (1981). Contextual family therapy. In A. Gurman & D. Kniskern (Eds.), *Handbook of family therapy* (pp. 159–187). New York: Brunner/Mazel.

legacy: The specific configuration of expectations that originate from generational rootedness and impinge on the offspring. The legacy's origins are multigenerational.
Example: Women may be expected to be successes while men are expected to be "ne'er-do-wells."
Source: Boszormenyi-Nagy, I., & Spark, G. (1973). *Invisible loyalties.* New York: Harper & Row.
Quoted: Boszormenyi-Nagy, I., & Ulrich, D. (1981). Contextual family therapy. In A. Gurman and D. Kniskern (Eds.), *Handbook of family therapy* (pp. 159–186). New York: Brunner/Mazel.

lethal games: A situation in which everyone agrees with everyone else, at the expense of one's own needs and satisfactions.
Source: Satir, V. (1967). *Conjoint family therapy.* Palo Alto, Calif.: Science and Behavior Books.

letter writing: A therapeutic technique in which the client is instructed to write a letter to a family member, even if that member is deceased. In the letter, the client expresses feelings about the relationship with that family member. The letter may be

assigned as a project to be worked on daily over a week, or it may be written in one sitting. The act of writing can be so cathartic as to allow the past to be put to rest. The letter may or may not be mailed. *Example:* Mrs. P. comes to therapy because of her preoccupation with what others think of her. When asked about her relationship with her parents, Mrs. P. says that her parents never took her seriously and constantly belittled her, which has resulted in considerable resentment. Mrs. P. is instructed to write a letter to her parents in which she is to be completely honest about her feelings toward them. She is given the choice of mailing the letter or not. In the next session, Mrs. P. reports that, although she decided not to mail the letter, writing it has allowed her to release a great deal of anger she felt toward her parents, resulting in a tremendous feeling of relief. As a result, Mrs. P. is able to develop a stronger sense of self-esteem, and her preoccupation with others' perceptions about her are diminished.
Source: Anonymous. (1972). Toward the differentiation of the self in one's own family. In J.L. Framo (Ed.), *Family interactions* (pp. 111–173). New York: Springer.
Quoted: Lange, A., & van der Hart, O. (1983). *Directive family therapy.* New York: Brunner/Mazel.

level of abstraction code: A code used to measure the similarity of verbal information processing among family members.
Source: Reiss, D. (1968). Individual thinking and family interaction, III. An experimental study of categorization performance in families of normals, those with character disorders, and schizophrenia. *Journal of Nervous and Mental Disease, 146,* 324–403.
Quoted: Riskin, M., & Faunce, E. (1972). An evaluative review of family interaction research. *Family Process, 11,* 365–455.

levels of intervention: Types of efforts to introduce systematically family change in individuals, social systems, populations, or networks of systems. The goal at each level is the improvement of the individual-family-environment fit. The family intervener is the person who assumes the greatest responsibility for initiating the change. The six levels of intervention are:

1. Individual interventions, such as family life education and job training.

2. Individual relocations, such as placing a child in a foster home when her natural parents are incapable of caring for her.
3. Population interventions, the focus of which is to change, prepare, or provide added resources to a population that is, or will be, in an inharmonious relationship with its social systems. Prevention programs are good illustrations of this kind of intervention, that is, they try to prepare people for future crises, e.g., late-middle-aged people for retirement, or parents and children for initial entry of the child into school.
4. Social systems interventions, which influence the structure of the social system (e.g., rearranging the power hierarchy, or changing the behavior of key personnel) rather than simply add new tasks or activities to the existing structure.
5. Intersystem interventions, such as intersystem assistance programs involving mothers with their children in the early stages of separation, upon entering school, or upon admission to a hospital; and intersystem coordination programs like suicide prevention centers or employment agency programs that are aimed at increasing employment opportunities for adolescents as a deterrent to juvenile delinquency.
6. Family network interventions, such as special reception systems for Vietnam immigrants to help them adapt to their new habitat.

Source: Sauber, S.R. (1977). The human services delivery system. *International Journal of Mental Health, 5,* 121–140.

life style: A personalized style of living that develops out of one's special life plan and characterizes everything one does. It refers to how the personality expresses itself in reaction to an external stimulus or to a stimulus that originates within the person.
Source: Anshacher, H., & Anshacher, R. (1956). *The individual psychology of Alfred Adler.* New York: Plastic Books.

likeness continuum: A continuum displaying the process of dyadic differentiation and individuation of self or personality. The continuum encompasses ranges: symbiosis ("I am you"), sameness ("I am like you"), similarity ("I am almost [but not quite] like you"), differentness ("I am not like you"), oppositeness ("I am the opposite [or contrary] of you"), and autism or alienation ("I am not").
Example: A father and son choose the same careers and share many personality characteristics and hob-

bies. They can be described as being like each other.
Source: L'Abate, L. (1976). *Understanding and helping the individual in the family.* New York: Grune & Stratton.

limerence: An emotional state of intense arousal brought about by an association with a romantic love object. The limerence state is characterized by a set of features that include physiological changes as well as subjective feelings. An individual experiencing limerence is obsessed with desire to be with the limerent object and is preoccupied with thoughts about that individual. Mood swings with respect to the state of the interpersonal relationship reflect changes in brain chemistry, as different neurotransmitters are produced in greater or lesser quantities. The limerent state lasts as long as there is instability in the relationship and is replaced by either long-term bonding or extinction of the feelings of attraction.
Example: A man meets a woman and is initially aroused by some aspect of her appearance or personality. Subsequent to the early encounters with her, he finds himself thinking more and more about her face, laugh, aroma, and other distinguishing characteristics that he believes are special about her. He finds he counts the hours until he can see her again, and in her absence he desires to call and speak with her. Any indication that she is interested in him creates great euphoria, while her rejection of his attentions immediately causes unusual discomfort and even depression.
Source: Tennov, D. (1980). *Love and limerence: The experience of being in love.* New York: Stein and Day.
Quoted: Silfen, R. (1980). Biopsychology of love and lust. Unpublished paper, New School for Social Research, New York.

linear statements: A straightforward honest statement about a client's behavior that is accepted by the client at face value.
Source: Weeks, G., & L'Abate, L. (1982). *Paradoxical psychotherapy.* New York: Brunner/Mazel.

linguistic tyranny: A situation in which language locks one into seeing reality in certain ways. Our language tends to be linear (simple cause-effect), digital (either/or), and content-oriented (ignores nonverbal behavior), rather than process-oriented.
Source: Selvini Palazzoli, M., Boscolo, L., Cecchin, G., & Prata, G. (1978). *Paradox and counterparadox,* New York: Jason Aronson.

Quoted: Weeks, G., & L'Abate, L. (1982). *Paradoxical psychotherapy.* New York: Brunner/Mazel.

linkage: A relationship that is considered temporary in its duration, usually less than one year in length. A link is the man and/or woman involved in a linkage relationship. In a linkage in which there is one natural parent and the other member of the linkage is not the biological parent, the child of the nonbiological parent is referred to as that parent's "linkette"; the child refers to the nonbiological parent as "Rex" for the man or "Regi" for the woman, both terms derived from the Latin translation for king and queen, respectively.
Example: A man goes out of town on a two-week business trip, and he and the woman in the link agree that they may engage in sexual relations with others until he returns from the trip. The man and woman do not have open sexual relationships with others when their link is available to them. In another situation, a man or woman going through a postdivorce adjustment may have a convenient partner move in with them for social/sexual purposes. Finally, a man and woman may have been linked for some time, intending to share their lives in the future, and they wish to have a "trial marriage," although their goal may not be to get married.
Source: Sauber, S.R., & Weinstein, C. (in press). Terminology for male/female relationships for the 1980's. *Family Review, 2*(1).

listening: A process that integrates physical, emotional, and intellectual inputs in a search for meaning and understanding. The listening process is more intricate and complicated than the physical process of hearing.
Example: A brother discerns and understands his sister's desire to buy something and gives her some money without question.
Source: Gordon, T. (1982). *Parent Effectiveness Training in action.* New York: Bantam.

lockage: A committed relationship between a man and a woman, as in marriage, in which the state is not a party. The man and woman may or may not have children as a result of their relationship. The two reside together, making a commitment similar to that of marriage in that there is an intention of a permanent "lock," in which the man and woman have generally been linked beyond one year in duration. A "lock" is the man and/or woman who are involved in a lockage relationship. In a lockage in which there is one natural parent and the other

member of the lockage is not the biological parent, the child of the nonbiological parent is referred to as that parent's "lockette," and the child refers to the nonbiological parent as "Rex" for the man or "Regi" for the woman, terms derived from the Latin translation for king and queen, respectively.
Source: Sauber, S.R., and Weinstein, C. (in press). Terminology for male/female relationships for the 1980's. *Family Review, 2*(1).

locus: The system or person for whom a problem is currently an issue. The locus excludes the generating structure of the problem as it first occurred and focus only on the here-and-now.
Example: The parent's are locked in conflict. They have a son who is now old enough to understand their problem. The son decides always to side with his mother, which in turn makes the problem worse. The locus of the current problem is now three people.
Source: Aponte, H., & Van Deusen, J. (1981). Structural family therapy. In A. Gurman and G. Kniskern (Eds.), *Handbook of family therapy* (pp. 310–360). New York: Brunner/Mazel.

long-brief therapy: Therapy consisting of a small number of sessions stretched over a long period of time.
Source: Selvini-Palazzoli, M. (1980). Why a long interval between sessions? In M. Andolfi & I. Zwerling (Eds.), *Dimensions of family therapy* (pp. 161–170). New York: Guilford Press.

loyalty binding: The act of inducing excessive breakaway guilt in the bound person and turning that person into a lifelong, self-sacrificing member of the relationship system.
Example: Every time a young adult son tries to learn how to lead his own life, his parents induce guilt in him by acting depressed over his gestures toward leaving.
Source: Stierlin, H. (1974). *Separating parents and adolescents.* New York: Quadrangle.

loyalty system: A powerful force operating upon the behavior of individuals in a family, characterized as an uninterrupted bookkeeping of obligations through the generations, with alternating positive and negative balances.
Example: A showing of concern and caring adds to the positive balance, and any form of exploitation depletes it, in marital or family relationships.
Source: Boszormenyi-Nagy, I., & Framo, J. (1966). *Intensive family therapy,* New York: Harper & Row.

machismo: In a very restricted sense, sexual prowess and aggressive behavior, equated with maleness; in a general sense, an ethos comprising traits and behaviors prized by and expected of men in Latin countries. The term is derived from macho, meaning male. Machismo is the fusion of two distinct elements, sexism and self-respect (respeto), of which the former is "destructive and reactionary" and the latter "benign and progressive." Among the macho ideals are courage, fearlessness, pride, honor, charisma, and the ability to be a leader of men. Whereas macho ideals are highly valued among Latin men, they are frequently ascribed negative values by others.
Example: If a man works and provides for his family, is a good role model for his children, protects and defends his family's interests and keeps his feelings to himself, he is a "man." By fulfilling his part of the bargain, he is entitled to respect and obedience from his family and the right to do as he pleases. Correspondingly, failure to fulfill his contract implies that he has failed as a man and a person. Dignity and self-respect, so important in Hispanic culture, is lost if he becomes dependent on his wife's earnings or on social service payments for support.
Source: Panitz, D.R., McChonchie, R.D., Sauber, S.R., & Fonseca, J.A. (1983). The role of machismo and the hispanic family in the etiology and treatment of alcoholism in hispanic American males. *American Journal of Family Therapy, 11*(1), 31–44.

madness mission: Recruitment of a child to embody and externalize the parent's feelings of badness or craziness. The parent seeks the embodiment of those feelings in the child.
Example: A father feels trapped and angry in his marriage but cannot admit these feelings to himself. He fears what might happen to the marriage if he lets the feelings out. His teenage son begins to get in trouble at school and with other boys on the weekend. The son is on a mission to act out his father's unacceptable feelings.
Source: Stierlin, H. (1974). *Separating parents and adolescents.* New York: Quadrangle.

madonna-prostitute complex: The traditional view of sex roles that dictates that males can be sexually

permissive, while females cannot. This view leads to a perceived distinction between "good girls" (Madonna) and "bad girls" (prostitutes). No such sexual distinction is perceived for men.
Source: Leiblum, S., & Pervin, L. (1980). *Principles and practice of sex therapy.* New York: Guilford Press.

magnetic field: A field of psychological force in which, if a child is too close to the mother, the child is suddenly "pulled into the mother" and loses her own identity; if the child is too far away from the mother, she develops no self at all.
Example: A 15-year-old son, while still at home, uses denial and isolation to escape his mother. He experiences psychotic helplessness after he fails to function without his mother.
Source: Bowen, M. (1978). *Family therapy in clinical practice.* New York: Jason Aronson.

male bridge maneuver: A treatment for retarded ejaculation in which, after the female manipulates her partner nearly to orgasm, she executes rapid intromission.
Source: Masters, W., & Johnson, V. (1970). *Human sexual inadequacy.* Boston: Little, Brown.

male sexual dysfunction: A male sexual disorder that can be subdivided into erectile failure, retarded ejaculation, premature ejaculation, and dyspareunia. Erectile failure (termed *impotence* in the past) refers to the inability of the male to achieve or maintain an erection and thus is unable to engage in satisfactory intercourse. Retarded ejaculation (RE), also termed "ejaculatory incompetence" or "ejaculative impotence," is a disorder in which the male suffers from delayed intravaginal ejaculation or the inability to ejaculate intravaginally. Premature ejaculation (PE) is topographically the opposite of RE: The patient suffering from PE ejaculates prior to or soon after inserting his penis into his partner's vagina. Dyspareunia, or painful intercourse, may be caused by organic factors.
Source: LoPiccolo, J., & LoPiccolo, L. (Eds.). (1978). *Handbook of sex therapy.* New York: Plenum.

maneuverability: The therapist's ability to take action despite obstacles and restrictions. As therapy progresses, the therapist may need to shift from one approach to another.
Example: The therapist begins by using a particular technique or approach but discovers it is not going to work. The therapist must be able to shift to another strategy without feeling trapped.

Source: Fish, R., Weakland, J., & Segal, L. (1982). *Doing therapy briefly.* San Francisco: Jossey-Bass.

manipulation: The act of successfully generating social reinforcement for one's maladaptive behavior. Individuals using manipulation get the message that, as long as they produce undesirable behaviors, others will show interest and concern. Manipulation may be a conscious or an unconscious act.
Source: Liebman, R. (1972). Behavioral approaches to family and couple therapy. In G. Erickson & T. Hogan (Eds.), *Family therapy: An introduction to theory and technique* (pp. 120–134). Belmont, Calif.: Wadsworth.

mapping strategy: A technique that graphically describes how the family system is organized and which particular subunit is most involved in a problem. Structural maps are useful in helping to organize family process data into elementary guesses about the structural features of the family. The maps should be quickly revised or discarded as new data appear.
Example: The map in Figure 6 shows "an open-family-unit boundary, enclosing a parental subsystem characterized by the mother's overinvolvement with her own mother, who in turn is in conflict with her daughter's husband, perhaps related to the diffuse tie between the spouses. The map also shows a normal open boundary between parents and children."
Source: Umbarger, C.C. (1984). *Structural family therapy.* New York: Grune & Stratton.

Figure 6 Structural Map of a Family

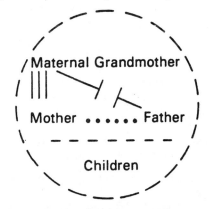

marathon sex therapy: Sex therapy combined with the use of group modalities, conducted during an extended period of time without interruption.
Example: A couple chose to experience continuous treatment for two days rather than hourly sessions once a week for two months.
Source: Kaplan, H. (1981). *The new sex therapy.* New York: Brunner/Mazel.

marital behavior modification: An approach that employs social learning and operant conditioning with couples. Treatment is based on the assumption that each partner does not know how to produce enough rewarding behavior to gratify the other.
Source: Lieberman, R. (1970). Behavioral approaches in family and couple therapy. *American Journal of Orthopsychiatry, 40,* 106–108.
Quoted: Barker, P. (1981). *Basic family therapy.* Baltimore: University Park Press.

marital coalition: The interactional pattern that spouses initially evolve for their mutual needs and satisfaction. Later, in the evolving structure and dynamics of the family, this coalition must serve the age-appropriate needs of the children and still maintain an area of exclusive relationship and mutuality between the parents.
Example: The parents form a sexual relationship that is exclusive of their relationship with the children.
Source: Fleck, S. (1972). An approach to family pathology. In G. Erickson & T. Hogan (Eds), *Family therapy: An introduction to theory and technique* (pp. 103–119). Belmont, Calif.: Wadsworth.

marital contract: Spousal agreement as to each spouse's expressed and unexpressed, conscious and unconscious concepts of that spouse's obligations within the marital relationship and the benefits the spouse expects to derive in exchange. In therapy, an explicit contract is worked out.
Example: A wife says to her husband, "I will allow you to engage in activities which I personally dislike—religious, spiritual, etc.—and you will not complain when I engage in activities you don't like."
Source: Sager, C.J. (1976). *Marriage contracts and couple therapy.* New York: Brunner/Mazel.

marital dyad: A relationship composed of a husband and wife.
Source: Glick, I., & Kessler, D. (1980). *Marital and family therapy.* (2nd ed.). New York: Grune & Stratton.

marital endogamy: The selection of marriage partners within one's own group.
Source: Eshleman, J.R. (1974). *The family: An introduction.* Boston: Allyn & Bacon.

marital enrichment group: A group specially designed to increase awareness and communication of the positive aspects in a marital relationship by use of a highly structured sequence of group procedures requiring a brief number of sessions. The group is developmental and preventive in nature. In a variety of group formations, as many as five or six couples may discuss the behaviors of the husband and wife that clearly express love, respect, and understanding; the qualities and traits that are highly valued in each other and appreciated in the relationship; and the ways in which the husband and wife meet each other's needs for love, acceptance, dependency, etc.

A marital enrichment group may be described as a "growth experience"; that is, the group procedures are not intended primarily to help couples resolve problems. Therefore, couples who are seeking marriage counseling or psychotherapy are discouraged from participating. However, husbands and wives who are concurrently in therapy may well find additional value in participating in a marital enrichment group. Most of the husbands and wives who join these groups are representative of the typical couple today. The group focuses on the expression of positive feelings and the recognition and sharing of positive aspects of the participants' selves and their relationship to create an emotional experience that is highly satisfying to both partners.
Sources: Clarke, C. (1970). Group procedures for increasing positive feedback between married partners. *Family Coordinator, 19,* 324–328. L'Abate, L., & Sloan, S. (1984). A workshop format to facilitate intimacy in married couples. *Family Relations, 33,* 245–250.
Quoted: Sauber, S.R. (1974). Primary prevention and the marital enrichment group. *Journal of Family Counseling, 12* (10), 39–44.

marital group therapy: Therapy in which the husband and wife are treated in a group with other couples.
Source: Lebedum, M. (1970). Measuring movement in group marital counseling. *Social Casework, 51,* 35–43.
Quoted: Barnard, C., & Corrales, R. (1979). *The theory and technique of family therapy.* Springfield, Ill.: Charles C Thomas.

marital maladjustment: Maladjustment may be the failure of the marital partners to prepare themselves adequately before marriage and cope with the current demands and the varied responsibilities they are assuming. Marital discontent is the difference between what couples want, what they expect, and what they get. The conventional concept of an innocent and a guilty party with relationship problems—the white sheep and the black sheep—does not stand up under close scrutiny. When marriage fails, it is usually because both spouses make mistakes, and the husband and the wife are caught in an emotional deadlock of circularity.

Real incompatibilities may be defined as those situations or conditions in which a marriage therapist literally cannot bring about any sort of change through acceptance, compromise, negotiation, or improved insight and communication. In such situations, there may be

- wide differences in intelligence that lead to different tastes, interests, and ways of thinking
- wide differences in education that lead to feelings of growing apart
- wide differences in age, to the extent that they may affect habits, sex drives, choice of friends, and activities
- physical handicaps of one partner that restrict that partner's activities, partially or completely, in one or more areas

In contrast, neurotic differences are subject to change through insight and therapy. These differences cause intelligent people to behave in confused, irrational, hostile, and marriage defeating ways toward each other. The neurotic interactions block each other's normal capacity for love, intimacy, and the need to belong and to be needed.
Example: One gets married expecting his spouse to love and respect him unconditionally, no matter how stupidly, boringly, or annoyingly he behaves. If his spouse does not respond to him with endless love in all of these situations, he decides his spouse doesn't love him at all.
Source: Sauber, S.R. (1972). *An honest guide to marriage counseling.* West Palm Beach, Fla.: Mental Health Association Press.

marital quality: The subjective evaluation of a married couple's relationship on a number of dimensions and evaluations. The range of evaluations constitutes a continuum reflecting numerous characteristics of marital interaction and functioning.

High marital quality is associated with good adjustment, adequate communication, a high level of marital happiness, integration, and a high degree of satisfaction with the relationship. Marital quality is not a fixed picture of discrete categories—i.e., a high- versus low-quality marriage—but rather a gradation of elements on a continuum ranging from high to low. See Figure 7.
Source: Lewis, R.A., & Spanier, G.B. (1979). Theorizing about the quality and stability of marriage. In N.R. Burr, R. Hill, F.I. Nye, & I.L. Reiss (Eds.), *Contemporary theories about the family (vol. 2)* (pp. 268–291). New York: Free Press.
Quoted: Spanier, G.B., & Lewis, R.A. (1980). Marital quality: A review of the seventies. *Journal of Marriage and the Family, 42,* 835.

marital quid pro quo: (1) A metaphorical statement of the marital relationship bargain, that is, how the couple have agreed to define themselves within the relationship. (2) A contract in which spouse behavior changes are cross-linked; the contract is written so that, if one spouse engages in the desired behavior, the other spouse will also change in the requested manner.
Example: Tom wants Sue to figure the household budget, and Sue wants Tom to play cards with her. A quid pro quo contract might be written as: (1) If Sue figures the household budget, then Tom will play cards with her for one hour, or (2) If Tom plays cards with Sue for one hour, then Sue will figure the household budget. The spouses' behavior changes are dependent on one another. If the first spouse does not honor the first part of the contract, the second spouse is under no obligation to change.
Sources: Lederer, W., & Jackson, D. (1968). *The mirages of marriage.* New York: Norton; Jackson, D. (1965). Family rules: The quid pro quo. *Archives of General Psychiatry, 12,* 589–594.

marital satisfaction: A state of satisfaction with one's marriage defined by an intrapersonal conceptualization (subjectively experienced reaction), or an interpersonal conceptualization (marital satisfaction as the congruence between one's expectations and another's behavior). The focus of marital satisfaction may be satisfaction with leisure, decision making, income, life style, communication, sex, or friends.
Source: Spanier, G.B., & Lewis R.A. (1980). Marital quality: A review of the seventies. *Journal of Marriage and the Family, 42,* 825–839.

Figure 7 Graphic Depiction of Marital Quality

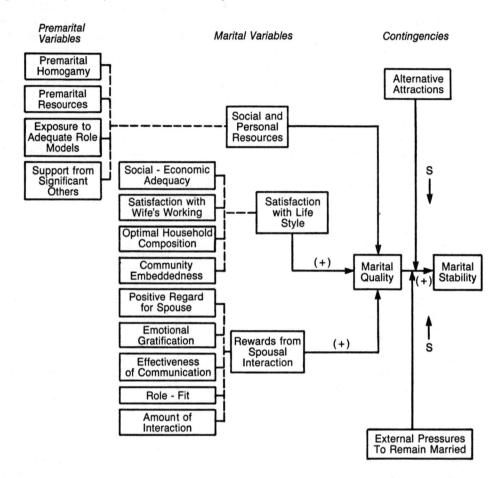

Source: From "Theorizing about the quality and stability of marriage" by R.A. Lewis and G.B. Spanier, in *Contemporary theories about the family* (vol. 1), ed. N.R. Burr, R. Hill, F.I. Nye, and I.L. Reiss, © 1979, New York: Free Press, p. 289. Reprinted by permission.

marital schism/skew: A mutual failure of the marital partners to meet each other's deep dynamic needs. A marital schism refers to the division of the family into two antagonistic and competing factions. A skew exists when one partner dominates the family to a striking degree. The two terms characterize the disturbed marital relationship in schizophrenic families.

Example: A family with a marital schism has the father and son aligned against the mother and daughter over household responsibilities.

Source: Lidz, T., Cornelison, A., Fleck, S., & Terry, D. (1957). Schism and skew in families of schizophrenics. *American Journal of Psychiatry, 114,* 241–248.

Quoted: Barker, P. (1981). *Basic family therapy.* Baltimore: University Park Press.

marital sociogram: A device employing nonverbal methodologies to depict each spouse's experience of self in relation to the other in the relationship. The device demonstrates for the therapeutic system the amount of distance (symbolic of emotional distance) each spouse desires in the relationship.

Example: One spouse is placed in a specific location and instructed to remain stationary. The other spouse is placed directly across from the first and told to move slowly toward the other until a comfortable distance is found.

Source: Barnard, C., & Corrales, R. (1979). *The theory and technique of family therapy.* Springfield, Ill.: Charles C Thomas.

marital stability: A state conceptualized as a function of the comparison between one's marital expectations and one's marital outcomes. Marital stability may be a function of the comparison between one's best available marital outcomes. An exchange typology of Marital Quality and Stability is shown in Figure 8.

Source: Spanier, G.B., & Lewis, R.A. (1980). Marital quality: A review of the seventies. *Journal of Marriage and the Family, 42,* 825–839.

marital therapy: A therapeutic approach in which the focus is on the marital relationship—the interactions and transactions that take place—rather than the intrapsychic forces within the individual. Marital therapy usually involves the therapist meeting with the two spouses conjointly.

Source: Haley, J. (1963). Marriage therapy. *Archives of General Psychiatry, 8,* 213–234.

Figure 8 An Exchange Typology of Marital Quality and Stability

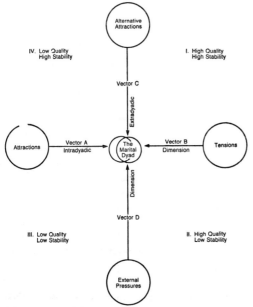

Source: From "Marital quality: A review of the seventies" by G.B. Spanier and R.A. Lewis, © 1980, *Journal of Marriage and the Family, 42,* p. 833. Reprinted by permission.

marriage: A complex of customs centering on the relationship between a sexually associating pair of adults within the family. Marriage defines the manner of establishing and terminating such a relationship, the normative behavior and reciprocal obligations within it, and the locally accepted restrictions upon its personnel.

Source: Murdock, G. (1949). *Social structure.* New York: Macmillan.

marriage counseling: The process whereby, within the context of an understanding and accepting face-to-face relationship, professional skills and experience are made available to spouses as they explore, evaluate, and clarify feelings and issues, as they seek to communicate verbally and emotionally, and as they learn to choose courses of action that will lead to some resolution of their problems. The ultimate goal of marriage counseling is the optimal development of the individual's potentialities and the enhancement of the marriage relationship. Its approaches include:

- Individual—Only one mate participates in counseling.
- Concurrent—Both the husband and the wife participate in counseling, but each spouse has separate sessions.
- Conjoint—Both partners participate together in counseling.
- Group—Counseling takes place when either a single mate joins a single mate's group or both mates join a couples' group.
- Combined—A combination of several of the above methods.

Sources: Sauber, S.R. (1972). *An honest guide to marriage counseling.* West Palm Beach, Fla.: Mental Health Association Press; L'Abate, L., & McHenry, S. (1983). *Handbook of marital interventions.* New York: Grune & Stratton.

martyr complex: A pattern of behavior in which the individual constantly communicates verbal or nonverbal messages designed to induce self-guilt.

Example: Individuals say they don't mind doing things for another but, each time they are asked to do something, they respond in a tone of voice that says they don't want to do it.

Source: Wahlroos, S. (1974). *Family communication.* New York: Macmillan.

masturbation: Self-stimulation and/or manipulation of the genital area, frequently engaged in as a sexual outlet. Masturbation commonly results in orgasm.

Source: Masters, W., & Johnson, V. (1970). *Human sexual inadequacy.* Boston: Little, Brown.

masturbation therapy: The treatment of erectile failure, premature ejaculation, retarded ejaculation, frigidity, general sexual dysfunction, primary orgasmic dysfunction, or secondary orgasmic dysfunction through masturbation techniques.
Source: LoPiccolo, J., & LoPiccolo, L. (Eds.). (1978). *Handbook of sex therapy.* New York: Plenum.

material reinforcers: Items like stars, points, tokens, or money that are used to reward desirable behavior patterns.
Example: When Jim brings home a paper with a score above a certain point, he is awarded stars on a chart that he can display to the whole family.
Source: LeBow, M. (1972). Behavior modification for the family. In G. Erickson & T. Hogan (Eds.), *Family therapy: An introduction to theory and technique* (pp. 347–376). Belmont, Calif.: Wadsworth.

matriarchy: A family system in which authority is based on a female as head of the family.
Source: Christensen, H. (1964). Development of the family field of study. In H. Christensen (Ed.), *Handbook of marriage and the family* (pp. 3–32). Chicago: Rand McNally.

matrilocal residence: A rule of residence that requires that a woman live with her mother and bring her husband to her mother's home to live.
Source: Zeldtich, M. (1964). Cross-cultural analyses of family structure. In H. Christensen (Ed.), *Handbook of marriage and the family* (pp. 462–500). Chicago: Rand McNally.

matrix of identity: The sense of belonging that comes with the child's accommodation to the groups within the family and with the child's assumption of the transactional patterns that form the family structure. Families mold and program the child's sense of identity early in the socialization process. The matrix of identity develops through participation in different family subsystems in different contexts, as well as through participation in extrafamilial groups. The family, then, is the matrix of its members' sense of identity—of belonging and of being different. Its chief task is to foster its members' psychosocial growth and well-being throughout their lives in common.
Source: Minuchin, S. (1974). *Families and family therapy.* Cambridge, Mass.: Harvard University Press.

Quoted: Bernard, C., & Corrales, R. (1979). *The theory and technique of family therapy.* Springfield, Ill.: Charles C Thomas.

maturation: The state in which human beings are fully in charge of themselves. Mature people are able to make choices and decisions based on accurate perceptions about themselves, about others, and about the contexts in which they find themselves. They acknowledge those choices and decisions as their own, and they accept responsibility for their outcomes.
Source: Satir, V. (1967). *Conjoint family therapy.* Palo Alto, Calif.: Science and Behavior Books.

mediation: The process by which disputants attempt to reach a consensual settlement of the issues in dispute with the assistance and facilitation of a neutral resource person or persons. At the very least, the process consists of systematically isolating points of agreement and disagreement, developing options, and considering accommodations. Generically, mediation is a goal-directed, problem-solving, helping intervention. The goal is to help the parties to resolve their dispute and to reduce the conflict between them. Even if all elements of the dispute cannot be resolved, the conflict may be reduced to a manageable level. However, resolution of the dispute does not always eliminate the conflict. Thus, some refer to mediation as a process not of dispute resolution but of conflict management. Mediation is also a time-limited process. It emphasizes the present and the future, not the past. Crisis and short-term therapies share some of mediation's parameters, but they differ from mediation in their goals, tasks, and issues and in the manner in which each commences. To reach a negotiated settlement, the clients and the mediator must deal throughout the process with tasks that are concrete; and their focus must be predominantly on external data and issues, not on internal psychological reactions.
Example: In order to identify and seek values for their separate and common assets and liabilities, married couples must focus on the important changes they desire in life insurance policies or titles of jointly held property. If they have children, they need to develop workable plans for postdivorce parenting that will meet the needs of each family member. If they value college education for their children, they will have to develop methods of financing that education.

Source: Kelly, J.B. (1983). Mediation & psychotherapy: Distinguishing the differences. *Mediation Quarterly, 1*(1), 33–44.

merging: A behavioral pattern that involves the active, yet unconscious, collaboration of two partners, wherein the first partner does not merely choose the second but enters into an implicit agreement to choose the second partner on the basis of the first partner's own unfulfilled needs and to form an implicit contract. People attached to one another in this manner share each other's feelings and motivations, instead of recognizing their differences.

Example: A couple merge in order to overcome their sense of emptiness. By sharing feelings about such things as family relationships, world views, etc., they validate each other's existence.

Source: Boszormenyi-Nagy, I. (1965). A theory of relationships: Experience and transaction. In I. Boszormenyi-Nagy & J. Framo (Eds.), *Intensive family therapy: Theoretical and practical aspects* (pp. 33–86). New York: Harper & Row. *See* **fusion.**

message symptom: A symptom that a client imagines to be something concrete. The client then changes aspects of the image in order to eliminate the symptom. Message symptoms are a focus of sex hypnotherapy.

Source: Araoz, D. (1982). *Hypnosis and sex therapy.* New York: Brunner/Mazel.

meta: Changed, transposed, or beyond something. In family systems therapy, meta (in recognition of Bateson's usage and influence) is used to mean "about," as in metacommunication, that is, a communication about communication, or as in metalanguage, that is, a language or symbolic system that is used to discuss, describe, or analyze another language or symbolic system (Bateson also used the prefix "meta" to refer to a higher level of generalization).

Source: Duhl, B.S. (1983). *From the inside out and other metaphors.* New York: Brunner/Mazel.

metacommunication: A message about a message. The second message qualifies what was said in the first message, for example, by commenting on the latent content of the message or on how the message was expressed. Metacommunication is conveyed by voice, inflection, or body language. It may convey:

- The sender's attitude toward the message: "The message I sent was a friendly one."

- The sender's attitude toward self: "I am friendly."
- The sender's attitude toward the receiver: "I see you as a friendly person."

Source: Watzlawick, J., Weakland, J., & Fisch, R. (1967). *Pragmatics of human communication.* New York: Norton.

metacomplementary relationship: A reciprocal relationship in which a person allows or forces a second person to be in charge.

Example: A husband says he is bored and wants to do something, but then refuses to suggest any activities. He forces his mate to make all the decisions regarding their entertainment.

Source: Watzlawick, J., Weakland, J., & Fisch, R. (1967). *Pragmatics of human communication.* New York: Norton.

metaphor: Verbal or physical similarities that a therapist uses to point up or clarify familial relationships.

Example: A therapist puts a table or chair between spouses in order to simulate the "wall" they have between them. Or the therapist uses such phrases as, "Your father stole your voice," or "You have very strong, but very sensitive wires connecting you to your family," to underscore a son's family relationships.

Source: Minuchin, A., & Fishman, H. (1981). *Family therapy techniques.* Cambridge, Mass.: Harvard University Press.

metasymmetrical relationship: A mutual relationship in which a person allows or forces a second person to be equal.

Example: A husband says he is bored and would like to go to a dance. His wife agrees without expressing her opinion. Because he sees her as his coequal, the husband forces her to tell him whether she would really like to go, and if not, what she would really like to do.

Source: Watzlawick, J., Weakland, J., & Fisch, R. (1967). *Pragmatics of human communication.* New York: Norton.

mimesis: A therapeutic skill used by the therapist to join with the family and become like the family members in the manner or content of their communications, e.g., joking with a jovial family, or talking slowly and sparsely with a slow-talking family. The therapist can also join with the family mimetically by conveying personal experiences to its members.

Source: Aponte, H., & Van Deusen, J. (1981). Structural family therapy. In A. Gurman & D. Kniskern (Eds.), *Handbook of family therapy* (pp. 310–360). New York: Brunner/Mazel.

mind reading: Making assumptions about the thoughts, feelings, and motives of a partner, then telling the partner what the partner thinks or feels, or ought to think or feel.

Example:

Wife:	Why did you forget my book?
Husband:	I had a lot to do and just forgot.
Wife:	That's not it at all. You just don't care about me.

Source: Bach, G., & Deutsch, R. (1970). *Pairing.* New York: Avon.

mirror image disagreement: An arrangement that allows parents to express their differences indirectly regarding their child's behavior. If, in their conflict over the child, the parents begin to struggle with each other directly, their own relationship might be imperiled.

Source: Haley, J., & Hoffman, L. (1967). *Techniques of family therapy.* New York: Basic Books.

model analysis: Attempts to discover the models that influenced family members in their early lives, gave them messages about the presence and desirability of growth, gave them the blueprints from which they learned to evaluate and act on new experience, and showed them how to become close to others.

Source: Satir, V. (1967). *Conjoint family therapy.* Palo Alto, Calif.: Science and Behavior Books.

modern nuclear family: A broad kinship model in which the entirety of individuals, extended families, community, and neighborhood is seen as the family.

Source: Glick, I., & Kessler, D. (1980). *Marital and family therapy* (2nd ed.). New York: Grune & Stratton.

monadic model: A model that assumes that psychological problems are a result of intrapsychic disturbances. Thus, the individual is the unit of treatment.

Source: Nichols, M. (1984). *Family therapy: Concepts and methods.* New York: Gardner Press.

monitoring/boundary control activity: An intra-system regulatory activity that involves checking an operating activity or taking action to institute a new or modified operating activity. Monitoring and boundary control regulatory activities are external to the operating activity of the system; they relate a system to its environment by controlling the input and output transitions across the system's boundary.

Example: A father who was previously weak and inefficient gains the strength in family therapy to assert himself and take control over the events that occur in his family.

Source: Sauber, S.R. (1983). *The human services delivery system.* New York: Columbia University Press.

monogamy: The marriage of one man to one woman at one time.

Source: In H. Christensen (Ed.). (1964). *Handbook of marriage and the family.* Chicago: Rand McNally.

moral codes: Rules developed by individuals or groups of individuals to sustain their philosophies or religious beliefs. If the rules are violated, the individuals lose their privileges or good standing.

Example: A couple may have a rule that extra-marital sex is acceptable, provided the other partner is told about the affair in advance. If one partner breaks the rule, the result is a lack of trust and withdrawal of affection.

Source: Bedford, S. (1969). The "new morality" and marriage counseling. In B. Ard, & C. Ard, (Eds.), *Handbook of marriage counseling* (2nd ed. pp. 83–87). Palo Alto, Calif.: Science and Behavior Books.

morphogenesis: A process by which a living system changes its basic structure in order to adapt to environmental conditions. The process involves positive feedback or sequences that serve to amplify deviation and functioning with a flexible structure that is open to growth and change and responsive to new stimulation.

Example: The family members come to therapy, recognizing their problems and their need for help and new ways to function.

Source: Speer, D. (1970). Family systems: Morphostasis and morphogenesis, or is homeostasis enough? *Family Process, 9,* 259–278.

Quoted: Beavers, W.R. (1976). A theoretical basis for family evaluation. In J.M. Lewis, W.R. Beavers, J.T. Gossett, & V.A. Phillips (Eds.), *No single thread: Psychological health in the family system* (pp. 46–82). New York: Brunner/Mazel.

morphostasis: The process by which a system maintains constancy through negative feedback in the face of environmental changes. It denotes a lack of change or stagnation of the structure of the system.

Example: The child is referred for treatment but the parents refuse to allow the child to go to the clinic. They thus deny the existence of any problems regarding the child, while blaming her school for not doing its job effectively.
Source: Speer, D. (1970). Family systems: Morphostasis or morphogenesis, or is homeostasis enough? *Family Process, 9,* 259–278.
Quoted: Beavers, W.R. (1976). A theoretical basis for family evaluation. In J.M. Lewis, W.R. Beavers, J.T. Gossett, & V.A. Phillips (Eds.), *No single thread: Psychological health in the family system* (pp. 46–82). New York: Brunner/Mazel.

mourning and empathy: A technique by which the therapist elicits unresolved grief to effect change. An attempt is made to release long-hidden feelings, expectations, and emotions.
Source: Paul, N. (1967). The use of empathy in the resolution of grief. *Perspectives in Biology and Medicine, 11,* 153–169.
Quoted: Bernard, C., & Corrales, R. (1979). *The theory and technique of family therapy.* Springfield, Ill.: Charles C Thomas.

movie directing: A sex hypnotherapy technique used to treat negative sexual processing. The client sees herself in a situation that elicits all her anxieties. She then takes over the scene as a director in an effort to change it so that it is pleasant. The client switches back and forth until the anxious aspects disappear.
Source: Araoz, D. (1982). *Hypnosis and sex therapy.* New York: Brunner/Mazel.

multifamily group therapy: Therapy in which several families are brought together in weekly group sessions. This has the advantage of fostering wholeness of the family rather than fragmentation. In this type of therapy, cross-influences and cross-interactions from family to family are more effective than techniques in individual family therapy in shaking up the rigid family systems that family members have a stake in maintaining and preserving.
Source: Leichter, E., & Schulman, G. (1968). Emerging phenomena in multifamily group treatment. *International Journal of Group Psychotherapy, 18,* 56–69.
Quoted: Leichter, E., & Schulman, G. (1972). Emerging phenomena in group treatment. In G. Erickson & T. Hogan (Eds.), *Family therapy: An introduction to theory and technique* (pp. 327–335). Belmont, Calif.: Wadsworth.

multigenerational therapy: A form of multiple family therapy utilizing the presenting family and its two preceding families in a single large-group therapeutic situation.
Source: Howells, J. (1975). *Principles of family psychiatry.* New York: Brunner/Mazel.

multigenerational transmission: The emergence of severe psychopathology in an individual family member as the outcome of generational influences. The principle of projection to different children in the family varies, depending on their levels of immaturity. The maximally involved child emerges with a lower level of self-differentiation.
Example: The mother of a schizophrenic child does not create the schizophrenia; she is seen as one involved person in a long line of involved persons down through the generations.
Source: Bowen, M. (1978). *Family therapy in clinical practice.* New York: Jason Aronson.
Quoted: Kerr, M. (1981). Family systems theory and therapy. In A. Gurman & D. Kniskern (Eds.), *Handbook of family therapy* (pp. 226–266). New York: Brunner/Mazel.

multilateral marriage: A voluntary group of three or more persons, each of whom is committed to and maintains a relationship with more than one person in the group in a manner regarded by the participants as being "married." Participants develop a structure for sharing economic and personal resources, and tend to live together in one residence. This marital arrangement is also called a group marriage.
Source: Constantine, L.L., Constantine, J.M., & Edelman, S.K. (1975). Counseling implications of alternative marriage styles. In A.S. Gurman & D.G. Rice (Eds.), *Couples in conflict* (pp. 124–134). New York: Jason Aronson.

multiorgasmic: Achievement of more than one orgasm by the female during coitus. New research suggests that males may also have multiple orgasms.
Source: Masters, W., & Johnson, V. (1970). *Human sexual inadequacy.* Boston: Little, Brown.

multiple family group counseling: A form of family treatment in which several families are brought together in a weekly group session. Its purpose is to assist families in developing a shared view of a client's difficulty and in evaluating a collaborative plan of changing maladaptive behaviors. Short-term, multiple family group counseling is an effective treatment for family problems of which the student is the "identified client." Such counseling is based on the premise that the worlds of the home and school are inseparable; yet, with the family as the primary influence, school personnel are often powerless unless communication has been established with the parents. The place to attack the problem is with the people whom it involves and the setting in which it occurs. Working with the problem student in a school situation offers students and parents the unique benefit of "sharing the responsibility" in an atmosphere of mutuality in which the concerns of the school and family can be integrated, discussed, and dealt with in an efficacious manner.

Example: Gary describes his feelings of being a failure as he presented his report card to his parents:

Therapist (to Gary):	Well, what happened when your parents saw your grades?
Gary's mother:	He silently and sullenly stalked out of the room.
Gary:	She asked me, Mom, not you!
Therapist:	Well, you were kind of nasty.
Gary:	I guess I was afraid of you, Dad.
Gary's sister:	The only time my parents ever show any interest in what I am doing in school is when I get into trouble or have bad grades.
Gary's father:	Gary is always up to something; he was recently caught lying to a teacher.
Therapist:	Let me stop you for a minute, Mr. P. (then to Gary): It seems to me that you are as much to blame as your father, Gary. Because you lied. . . .
Gary:	I don't know (sighing). But, Dad, you make me feel like a failure, like I'm just no good at anything. This is the same way I feel in school. My teachers get on my back. I just don't like school. And you and Mom just yell at each other about me; and it makes me so angry, I just have to get away.

Source: Sauber, S.R. (1971). Multiple family group counseling. *Personnel and Guidance Journal, 49,* 459–465.

multiple family group sensitivity procedures: A set of group procedures used to stimulate awareness and communication of positive feelings between parents and adolescents. The procedure is used for families in which the generation gap has broken down communication lines between the members. It can involve as many as six families, or a total of 12 parents and 9 adolescents. To get the parents and adolescents to talk to each other, six different group formations are utilized during five two-hour sessions. For example, the "simulated family group" may consist of an unrelated father, mother, and one or two adolescents. The "role group in concentric circles" may consist of all the mothers talking among themselves in the inner circle while the fathers and adolescents sit observing in the outer circle. A number of topics may be discussed in the various groupings, within the context of all possible relationships.

Example: A son's perspective of a father-son relationship includes the following: (1) the father's and son's positive behavior, which makes the son feel loved, appreciated, valued, and understood; (2) the positive characteristics that his father likes, admires, and respects; (3) the commitment behavior and wished-for behaviors; and (4) the feedback from all participants revealing their feelings about the session, themselves, and other members.

Source: Clarke, C. (1969, October). Group procedures for stimulating awareness and communication of positive feelings between parents and young adults. Paper presented at the meeting of the Family Life Council, Goldsboro, N.C.

Quoted: Sauber, S.R. (1971). Multiple group family counseling. *Personnel and Guidance Journal, 49,* 459–465.

multiple family group therapy: A form of therapy in which several families (or married couples) are seen in groups. This type of therapy is particularly effective in pathologically homogeneous families in which there is profound mental and emotional sex or generational differences. It affords a sense of camaraderie among the sexes (or generations), as well as an increased awareness and acceptance of differences among the participants.

Source: Laqueur, H.P. (1976). Multiple family therapy. In P.J. Guerin (Ed.), *Family Therapy: Theory and Practice* (pp. 405–416). New York: Gardner Press.

multiple family therapy: Therapy for multiple members of multiple families who meet together for discussion of individual and joint problems. The therapy is designed to help the individual family members achieve higher levels of functioning. The therapist works with each family separately, dividing the time between the several families, but avoiding communication exchanges between them. Emotional exchanges between the families would encourage a group process, which would overshadow the family process and impair or block individuation. The advantages of this type of therapy are faster progress in each family due to observing others and a net saving in time. The disadvantages are the additional work in scheduling and the energy required of the therapist in maintaining structure.

Sources: Bowen, M. (1975). Family therapy after twenty-five years. In J. Dyrud and D. Freedman (Eds.), *American handbook of psychiatry* (2nd ed., vol. 5, pp. 367–392); New York: Basic Books. Laqueur, H.P. (1972). Mechanisms of change in multiple family therapy. In C.J. Sager & H.S. Kaplan (Eds.), *Progress in group and family therapy* (pp. 400–415). New York: Brunner/Mazel.

multiple impact therapy: Therapy in which families are seen on an intensive basis and in different combinations over a two- or three-day period by members of a therapy team, including a psychiatrist, a psychologist, a social worker, and a vocational counselor. The techniques focus on bringing about rapid change. This approach has generally been used with families in crisis.
Source: MacGregor, R., Ritchie, A., Serrano, A., & Schuster, F. (1964). *Multiple impact therapy with families.* New York: McGraw-Hill.
Quoted: Barker, P. (1981). *Basic family therapy.* Baltimore: University Park Press.

mutuality: A relationship characterized by convergence of self-interests and a willingness to accommodate to one another without loss of individuality, or fear of criticism.
Example: The spouses' interactive patterns on implicit and explicit levels resulted in the sharing of feelings and the conveying of respect and appreciation for one another as well as to other people.
Sources: Wynne, L., Ryckoff, I., Day, J., & Hirsch, S. (1958). Pseudomutuality in the family relations of schizophrenics. *Psychiatry, 21,* 205; Fleck, S. (1972). Family pathology. In G. Erickson and T. Hogan (Eds.), *Family therapy: An introduction to theory and technique* (pp. 103–119). Belmont, Calif.: Wadsworth.
Quoted: Foley, V. (1974). *An introduction to family therapy.* New York: Grune & Stratton.

mystification: Misdefinition of the issue of who is doing what to whom. Mystification is accomplished in three steps:

1. attribution: attributing to an individual a characteristic or role that is functional to or for the attributor

2. invalidation: disqualifying any action that is manifested by the individual who is being mystified

3. induction: actively recruiting and seducing the person into accepting the attribution, or at least part of it.

Example: A child is playing noisily in the evening. His mother is tired and wants him to go to bed. A straight statement by the mother would be: ''I am tired. I want you to go to bed,'' or, ''Go to bed, because I say so,'' or, ''Go to bed, because it's your bedtime.'' A mystifying way to induce the child to go to bed would be: ''I'm sure you feel tired, darling, and you want to go to bed now, don't you?'' Mystification occurs here in different ways. What is ostensibly an attribution about how the child feels (''You are tired'') is really a command (''Go to bed''). The child is told how he feels (he may or may not feel tired), and what he is told he feels is what mother feels herself (projective identification). If we suppose he does not feel tired, he may contradict his mother's statement. He may then become liable to a further mystifying ploy such as: ''Mother knows best.''
Source: Laing, R. (1965). Mystification, confusion and conflict. In I. Boszormenyi-Nagy & J. Framo (Eds.), *Intensive family therapy* (pp. 343–368). New York: Harper & Row.

N

narcissistic involvement: An investment in others that is egocentric or centered; the person so invested has no feeling of the meaning a particular situation holds for others.
Example: A man is interested in his wife only to the extent that she bolsters his ego by being attractive and attentive and by praising his accomplishments.
Source: Epstein, N., Bishop, D., & Levin, S. (1978). The McMaster model of family functioning. *Journal of Marriage and Family Counseling, 4,* 19–31.
Quoted: Epstein, N., & Bishop, D. (1981). Problem-centered systems therapy of the family. In A. Gurman & D. Kniskern (Eds.), *Handbook of family therapy* (pp. 444–482). New York: Brunner/Mazel.

narcissistic patients: A patient whose capacity to fall and stay in love in adult life becomes impaired due to abnormal early emotional development.
Source: Kaplan, H. (1979). *Disorders of sexual desire.* New York: Brunner/Mazel.

narcissistic relationship: A relationship in which each person acts to validate an image-derived expectation of the other, that is, each person serves to validate and bolster the image projected by the other.
Example: A wife puts her husband on a pedestal, referring to him as handsome, intelligent, social, kind, and successful in everything. The higher in esteem she places her husband, the higher becomes her own self-image (much like the "doctor's wife" syndrome), in which the husband's status is used as an expression of the wife's own status.
Source: Brody, W. (1961). The family as the unit of study and treatment: Image, object, and narcissistic relationship. *American Journal of Orthopsychiatry, 31,* 69–73.
Quoted: Searles, H. (1965). Contributions of family treatment to the psychotherapy of schizophrenia. In I. Boszormenyi-Nagy & J. Framo (Eds.), *Intensive family therapy: Theoretical and practical aspects* (pp. 463–497). New York: Harper & Row.

negation/retraction code: A code to measure the amount of negating words (no, don't, not) or retractors (although, except, nevertheless) present in verbal interaction.
Source: Mishler, E., & Waxler, N. (1968). *Interaction in families: An experimental study of family processes and schizophrenia.* New York: John Wiley & Sons.
Quoted: Riskin, M., & Faunce, E. (1972). An evaluative review of family interaction research. *Family Process, 11,* 365–455.

negative consequence of change: A client's ambivalence about change by which positive consequences are framed negatively. The technique used to resolve this condition increases the client's motivation to change.
Example: A client who has been withdrawn and depressed for many years says he wants to change. The therapist points out that if he becomes stronger he would demand more of his wife, which in turn could lead to arguments—a negative consequence stemming from a positive one. The client actively fights this view of what would happen.
Source: Weeks, G., & L'Abate, L. (1982). *Para-doxical psychotherapy.* New York: Brunner/Mazel.

negative feedback: The family system continually receives information from the environment that helps it adjust and take corrective actions on deviations from a prescribed course. In feedback, a portion of the output (e.g., behavior of a family member) is returned to the system as input, which functions to modify succeeding outputs of the system. Negative feedback is informational input looping back to the family system in such a way as to decrease the deviation of output from the family's steady state. In contrast to positive feedback, signals are fed back over a feedback channel in such a way that they increase the deviation of the output from a steady state.
Example: The mother observed her son at nursery school and told him that certain actions should be done differently.
Source: Sauber, S.R. (1983). *The human services delivery system.* New York: Columbia University Press.

negative processing: A mental activity connected with any aspect of behavior that leads to guilt, anxiety, anger, or any other negative feeling. The processing is a continuum ranging from (1) detection or awareness of a situation, (2) the labeling of it, (3) attribution or the interpretation of it, and (4) evaluation. Sexual negative processing is this mental process in the area of sex.
Example: A man thinks, She (detection) turns me off (labeling) by being seductive (attribution). I don't like to be manipulated by a woman (evaluation).
Source: Araoz, D. (1982). *Hypnosis and sex therapy.* New York: Brunner/Mazel.

negative projection: The projection of one's own feared identity onto another group, which can lead to extensive intergroup fear and hostility.
Example: A man feels as if he is going crazy. Rather than deal with this feeling, he begins to say it is his family that is crazy.
Source: Wallace, A., & Fogelson, R. (1965). The identity struggle. In I. Boszormenyi-Nagy & J. Framo (Eds.), *Intensive family therapy: Theoretical and practical aspects* (pp. 365–406). New York: Harper & Row.

negative reinforcement trap: The use of reinforcement to terminate an aversive event, which in turn reinforces the behavior leading to the event.

Example: A child wants a candy bar in a store but the mother refuses. The child has a tantrum. The mother does not want the child to have the candy, but neither does she want the tantrum. She decides to give the child the candy. This action reinforces the probability that the child will have other tantrums.
Source: Wahler, R. (1976). Deviant child behaviors within the family. In H. Leitenberg (Ed.), *Handbook of behavior modification and therapy* (pp. 516–546). Englewood Cliffs, N.J.: Prentice-Hall.

negative self-hypnosis: Negative thoughts, both affirmations and imagery, that lie outside of awareness and become part of one's belief system. These thoughts act as powerful hypnotic suggestions because (1) they have been accepted by the inner mind without critical evaluation or rational analysis; (2) they activate negative imagery; and (3) they affect mood, motivation, and behavior in such a way that a person cannot break through.
Source: Araoz, D. (1982). *Hypnosis and sex therapy.* New York: Brunner/Mazel.

negativistic: A person's resistance to a family task, as measured or reduced to an attitude of mind marked by skepticism about nearly everything affirmed by others in the family.
Source: Singer, M., & Wynne, L. (1966). Communication styles in parents of normals, neurotics, and schizophrenics. *Psychiatric Research Reports, 20,* 25–38.
Quoted: Riskin, M., & Faunce, E. (1972). An evaluative review of family interaction research. *Family Process, 11,* 365–455.

negentropic family: A family in which members combine intimacy and individuality.
Source: Beavers, W.R. (1977). *Psychotherapy and growth.* New York: Brunner/Mazel.

neolocal residence: A residence in which a nuclear family lives independently of either the husband's or wife's parents.
Source: Zeldtich, M. (1964). Cross-cultural analyses of family structure. In H. Christensen (Ed.), *Handbook of marriage and the family* (pp. 462–500). Chicago: Rand McNally.

neomarital programs: Marital-enrichment programs designed to help newly-married couples preview their upcoming developmental tasks, as well as a wide range of behavioral skills.
Source: Levant, R.F. (1984). *Family therapy: A comprehensive overview.* Englewood Cliffs, N.J.: Prentice-Hall.

neoparental program: A program consisting of various forms of childbirth education classes. Such programs are offered by prenatal clinics, maternity hospitals, the Red Cross, and the Childbirth Education Association. Their content typically encompasses the health needs of the expectant mother, her labor and delivery, and the care of the newborn infant. Some programs also attempt to prepare the expectant parents for the developmental transition to parenthood.
Source: Levant, R.F. (1984). *Family therapy: A comprehensive overview.* Englewood Cliffs, N.J.: Prentice-Hall.

network therapy: Therapy in which members of the kinship system, friends, and significant others work together on the patient's problem.
Source: Speck, R., & Attneave, C. (1973). *Family networks.* New York: Pantheon.

neurogenic disorders: Neurological disorders primarily affect the sex centers of the brain and the lower neural structures that serve the genital reflexes. In some way, they impair or affect certain phases of the sexual response.
Source: Kaplan, H. (1979). *Disorders of sexual desire.* New York: Brunner/Mazel.

neurolinguistic programming: The neurological process of organizing the structure of subjective experience in humans. The human system's neural processes are represented, ordered, and sequenced into models and strategies through language and communications systems.
Source: Dilts, R., Grinder, J., Bandler, R., Cameron-Bandier, L., & DeLozier, I. (1980). *Neurolinguistic programming* (Vol. 1). Cupertino, Calif.: Meta Publications.

neurotic complementarity: The relationship of a person who feels inadequate, incomplete, and unable to live a whole life, with another person who can complement or complete the syndrome of personality need, also referred to as "negative complementarity."
Example: A woman with strong, repressed sexual needs chooses a man who becomes an alcoholic, has affairs, or is sexually perverted.
Sources: Rutledge, A. (1969). Male and female roles in marriage counseling. In B. Ard and C. Ard (Eds.), *Handbook of marriage counseling* (pp. 120–127). Palo Alto, Calif.: Science and Behavior Books; White, S.G., & Hatcher, C. (1984). Couple complementarity and similarity: A review of the literature. *American Journal of Family Therapy, 12,* 15–25.

neurotic marital interaction: The expression of neurotic needs in marriage. The interaction may involve an individual unconsciously seeking a parental figure, trying to prove something about the individual, or replicating an old conflictual relationship.

Example: A daughter feels she was never fully loved and accepted by her father. In her marriage, she makes every effort to please her husband in order not to lose his affection.

Source: Kubie, L. (1956). Psychoanalysis and marriage: Practical and theoretical issues. In V. Eisenstein (Ed.), *Neurotic interaction in marriage* (Chapter 2). New York: Basic Books.

Quoted: Framo, J. (1965). Rationale and technique of intensive family therapy. In I. Boszormenyi-Nagy & J. Framo (Eds.), *Intensive family therapy: Theoretical and practical aspects* (pp. 143–212). New York: Harper & Row.

new hypnosis: An approach in hypnosis that deemphasizes the ritual of induction. It induces a state in which one lets oneself go into goal-directed daydreams to the extent that one dissociates oneself from the surrounding reality and becomes engrossed in one's inner reality.

Source: Araoz, D. (1982). *Hypnosis and sex therapy.* New York: Brunner/Mazel.

nocturnal penile tumescence: Erectile episodes typically occurring in healthy boys and men every 90-100 minutes during sleep. These episodes are often used to aid the diagnosis of the etiology of impotence.

Source: Karacan, I. (1978). Advances in the psychophysiological evaluation of male erectile impotence. In J. LoPiccolo, & L. LoPiccolo (Eds.), *Handbook of sex therapy* (pp. 137–146). New York: Plenum Press.

no-fault divorce: A form of divorce granted without the establishment of blame. In 1970, California was the first state to abandon traditional grounds for divorce—adultery, desertion, cruelty, drunkenness—and substitute one comprehensive basis: the breakdown of the marriage. In a no-fault divorce, it is not necessary to find blame for the marital failure. Emphasis is rather placed on an equitable determination of financial rights and child-care responsibilities. In the past decade, all but two states have enacted some form of no-fault divorce procedure.

Source: Marlow, L., & Sauber, S.R. (in press). *Handbook on divorce mediation.* New York: Brunner/Mazel.

no-gossip principle: The principle underlying the behavioral pattern in which persons with problems in their relationships either fail to communicate or communicate through a third party. Despite the clients' initial resistance, the therapist must disrupt the pattern by forcing them to address each other directly, not through the therapist.

Example: A young lady complains to her therapist that she cannot discuss with her mother certain important subjects. When the therapist suggests that she try to discuss these subjects with her mother, she insists that she cannot. The therapist then asks her to go to her mother and tell her that she finds it difficult to discuss the subjects with her. The result is a highly significant, and mutually rewarding, conversation between the young lady and her mother.

Source: Kempler, W. (1974). *Principles of gestalt family therapy.* Oslo, Norway: A.S. John. Nordahl Trykkery.

Quoted: Lange, A., & van der Hart, O. (1983). *Directive family therapy.* New York: Brunner/Mazel.

nondemand ambience: A condition induced by therapeutic treatment that structures a couple's interactions around sensual pleasure instead of performance goals and orgasm.

Example: A couple is told simply to enjoy the sensation of intercourse without trying to achieve orgasm.

Source: Kaplan, H. (1974). *The new sex therapy.* New York: Brunner/Mazel.

nontherapeutic coalition: An alliance between two or more family members, usually with the exclusion of the other family members.

Example: The mother and son are united in keeping the father excluded from their emotional involvement. As a result, the father becomes more punitive, and mother more permissive, toward the son.

Source: Minuchin, S., & Fishman, H. (1981). *Family therapy techniques.* Cambridge, Mass.: Harvard University Press.

nonverbal communication: Communication through physical movement or gesture of a portion of the body—through facial expressions, glances of the eyes, hand and arm movements, or the manner of sitting or walking.

Source: Ard, C. (1969). The role of nonverbal communication in marriage counseling. In B. Ard and C. Ard (Eds.), *Handbook of marriage counsel-*

ing (pp. 128–138). Palo Alto, Calif.: Science and Behavior Books.

normalizing: A therapeutic technique by which a symptom or problem is redefined as normal or quasi-normal behavior.
Example: A teenage boy is brought into the office for truancy and smoking pot. The boy is depressed and is admitted to the day hospital; but he arrives late each morning, saying that he cannot motivate himself. The therapist "normalizes" this behavior by explaining to the boy that he is a night person—more alive, awake, and ready to do things at night.
Source: Minuchin, S., & Fishman, H. (1981). *Family therapy techniques.* Cambridge, Mass.: Harvard University Press.

norms: Societal controls to enforce certain attitudes and behaviors that would not normally exist. Normative controls require (1) an initial definition of the attitudes and behaviors in question (for example, dinner is at 6 P.M.), (2) some way of monitoring those members who conform and those who do not (Dad sees who is 15 minutes late), and (3) rewards or punishment for conformity or nonconformity (those who are late go without dinner). Normative controls exist in families whose members have come to depend on the family for need satisfaction. The family members abide by the normative structure because of their mutually satisfying contract, and they disapprove of interference with their satisfaction. Family researchers refer to this phenomenon as homeostasis. Initially, each family is likely to have a firm or cohesive normative structure.
Source: Thibault, J., & Kelly, H. (1959). *The social psychology of groups.* New York: John Wiley & Sons.

now rule: The therapeutic rule that stipulates that self-expressions should be made in the present tense. The use of past or future tenses can create a distance in verbal communication—a situation in which one divests oneself of at least part of the responsibility for the words one speaks. Staying in the present tense increases openness and reduces potential defensiveness on the part of the listener.
Source: Nierenberg, G.I., & Calero, H.H. (1973). *Meta-talk: Guide to hidden meanings on conversations.* New York: Simon and Schuster.
Quoted: Baruth, L.G., & Huber, C.H. (1984). *An introduction to marital theory and therapy.* Monterey, Calif.: Brooks/Cole.

nuclear family: A family consisting of a husband, a wife, and their immediate children. The nuclear family is sometimes referred to as the conjugal family.
Source: Christensen, H. (1964). Development of the family field of study. In H. Christensen (Ed.), *Handbook of marriage and the family* (pp. 3–32). Chicago: Rand McNally.

nuclear family emotional system: The patterns of emotional functioning in a family in a single generation. These patterns are replicas of past generations and are repeated in future generations.
Example: The fathers in a vertical family system are all distant emotionally from others in their respective families.
Source: Bowen, M. (1976). Theory in the practice of psychotherapy. In P. Guerin (Ed.), *Family therapy* (pp. 388–404). New York: Gardner Press.

number of meanings: A code category indicating whether or not individuals recognize the fact that the "rolling stone" proverb has two mutually exclusive interpretations. This code category was developed by Sojit specifically for use in analyzing parental interaction during the proverb task.
Source: Sojit, C. (1971). The double bind hypothesis and the parents of schizophrenics. *Family Process, 10,* 53–74.
Quoted: Riskin, M., & Faunce, E. (1972). An evaluative review of family interaction research. *Family Process, 11,* 365–455.

nupercainal cream: A cream used by males who suffer from premature ejaculation. The cream helps to deaden the sensations of the penis.
Source: Perelman, M. (1980). Treatment of premature ejaculation. In S. Leiblum & L. Pervin (Eds.), *Principles and practice of sex therapy* (pp. 199–234). New York: Guilford Press.

nurturant functions: Functions encompassing, in addition to the ingestion of food and the psychological aspects of feeding, the early nurturance of the child (helping the child learn how to manage and control the body and to observe, distinguish, and communicate about inner and external experiences), the provision of appropriate experiences and learning opportunities, and the establishment of basic trust.
Source: Fleck, S. (1972). An approach to family pathology. In G. Erickson & T. Hogan (Eds.), *Family therapy: An introduction to theory and technique* (pp. 103–119). Belmont, Calif.: Wadsworth.

O

object relations theory: A theory that views the internalization of basic parent-child relationships as eventually repeated from the family of origin to the family of procreation. This theory is a British variation of psychoanalytic concepts based on the writings of Klein, Bowlby, Fairbairn, Winnicott, Dick, and others. It is best represented in this country by James Framo.
Sources: Hansen, J.C., and L'Abate, L. (1982). *Approaches to family therapy.* New York: Macmillan; Pearce, J.K., & Friedman, L.J. (Eds.). (1980). *Family therapy: Combining psychodynamic and family systems approaches.* New York: Grune & Stratton.

object sorting task: A task in a standard psychological test that has been used by some researchers to generate interaction between the subject and the tester for the purpose of measuring disordered styles of thinking.
Source: Reiss, D. (1981). *The family's construction of reality.* Cambridge, Mass.: Harvard University Press.

object-focused family: A family characterized by overemphasis on the children (child-centered), the outside community, or the self (narcissistic). The motivation for treatment depends on the willingness of the marital couple to form an effective coalition.
Source: Cuber, J., & Harroff, P. (1966). *Sex and the significant Americans.* Baltimore: Penguin.
Quoted: Glick, I., & Kessler, D. (1980). *Marital and family therapy* (2nd ed.). New York: Grune & Stratton.

objectification: The process of taking a thoroughly and completely rational, nonemotional stance, in which a logical analysis of cost-rewards is made without attention or recourse to personal, emotional, or interpersonal factors.
Example: A father makes a global assessment that his son is lazy. In fact, the son is seen as lazy because a particular behavior occurs at a low frequency. It is logical to the father that, if his son is lazy in one area, he will be lazy in all areas.
Source: Weiss, R. (1978). The conceptualization of marriage from a behavioral perspective. In T. Paolino & B. McCrady (Eds.), *Marriage and marital therapy* (pp. 165–239). New York: Brunner/Mazel.

obligatory relationship: A tradition-controlled, role-structured form of commitment in which success and satisfaction are measured by living up to external standards of excellence, or the appearance of excellence. Doing what is correct is more important than the expression of self.
Example: Going to church and presenting a facade of togetherness is more important to a family than each member's individuality.
Source: Weiss, R. (1978). The conceptualization of marriage from a behavioral perspective. In T. Paolino & B. McCrady (Eds.), *Marriage and marital therapy* (pp. 165–239). New York: Brunner/Mazel.

observational blindness: The therapist or patient fails to see the obvious unless it fits into the therapist's or patient's theoretical frame of reference.
Example: The therapist's theoretical background is based on the individual orientation of psychoanalysis, which does not recognize the possibilities of family dynamics and family system intervention.
Source: Bowen, M. (1978). *Family therapy in clinical practice.* New York: Jason Aronson.

observing family mealtimes: The technique of monitoring the family mealtime as a microcosm of the family in sociological and dynamic terms. The clinician observes the mealtime to assess the family's way of relating.
Example: In one family, the members do not eat together. The members eat separately as they come home and then go their separate ways.
Source: White, S. (1976). Family dinner time: A focus for life space diagrams. *Journal of Clinical Social Work, 4,* 93–101.
Quoted: Glick, I., & Kessler, D. (1980). *Marital and family therapy* (2nd ed.). New York: Grune & Stratton.

one parent against another: A situation in which one parent sides with a child against the other parent.
Example: A mother and son are engaged in a struggle over the son staying out late at night. Father is called in to help settle the issue, but the mother says his solution is inappropriate. The father and mother end up at odds with each other, while the situation with the son reaches an impasse.
Source: Haley, J. (1976). *Problem-solving therapy.* San Francisco: Jossey-Bass.

one-way mirror: A device by which family members can observe each other objectively. One-way mirrors have been used in child guidance clinics and have been adopted more recently by the family therapy movement. The device is also useful in the supervision of family therapy trainees.

Example: A family is given a specific task to work on while one member of the family observes from behind a mirror. The mother believes the father cannot discipline their son. By giving the father a task involving discipline, the mother can see his behavior objectively.

Source: Minuchin, S., Montalvo, B., Guerney, B., Rosman, B., & Schumer, F. (1967). *Families of the slums: An exploration of their structure and treatment.* New York: Basic Books.

open family system: A family system permitting honest self-expression by the participating members. In such a family, differences are viewed as natural, and open negotiation occurs to resolve the differences before they are allowed to develop without limits in the family.

Source: Kantor, D., & Lehr, W. (1975). *Inside the family: Toward a theory of family process.* San Francisco: Jossey-Bass.

open system: A system in which there is an exchange of material, energy, and information with the environment. Open systems have three properties: wholeness, relationship, and equifinality. Wholeness implies that the whole is greater than the sum of the parts. Relationship refers to the fact that one must understand connections and interactions between the parts in order to understand the system. Equifinality means that, no matter where one begins, the conclusions will be the same. Thus, in family theory, if a systems view is taken of an ongoing interrelationship such as marriage, the pattern of behavior will be the same regardless of the specific subject matter (e.g., money, in-laws, sex, children). Thus, in family systems work, the therapist looks for wholeness, interrelationships between individuals, and patterns of behavior.

Example: The parents did everything possible to raise their daughter in a healthy way, but her adolescent peer group influenced her values to the extent that she became drug addicted. Her parents continued to be supportive in hopes of her learning from the difficult experiences she is now going through.

Source: Sauber, S.R. (1983). *The human services delivery system.* New York: Columbia University Press.

operant behavior: Behavior that has a statistical frequency of occurrence over time when an eliciting stimulus is either unknown or not present. Operant behavior can be reinforced independently of the intention of others.

Example: A person cries frequently but does not know why. It could be that, each time the person cries, a great deal of attention is given, which reinforces the behavior.

Source: Weiss, R. (1978). The conceptualization of marriage from a behavioral perspective. In T. Paolino & B. McCrady (Eds.), *Marriage and marital therapy* (pp. 165–239). New York: Brunner/Mazel.

opinion asking or giving: A category of the Interaction Process Analysis (IPA) coding system that encompasses asking for or giving of opinions, evaluations, analyses, or feelings.

Source: Bales, R. (1950). *Interaction process analysis: A method for the study of small groups.* Reading, Mass.: Addison-Wesley.

Quoted: Riskin, M., & Faunce, E. (1972). An evaluative review of family interaction research. *Family Process, 11,* 365–455.

optimal balance theory: The theory that agreements must outnumber disagreements, and that answers must outweigh questions, for effective group functioning.

Source: Lennard, H., & Bernstein, A. (1969). *Patterns in human interaction.* San Francisco: Jossey-Bass.

Quoted: Riskin, M., & Faunce, E. (1972). An evaluative review of family interaction research. *Family Process, 11,* 365–455.

optimal functioning: A pattern of adapting to circumstances in a way that reaches toward change, intrasystem determinism, and innovation. Optimal functioning is characterized by flexible marital and parental coalitions, clear boundaries, spontaneous and free interchange, and respect for the individuality of family members.

Source: Lewis, J.M., Beavers, W.R., Gossett, J.T., & Phillips, V.A. (1976). *No single thread: Psychological health in the family system.* New York: Brunner/Mazel.

ordinal position: According to the theory of Alfred Adler, a rank one holds in the family, determines the situation in which one finds oneself. The ordinal position is not a "cause" of behavior disturbances but a fact of life to which the family member responds. Five ordinal positions can be considered basic; all other positions can be seen as variations, combinations, or permutations of these five. The five are (1) an only child, (2) the eldest child, (3) the second child, (4) the middle child and (5) the youn-

gest child. A child may occupy two positions (second and youngest child), or a child may be several years in one position and then move to another (a youngest child becomes a middle child or a middle child becomes the youngest child when a younger sibling dies). Finally, a child may be overrun by a younger sibling who is more intelligent.
Source: Shulman, B.H., & Nikelly, A.G. (1971). Family constellation. In A.G. Nikelly (Ed.), *Techniques for behavior change: Applications of adlerian theory.* Springfield, Ill.: Charles C Thomas.

orgasm of the female: Sexual release, reached at an increment peak of pelvic tissue vasocongestion and myotonia, in which the orgasmic platform in the outer third of the vagina and the uterus contract with a regularly recurring rhythmicity.
Source: Masters, W., & Johnson, V. (1970). *Human sexual inadequacy.* Boston: Little, Brown.

orgasmic phase: The third stage of the sexual response cycle, usually referred to as the climax. This stage is marked by pleasurable rhythmic contractions localized in the pelvic area.
Source: Masters, W., & Johnson, V. (1970). *Human sexual adequacy.* Boston: Little, Brown.

orgastic threshold: The amount of stimulation required to elicit the female orgasm. This threshold varies widely from woman to woman.
Source: Kaplan, H. (1974). *The new sex therapy.* New York: Brunner/Mazel.

orientation asking: A category of the Interaction Process Analysis (IPA) coding system that encompasses asking for orientation, information, repetition, and confirmation.
Source: Bales, R. (1950). *Interaction process analysis: A method for the study of small groups.* Reading, Mass.: Addison-Wesley.
Quoted: Riskin, M., & Faunce, E. (1972). An evaluative review of family interaction research. *Family Process, 11,* 365–455.

orientation giving: A category of the Interaction Process Analysis (IPA) coding system that encompasses the giving of orientation, information, repetition, clarification, or confirmation.
Source: Bales, R. (1950). *Interaction process analysis: A method for the study of small groups.* Reading, Mass.: Addison-Wesley.
Quoted: Riskin, M., & Faunce, E. (1972). An evaluative review of family interaction research. *Family Process, 11,* 365–455.

out-of-control families: Families characterized by issues of control that are usually systemic, not individual, in nature. The developmental stages of family members tend to define the types of problems encountered. For example, in families with young children, the controlling youngster often elicits support from one of the adults. The adults are "disqualified," which leaves the position of control to the child. In families with adolescents, a major issue of control is the "inability of the parents to move from the stage of concerned parents of young children to respectful parents of young adults." Problems with control are also found in families with delinquent children, in which "the parent's control is dependent on their presence." Families in which there is child abuse also have a great deal of difficulty with control issues. In such cases, the family is the only place in which the abusive parent feels in control, and subsequently that control becomes aggression. Out-of-control families are characterized by chaotic communication patterns. Contact becomes unimportant, since the members of the family do not expect to be heard, and only relationship messages are apparent. Communication is limited to "small, disconnected, affect-carrying bits or transactions."
Source: Minuchin, S., & Fishman, H.C. (1981). *Family therapy techniques.* Cambridge, Mass.: Harvard University Press.

outsight: The act of understanding the motives of others, of comprehending them in depth. Outsight differs from empathy, in that it is more intellectual than emotional. It also differs from idiopanima, which refers to A's perception of B's perception of A. Outsight is the analogue of insight.
Source: Corsini, R.J. (1966). *Roleplaying in psychotherapy: A manual.* Chicago: Aldine.

overadequate-inadequate reciprocity: A relational pattern in which both parents are equally immature. The one who makes the decisions for the two of them becomes the overadequate parent and the other one becomes the inadequate parent. Neither is able to find a midground between the two extremes—domineering, authoritative, and stubborn versus helpless, compliant, and submissive.
Example: A father has no problem in making important decisions at work, but he ends up in an emotional, paralyzing deadlock when he and his wife (the "mother") try to decide which movie the family should see together.
Source: Bowen, M. (1978). *Family therapy in clinical practice.* New York: Jason Aronson.

overfocusing: A narrowing of a family's experience of reality due to focusing on a specific problem. The intensity of the family's experiences around the symptom and the symptom's bearer causes the family members to ignore other significant aspects of their transactions.
Source: Minuchin, S., & Fishman, H.C. (1981). *Family therapy techniques.* Cambridge, Mass.: Harvard University Press.

overinvolvement: An intrusive, overly warm, dependently affective engagement with another person.
Example: A man constantly attends to his wife's moods, for example, by asking her, "Is everything OK now?" He cannot operate as a separate emotional entity.
Source: Epstein, N., Bishop, D., & Levin, S. (1978). The McMaster model of family functioning. *Journal of Marriage and Family Counseling, 4,* 19–31.
Quoted: Epstein, N., & Bishop, D. (1981). Problem-centered systems therapy of the family. In A. Gurman, & D. Kniskern (Eds.), *Handbook of family therapy* (pp. 444–482). New York: Brunner/Mazel.

overprotection: An extreme degree of concern for somebody's welfare. In children, overprotection produces dependency, submissiveness, shyness, and possibly disobedience.
Example: A mother does not let her child assume any age-appropriate activities; she keeps the child at a level appropriate for a much younger age by limiting the child's play with neighborhood children ("They are too rough") or by controlling food intake ("It's no good for you"), appearances ("You may catch a cold"), or behavior ("You cannot go because it is dangerous for you").
Source: Parker, G. (1983). *Parental overprotection: A risk factor in psychosocial development.* New York: Grune & Stratton.

overt fusion: The condition of being overly trapped in the family emotional system. The person involved stresses belongingness, relatedness, and togetherness. Although an adult, the person is unable to assume the adult tasks of dealing with marriage, career options, care of parents, or the assumption of a different role in the family.
Source: Minuchin, S. (1974). *Families and family therapy.* Cambridge, Mass.: Harvard University Press.

Quoted: Barnard, C., & Corrales, R. (1979). *The theory and technique of family therapy.* Springfield, Ill.: Charles C Thomas.

overwhelmed mother: A mother who is in charge of everyone, with no hierarchy established among the children. In her role as the hub of the family, the mother must settle all issues with her children, individually and collectively.
Example: A mother asks her child to do a simple task, such as play with some toys. The child constantly interrupts his mother to ask her something, show her something, and check out her next activity. If another child tries to become involved in the play, the child will return to his mother to ask questions about the situation rather than deal himself with the other child.
Source: Haley, J. (1976). *Problem-solving therapy.* San Francisco: Jossey-Bass.

ownership: The act of being responsible for one's own perceptions, feelings, thoughts, and deeds.
Example: The assertion, "You make me angry," is not a statement of ownership. However, if one says, "When you don't act as I expect, I become angry," one is asserting ownership, because one is making a statement about one's own feeling and assuming responsibility for it.
Source: Duhl, B., & Duhl, F. (1981). Integrative family therapy. In A. Gurman & D. Kniskern (Eds.), *Handbook of family therapy* (pp. 483–516). New York: Brunner/Mazel.

P

paradigm: A frame of reference used to organize perceptions. Different paradigms produce different perceptions. Levenson suggests three paradigms in therapy—the work machine model, the communication model, and the organismic model. In the first model, cure involves undoing the past; in the second, cure occurs by staying in the present; and in the third model, the emphasis is on organization. This concept is used to distinguish the "family" concept from the "individual" conceptualization.
Source: Levenson, E. (1972). *The fallacy of understanding.* New York: Basic Books.
Quoted: Foley, V. (1974). *An introduction to family therapy.* New York: Grune & Stratton.

paradox: A contradiction that follows correct deduction from consistent premises. There are three types of paradoxes: (1) logico-mathematical antinomies, (2) paradoxical definitions (semantical antinomies), and (3) pragmatic paradoxes (paradoxical injunctions and paradoxical predictions).
Source: Watzlawick, J., Weakland, J., & Fisch, R. (1967). *Pragmatics of human communication.* New York: Norton.

paradoxical definition: A definition in which the same concept is used to refer both to a member of a class and to the class itself, thus creating an illusion of identity.
Example: The statement, ''I am lying,'' is a paradoxical definition of self. The statement is true only if it is not true, and vice versa.
Source: Watzlawick, J., Weakland, J., & Fisch, R. (1967). *Pragmatics of human communication.* New York: Norton.

paradoxical injunction: A communication that must be obeyed, but must be disobeyed to be obeyed. Two conditions are required for a paradoxical injunction: (1) There must be a strong complementary relationship (e.g., father-son), and (2) the person who receives the injunction cannot step outside the frame of reference or metacommunicate.
Example: A father advises his daughter, ''Be yourself'' but then qualifies the injunction by limiting the kind of friends she can make, the places she can visit, and the curfews she must keep. Consequently, there is no way she can be herself. If she is herself, she may make choices that go counter to her father's wishes. If she does what her father wants her to do, she may not have a will or personality of her own. Thus, she is offered a digital choice, i.e., being either what her father wants her to be, or the opposite of what her father wants. Being herself would be tantamount to being the opposite of her father. If she does what he wants, she cannot be herself. The same kind of logic is present in therapeutic situations where the therapist obtains change by asking for sameness, i.e., no change. For example, a prescription of the symptom may put a family in the same situation. If the family members follow the prescription, they are under the control of the therapist; if they start, rather than stop, the symptom, they learn to acquire control. Either way, they win.
Source: Watzlawick, P., Weakland, J., & Fisch, R. (1967). *Pragmatics of human communication.* New York: Norton.

Quoted: Weeks, G., & L'Abate, L. (1982). *Paradoxical psychotherapy.* New York: Brunner/Mazel.

paradoxical intention: A special technique of logotherapy that is used when a client is concerned about the frequency of an undesired response. When the client wants to reduce the frequency of a behavior, the therapist requires that the client attempt to increase its occurrence.
Example: A man perspires excessively when he meets authority figures. He wants to eliminate this response. The therapist asks him to sweat out as much as he can when he meets an authority figure. This tactic removes the anticipatory anxiety, hence, the problem.
Source: Frankl, V. (1955). *The doctor and the soul: From psychotherapy to logotherapy.* New York: Knopp.
Quoted: Ascher, L. (1980). Paradoxical intention. In A. Goldstein & E. Foa (Eds.), *Handbook of behavioral interventions* (pp. 266–321). New York: John Wiley & Sons.

paradoxical letter: A written paradoxical intervention that is given directly or mailed to a client. Such letters are used after verbal paradoxical interventions have failed.
Example: The following is a typical paradoxical letter, with a subsequent analysis keyed to specific statements:

> Dear Norma, Sara, Ann, and Dave:
> I was very impressed with the sadness and hurt in your family in our last session. I am glad that two of you were able to express your sadness.[1] It is important when you are sad and hurt to be able to share your feelings with other family members. Family members that share their hurts really love one another.[2]
> However, I have grave misgivings about how much you should share at this time. I think it is much too soon for you to communicate these feelings to each other.[3] Instead, each of you should continue to protect the family from its sadness by distracting or keeping each other busy.[4] You might even select one family member on whom you can focus all your attention, or maybe someone in the family has already decided to take this role. This person could be responsible for starting fights and misbehaving.[5] The person selected should be a very responsible and loyal member of the family; this should make the choice easy, since one of you is already acting in an overtly responsible manner (but enjoying it.)[6]

Your family is also in a silent crisis.[7] Someone has changed recently, which has the family confused and uncertain about the future. The confusion and chaos in the family are actually part of the preparation for the family's forthcoming growth and change.[8] *Warning:* The family should be prepared for a big fight on Wednesday night.[9]

1. Cryptic statement—Raises the question of who expressed sadness, is designed to unite the family in guessing who it was.
2. Relabeling—Sharing hurt is equated to love.
3. Restraining—Previous statement tells the family members it is good to share hurt, but now they are warned that it may be risky.
4. Positive connotation—Distraction is said to protect the family, which puts them all on the same level.
5. Prescription—The fighting is prescribed.
6. Relabeling—The most distracting member of the family is relabeled as the one who is responsible and loyal.
7. Cryptic statement—What is a "silent crisis"?
8. Relabeling—Remember this is a chaotic family; there is no predictability or certainty; the confusion is relabeled as preparation for growth.
9. Paradoxical question—Our next session is scheduled for Thursday; the oldest daughter said she would not return; hence, we expect a fight about her attendance on Wednesday night, if not earlier.

Source: Weeks, G.R., & L'Abate, L. (1982). *Paradoxical psychotherapy.* New York: Brunner/Mazel.

paradoxical prescription: A statement to the family that overtly strengthens or promotes the family homeostatic defenses and does not arouse resistance. The prescription reveals the secondary gain of the patient's symptomatic behavior for the family; hence, covertly, change is expected. Paradoxical prescriptions (also called therapeutic double binds) are used in strategic family therapy.
Example: A therapist tells a son to continue to fail, since in that way he is helping his father feel good about himself.
Source: Weeks, G., & L'Abate, L. (1982). *Paradoxical psychotherapy: Theory and practice with individuals, couples and families.* New York: Brunner/Mazel.

parallel relationship: A relationship in which the spouses alternate comfortably between symmetrical and complementary relationships as they adapt to changing situations. At times, one partner assumes a one-up relationship vis-à-vis the other; at other times, they are on equal terms.
Example: A husband decides which model car to buy, but the decision to buy the car is reached mutually with his wife.
Source: Lederer, W., & Jackson, D. (1968). *The mirages of marriage.* New York: Norton.
Quoted: Bodin, A. (1981). The interactional view: Family therapy approaches of the Mental Research Institute. In A. Gurman & D. Kniskern (Eds.), *Handbook of family therapy* (pp. 267–309). New York: Brunner/Mazel.

parataxic distortion: Projections, stemming from early life experiences, that are placed upon another person. Such distortions generally occur in new relationships.
Example: A woman claims her husband is rejecting her because she was rejected by her father.
Source: Sullivan, H. (1956). *Clinical studies in psychiatry.* New York: Norton.
Quoted: Beavers, W.R. (Ed.). (1977). *Psychotherapy and growth: A family systems perspective.* New York: Brunner/Mazel.

parent effectiveness training: A communications method to assist parents in getting along with and in better disciplining their children. The training develops parental guidelines from theories of client-centered behavioral and communication models. The approach is similar to that used in systematic training for effective parenting, developed by Dinkmeyer and McKay and based on the writings of Alfred Adler and Rudolph Dreikurs.
Source: Gordon, T. (1970). *Parent effectiveness training.* New York: Peter H. Wyden.
Quoted: L'Abate, L. (1981). Skill training programs for couples and families. In A. Gurman & D. Kniskern (Eds.), *Handbook of family therapy* (pp. 631–662). New York: Brunner/Mazel.

parent surrogate: An adult who fills the role of an absent parent in the development of the child.
Example: The husband's sister assumes the role of the mother after the wife leaves the husband and fails to return to the family.
Source: Glick, I., & Kessler, D. (1974). *Marital and family therapy.* New York: Grune & Stratton.

parental child: An older child who functions as parent for the younger children. Though not yet an adult and lacking the relevant power, the parental child assumes responsibility for the younger children. The child is thus caught in the middle between misbehaving children and a mother who has failed to delegate the requisite power.

Source: Minuchin, S., Montalvo, B., Guerney, B., Rosman, B., & Schumer, F. (1967). *Families of the slums.* New York: Basic Books.
Quoted: Haley, J. (1976). *Problem-solving therapy.* San Francisco: Jossey-Bass.

parental coalition: A clearly defined husband-wife subsystem within the family. The parents are able to create well-defined generational boundaries, which help the children maintain their own identity within the sibling subsystem.
Example: The parents in a family are careful not to discuss such issues as sex, money, and parental conflict with their children. They have established a strong bond between themselves, and this serves to keep such issues at their generational level.
Source: Lidz, T., Fleck, S., & Cornelison, A. (1965). *Schizophrenia and the family.* New York: International Universities Press.
Quoted: Barnard, C., & Corrales, R. (1965). *The theory and technique of family therapy.* Springfield, Ill.: Charles C Thomas.
See also **marital schism/skew.**

parental dyad: A relationship composed of a father and a mother.
Source: Glick, I., & Kessler, D. (1974). *Marital and family therapy.* New York: Grune & Stratton.

parental group therapy: A form of therapy in which each parent is seen in a group with other same-sex parents. This type of therapy is often conducted with parents of severely disturbed children, who simultaneously receive either individual or group psychotherapy. Parental group therapy affords emotional support to the parents; within the group, the parents often become aware of their own dependency needs and feelings of isolation.
Source: Speers, R.W., & Lansing, C. (1964). Group psychotherapy with preschool psychotic children and collateral group therapy of their parents: A preliminary report of the first two years. *American Journal of Orthopsychiatry, 34,* 659–666.

parental identification: Internalization of the personality characteristics of a given parent. The person who does this makes unconscious reactions similar to those of that parent.
Example: A son becomes hostile and sarcastic toward his mother because he identifies with his father's similar behavior.

Source: Lynn, D. (1969). *Parental and sex role identification: A theoretical formulation.* Berkeley, Calif.: McCutchan.

parental loading: The tendency of parental standards to be more rigid for the eldest child in the family.
Source: Glick, I., & Kessler, D. (1974). *Marital and family therapy.* New York: Grune & Stratton.

parental preference: The child's desire to adopt behavior characteristics of a particular parent.
Example: A child prefers to adopt her mother's emotional approach to other people, rather than her father's cold and aloof stance.
Source: Lynn, D. (1969). *Parental and sex role identification: A theoretical formulation.* Berkeley, Calif.: McCutchan.

parentification: Fantasizing or behaving as if one's partner or child were one's parent. This subjective distortion, the result of wishful fantasy or dependent behavior, can be either a pathological condition or a component of the regressive core of an evenly balanced, reciprocal relationship.
Example: A single parent asks the oldest child to assume parental duties and responsibilities, such as sharing the parent's anxieties and financial problems, taking care of the younger siblings, and acting in general as a confidant and friend, without generational boundaries. These duties and responsibilities are beyond the age and maturity level of the child; but, as a result of assuming them, the child displays adult-like behavior much earlier than expected.
Source: Boszormenyi-Nagy, I., & Spark, G.M. (1973). *Invisible loyalties.* New York: Harper & Row.

parentification of child: Unconscious attempts by parents who have been deprived of their own parents through loss or separation to transform their own children into parent-like figures. Such identification is especially likely if the marital partner fails to gratify the need to recover the lost parents. Parentification of a child normally occurs in large families or in families where the parents work and an older child is given authority over the younger children. It occurs abnormally when a parent abdicates a position of authority or assigns an adult role to a child, thereby breaching generational boundaries.
Example: Mary lost her parents at the age of four. She was forced to grow up fast, feeling she could never depend on anyone. She now has a 12-year-old child and finds that she can use this child to gratify her frustrated dependency needs.

Source: Boszormenyi-Nagy, I., & Spark, G. (1973). *Invisible loyalties.* New York: Harper & Row.

participation rate: The relative amount of communication contributed by each family member to the family's total interaction.
Source: Mishler, E., & Waxler, N. (1968). *Interaction in families: An experimental study of family processes and schizophrenia.* New York: John Wiley & Sons.

parts technique: A technique in which family members are asked to visualize and define parts of themselves.
Example: A mother feels that one part of her, her household self, is inefficient. She is asked to sculpt one of her children to represent her felt inefficiency. The sculpting leads to a discussion of her feelings.
Source: Dodson, L., & Kurpius, D. (1977). *Family counseling: A systems approach.* Muncie, Ind.: Accelerated Development.

passive-congenial marriage: A marital relationship in which one member is passive and somewhat withdrawn, and the other partner is gregarious and "happy-go-lucky."
Example: The wife practices as a Jehovah's Witness, the husband excludes himself by choice from all of the religious activities of his wife and children. He spends most of his time drinking with his friends.
Source: Glick, I., & Kessler, D. (1980). *Marital and family therapy* (2nd ed.). New York: Grune & Stratton.

past-present switch: A device in which, in answer to a question, present and past difficulties are connected in a very illogical fashion.
Example: A school-age girl is brought into therapy because she has been acting strangely and talking in riddles. When the mother is asked, "When did you notice that your child was not developing as she should?", she replies, "Well, she was a seven-month-old baby, and she was in an incubator for six weeks." The child's present and past difficulties are thus connected illogically.
Source: Watzlawick, P. (1963). *An anthology of human communication.* Palo Alto, Calif.: Science and Behavior Books.
Quoted: Satir, V. (1967). *Conjoint family therapy.* Palo Alto, Calif.: Science and Behavior Books.

paternal rejection: A pattern of paternal behaviors ranging from physical abuse, distancing, lack of interest and concern, to uninvolvement vis-à-vis a child.

Source: L'Abate, L. (1975). Pathogenic role rigidity in fathers: Some observations. *Journal of Marriage and Family Counseling, 1,* 69–79.

pathogenic family: A family whose adaptive and coping mechanisms have been exhausted. The family members are chronically trapped in stereotyped patterns of interaction that severely limit their range of choice, but no alternatives seem possible. This situation produces extremely dysfunctional behaviors in the offspring.
Source: Minuchin, S., Rosman, B., & Baker, L. (1978). *Psychosomatic families.* Cambridge, Mass.: Harvard University Press.

pathogenic relating: A destructive behavioral process between family members. A pervasive form of this type of relating is silence.
Example: A son is acting-out. Every time the parents raise the issue of their son's misbehavior, he becomes sullen, withdrawn, and silent.
Source: Zuk, G. (1971). *Family therapy.* New York: Behavioral Publications.

pathologic need complementarity: Unconscious needs of the parent to shape the psychic structure of the child. The parent's unconscious needs are transferred to the child as rigid superego demands that the child accepts in a passive way. By accepting such demands, the child's dependent needs are gratified. The parent and child thus feed each other's narcissistic demands. This helps to overcome loneliness, helplessness, and isolation.
Source: Boszormenyi-Nagy, I. (1962). The concept of schizophrenia from the perspective of family treatment. *Family Process, 1,* 103–113.
Quoted: Zuk, G., & Rubenstein, D. (1965). A review of concepts in the study and treatment of families of schizophrenics. In I. Boszormenyi-Nagy & J. Framo (Eds.), *Intensive family therapy: Theoretical and practical aspects* (pp. 1–32). New York: Harper & Row.

patriarchal family: A family or clan marked by the supremacy of the father.
Source: Garrett, W. (1982). *Seasons of marriage and family life.* New York: Holt, Rinehart, & Winston.

patrilineal descent group: A group based upon parent-child genealogical relationships in which membership is determined solely through male genealogical relationships.
Source: Zelditch, M. (1964). Cross-cultural analyses of family structure. In H. Christensen (Ed.), *Handbook of marriage and the family* (pp. 3–32). Chicago: Rand McNally.

patrilocal residence: A rule of residence that requires that a man live with his father and that when he is married, he bring his wife home with him.
Source: Zelditch, M. (1964). Cross-cultural analyses of family structure. In H. Christensen (Ed.), *Handbook of marriage and the family* (pp. 3–32). Chicago: Rand McNally.

pattern of alignment: The distribution of ties among members of a family. It refers to any basis on which family members line up with each other—unconsciously or consciously, in fantasy or in action, for reasons of comfort, affection, or power—to enhance or defeat each other.
Example: A child aligns himself with his father in order to get what he wants, because he believes his father will override his mother's prohibitions.
Source: Hess, R., & Handel, G. (1959). *Family worlds: A psychological approach to family life.* Chicago: University of Chicago Press.

pattern recognition task: A task used by Reiss to test family problem-solving effectiveness. In the task, each family member is given a sample card with a sequence of letters on it; the children are given one type of sequence and the parents another type. Each person is then asked to conceptualize and identify the correct sequences. This is done without any verbal communication. A variation of this task is to give each family member a series of 15 cards with sequences on them and to ask each member to sort the cards into patterns. Then the family is asked to sort the same 15 cards as a group, discussing the sort as they do it. Finally, each member is asked to sort the cards separately a second time.
Source: Reiss, D. (1981). *The family construction of reality.* Cambridge, Mass.: Harvard University Press.

pattern regulators: Non-symbolic, routinized sequences of behavior that determine space and distance among family members and between the family and the outside world. These sequences of behavior are manifested by all family members. However, they occur continuously and are beyond the members' awareness.
Example: In a family with a handicapped child, certain remedial motor exercises are performed with the child. These exercises are conducted only by the parents or by the oldest child, thus determining a clear hierarchy within the family. No one outside the family helps the handicapped child with his daily exercises, which defines the family's boundary with the outside world.
Source: Reiss, D. (1981). *The family's construction of reality.* Cambridge, Mass.: Harvard University Press.

patterns of interaction: Redundant sequences of behavior or interaction patterns in the family that define who talks to whom, when, about what, and in what manner.
Example: At the dinner table, the oldest child, Rob, begins to talk about an experience he had at school. Mom listens attentively while Dad continues eating and Rob's two sisters begin to whisper about a boy they like. Rob gets upset and complains that Dad and his sisters are not paying attention. Mom fusses at the girls and gives Dad a warning glance. Everyone then listens more carefully to Rob's story. This fairly simple interaction pattern is repeated over and over in the family.
Source: Hoopes, M.H., Fisher, B.L., and Barlow, S.H. (1984). *Structured family facilitation programs: Enrichment, education, and treatment.* Rockville, Md.: Aspen Systems Corp.

pause: A break between sentences spoken by the same speaker or a break between two or more speakers. Any silence in which it is felt that someone "should" be speaking.
Source: Mishler, E., & Waxler, N. (1968). *Interaction in families: An experimental study of family processes and schizophrenia.* New York: John Wiley & Sons.

peak experience: A personal and private experience of great emotional significance that may lead to rapid changes in personality, e.g., a religious conversion.
Source: Maslow, A.H. (1959). *New knowledge in human values.* New York: Harper & Row.

peculiar forms of verbalization: A code used by Singer and Wynne to denote statements with odd grammatical constructions, mispronunciations, slips of the tongue, or violations of conventional usage and logic.
Source: Singer, M., & Wynne, L. (1966). Principles of scoring communication defects and deviances in parents of schizophrenics: Rorschach and TAT scoring manuals. *Psychiatry, 29,* 260–288.

penalty deposit system: A system that maintains patient compliance in treatment by requiring patients to pay the therapist a deposit that is refunded in full if they comply with, but is forfeited if they violate, a therapeutic prescription.

Source: Lobitz, W., & LoPiccolo, J. (1972). New methods in the behavioral treatment of sexual dysfunctions. *Journal of Behavior Therapy and Experimental Psychiatry, 3*, 265–271.
Quoted: LoPiccolo, J. (1978). Direct treatment of sexual dysfunction. In LoPiccolo, J., & LoPiccolo, L. (Eds.), *Handbook of sex therapy* (pp. 1–18). New York: Plenum Press.

penchant for closure: A family's proclivity to suspend or apply ordered and coherent concepts to raw sensory experience. A penchant for closure is a dimension of family consensual experience.
Source: Reiss, D. (1981). *The family construction of reality.* Cambridge, Mass.: Harvard University Press.

peoplemaking: An attempt to explicate the procedures by which a family might extricate itself from a dysfunctional system. This is not easily accomplished and may require an outside intervention by one who is not part of the family system.
Example: The wife was advised to move out of her parents' home, stop following her mother's dictates, and begin to relate to her husband as a capable man instead of as her son.
Source: Satir, V. (1967). *Conjoint family therapy.* Palo Alto, Calif.: Science and Behavior Books.

perceived parental similarity: Perception of oneself as being similar to a particular parent, whether or not an actual similarity exists.
Source: White, S.G., & Hatcher, C. (1984). Couple complementarity: A review of the literature. *American Journal of Family Therapy, 12*, 15–25.

perceived sex role similarity: Perception of oneself as being similar to others of a given sex, whether or not an actual similarity exists.
Example: The husband and wife are equally responsible for financial decisions; the wife is in charge of spending the money, and the husband earns it.
Source: Lynn, D. (1969). *Parental and sex role identification: A theoretical formulation.* Berkeley, Calif.: McCutchan.

perceptual distortion: A condition in which the mates in dysfunctional marital pairs see their spouses as they expect them to be, rather than as they really are, and treat them accordingly.
Example: A woman sees her husband as cold and rejecting and thus does not have to confront her lack of sexual desire for him.
Source: Satir, V. (1965). Conjoint marital therapy. In B. Green (Ed.), *The psychotherapies of marital disharmony* (pp. 121–134). New York: Free Press.

perineometer: A cylindrical instrument that is inserted into the vagina to provide a simple means of exercising the pubococcygeus muscle against resistance.
Source: Kegel, A.H. (1952). Sexual functions of the pubococcygeus muscle. *Western Journal Surgery Obstetrics and Gynecology, 60*, 521.
Quoted: Kline-Graber, G., & Graber, B. (1978). Diagnosis and treatment procedures of pubococcygeal deficiencies in women. In J. LoPiccolo & L. LoPiccolo (Eds.), *Handbook of sex therapy* (pp. 222–238). New York: Plenum Press.

peripheral person: A relatively uninvolved or less involved outside person whom a therapist uses to achieve an objective.
Example: A therapist interviews a whole family presenting a child problem and sees the mother and child as overinvolved and the father as more peripheral. The therapist tells the family that the child needs to identify more with the father by structuring father-son activities that exclude the mother.
Source: Haley, J. (1976). *Problem-solving therapy.* San Francisco: Jossey-Bass.

permeability: The extent to which family members and nonmembers can move freely into and out of the family. Family boundaries necessarily vary, both across family systems and within families over time. Across family systems, permeability relates to the degree of system organization; overorganized systems have relatively impermeable boundaries (with reference to nonfamily members) and underorganized systems have extremely permeable boundaries. These boundaries are in part determined by the environment—particularly cultural, ethnic, and occupational systems.
  Family boundaries tend to ebb and flow through time, expanding and becoming more permeable with the addition of members and becoming more impermeable with loss of members. A family system that is relatively permeable at the level of interaction may be equally "open" at the level of meaning, affect, and communication. But such covariation does not always occur; at times, permeability at the level of interaction and communication may be associated with impermeability at the level of meaning and affect.
Example: The father is not open to any kind of influence from his in-laws when they want to give him advice on child-rearing because he knows the

kind of parents they were with his wife, their daughter.

Source: Benjamin, M. (1982). General systems theory, family system theories, and family therapy. In A. Bross (Ed.), *Family therapy: Principles of strategic practice* (pp. 34–88). New York: Guilford.

permeability to others: The ability to hear and respond to others within the family system.

Source: Beavers, W.R. (1976). A theoretical basis for family evaluation. In J.M. Lewis, W.R. Beavers, J.T. Gossett, & V.A. Phillips (Eds.), *No single thread: Psychological health in the family system* (pp. 46–82). New York: Brunner/Mazel.

permeable boundaries: Ambiguity regarding stepfamily boundaries when there is an emotionally or legally important adult living elsewhere as a result of a previous marriage relationship. When a family system has permeable boundaries, flexibility exists with respect to individuals and events of influence entering and existing within the system.

Example: A child lives with a mother who usually exercises parental control over the child. However, this boundary may shift from time to time when the father reenters the system to assume responsibility.

Source: Visher, E., & Visher, J. (1979). *Stepfamilies: A guide to working with stepfamilies and stepchildren.* New York: Brunner/Mazel.

person control strategy: The use of successful interruptions (direct control) and questions (indirect control) to influence others.

Example: A person is talking about a serious subject when another, in order to change the subject, interrupts to ask about the time.

Source: Mishler, E., & Waxler, N. (1968). *Interaction in families: An experimental study of family processes and schizophrenia.* New York: John Wiley & Sons.

perverse triangle: A family relationship triangle in which the separation between the generations is blocked in a covert way. The presence of the triangle coincides with undesirable manifestations of violence, symptomatic behavior, or dissolution of the system. A perverse triangle has the following characteristics: (1) it comprises two members from one generation and one from another, (2) two members from different generations form a coalition excluding the third party, and (3) the coalition is kept hidden or denied.

Example: Two parents (same generation) and a child (different generation) go to the maternal grandparents' house for a special Sunday dinner. The child becomes restless during dinner and starts to complain. The father does not like his in-laws but is much too courteous and polite to reveal his feeling. As the meal proceeds, the father supports the child's complaints indirectly by attending closely to every word the child says and failing to set any limits (hidden coalition). The mother becomes increasingly frustrated and angry. Her attempts to discipline the child are undermined by the father (different generation in coalition).

Source: Haley, J. (1977). Toward a theory of pathological systems. In P. Watzlawick & J. Weakland (Eds.), *The interactional view* (pp. 11–27). New York: Norton.

Quoted: Hoffman, L. (1981). *Foundations of family therapy.* New York: Basic Books.

petrification: The process of turning oneself or another person into a stone, a robot—a thing, without subjectivity. The act of petrifying a person negates that person's autonomy and ignores the person's feelings.

Example: A psychotic patient dreams that members of her family had turned into inanimate objects.

Source: Laing, R. (1969). *The divided self.* New York: Penguin Books.

phantom orgasm: An orgasm or orgasm-like response in an individual with spinal cord injury that is assumed to be purely cerebrocognitional and that serve intrapsychic functions.

Source: Money, J. (1960). Phantom orgasm in dreams of paraplegic men and women. *Archives of General Psychiatry, 3,* 373–382.

Quoted: Higgins, G. (1978). Aspects of several responses in adult with spinal cord injury: A review of the literature. In J. LoPiccolo & L. LoPiccolo (Eds.), *Handbook of sex therapy* (pp. 387–410). New York: Plenum Press.

phase differentiation: Sequential changes that two people or a group go through in a given time period.

Example: The first phase in a group's development is one in which the members get to know one another and then set some tasks for the group.

Source: Lennard, H., & Bernstein, A. (1969). *Patterns in human interaction.* San Francisco: Jossey-Bass.

Quoted: Riskin, M., & Faunce, E. (1972). An evaluative review of family interaction research. *Family Process, 11,* 365–455.

phasic relational process: A process in which all relationships go through phases of unrelatedness

(autistic phase), affiliative overinvolvement (symbiotic phase), growth of autonomy in members (individuation phase), and dissolution (separation phase), leading to reinvolvement in new groups.
Source: Boszormenyi-Nagy, I. (1965). A theory of relationships: Experience and transactions. In I. Boszormenyi-Nagy & J. Framo (Eds.), *Intensive family therapy: Theoretical and practical aspects* (33–86). New York: Harper & Row.

physical symptoms: An adaptive mechanism for a current life situation.
Example: A woman complains that she has difficulty swallowing. Her family members call her every day to unload their problems. She can no longer "swallow" their problems or express her feelings toward them.
Source: Haley, J. (1976). *Problem-solving therapy.* San Francisco: Jossey-Bass.

planning: An activity in which the therapist makes initial hypotheses on the basis of a minimum awareness of the family structure. Clues that may lead to information about the family may be the age of the family members, the number of family members, where they live, and the composition of the family.
Source: Minuchin, S., & Fishman, H.C. (1981). *Family therapy techniques.* Cambridge, Mass.: Harvard University Press.

plan-something-together task: The first task of the Structured Family Interview (developed at the Mental Research Institute for therapy and research purposes), in which the family members are seated around a table in the interview room and asked by the interviewer to "plan something you could all do together as a family; all of you please participate in the planning." The interviewer then leaves the room, and the family is given ten minutes to deal with the task.
Source: Riskin, J., & Faunce, E. (1970). Family interaction scales, I. Theoretical framework and method. *Archives of General Psychiatry, 22,* 504–512.

plautean phase: The second stage of the sexual response cycle, generally characterized by high levels of sexual arousal.
Source: Masters, W., & Johnson, V. (1970). *Human sexual adequacy.* Boston: Little, Brown.

p-li-ss-it model: A treatment model that provides four levels of approach with suggested methods for handling sexual concerns. The four levels are (1) permission, (2) limited information, (3) specific suggestion, and (4) intensive therapy. The first three levels constitute brief therapy.
Source: Annon, J., & Robinson, C. (1978). The use of vicarious learnings in the treatment of sexual concerns. In J. LoPiccolo & L. LoPiccolo (Eds.), *Handbook of sex therapy* (pp. 35–56). New York: Plenum Press.

polyandry: A type of polygamous marriage in which a woman is simultaneously married to two or more husbands.
Source: Christensen, A. (1964). Development of the family field of study. In H. Christensen (Ed.), *Handbook of marriage and the family* (pp. 3–32). Chicago: Rand McNally.

polygramy: The joining of nuclear families into larger social units. A polygramous relationship exists if the joining is at the point of the marriage relationship, so that one person has two or more spouses and hence membership in two or more nuclear families.
Source: Christensen, A. (1964). Development of the family field of study. In H. Christensen (Ed.), *Handbook of marriage and the family* (pp. 3–32). Chicago: Rand McNally.

polygyny: A type of polygamous marriage in which a man is simultaneously married to two or more wives.
Source: Christensen, A. (1964). Development of the family field of study. In H. Christensen (Ed.), *Handbook of marriage and the family* (pp. 3–32). Chicago: Rand McNally.

positioning: A paradoxical strategy in which the therapist accepts and exaggerates the clients' position or self-assertion.
Example: A woman who said all her friends hated her is told by the therapist that perhaps they did. The therapist then suggests that she list all the ways people have expressed their hate toward her.
Source: Rohrbaugh, M., Tennen, H., Press, S., White, L., Raskin, P., & Pickering, M. (1977, August). Paradoxical strategies in psychotherapy. Paper presented at the American Psychological Association, San Francisco, Calif.
Quoted: Weeks, G., & L'Abate, L. (1982). *Paradoxical psychotherapy.* New York: Brunner/Mazel.

positive connotation: Emphasizing the homeostatic goal of the family, a statement of positive connotation to the family defines the relationships among the family members in a positive way, while shifting the context of therapy to the systemic level. The statement is based on the assumption that pathology helps to preserve the stability or cohesion of the group.

Example: A ten-year-old boy is presented with psychotic symptoms following the death of his grandfather. The following message is given to the family: "You are doing a good thing. We understand that you considered your grandfather to be the central pillar of your family. He kept it together, maintaining a certain balance. Without your grandfather's presence, you were afraid something would change. Perhaps because of the fear that the balance in the family would change, you thought of assuming his role. For now, you should continue this role that you've assumed spontaneously."

Source: Selvini Palazzoli, M., Boscolo, L., Cecchin, L., & Prata, G. (1978). *Paradox and counterparadox.* New York: Jason Aronson.

Quoted: Weeks, G., & L'Abate, L. *Paradoxical psychotherapy.* New York: Brunner/Mazel.

positive feedback: Feedback that leads to change or loss of stability. As a crisis-inducing mechanism, it counteracts negative feedback.

Example: Two married partners who are constantly fighting somehow find that this behavior protects their marriage from change. When a therapist tells them how well they are fighting and that they should continue, this prescription creates a crisis in the couple leading to change.

Source: Watzlawick, P., Weakland, J., & Fisch, R. (1967). *Pragmatics of human communication.* New York: Norton.

See also **negative feedback.**

positive feedback loop: A mechanism that relates two events in a circular, amplifying manner. An increase in any component part of the circular sequence increases, in turn, the next event in the sequence. In this deviation-amplifying situation, the positive feedback loop is primarily a self-destruction mechanism. It sets up a runaway situation that eventually drives the system beyond the limits or range within which it can function.

Source: Maruyama, M. (1963). The second cybernetics: Deviation-amplifying mutual causal processes. *American Scientist, 51,* 164–179.

Quoted: Steinglass, P. (1978). The conceptualization of marriage from a system theory perspective. In T. Paolino & B. McCrady (Eds.), *Marriage and marital therapy* (pp. 292–366). New York: Brunner/Mazel.

See **positive feedback.**

positive reinforcement: Material reinforcers (tokens, stars, points, money) or social reinforcers (praise, smiles) to increase desired behavior.

Example: Henry's parents want him to study more. They begin systematically to praise him for doing his homework and engaging in other school-related activities.

Source: LeBow, M. (1972). Behavior modification for the family. In G. Erickson & T. Hogan (Eds.), *Family therapy: An introduction to theory and technique* (pp. 326–376). Belmont, Calif.: Wadsworth.

positive statement procedure: A procedure requiring that the client make a positive statement for every negative statement the client makes.

Source: Azrin, N., Naster, B., & Jones, R. (1973). Reciprocity counseling: A rapid learning based procedure for marital counseling. *Behavioral Research and Therapy, 11,* 365–382.

Quoted: O'Leary, K., & Turkewitz, H. (1978). Marital therapy from a behavioral perspective. In T. Paolino & B. McCrady (Eds.), *Marriage and marital therapy* (pp. 240–297). New York: Brunner/Mazel.

positivity: Positive socioemotional responses. An "index of positivity" is the net total of positive socioemotional responses of individuals and/or groups, i.e., the total number of positive socioemotional acts (coded according to Bales' IPA) minus the total number of negative socioemotional acts (coded according to Bales' IPA) divided by the total number of all coded acts.

Source: O'Rourke, J. (1973). Field and lab: The decision-making behavior of family groups in two experimental conditions. *Sociometry, 26,* 422–435.

Quoted: Riskin, M., & Faunce, E. (1972). An evaluative review of family interaction research. *Family Process, 11,* 365–455.

power: A behavioral syndrome consisting of authority (who makes the decisions) and responsibility (who carries out the decisions). It involves orchestration decisions (where shall we live, who should work, etc.), instrumental decisions (everyday routines), negotiation potential (degree of functionality-dysfunctionality), ability to negotiate (skill), motivation to negotiate (will), and the content of what is being negotiated.

Source: L'Abate, L., Hansen, J.C., and Ganahl, G. (in press). *Key concepts and methods in family psychology.* Englewood, N.J.: Prentice-Hall.

pragmatics: The behavioral effects of communication. All behavior is considered communication. The data of pragmatics are words, their configurations and meanings, their nonverbal concomitants, and body language.

Source: Watzlawick, P., Weakland, J., & Fisch, R. (1967). *Pragmatics of human communication.* New York: Norton.

praxis: The intentions of a person or a group of persons, e.g., a family, toward another person or group, based on the experiences the first person or group has had regarding that other person.

Example: Every time the daughter says something about her feelings, her mother switches the topic. The mother's experience of her daughter is that she will raise painful issues as she did some time ago.

Source: Esterson, A. (1970). *The leaves of spring.* London: Pelican.

preempting: A strategy in which the client's thoughts, feelings, attitudes, and positions are anticipated and stated by the therapist or mediator in a neutralizing context before the client has a chance to state them. The best strategy for dealing with undesirable conflict is to prevent it in the first place. Preempting is useful, not only for structuring the context of mediation in a general way, but for preventing conflict by removing the stingers before antagonizing words can be uttered. Thus, the technique minimizes the client's opportunity to develop and manifest resistance to change or compromise.

Example: The mediator begins the mediation by informing both spouses, in an informed and authoritative manner, of the current understandings of the children's needs in the divorce situation and of the irrelevance of the various negative and incriminating comments and interpretations the spouses have made about each other. In this way, the spouses' resistance is minimized. Alternatively, the mediator presents to the parents the assumption that their child needs regular and continuing contact with both parents. It then becomes very difficult for the mother to state that the children do not need their father. In effect, that statement has been preempted.

Source: Saposnek, D.T. (1983). Strategies in child custody mediation: A family systems approach. *Mediation Quarterly, 1*(2), 29–54.

Quoted: Marlow, L., & Sauber, S.R. (in press). *Handbook on divorce mediation.* New York: Brunner/Mazel.

premarital counseling: Counseling to help a couple prepare for marriage. Such counseling may be problem-focused (remedial) or prevention-oriented.

Sources: L'Abate, L. (1981). Social skills training programs for couples and families. In A. Gurman

& D. Kniskern (Eds.), *Handbook of family therapy* (pp. 631–661). New York: Brunner/Mazel; L'Abate, L., & McHenry, S. (1983). *Handbook of marital intervention.* New York: Grune & Stratton.

premonitory sensations: The sensations that occur just before ejaculation and serve as feedback to the man to indicate that ejaculation is near.

Source: Masters, W., & Johnson, V. (1970). *Human sexual inadequacy.* Boston: Little, Brown.

prescribing the defense: Recognition of a defense and requesting the patient to maintain his or her "line of defense."

Example: A withdrawn husband shuts off his feelings, and his frantic wife continually tries to get through to him by constantly expressing hers, much like his mother used to do. The therapist acknowledges the importance of controlling feelings: "It takes independence and courage not to allow your wife to infringe on you. . . ."

Source: Papp, P. (1980). The use of fantasy in a couples group. In M. Andolfi & I. Zwerling (Eds.), *Dimensions of family therapy* (pp. 73–90). New York: Guilford Press.

prescribing the role: If the therapist senses a high degree of rigidity in the roles, rather than attempting to modify them directly, it is better to define one aspect of the role positively and ask the client to act it out.

Example: The husband was proud of protecting his wife, "shepherding" her all these years. The therapist said he had not gone far enough in his shepherding. He had only shepherded one side of her, her moral side, and neglected to shepherd the other side, her desire for pleasure.

Source: Papp, P. (1980). The use of fantasy in a couples group. In M. Andolfi & I. Zwerling (Eds.), *Dimensions of family therapy* (pp. 73–90). New York: Guilford Press.

prescribing the symptom: Directing the client to engage voluntarily in the symptomatic behavior. The behavior is then no longer spontaneous, because the client has stepped outside of the client's frame of the symptomatic game-without-end.

Example: A woman complains about worrying off and on throughout the day. These worries interfere with her daily activities and she enters therapy to eliminate them. She has already tried to put her worries aside, but with no success. The therapist tells her these worries are trying to tell her something important about her life. Rather than attempt to get rid of them, however, she is told to worry more. In fact, she is to concentrate on her wor-

risome thoughts completely and exclusively whenever they occur. She is to worry about as many things as possible. In fact, in the hope that she will get the message sooner, she is instructed to amplify her worries.
Source: Watzlawick, P., Weakland, J., & Fisch, R. (1967). *Pragmatics of human communication.* New York: Norton.
Quoted: Weeks, G., & L'Abate, L. (1982). *Paradoxical psychotherapy.* New York: Brunner/ Mazel.

pretense of problems: A therapeutic situation created by a paradoxical strategy in which an individual, usually a child, is asked to pretend to have a problem. The strategy is based on the assumption that the child's problem is helping to protect the family. There are three ways to create a pretense of problems:

1. The parents request that the child have the problem. That is, the parents ask the child to consciously and voluntarily enact the problem behavior. For example, a child who is bedwetting might be asked to urinate and sleep in a wet bed.
2. The parents request that the child pretend to have the problem. A child who has stomachaches might be asked to fake stomachaches at particular times.
3. The parents request that the child pretend to help the parent. This involves making an overt shift in the family hierarchy. The strategy makes the child superior, while the parent takes a one-down position. For example, a young boy develops chronic headaches, which take attention away from the father's unhappiness. The father is instructed to pretend to have a headache every evening so that his son can be helpful to him.

Source: Madanes, C. (1981). *Strategic family therapy.* San Francisco: Jossey-Bass.

pretherapy training: Training procedures (e.g., role induction interview, videotaped recordings for vicarious learning and modeling, and therapeutic reading) for the purpose of maximizing the initial stage of the therapeutic relationship. With these procedures, the therapist prepares the patient "to attend to, react to, and concern himself with the 'right' things in therapy."
Example: A resistant spouse views a videotape of a marital therapist describing what to expect in therapy and conducting a session.

Source: Sauber, S.R. (1974). Approaches to pretherapy training. *Journal of Contemporary Psychotherapy, 6,* 190–197.

prevention: Strengthening of factors that encourage individual ability to cope with situations, or the reduction of factors that impair treatment. In standard public health terms, primary prevention is focused on reducing the incidence of new cases of mental disorders in a community; secondary prevention is aimed at decreasing the prevalence of existing cases in the population; and tertiary prevention is focused on reducing the duration of additional negative side effects or other impairments following treatment. Prevention is also sometimes defined on the basis of the population or target—primary prevention as that aimed at the "population at large"; secondary as that aimed at "identified vulnerable, high-risk groups;" and tertiary as that focused on "treatment and rehabilitation." Within this framework, primary prevention focuses on both modifying the environment and strengthening individual capacities to cope with situations.
Example: Consider that changes in one subsystem, designed to improve a situation, may lead to a change in other subsystems such that the overall result may be a more negative or more positive state of affairs than existed before the change. Helping a couple to alter their neurotic marital relationship may disrupt an adaptive family lifestyle and lead to divorce. The divorce may be viewed as a positive or negative outcome of prevention. Primary prevention may include outreach to children of divorced parents in the school as in lag detection; secondary prevention may audit further exacerbation of the inherent problems; and tertiary prevention may include psychotherapy for divorced spouses unable to enter the singles world.
Sources: Sauber, S.R. (1973). *Preventive educational intervention for mental health.* Cambridge, Mass.: Ballinger; L'Abate, L. Prevention of remarriage and family problems. (In press). In B. Edelstein & L. Michaelson (Eds.), *Handbook of prevention.* New York: Plenum Press.

priapism: A pathologic erection unassociated with sexual desire.
Source: Kaplan, H. (1979). *Disorders of sexual desire.* New York: Brunner/Mazel.

primary family tasks: Tasks that involve socialization of the children and the stabilization of adult personalities.
Example: A primary task of the family is to teach the child to be independent.

Source: Parsons, T., & Bales, R. (1955). *Family socialization and interaction process.* Glencoe, Ill.: Free Press.
Quoted: Lewis, J.M., Beavers, W.R., Gossett, J.T., & Phillips, V.A. (1976). *No single thread: Psychological health in the family system.* New York: Brunner/Mazel.

primary impotence: The male sexual dysfunction of being unable to achieve coitus because of an inability to obtain or maintain an erection.
Source: Masters, W., & Johnson, V. (1970). *Human sexual adequacy.* Boston: Little, Brown.

primary locus: The status of being structurally engaged in the essential and habitual generation and maintenance of a problem. The primary locus locks systems in relationships that generate the problem for all or some of those systems.
Example: The grandparents and parents in a family are locked in a struggle over who has ultimate control and authority over the children. This produces confusion in the family's hierarchy, which in turn leads the children to develop symptoms.
Source: Aponte, H., & Van Deusen, J. (1981). Structural family therapy. In A. Gurman & D. Kniskern (Eds.), *Handbook of family therapy* (pp. 310–360). New York: Brunner/Mazel.

primary reinforcement: Provided by stimuli that initially reinforce an organism. These stimuli, which reinforce without any prior learning taking place, satisfy such basic needs as food, water, and sex.
Source: LeBow, M. (1972). Behavior modification for the family. In G. Erickson & T. Hogan (Eds.), *Family therapy: An introduction to theory and technique* (pp. 347–376). Belmont, Calif.: Wadsworth.

primary relationships: Relationships in which there are exchanges of intimacy, love, and services and in which there are everyday activities involving marital or other close physical relationships of an intimate and prolonged nature.
Source: Cooley, C. (1909). *Social organization.* New York: Scribner.
Quoted: Garrett, W. (1982). *Seasons of marriage and family life.* New York: Holt, Rinehart, & Winston.

priorities: Degrees of importance of different component roles in the family system. The functional priorities are: self as person, self as partner, self as parent. Deviations from this sequence may produce family dysfunctionality.

Example: A woman is highly involved with her children. She sees herself only as a mother. She is unable to see herself as a person or partner, separate and apart from her parental role. By the same token, her husband sees himself as a provider and not as a source of emotional nurturance.
Source: L'Abate, L. (1976). *Understanding and helping the individual in the family.* New York: Grune & Stratton.

problem behavior: Behavior that is part of a sequence of acts between several people. The repeating sequence of behavior is the focus of the therapy. The problem is not viewed as existing in a social vacuum.
Source: Haley, J. (1976). *Problem-solving therapy.* San Francisco: Jossey-Bass.

problem list: An inventory of a family's problems and strengths that is generated at the outset of therapy and agreed upon by the family members.
Source: Barker, P. (1981). *Basic family therapy.* Baltimore: University Park Press.

problem-centered systems therapy of the family: Therapy that focuses on (1) assessing, (2) contracting, (3) treating, and (4) establishing closure with respect to a presented family problem. The first stage, assessment, involves investigation of not only the presenting problem of the family but also of a wide range of aspects of family functioning as described in the McMaster model of family functioning. In the assessment stage, areas of strength and deficit are examined in detail and highlighted. Comprehensive evaluations are made of as many levels of the family system as possible. At the end of the assessment, the family and the therapist construct and agree on a problem list. The second stage, contracting, deals with establishing the therapy's goals, expectations, and commitments, to which both the family and the therapist agree. Treatment, the third stage, makes use of the strengths identified in the assessment and focuses on shoring up the weak areas that have been identified in the problem list. In closure, the fourth stage, the family sets long-term goals and procedures for self-monitoring. A distinctive feature of this model is that the therapy involves an active collaboration between the family and the therapist. The therapist takes the role of mediator and facilitator. At each stage, the therapist explains what is being done and why. Assessment and diagnostic impressions are clearly spelled out and agreed upon before treatment proceeds.

Source: Epstein, N.B., & Bishop, D. (1981). Problem-centered systems therapy of the family. In A. Gurman & D. Kniskern (Eds.), *Handbook of family therapy* (pp. 444–482). New York: Brunner/Mazel.

problem-solving dimension: The level of a family's ability to resolve problems in order to maintain effective family functioning. The problems may be either instrumental problems (mechanical problems of everyday life) or affective problems (problems related to feelings).
Source: Epstein, N., & Bishop, D. (1981). Problem-centered systems therapy of the family. In A. Gurman & D. Kniskern (Eds.), *Handbook of family therapy* (pp. 444–482). New York: Brunner/Mazel.

process: A discrete, time-limited sequence of behaviors that constitute particular transactions among system components. A process consists of linked behavioral exchanges. In contrast to structure, which has the qualities of repetition and duration, a process is a sequence of single behavioral temporal transactions.
Example: A family decision process is seen to consist of several linked behaviors: the father makes some opening statement, his oldest son opposes him, and the mother comes to the support of her son; the mother-son arrangement has enough force to determine an outcome. When a temporal dimension is added, a distinction may be made between structure and process and between process and content.
Source: Umbarger, C.C. (1984). *Structural family therapy.* New York: Grune & Stratton.

process model: A model of the interactions and transactions (translated into methods and procedures) that move the individuals in the family and the family system from a symptomatic base toward one of wellness.
Source: Satir, V. (1982). The therapist and family therapy: Process model. In A.M. Horne & M.M. Ohlsen (Eds.), *Family counseling and therapy* (pp. 12–42). Itasca, Ill.: F.E. Peacock.

process research: An investigation that uses, totally or in part, data from direct or indirect measurement of patient, therapist, or dyadic (patient-therapist interaction) behavior in the therapy interview.
Source: Kiesler, D. (1973). *The process of psychotherapy: Empirical foundations and systems of analysis.* Chicago: Aldine.
Quoted: Pinsof, W. (1981). Family therapy process research. In A. Gurman & D. Kniskern (Eds.), *Handbook of family therapy* (pp. 699–741). New York: Brunner/Mazel.

process variables: Variables that "focus on the process of intrafamilial or interpersonal transaction," e.g., who speaks to whom, who interrupts whom, who agrees with whom.
Source: Pinsof, W. (1981). Family therapy process research. In A. Gurman & D. Kniskern (Eds.), *Handbook of family therapy* (pp. 699–741). New York: Brunner/Mazel.

process-oriented marriage counseling: Counseling that directs its attention to the quality and direction of the changing activity, the dynamic behavior, and the life styles of the individuals who make up a marriage relationship.
Source: Harper, R. (1969). Marriage counseling as rational process-oriented psychotherapy. In B. Ard & C. Ard (Eds.), *Handbook of marriage counseling* (pp. 115–119). Palo Alto, Calif.: Science and Behavior Books.

product variables: The outcome or end results of interaction, i.e., outcome variables, such as participation rate, total number of questions, and who wins in arguments.
Source: Riskin, M., & Faunce, E. (1972). An evaluative review of family interaction research. *Family Process, 11,* 365–455.

projective identification: Marital partners' projection of certain aspects of themselves onto their mates. The first partner thus views the mate as an embodiment of the projected characteristic. This projection is often part of self-object representation based on early family relationships (i.e., one's own family of origin). Through the process of projective identification, one or both partners misperceive important aspects of the other's character. Since the misperceptions serve to meet certain denied needs, the partners are strongly motivated to sustain them, regardless of the actual behavior manifested.
Example: A 32-year-old woman, married for 8 years, has been reared by an overprotective mother. She perceives her husband as being like her mother and in anger often describes him as a "mother hen" or as a person who would have made a "good wife." No matter how masculine the husband's pursuits are, the wife's perception blinds her to those aspects of his character that do not fit her projected image of him. Their interactions take on a pseudorealistic quality as the wife undermines the husband's confidence and encourages him to behave in ways similar to her projected image.

Source: Greenspan, S., & Mannino, M. (1974). A model for brief intervention with couples based on projective identification. *American Journal of Psychiatry, 131,* 1103–1106.

protectiveness: Behavior based on the need to protect an intimate other from hurt. Protectiveness can be a positive antecedent of pathology. When protectiveness is carried to an extreme, the relationship cannot be negotiated.
Source: Weeks, G., & L'Abate, L. (1982). *Paradoxical psychotherapy.* New York: Brunner/Mazel.

proverb: One of the tasks of the structured family interview. The parents are asked to discuss by themselves the meaning of the proverb, A rolling stone gathers no moss; they then are asked to call in their children and teach the agreed-upon meaning to them. Although other proverbs have been used, the rolling-stone proverb is the most commonly used because it has two valid but mutually exclusive meanings. These introduce the possibility of disagreement, which then has to be dealt with in some way.
Source: Watzlawick, P. (1966). A structured family interview. *Family Process, 5,* 256–271.

pseudo-democratic family: A family in which all channels of communication seem to be of about equal importance, with the marital coalition and the parental role not particularly well-differentiated.
Source: Glick, I., & Kessler, D. (1980). *Marital and family therapy* (2nd ed.). New York: Grune & Stratton.

pseudo-dyspareunia: The female use of "pain during sex" as an excuse to avoid frequent or further contact with a husband or lover.
Source: Lazarus, A. (1980). Psychological treatment of dyspareunia. In S. Leiblum & L. Pervin (Eds.), *Principles and practice of sex therapy* (pp. 147–166). New York: Guilford Press.

pseudohostility: Continuous bickering and turmoil to maintain relatedness. Quarreling and disruption can maintain a relationship without opening up the possibility of genuinely expressing the tender, deep relationship feelings involved. Pseudohostility actually serves to cover up the need for intimacy and affection that family members cannot deal with easily.
Source: Wynne, L., Ryckoff, I., Day, J., & Hirsch, S. (1958). Pseudo-mutuality in the family relations of schizophrenics. *Psychiatry, 21,* 205–220.

pseudoidentification: A phenomenological shift in a close, intimately interdependent relationship by a partner who begins to function with a facade of exaggerated strength and assertion, while the other partner seems to lose identity and become a relative nonentity.
Example: A wife is overshadowed by her husband who has suddenly become flirtatious with other women, and she feels increasingly insecure.
Source: Nadelson, C. (1976). Marital therapy from a psychoanalytic perspective. In T. Paolino & B. McCrady (Eds.), *Marriage and marital therapy* (pp. 89–164). New York: Brunner/Mazel.

pseudomarriage: A marriage in which the couple's relationship is void of intimacy and the marriage is maintained either for convenience or for appearance.
Source: Stahman, R.F., & Hiebert, W.J. (1977). Commonly recurring couple interaction patterns. In R.F. Stahman & W.J. Hiebert (Eds.), *Klemer's counseling in marital and sexual problems: A clinical handbook* (2nd ed.) (pp. 17–33). Baltimore: Williams & Wilkins.
Quoted: Okun, B.F., & Rappaport, L.J. (1980). *Working with families: An introduction to family therapy.* Belmont, Calif.: Brooks/Cole.

pseudomutuality: A process by which families seek to maintain a form of homeostasis. Pseudomutuality is a type of surface alignment that blurs and obscures from recognition and conscious experience both underlying splits and divergencies and deeper affection and alignment. Through this mechanism, the family wards off real or imagined threats to its unity, thus avoiding the discomforts of intimate relations, which often are highly loaded with emotional positive or negative forces.
Example: In the following illustration, the father seeks to avoid disagreement between himself and his wife. The mother seeks to avoid open conflict with her daughter. The underlying disagreement between the parents and the daughter is disguised so that the real issue—which boys are acceptable—is avoided. Discussion of this issue would create an open conflict whose impact on their relationships all the family members fear.

Mother: I think Mary is old enough to have dates—if the boy friends are of a high-class type.

Mary: But, Mother, you told me I couldn't date Tom, and I don't see anything wrong with him.

Mother: Your father was the one who objected.

Father: Well, I don't really object. I think I said she would have to ask you. I really think your mother knows best.

Mary: But she always says to ask you.

Mother: Well, I think your father and I agree on what kind of boys you can date. You wouldn't want to go out with Tony, would you?

Mary: Gee whiz, no. He's a drip.

Mother: Well, I think you'd agree with dad and me—most of the time anyway.

Source: Wynne, L.C., Ryckoff, I.M., Day, J., & Hirsch, S.I. (1958). Pseudomutuality in the family relations of schizophrenics. *Psychiatry, 1,* 205–220.

pseudoself: A very low level of differentiation of self. Individuals with pseudoselves manage to function fairly well in their life adjustments. As children, they do not "grow away" from the family ego mass as do their more differentiated siblings. They remain emotionally attached and dependent upon their parents. After adolescence, they "tear themselves away" to attain a "pseudoseparation" from the family ego mass.

Example: A husband and wife with equally poor differentiations of self become deeply involved emotionally and "fuse together" into a new undifferentiated family ego mass. Their separation from their parents is maintained only by finding new dependent attachments.

Source: Bowen, M. (1978). *Family therapy in clinical practice.* New York: Jason Aronson.

pseudotherapeutic marriage: A reform-based marital relationship in which one partner tries to change the other's habits.

Example: A professional man brings his wife to therapy, complaining that he wanted an intellectual companion but has ended up with an empty-headed, emotional cripple. He requests that the therapist help him reform her so she will be what he wanted.

Source: Rutledge, A. (1969). Male and female roles in marriage counseling. In B. Ard & C. Ard (Eds.), *Handbook of marriage counseling* (pp. 120–127). Palo Alto, Calif.: Science and Behavior Books.

psychoanalytic family therapy: Family therapy that is concerned with the social and cultural aspects of personality development and functioning. This form of therapy is derived from the psychoanalytic theories of Alfred Adler, Carl Jung, Franz Alexander, Eric Fromm, Karen Horney, Abram Kardiner, Clara Thompson, and Harry Stack Sullivan.

Influenced by these culturalists and neo-Freudian thinkers, many early analysts started working therapeutically with both spouses. (It is reported that Freud himself did concurrent marital therapy.) Nathan W. Ackerman, Don D. Jackson, Theodore Lidz, and Murray Bowen, who pioneered family therapy, were trained in psychoanalysis.

The aim of psychoanalytic family therapy is to establish a collaborative working alliance with the family members in order to explore the relationship of individual and interpersonal factors in current relationships, provide insight into genetic and unconscious factors from past conflicts, and help the members function more freely and authentically in terms of emotions and thoughts. Change occurs internally by working through old conflicts that influence current relationships. In directive family therapy, in contrast, change is imparted from the outside by providing solutions to problems, teaching skills, manipulating power and communication structures, or applying paradoxical prescriptions. It is assumed that the changes resulting from the growth in the family members will result in greater and more permanent personality strengths and individualism.

Source: Meissner, W.W. (1978). The conceptualization of marriage and family dynamics from a psychoanalytic perspective. In T.J. Paolino & B.S. McCrady (Eds.), *Marriage and marital therapy.* New York: Brunner/Mazel.

psychological contagion: Individual psychopathology that affects others in the family system.

Example: The presence of maladjustment in the parents can increase the probability of disorders or maladjustments in their children. In other cases, if one family member in treatment improves, another member may develop symptoms of pathology; or improvement in a sick member may bring shifts in family alignments. The family members may resist changes because of their unconscious needs to keep a patient member ill. Thus, parents sometimes use a child's symptoms as a defense against their own anxiety, shifting their problems to the child and resisting the therapist's attempts to clarify their emotional conflicts.

There are two types of marital situations that, through psychological contagion, can lead to disorders in children: (1) marital schism, the failure to work out complementary role relationships which results in open conflict; and (2) skewed relationships between husband and wife, with one partner very dependent or masochistic and the other independent and supportive. In the latter case, overt conflict seldom appears.

Sources: Ehrenwald, J. (1958). Neurosis in the family: A study of psychiatric epidemiology. *American Journal of Psychiatry, 115,* 134–142; Lidz, T., Cornelison, A., Terru, D., & Fleck, S. (1958). Intrafamilial environment of the schizophrenic patient.   VI. Parental personalities and family interaction. *American Journal of Orthopsychiatry, 28,* 764–776.

psychosomatic family: A family in which emotional conflicts are transformed into somatic symptoms. Characteristics of a psychosomatic family are enmeshment, overprotectiveness, rigidity, and lack of conflict resolution.

Example: The parents in a family experience covert conflict but are overtly pleasant and conflict-free. Their daughter develops anorexia, which diverts the parents' attention. They now fight with her over not eating.

Source: Minuchin, S., Rosman, B., & Baker, L. (1978). *Psychosomatic families: Anorexia nervosa in context.* Cambridge, Mass.: Harvard University Press.

psychotic family: Commonly cited characteristics include failure to form a nuclear family; family schism and skew; blurring of generational lines; pervasion of the entire atmosphere with irrational, usually paranoid, ideation; persistence of unconscious incestuous preoccupation; and sociocultural isolation.

Example: A family in which the grandparents are crossing generation lines, the parents are in conflict over a child, and a parental child is saving the child from the parents.

Sources: Haley, J. (1976). *Problem-solving therapy.* San Francisco: Jossey-Bass; Fleck, S. (1960). Family dynamics and origin of schizophrenia. *Psychomatic Medicine, 22,* 333–344.

pubococcygeal muscle hypothesis: The hypothesis that the poor tone of the pubococcygeal muscle accounts for a substantial number of cases of female sexual inadequacy.

Source: Kaplan, H. (1974). *The new sex therapy.* New York: Brunner/Mazel.

punching-bag marriage: A marriage based on the idea that one sex is superior and has special rights. If the rights of the partner of that sex are not respected, the other partner is physically or verbally beaten.

Source: Rutledge, A. (1969). Male and female in marriage counseling. In B. Ard & C. Ard (Eds.), *Handbook of marriage counseling* (pp. 120–127). Palo Alto, Calif.: Science and Behavior Books.

punctuation: What one defines as stimulus and response when the two are not clearly distinguishable. Punctuation is a concept in family communication.

Example: A wife nags her husband because he comes home late, but he says he comes home late because she is a nag. They punctuate this sequence differently, each blaming the other.

Source: Watzlawick, P., Weakland, J., & Fisch, R. (1967). *Pragmatics of human communication.* New York: Norton.

punisher: A stimulus that decreases the probability of a behavior occurring.

Example: When a man approaches his wife sexually, she becomes hostile, telling him that the only time he approaches her is when he wants sex. Her behavior decreases the chances that he will approach her, except to meet overriding needs.

Source: Weiss, R. (1978). The conceptualization of marriage from a behavioral perspective. In T. Paolino & B. McCrady (Eds.), *Marriage and marital therapy* (pp. 165–239). New York: Brunner/Mazel.

pursuer-distancer: A relational system based on a pursuer-distance polarity. The pursuer believes the solution to anxiety lies in external action or in moving toward another for comfort. The distancer tries to avoid anxiety by withdrawing and moving away from others.

Example: In a marriage, one spouse moves toward the other, while the other moves away. They may alter the roles they play, but the pattern of interaction remains stable.

Source: Fogarty, T. (1976). Marital crisis. In P.J. Guerin (Ed.), *Family therapy, theory, and practice* (pp. 335–350). New York: Gardner.

Quoted: L'Abate, L., & McHenry, S. (1983). *Handbook of marital interventions.* New York: Grune & Stratton.

quantity of speech: The amount of speaking each individual contributes to the family discussion.

Source: Ferreira, A., Winter, W., & Poindexter,

E. (1966). Some interaction variables in normal and abnormal families. *Family Process, 5,* 65–70.
Quoted: Riskin, M., & Faunce, E. (1972). An evaluative review of family interaction research. *Family Process, 11,* 365–455.

quid pro quo: In a marital relationship, what each spouse gives and receives in the initial bargain made between the two spouses. The quid pro quo specifies in very general terms the rules, implicit or explicit, of the relationship. When the rules are formalized, the couple is said to have a marital contract.
Example: A husband agrees to help with the children if his wife agrees to help with the family budgeting.
Source: Jackson, D. (1965). Family rules: The marital quid pro quo. *Archives of General Psychiatry, 12,* 589–594.
Quoted: Gerson, M., & Barsky, M. (1979). For the new family therapist: A glossary of terms. *American Journal of Family Therapy, 7,* 15–30.

R

racket system: In transactional analysis, a self-reinforcing, distorted system of feelings, thoughts, and actions that is maintained by individuals who are functioning in a script or longitudinal life plan. A racket system has three interrelated and interdependent components: script beliefs and feelings, the rackety display, and the reinforcing experiences. The racket system stipulates how the script is lived out day-by-day. It shows how the script plot is reinforced and how others are manipulated into the roles the script requires. Identification of a client's racket system can provide useful guideposts for therapeutic intervention.
Example: A person acts in a way defined by the script beliefs, e.g., saying, "I don't know," when believing, "I'm stupid"; or the person acts in a way that socially defends against the script beliefs, e.g., by excelling in school and acquiring numerous degrees.
Source: Erskine, R.G., & Falcman, M. (1979). The racket system: A model for racket analysis. *Transactional Analysis Journal, 9,* 1.
Quoted: Erskine, R.G. (1982). Transactional analysis and family therapy. In A.M. Horne & M.M.

Ohlsen (Eds.), *Family counseling and therapy* (pp. 245–275). Itasca, Ill.: F.E. Peacock.

random type family: A family structural arrangement in which space is dispersed; that is, the members separately develop their individual boundary patterns in defending their own and their family's territory. Since the random family's territorial pattern is an aggregate of individual styles, including the effect of each on each other, there may be as many territorial guidelines as there are members of the family.
Example: The family den contains papers, books, unopened letters, garden and carpentry tools, a movie projector, several dead plants, and other seemingly unconnected items—some of which are swept by the wind into messy confusion every time the children pass through the room on their way to the backyard.
Source: Kantor, D., & Lehr, W. (1976). *Inside the family.* San Francisco: Jossey-Bass.

rational sex ethics: A humanistic, empirical, and scientific approach to the resolution of ethical dilemmas having to do with sex. Rather than look at revelations, intuition, religion, or feelings, rational sex ethics looks to the basic sciences revelant to sex, e.g., psychology, sociology, psychiatry, sexology, and anthropology. With these basic resources at hand, rational sex ethics then applies rigorous logic and clear thinking to arrive at humanistic, empirical conclusions.
Example: Masturbation was long considered to be a sin, an affront to God, and for the cause of all sorts of illnesses, from acne to blindness to insanity. Rational sex ethics examines all the scientific evidence and concludes that masturbation is not a sin and is neither harmful nor a causative factor with regard to illness or disease but is rather a normal, natural phenomenon.
Source: Ard, B.N., Jr. (1978). *Rational sex ethics.* Washington, D.C.: University Press of America.

rational-emotive family therapy: A comprehensive system of therapy that consciously and actively employs cognitive, emotive, and behavioral methods. The intent is not to effect symptom removal but rather to bring about profound philosophic changes in all involved family members. In rational-emotive family therapy (RET), the husband and wife are shown how they usually create their own disturbances and are not (as they often erroneously believe) emotionally upset by other family members. Their children, if old enough, are shown how

they upset themselves *about,* rather than get disturbed *by,* their parents' and siblings' actions and verbalizations. All participants in the therapy are taught how to recognize clearly and dispute their own irrational beliefs about themselves, about others, and about the world. In particular, they are shown that their emotional disturbances almost always arise from their self-defeating way of turning their desires and preferences into absolutistic shoulds, oughts, and musts.
Source: Ellis, A., & Grieger, R. (1977). *Handbook of rational emotive therapy.* New York: Springer.

reactance: The need to maintain one's freedom. The degree of reactance is a function of three variables that can be manipulated by the therapist: (1) the importance of free behavior to the individual, (2) the number of freedoms threatened, and (3) the magnitude of threat.
Source: Rohrbaugh, M., Tennen, H., Press, S., White, L., Raskin, P., & Pickering, M. (1981). Compliance, defiance, and therapeutic paradox. *American Journal of Orthopsychiatry, 51,* 454–467.
Quoted: Weeks, G., & L'Abate, L. (1982). *Paradoxical psychotherapy.* New York: Brunner/Mazel.

reality impairment: Distortions in family attitudes toward or perceptions of reality. Frequently, parental unrealities can be imposed on the child. Powerful guilt pressures and implications of treason or disloyalty can be brought to bear upon the child if the child persists in pursuing reality. These pressures can not only force the child to renounce reality but also block off the higher levels of reasoning associated with abstract thinking.
Example: A girl who has always allowed her mother to set her hair now refuses to let her do so. The mother perceives this as a threat to her symbiotic tie to her daughter. The mother deals with her daughter's refusal by stating that the daughter must be getting sick again since stubbornness and rebelliousness are signs that something is happening. The daughter accepts the reality of her mother's statements, feeling that something is wrong with her just because her mother said it was true.
Source: Framo, J. (1965). Rationale and techniques of intensive family therapy. In I. Boszormenyi-Nagy & J. Framo (Eds.), *Intensive family therapy: Theoretical and practical aspects* (pp. 143–212). New York: Harper & Row.

reciprocity awareness procedure: A procedure in which each spouse is asked to make a list of behaviors of that spouse's partner that are satisfying. The spouses read their lists in subsequent sessions with the therapist. The procedure is designed to facilitate positive interaction between the spouses.
Source: Azrin, N.H., Naster, B.J., & Jones, R. (1973). Reciprocity counseling: A rapid learning-based procedure for marital counseling. *Behavior Research and Therapy, 11,* 365–382.
Quoted: O'Leary, D., & Turkewitz, H. (1978). Marital therapy from a behavioral perspective. In T. Paolino & B. McCrady (Eds.), *Marriage and marital therapy* (pp. 240–297). New York: Brunner/Mazel.

reconstituted family: A family in which the spouses have custody of their children from previous marriages. Structurally, these families are characterized by a relatively open system regarding the inclusion of members. The family members are not clearly defined, since there may not be a consensus about who is in the family. The family is influenced by a network of people and relationships created through the prior divorce(s) and the formalization of the remarriage. This family network is called the "rem supra system," a system comprising the different individuals and functionally related people (subsystems) who impinge on the reconstituted family. Some of these subsystems may cross two or more households.
Example: Reconstituted families must frequently solve problems that result directly from the "ghosts" of past relationships, from inadequate or incomplete mourning of the lost relationship, or from the complexities of stepkin relationships.
Source: Sager, C., Brown, H., Brohn, H., Engel, T., Rodstein, E., & Walker, L. (1983). *Treating the remarried family.* New York: Brunner/Mazel.
Quoted: Baptiste, D.A. (1983). Family therapy with reconstituted families: A crisis-induction approach. *American Journal of Family Therapy, 11,* 3–9.

recursive language: Language that describes relationships in terms of other relationships. Recursive language is contextual, multicausal, and reciprocal or circular.
Example: A man yells at his wife, who yells back in response. Each influences and is influenced by the other.
Source: Bateson, G. (1978). The birth of a double bind. In M. Berger (Ed.), *Beyond the double bind* (p. 53). New York: Brunner/Mazel.

Quoted: Hoffman, L. (1981). *Foundations of family therapy.* New York: Basic Books.

redefinition: In clinical theory, a shift of perspective from the individual patient to the family system, resulting in a new meaning of the individual symptom. In clinical practice, redefinition may be shared with the family as a reframing of the presenting problem so that individual behaviors may be seen as linked to a meaningful family pattern.
Example: The six-year-old daughter refuses to eat most of the food her mother prepares for her. The therapist redefines her eating difficulty in terms of her older sister excelling in school and gaining all of her mother's positive attention.
Source: Umbarger, C.C. (1984). *Structural family therapy.* New York: Grune & Stratton.

reeducating the inner child: A sex hypnotherapy technique used to treat negative sexual processing. The client imagines that she is a child and that the adult self is bringing her up free of sexual guilt and anxiety.
Source: Araoz, D. (1982). *Hypnosis and sex therapy.* New York: Brunner/Mazel.

referee system: A system in which all family members are subjugated to standards of thought, behavior, and feelings that are pathetically insensitive to their needs. The system does not limit itself to behavioral control; it also disciplines feelings and thoughts, continually trying to bring everyone's inner life into agreement with the rules. In such a family, feelings are rarely expressed spontaneously.
Source: Beavers, W.R. (1977). *Psychotherapy and growth: A family systems perspective.* New York: Brunner/Mazel.

reflected appraisal: The perception of self as shaped by the parts of one's behavior to which others respond, positively or negatively. The child grows in response to shifting social situations as he matures.
Example: In a family, the siblings and parents observe how the oldest child takes charge. The child's friends also see him as a natural leader.
Source: Sullivan, H. (1953). *Interpersonal theory of psychiatry.* New York: Norton.
Quoted: Broderick, C., & Schrader, S. (1981). The history of professional marriage and family therapy. In A. Gurman & D. Kniskern (Eds.), *Handbook of family therapy* (pp. 5–38). New York: Brunner/Mazel.

reframing: Relabeling or redefining a concept or reality so as to give it a slightly different and more constructive perspective. The process by which we label feelings, thoughts, attitudes, behaviors, and events has, in recent years, been recognized by cognitive psychologists as having an extraordinarily significant influence on the way in which we perceive reality. It appears that, to a large extent, we construct our own reality on the basis of the frames or points of view that we impose on our experiences.
Example: If, in talking with a couple about the couple's child-sharing plans in a divorce situation, one spouse says, "I want to keep custody of my children!" the therapist can reframe the statement as, "You would like the children to share a significant amount of time with you." When one spouse says to the other, "You can visit the kids every other weekend," the therapist can reframe it, "The children will be able to share time with their dad for two weekends every month."
Source: Watzlawick, P. (1978). *The language of change: Elements of therapeutic communication.* New York: Basic Books.
Quoted: Marlow, L., & Sauber, S.R. (in press). *Handbook on divorce mediation.* New York: Brunner/Mazel.

reification: The process by which an idea is almost made into a thing, that is, it is false in terms of reality but contains a grain of truth.
Example: The idea that life is precious has been reified in every individual, including in some cases the fetus, in our society.
Source: Bateson, G. (1972). *Steps to an ecology of mind.* New York: Ballantine Books.

reinforcement schedule: The relationship (either temporal or as determined by response frequency) between responding and the occurrence of consequences.
Example: Each time the husband takes his wife shopping, she initiates sexual advances toward him that evening.
Source: Weiss, R. (1978). Marriage from a behavioral perspective. In T. Paolino & B. McCrady (Eds.), *Marriage and marital therapy* (pp. 165–239). New York: Brunner/Mazel.

rejunction: Movement toward trustworthy relatedness. In contextual family therapy, trustworthiness is seen as the basic dynamic among families members.

Example: A husband who strives to enhance his wife's trust in her parents also improves her trust in his familial relationships.
Source: Boszormenyi-Nagy, I., & Ulrich, D. (1981). Contextual family therapy. In A. Gurman & D. Kniskern (Eds.), *Handbook of family therapy* (pp. 159–186). New York: Brunner/Mazel.

relabeling: Changing the label attached to a person or problem without necessarily changing the frame of reference. Relabeling usually involves changing the label from negative to a positive.
Example: A person who is upset because he is confused is told that confusion is part of the preparation required for new growth.
Source: Weeks, G., & L'Abate, L. (1982). *Paradoxical psychotherapy.* New York: Brunner/Mazel.

relapse prediction: A paradoxical intervention in which a client is told that a problem will reappear, thereby reducing the likelihood of its reappearance or of placing it under the therapist's control if it does. This intervention is made only after a successful paradoxical prescription has been given.
Example: A couple stops fighting in response to an intervention. The two partners are then told they may experience a relapse, fighting even more because they have saved up some fights.
Source: Weeks, G., & L'Abate, L. (1982). *Paradoxical psychotherapy.* New York: Brunner/Mazel.

relatedness, expressive: Having "meaningful feelings, i.e., relating on a feeling level."
Source: Wynne, L. (1970, March). *Communication disorders and the quest for relatedness in families of schizophrenics.* Paper presented at the Association for the Advancement of Psychoanalysis, New York.

relatedness, instrumental: Interaction that emphasizes the nonpersonal aspects of a task.
Source: Wynne, L. (1970, March). *Communication disorders and the quest for relatedness in families of schizophrenics.* Paper presented at the Association for the Advancement of Psychoanalysis, New York.

relation: A coding category, devised by Loveland to analyze the Relation Rorschach, that measures the affective stand a speaker takes in relation to other participants and the task.
Source: Loveland, N. (1967). The Relation Rorschach: A technique for studying interaction. *Journal of Nervous and Mental Disease, 142,* 93–105.

Quoted: Riskin, M., & Faunce, E. (1972). An evaluative review of family interaction research. *Family Process, 11,* 365–455.

relational corruption: A situation in which a person is so bound to a legacy of familial corruption that the person feels entitled to be unfair to everybody. In a contextual family therapy session, a person may give a caring response only to be cut down by another who feels entitled to be unfair.
Source: Boszormenyi-Nagy, I., & Ulrich, D. (1981). Contextual family therapy. In A. Gurman & D. Kniskern (Eds.), *Handbook of family therapy* (pp. 159–186). New York: Brunner/Mazel.

relational ethics: Long-term preservation of an oscillating balance of equitable fairness among family members, whereby the basic interests of each member are taken into account by the others. Relational ethics is a focus in contextual family therapy.
Source: Boszormenyi-Nagy, I., & Ulrich, D. (1981). Contextual family therapy. In A. Gurman & D. Kniskern (Eds.), *Handbook of family therapy* (pp. 159–186). New York: Brunner/Mazel.

relational need templates: Projecting the inner need confirmation onto a legal relationship. A real (interpersonal) relationship passes through a period of adjustment—on the one hand, between each person's relational need templates and, on the other hand, between each person's internal and real demands. The internal relational need template (or its fitting object) may or may not be consciously represented in a patient's mind.
Example: Paranoid hallucinations may be projected onto real others in the process of trying to relate to them.
Source: Boszormenyi-Nagy, I. (1965). A theory of relationships: Experience and transaction. In I. Boszormenyi-Nagy & J. Framo (Eds.), *Intensive family therapy: Theoretical and practical aspects* (pp. 33–86). New York: Harper & Row.

relational stagnation: In contextual family therapy, familial disengagement from concern about fairness, thereby blocking out moves toward greater trust.
Example: A husband demands that his wife contribute to the family equally in financial terms, although it is impossible for her to do so.
Source: Boszormenyi-Nagy, I., & Ulrich, D. (1981). Contextual family therapy. In A. Gurman & D. Kniskern (Eds.), *Handbook of family therapy* (pp. 159–186). New York: Brunner/Mazel.

relationship enhancement: A method to help couples and families deal with problems more effectively. Participants are taught to (1) express clearly their feelings and thoughts, (2) accept the expressions of others, (3) facilitate and criticize their own communication skills, and (4) discuss constructive resolutions of conflicts.
Source: Guerney, B. (1977). *Relationship enhancement.* San Francisco: Jossey-Bass.
Quoted: L'Abate, L., & McHenry, S. (1983). *Handbook of marital interventions.* New York: Grune & Stratton.

remarried (REM) family: A blended or reconstituted family or a stepfamily that is formed by the marriage or living together of two adults—one or both widowed or divorced—with their custodial or visiting children.
Source: Sager, C., Brown, H., Crohn, H., Engel, T., Rodstein, E., & Walker, L. (1983). *Treating the remarried family.* New York: Brunner/Mazel.

replacement partner: The partner of choice brought by a sexually inadequate unmarried man or woman to share the experiences and the education of a sex therapy program.
Source: Masters, W., & Johnson, V. (1970). *Human sexual adequacy.* Boston: Little, Brown.

replay: A scenario in which a couple presents a frustrating discussion or hostile argument they had during the week and are asked to replay the sequence. The therapist interrupts the interaction to help the spouses pinpoint the destructive behaviors that contributed to the negative chain, and the couple is asked to generate alternative responses that would be more productive.
Source: O'Leary, K., & Turkewitz, H. (1978). Marital therapy from a behavioral perspective. In T. Paolino & B. McCrady (Eds.), *Marriage and marital therapy* (pp. 240–297). New York: Brunner/Mazel.

report level: The verbal message of a communication, especially the dictionary meaning of the words.
Example: A wife asks her husband to tell their son to assist his sister in completing her homework from school.
Source: Haley, J. (1959). An interactional description of schizophrenia. *Psychiatry, 22,* 321–332.
Quoted: Barnard, C., & Corrales, R. (1979). *The theory and technique of family therapy.* Springfield, Ill.: Charles C Thomas.

representational system: The manner in which one typically represents or interprets one's input into a system. Input may be interpreted kinesthetically, visually, or auditorily. In order to increase rapport with a client, the therapist tries to match the client's dominant representational system.
Example: A client says, "I see," repeatedly and is thus visually oriented. The therapist decides to use visual verbs in talking with this person, i.e., "Let's get a clear picture of this problem."
Source: Grinder, J., & Bandler, R. (1976). *The structure of magic* (Vol. 2). Palo Alto, Calif.: Science and Behavior Books.
Quoted: Weeks, G., & L'Abate, L. (1982). *Paradoxical psychotherapy.* New York: Brunner/Mazel.

rescue games: Situations in which one member of the original family triad always agrees, a second member always disagrees, and a third's statements are always irrelevant. In most interactional systems, the same person plays by the same rule most of the time.
Source: Satir, V. (1967). *Conjoint family therapy.* Palo Alto, Calif.: Science and Behavior Books.

resistance: Any block to change. Resistance has been seen as "located" in the client; it has been described as something the client is doing rather than as a product of client-therapist interaction, a result of splitting the ecosystem by placing the boundary between therapist and client, thus creating "imaginary oppositions" between the two components of the ecosystem. However, resistance also includes some of the therapist's behavior in the situation. The therapist may suggest that clients withhold—and they do. The therapist may also suggest that they tell—and they do. But they withhold and tell responsively. Thus, as long as they are going to withhold, the therapist ought to encourage them to withhold. Psychoanalytically oriented therapists see resistance as a transference reaction, while systemic therapists view it as the therapist's poor choice of an intervention.
Example: (1) In more than one sense, this form of problem resolution is similar to the philosophy and technique of judo, where the opponent's thrust is not opposed by a counterthrust of at least the same force, but rather is accepted and amplified by yielding to and going with it. This the opponent does not expect; he is playing the game of force against force, of more of the same, and by the rules of his game he anticipates a counterthrust and not a different game altogether. (2) In a therapeutic context, resistance can be illustrated by a situation in which a patient explains how busy he is at work and says he can't do something suggested by the therapist, even

though he thinks the therapist's suggestion is a good one.
Source: Erickson, M.H., & Rossi, E. (1979). *Hypnotherapy: An exploratory casebook.* New York: Irvington.
Quoted: de Shazer, S. (1982). *Patterns of brief family therapy: An approach.* New York: Guilford Press.

resolution phase: The fourth and final stage of the sexual response cycle, characterized by the body returning to its normal unstimulated state. During this phase, no amount of sexual stimulation can initiate sexual excitement in the male. The length of the resolution phase varies greatly and extends with age.
Source: Masters, W., & Johnson, V. (1970). *Human sexual adequacy.* Boston: Little, Brown.

resource exchange theory: A theory developed by Foa and Foa (1974) that stipulates six categories or classes of resources that are exchanged between and among people: (1) love, (2) status, (3) money, (4) possessions, (5) services, and (6) information. L'Abate, Sloan, Wagner, and Malone (1980) reduced these to three: being (love and status), having (money and possessions), and doing (information and services). Most interpersonal and family dysfunctions derive from deficits and disturbances in being.
Source: Foa, U., and Foa, M. (1974). *Societal structures of the mind.* Springfield, Ill.: Charles C Thomas.
Quoted: L'Abate, L., Sloan, S.Z., Wagner, V., and Malone, K. (1980). The differentiation of resources. *Family Therapy, 7,* 237–246.

resource theory: A theory based on three major assumptions: (1) "Every individual is continually attempting to satisfy his needs and desires to attain goals"; (2) "Most of the individual's needs are satisfied through social interaction with other persons or groups"; and (3) "During this interaction, there is a continual exchange of 'resources' which contribute to the satisfaction of individual need; and to the attainment of individual or group goals." The theory asserts that "the balance of power (in decision-making) will be on the side of the partner who contributes the greatest resources to the marriage." The family member with the greatest command of resources to meet another's needs and goals is defined as having the greater power. The basic idea is that one person possesses resources that are instrumental to the attainment of another person's goals, needs, desires, or interests.

Example: In desiring the economic resources that the husband provides, but lacking the opportunities to gain those resources in other ways, women relinquish power to (and freedom from) their husbands in order to fulfill their needs.
Source: Cromwell, E., & Olson, D.H. (1975). *Power in families.* New York: Halsted Press.

respondent: A person who is responding under the control of an eliciting stimulus and therefore responds "on call," i.e., the frequency of the stimulus equals the frequency of the response.
Example: Whenever a wife looks depressed the husband becomes angry and wants to know what he has done wrong. His response has become conditioned to her depressions.
Source: Weiss, R. (1978). Marriage from a behavioral perspective. In T. Paolino & B. McCrady (Eds.), *Marriage and marital therapy* (pp. 165–239). New York: Brunner/Mazel.

response cost: The taking away of positive reinforcers from an individual's pool of available reinforcers when a specific undesirable behavior occurs.
Example: Each time a boy strikes a match, one penny is removed from a stack of pennies which has been given.
Source: LeBow, M. (1972). Behavior modification for the family. In G. Erickson & T. Hogan (Eds.), *Family therapy: An introduction to theory and technique* (pp. 347–376). Belmont, Calif.: Wadsworth.

restraining: A paradoxical intervention in which the therapist keeps the client from change. There are several ways to restrain change. The therapist can (1) point out the negative consequences of change, even though the client might define them as positive; (2) inhibit and forbid change; (3) predict and prescribe a relapse; or (4) declare that change is hopeless. The underlying message in a restraining statement is, "In order to change, stay the same or give up." This type of intervention may be used at any point in therapy, but it is recommended after the use of symptom prescription.
Example: A client enters therapy, stating that her main problem is doing the opposite of what everyone tells her to do. She acts as if she wants to stop this pattern immediately and completely. The therapist forbids her to change by stating that an abrupt change would be too painful. Hence, she is permitted to cooperate with another on only one small request. By implication, her spontaneous opposition to another's requests is prescribed, which places it under her voluntary control.

Source: Rohrbaugh, M., Tennen, H., Press, S., White, L., Raskin, P., & Pickering, M. (1977, August). *Paradoxical strategies in psychotherapy.* Paper presented at the American Psychological Association, San Francisco.
Quoted: Weeks, G., & L'Abate, L. (1982). *Paradoxical psychotherapy.* New York: Brunner/Mazel.

retribalization: A basic strategy of network therapy in which a large number of people who have some connection to a troubled family are brought together to help reestablish network ties.
Source: Speck, R., & Attneave, C. (1973). *Family networks.* New York: Pantheon Books.

revealed differences: The result of a technique by which subjects who have shared experiences are asked to make individual evaluations of them and then to reconcile any differences in interpretations that may have occurred. By presenting only one of two alternatives for problems that require commitment, personal involvement is maximized, the possibility of compromise on a given question is perceived, and a simple way is provided to determine who has "won" a given decision.
Source: Strodtbeck, F. (1954). The family as a three-person group. *American Sociological Review, 19,* 23–29.

revivification: A sex hypnotherapy technique that is used to treat sexual desire dysfunction. The client is requested to replay an old sexual experience that was very pleasant.
Source: Araoz, D. (1982). *Hypnosis and sex therapy.* New York: Brunner/Mazel.

revolving slate: A legacy of patterns repeated from one generation to the next. From the viewpoint of contextual family therapy, the revolving slate is a chief factor in marital and familial dysfunction.
Example: A parent abandons his children because he too was abandoned.
Source: Boszormenyi-Nagy, I., & Ulrich, D. (1982). Contextual family therapy. In A. Gurman and D. Kniskern (Eds.), *Handbook of family therapy* (pp. 159–187). New York: Brunner/Mazel.

rigid complementarity: A relationship based on inequality, e.g., doctor-patient, well one-sick one. This type of relationship is usually based on the traditions of the culture. It is a highly dysfunctional interaction in which one person disconfirms the other by making a disinterested, illogical, irrelevant, or contradictory statement.

Example: The husband says to his wife, "Do you care how I feel?" The wife responds, "Well, I'm just so upset about everything these days."
Source: Watzlawick, P., Weakland, J., & Fisch, R. (1967). *Pragmatics of human communication.* New York: Norton.
See also **neurotic complementarity.**

rigid family: A family that permits only very stereotyped and limited interactions, in which the patient's personality is usually an extension of that of one of the parents.
Source: Alanen, Y. (1958). The mothers of schizophrenic patients. *Acta Psychiatry Neurological Scandinavian Supplement, 12*(4), 124.
Quoted: Fleck, S. (1972). An approach to family pathology. In G. Erickson & T. Hogan (Eds.), *Family therapy. An introduction to theory and technique* (pp. 103–119). Belmont, Calif.: Wadsworth.

rigid triad: A family triangle in which members are locked into pathogenic roles. In structured family therapy, triads include triangulations, parent-child coalitions, detouring attacking coalitions, and detouring supportive coalitions.
Source: Minuchin, S., Rosman, B., & Baker, L. (1978). *Psychosomatic families.* Cambridge, Mass.: Harvard University Press.

role complementarity: The assumption that a role does not exist in isolation but is always patterned to gear in with the complementary or reciprocal role of a role partner. Spiegel notes that role complementarity is chiefly responsible for the degree of harmony and stability that exists in interpersonal relations. He cites five causes for the failure to develop complementarity in role systems within the family: (1) cognitive discrepancy, (2) discrepancy of goals, (3) allocative discrepancy, (4) instrumental discrepancy, and (5) discrepancy in cultural value orientations.
Source: Spiegel, J. (1971). *Transactions.* New York: Science House.

role conflict: Conflict arising from disparities between family members' perceptions of each other's roles. Each member has a conception of that member's role in the family. A father may follow his father's example and be a strict disciplinarian. He may consider his role in the context of his assets and competencies. For example, he may regard his wife as a more efficient manager than himself and delegate to her the tasks of budgeting the family income. He may still regard this as his function, but he delegates those tasks to her because of a realistic consideration of his own limitations.

Each family member also has a conception of the roles of the other members. Such conceptions are based on factors similar to those affecting one's conception of one's own role—family or origin, sexual identification, sense of personal identity, and social expectations. However, one's conception of one's own role and the conceptions of other members of that role may differ. In some families, the roles are complementary, and the family functions adequately. But, if the family lacks complementarity, conflict becomes highly probable.

Families deal with conflict in one or more ways. The conflict may be:

- expressed openly and resolved through normal channels of communication
- recognized but obscured through patterns of communication that conceal or evade conflict
- expressed by acting out problems rather than through a rational consideration of solutions
- projected upon a member in the form of a neurotic or psychotic disorder
- evaded by limiting or avoiding physical or psychological contact with members

Sources: Thorman, G. (1965). *Family therapy: A handbook.* Beverly Hills, Calif.: Western Psychological Services; Stuart, R.B. (1980). *Helping couples change.* New York: Guilford Press.

role cycling: Attempts by couples to mesh the demands of their individual career cycles with the changing responsibilities of the different family life cycle stages. Many dual-career couples attempt to avoid additional strain by staggering their career and family cycles so that peak career and family stress times do not occur simultaneously.
Example: The husband tries to cycle his role at work, given his new promotion and the added responsibilities stemming from the birth of his second child.
Source: McCubbin, H.I., & Figley, C.R. (1983). *Stress and the family: Coping with normative transitions* (Vol. 1). New York: Brunner/Mazel.

role equilibrium: The family is a small-scale system that is constantly shifting its equilibrium. When there is role equilibrium, decision making takes place at a low level, events tend to occur in automatic fashion, and there is considerable spontaneity in family members interacting with each other. When complementarity fails through role conflict,

the interpersonal relations move toward disequilibrium. The failure of complementarity is so disruptive that it is almost always accompanied by processes of restoration or reequilibrium, e.g., role reversal, coercion, coaxing, or postponement.
Source: Spiegel, J. (1971). *Transactions.* New York: Science House.

role induction: Changing another's concept of a role—e.g., by coaxing, coercing, masking, evaluating, or postponing—in order to induce complementarity.
Source: Spiegel, J. (1971). *Transactions.* New York: Science House.

role induction interview: This pretherapy training procedure is used for couples in order to prepare them for conjoint therapy by providing a general explanation of the process, as well as a description and exposition of the behavior expected of the patient and therapist, and by preparing them for such typical therapeutic phenomena as resistance and induction expectancies or improvement within several months. The session may take place with one couple or as many as five couples.
Example: The husband did not want to participate in therapy because he believed his wife had the problem. His wife said they could overcome their difficulties if he would attend one or two sessions. The therapist requested that the couple attend a group role induction interview in order for the couple to learn to be more realistic about marital and individual therapy and experience what other couples are questioning and wish to achieve.
Source: Sauber, S.R. (1972). Patient training prior to entering psychotherapy. *Social Psychiatry, 7,* 139–143.

role model: An individual whose behavior in a particular role provides a pattern or model upon which another individual bases behavior in performing the same role.
Example: An ex-alcoholic is a role model for a recovering alcoholic.
Source: Amaranto, E. (1971). Glossary. In H. Kaplan & B. Sadock (Eds.), *Comprehensive group psychotherapy* (pp. 823–872). Baltimore: Williams & Wilkins.

role modification: A therapeutic technique to produce a change that will induce complementarity, e.g., by exploring, compromising, or consolidating or by referral to a third party.
Example: A husband feels he has fulfilled his marital role simply by bringing home the paycheck. He and his wife consult a therapist, who helps them

reach a compromise over how much and what kind of housework the husband can or should do.

Source: Spiegel, J. (1957). The resolution of role conflict within the family. *Psychiatry, 20,* 1–16.

Quoted: Foley, V. (1974). *An introduction to family therapy.* New York: Grune & Stratton.

role playing: An action technique in which family members act out a problem. The essence of role playing is "making believe" that the situation is real—i.e., acting in a spontaneous manner. Role playing is useful when other techniques have been ineffective in families that operate on an intellectual level.

Example: A couple has an argument every day when the husband arrives home from work. The couple plays this scene in the therapist's office so that the therapist can observe the patterns of interaction.

Source: Satir, V. (1957). *Conjoint family therapy.* Palo Alto, Calif.: Science and Behavior Books.

role reversal: The exchange of roles with another family member to facilitate seeing the other member's viewpoint and to increase empathy between the members. Role reversal enables the individual who has played one role to move into the other role and demonstate how that individual would like to have been treated. If the role reversal takes place during the enactment, it is known as "switching." Role reversal may also occur when a passive partner is allowed to assume the role of the dominant partner.

Example: Exchange of roles in switching when father/mother and son/daughter interact, and father and mother change roles, to father/daughter and mother/son there is a role reversal among the family members during the course of action. In some family scenes, members may switch roles several times. The daughter said the vacation was too expensive. The son complained about how boring his household duties were.

Source: Corsini, R.J. (1966). *Role playing in psychotherapy: A manual.* Chicago: Aldine.

role reversal theory: A theory that postulates that, in schizophrenogenic families, the mother usurps the father's role as the authority figure in the household. Role reversal theory derives from the clinical tradition of working with families with a schizophrenic member.

Source: Lidz, T., Fleck, S., & Cornelison, A. (1965). Family studies and a theory of schizophrenia. In T. Lidz, S. Fleck, & A. Cornelison (Eds.), *Schizophrenia and the family*

(pp. 362–376). New York: International Universities Press.

role strain: Stress produced by confronting a task that has not been a part of one's normal role.

Example: A new single-parent mother takes her son to a baseball practice where all of the other boys have been brought by their fathers.

Source: Goode, W. (1960). A theory of role. *American Sociological Review, 25,* 423–496.

Quoted: Blechman, E.A., & Manning, M. (1976). A reward-cost analysis of the single-parent family. In E.L. Mash, L. Hamerlynck, & L. Handy (Eds.), *Behavior modification and families* (pp. 61–90). New York: Brunner/Mazel.

role theory: A theory that focuses on role functioning in the study and analysis of family disorders. The following concepts of role theory are incorporated in family therapy.

- An individual has a fairly well-defined role in the family. This role involves obligations to be met and expectations to be fulfilled.
- There may be confusion in identifying, accepting, or enacting roles.
- Conflict in roles may result. For example, a wife may assume responsibility for disciplining the children, while the husband may regard this function as part of his role as father.
- Roles may be complementary.
- Roles may be stereotyped and inflexible.
- Family therapy aims at the modification of role functioning. The achievement of complementarity helps the family to achieve a balance of role functioning so as to maximize the mutual gratification of needs and opportunities for growth.

Sources: Thorman, G. (1965). *Family therapy: A handbook.* Beverly Hills, Calif.: Western Psychological Services; Glick, I.D., & Kessler, D.P. (1980). *Marital and family therapy* (2nd ed.). New York: Grune & Stratton.

roles: The expected behaviors of family members. For example, Mom is the caretaker, Dad is the breadwinner, the daughter Cindy is the clown, and the daughter Julie is the peacemaker. Sociologists divide roles into two basic types: achieved and ascribed. Ascribed roles are assigned on the basis of factors over which the individual has no control, for example, sex and race. Achieved roles are earned on the basis of individual achievement, for example, becoming a boss, peacemaker, breadwinner, or scapegoat. The two kinds of roles overlap in families. However, family role structure is often so obscured in its early development that the family members may not know the origins of their roles, and they may feel trapped in them.

Role differentiation is important as a defensive effort to restore a sense of self in families. The cost of such differentiation to both the individual and the family is that, in order to remain a part of the family yet still have individually unique qualities, the individual may distort or simplify personal emotions. Each member experiences pressure to be both a unique individual and a valued member of the family.

Source: Hoopes, M.H., Fisher, B.L., and Barlow, S.H. (1984). *Structured family facilitation programs: Enrichment, education, and treatment.* Rockville, Md.: Aspen Systems Corp.

romantic concepts: Concepts that lead to unrealistic and false expectations, and thus to subsequent disillusionment.

Source: Crosby, J. (1976). *Illusion and disillusion in marriage* (2nd ed.). Belmont, Calif.: Wadsworth.

romantic success: A problem symbolically equated with the dangerous competition for sex and power that the patient experienced with the same gender parent in the oedipal situation. Most persons who suffer from success problems show evidence of unresolved oedipal problems.

Source: Kaplan, H. (1979). *Disorders of sexual desire.* New York: Brunner/Mazel.

rosaphrenia: A psychosexual disorder common to women that is characterized by inadequate sexual psychology, exaggeration of sexual tendencies, and inability to achieve orgasm. Self-worth exists in the woman's sexuality, and she reacts passively or aggressively to that perception by adopting attitudes and behaviors typical of frigidity or nymphomania. Her manner of dress and behavior usually either exaggerates or masks feminine attributes. The rosaphrenian woman can be identified by her stereotypical female roles—for example, the ultimately feminine secretarial type who dresses to provoke male admiration, or the matronly type who looks and acts as if she has nothing to do with sex or men.

Example: A woman who promises sexual favors for economic or social gain or who withholds sex as punishment for her mate.

Source: Baisden, M. (1971). *The world of rosaphrenia: The sexual psychology of the female.* Sacramento, Calif.: Allied Research Society.

Quoted: Baisden, M., & Baisden, J. (1979). A profile of women who seek counseling for sexual dysfunctions. *American Journal of Family Therapy, 7,* 62–76.

rotary depression: Feelings of dysphoria that seem to rotate among family members in a way that may be used to predict which family member other than the nominal patient may become either an identified patient requiring special help or a particularly strong resource in the family. Rotary depression is viewed as a part of a natural self-rehabilitation process by which a family rids itself of obsolete mechanisms and its members return to accessibility to outside stimuli. It is a cooperative process that serves as a natural model from depression through grief.

Source: MacGregor, R., Ritchie, A., Serrano, A., & Schuster, F. (1964). *Multiple impact therapy with families.* New York: McGraw-Hill.

roundtable discussion: A therapeutic technique used to summarize the facts that have been obtained in separate interviews involving both marital partners and the cotherapists.

Source: Masters, W., & Johnson, V. (1970). *Human sexual adequacy.* Boston: Little, Brown.

rubber fence: Lyman Wynne's term for the family's collective and unconscious dynamic equilibrium between the intense need to maintain a collective ego (symbiotic ego) and the members' strivings for individuality. In schizophrenic families, the members act as if they are a self-sufficient social system with completely encircling boundaries. In a rubber fence situation, the persons who do not follow family rules (myths) are experienced as psychologically excluded. The specific location of the family's boundaries may shift, as if made of rubber, always encircling but without clearly defined gates for entry or exit.

Source: Wynne, L., Ryckoff, I., Day, J., & Hirsch, S. (1952). Pseudomutuality in the family relations of schizophrenics. *Psychiatry, 21,* 204–220.

Quoted: Searles, H. (1965). The contribution of family treatment to the psychotherapy of schizophrenia. In I. Boszormenyi-Nagy & J. Framo (Eds.), *Intensive family therapy: Theoretical and practical aspects* (pp. 463–496). New York: Harper & Row.

rule: A persistent patterning in family interactions, deviation from which evokes awareness that something new has occurred. Some rules are intentionally announced and followed, as in a family that describes itself as "close-knit and without fighting." The more important rules, however, are often outside of the family's awareness and are composed of the repetitive behaviors that make up the routines of daily family life.

Example: The children are not allowed t᾽ watch TV until they complete their homework.

Source: Umbarger, C.C. (1984). *Structural family therapy.* New York: Grune & Stratton.

runaway technique: A crisis-inducing therapeutic maneuver that brings about a positive feedback process. The family symptom is so escalated that a breakdown or a blowup in the family system results, and the family is then ready for change.

Example: A wife is suspicious every time her husband leaves the house. She does not tell her husband directly about her suspicions, but expresses them indirectly. The therapist directs her to be overtly suspicious and to ask "20 questions" when he returns home in order to precipitate a crisis.

Source: Haley, J. (1963). *Strategies of psychotherapy.* New York: Grune & Stratton.

S

sabotage: A marital partner's subtle reinforcement of a spouse's dysfunction in ways that are not apparent to the sabotaging partner, due to the latter's unconscious fears or underlying conflicts.

Example: A man tells his wife that he wants her to initiate sex, but when she tries he finds a reason for not being interested.

Source: Kaplan, H. (1974). *The new sex therapy.* New York: Brunner/Mazel.

saint syndrome: A situation in which the entire family agrees that a particular family member is more gracious, more loving, more generous, and more self-sacrificing than any ordinary mortal. The family member is assumed to possess no negative traits and to be capable of an even better performance if the member were not surrounded by less worthy people.

Example: A father is a physician who is worshipped by his patients. At home, he is greatly admired by his family members, who assume the roles of either children or sinners.

Source: Beavers, W.R. (1977). *Psychotherapy and growth.* New York: Brunner/Mazel.

say-ask rule: The principle that, when a question must be asked, it is best for it to be preceded by a self-statement. This increases the level of responsibility the speaker assumes for the messages the speaker sends and thus lowers the need for defensiveness on the part of the listener.

Example: The husband says to his wife, "I have the feeling you don't want to go. What would you like to do?"

Source: Baruth, L.G., & Huber, C.H. (1984). *An introduction to marital theory and therapy.* Monterey, Calif.: Brooks/Cole.

scapegoating: A process in which an external target—a spouse, child, or parent—is chosen by members of a family system to assume responsibility for whatever is wrong in the system. The scapegoat not only assumes and accepts this role but often becomes so entrenched as to be unable to behave otherwise.

Example: A mother and father cannot deal with the anger they experience in their marriage. They begin to blame their child for all kinds of misconduct in order to ventilate their anger.

Sources: Ackerman, N. (1966). *Treating the troubled family.* New York: Basic Books; Vogel, S.E., & Bell, N. (1960). The emotionally disturbed child as family scapegoat. In N. Bell & S.E. Vogel (Eds.), *A modern introduction to the family* (pp. 382–397). Glencoe, Ill.: Free Press.

Quoted: L'Abate, L., Weeks, G., & Weeks, K. (1979). Of scapegoats, strawmen, and scarecrows. *International Journal of Family Counseling, 1,* 86–96.

schism: (1) A relationship marked by failure to achieve mutuality, with a consequent outbreak of unresolved conflict and a chronic state of marital separation at the emotional level. This situation is eventually transmitted or projected upon the children. The spouses' status and worth are undercut, and there is a tendency to compete for and to form alliances with the children, thereby breaching generational boundaries. (2) A relationship marked by chronic failure to achieve complementarity of purpose or role reciprocity or by excessive attachment of the children to the parental home. In the latter case, the attachment is used to delay or prevent the threatened breakup of the marriage. It thus becomes a rescue maneuver on the part of the children.

Source: Lidz, T., Fleck, S., & Cornelison, A. (1965). *Schizophrenia and the family.* New York: International Universities Press.

schismatic coalition: A family pattern in which the marital coalition is absent or relatively weak and in which strong alliances exist across the generations and sexes.
Example: The marital partners have an emotionally distant relationship but feel close to their opposite sex children.
Source: Glick, I., & Kessler, D. (1974). *Marital and family therapy.* New York: Grune & Stratton.

schismatic family: A family in which the parents fill complementary roles, undercut each other, and compete for the children. The family is in two camps, and the identified patient cannot use one parent as a model for identification or as a love object without losing the support of the other parent. There are two types of schismatic families. In one, the marital coalition is weak or absent and there are strong alliances across the generations and sexes. In the other type, there are cross-generational alliances between same-sexed parent and child.
Source: Lidz, T., Fleck, S., & Cornelison, D. (1965). *Schizophrenia and the family.* New York: International Universities Press.

schizogenia: A pathologic process that occurs in the family. In contrast, schizophrenia denotes a psychotic disorder in the individual.
Source: Rubinstein, D. (1960, January). *The family of the schizophrenic.* Paper read at the Second Cuban Congress of Neurology and Psychiatry, Havana.
Quoted: Zuk, G., & Rubinstein, D. (1965). A review of concepts in the study and treatment of families of schizophrenia. In I. Boszormenyi-Nagy & J. Framo (Eds.), *Intensive family therapy: Theoretical and practical aspects* (pp. 1–32). New York: Harper & Row.

schizophrenic omnipotence: Assumption by a primary patient of the exalted position, power, and privileges accorded a superparent. The price paid by the patient is a burden of guilt so overwhelming that it helps to bring about ego disruption.
Example: The schizophrenic assumes the position of master decision maker in the family.
Source: Framo, J. (1965). Systematic research on family dynamics. In I. Boszormenyi-Nagy & J. Framo (Eds.), *Intensive family therapy: Theoretical and practical aspects* (pp. 407–463). New York: Harper & Row.

schizophrenogenic mother: A mother in a schizophrenic family who is aggressive, domineering, insecure, and rejecting. This type of mother is viewed as an important causal factor in the development of schizophrenia. In a family with a schizophrenogenic mother, the father is seen as inadequate, passive, and indifferent.
Source: Fromm-Reichmann, F. (1948). Notes on the development of schizophrenia by psychoanalytic psychotherapy. *Psychiatry, 11,* 267–277.
Quoted: Zuk, G., & Rubinstein, D. (1965). A review of concepts in the study and treatment of families of schizophrenics. In I. Boszormenyi-Nagy & J. Framo (Eds.), *Intensive family therapy: Theoretical and practical aspects* (pp. 1–32). New York: Harper & Row.

script: In transactional analysis, a life plan formulated from what one experiences as a child and from decisions made under stress. A script limits spontaneity and flexibility in problem solving and in relating to people because the story, including all the major events and the ending, has already been written in early childhood. In essence, the script answers the question, "What does a person like me do in a family like this with people like you?"
Example: A mother says to the child, "You don't need anything," and the child accepts it literally, developing a life plan of denying wants and needs. Or the message can be inferred, as when a boy whose father continually ignores him concludes that the father is saying to him, "Don't exist."
Source: Erskine, R.G. (1982). Transactional analysis and family therapy. In A.M. Horne & M.M. Ohlsen (Eds.), *Family counseling and therapy* (pp. 245–275). Itasca, Ill.: F.E. Peacock Publishers.

sculpting: A technique in which family members are molded during the therapy session into positions symbolizing their actual relationships as seen by one or more members of the family. Through the sculpturing process, past events and attitudes as they affect the present are immediately and directly perceived and experienced. The sculpting inevitably provides new meanings, and new imagery of family relations in a way that verbal sharing alone cannot.
Example: A fragmented family is sculpted in such a way that the members are placed in different parts of a room facing different directions, or even in different rooms.
Source: Duhl, K., Kantor, D., & Duhl, B. (1973). Learning, space and action in family therapy. A primer of sculpture. In D. Bloch (Eds.), *Techniques of family psychotherapy* (pp. 47–63). New York: Grune & Stratton.

Quoted: Gerson, M., & Barsky, M. (1979). For the new family therapist: A glossary of terms. *American Journal of Family Therapy, 7,* 15–30.

secondary gain: A secondary advantage arising from an illness or symptom presentation, such as gratification of depending yearnings or attention seeking. A secondary gain offers a way of obtaining some particular intrafamilial benefit.
Example: When the husband comes home from work, his wife complains of chronic back pain in order to get him to assist her in household chores and thereby pay attention to her.
Source: Framo, J. (1965). Rationale and techniques of intensive family therapy. In I. Boszormenyi-Nagy & J. Framo (Eds.), *Intensive family therapy* (pp. 143–212). New York: Harper & Row.

secondary locus: The part of a system that supports, but is not essential to, the generation and maintenance of a problem.
Example: Each time the husband and wife engage in an upsetting disagreement, the wife confides in her neighbor, who provides the wife support and reassurance of her correct position.
Source: Aponte, H., & Van Deusen, J. (1981). Structural family therapy. In A. Gurman & D. Kniskern (Eds.), *Handbook of family therapy* (pp. 310–360). New York: Brunner/Mazel.

second-order change: A change in the frame of reference or system itself.
Example: Moving from a dream state to a working state; in therapy, defining a symptom as something that is "good" rather than "sick" or "bad."
Source: Watzlawick, P., Weakland, J., & Fisch, R. (1967). *Pragmatics of human communication.* New York: Norton.
Quoted: Weeks, L., & L'Abate, L. (1982). *Paradoxical psychotherapy.* New York: Brunner/ Mazel.

secrets in the family: Include those that are acknowledged as actual events by a family member who keeps them secret from others, and those that have no such factual foundation. The latter arise from fantasies that cannot be expressed due to feelings from a time when jealousy, rivalry, love, and hate within one family were faced. Such secrets may be unconsciously shared by parents and children for generations and are sometimes difficult to distinguish from family myths. There are open and closed secrets in the family that determine group behavior.
Source: Pincus, L., & Dare, C. (1978). *Secrets in the family.* New York: Pantheon Books.

self-blamer: One who accepts the blame for something without being able to look outside one's self.
Example: Two people are equally responsible for an embarrassing situation. The self-blamer thinks, "If I had not been so awkward, this would not have happened."
Source: Bowen, M. (1965). Family psychotherapy with schizophrenia in the hospital and in private practice. In I. Boszormenyi-Nagy & J. Framo (Eds.), *Intensive family therapy: Theoretical and practical aspects* (pp. 213–244). New York: Harper & Row.

self-concept: "The organized, consistent conceptual gestalt composed of perceptions of the characteristics of the 'I' or 'me' and the perceptions of the relationships of the 'I' or 'me' to others and to various aspects of life, together with the values attached to these perceptions." Thus, the self-concept involves a changing and fluid process. In general, self-experiences are the raw material from which the organized self-concept is formed. The ideal self is "the self-concept which the individual would most like to possess, upon which he places the highest value for himself."
Source: Rogers, C.P. (1959). A theory of therapy, personality and interpersonal relationships, as developed in the client-centered framework. In S. Koch (Ed.), *Psychology: A study of a science: vol. 3. Formulations of the person and the social context* (pp. 184–256). New York: McGraw-Hill.
Quoted: Thayer, L. (1982). A person-centered approach to family therapy. In A.M. Horne & M.M. Ohlsen (Eds.), *Family counseling and therapy* (pp. 175–213). Itasca, Ill.: F.F. Peacock Publishers.

self-confrontation: A technique that forcibly provides one with a means by which one can observe the supportive or maladaptive impact one makes on others and the types of stimuli that provoke different responses from oneself, e.g., videotape or playback of sound recordings.
Example: A mother who constantly interrupts her husband is unaware of her behavior. Audio playback is used to enhance her awareness.
Source: Paul, N. (1972). Effects of playback on family members of their own previously recorded conjoint therapy material. In G. Erickson & T. Hogan (Eds.), *Family therapy: An introduction to theory and technique* (pp. 251–264). Belmont, Calif.: Wadsworth.

self-control: A psychological process that, in cases where there is conflict between possible behavioral choices, involves behavioral shifts in which external influences are supplemented by self-generated cues and reinforcers. The outcome of the process is either that (1) the probability of a response with initial high likelihood of occurrence is decreased, or that (2) the probability of a response with initially low likelihood is increased by the execution of self-generated behaviors. Usually, the initial behaviors are well-established by prior learning, have been supported for a long time by immediate reinforcement, or have been maintained by socially or physiologically determined contingencies. Self-control (also called self-management) methods are used to train individuals to become better problem solvers and behavior analysts by becoming more independent of their immediate environment and other persons.

Example: An alcohol-prone man passes up a drink so that he can later boast to his spouse about his major feat of self-management. However, he thereby demonstrates not self-control but a choice between a lesser (alcohol) and a major (attention by a significant other) reinforcement.

Source: Kanfer, F.H. (1977). The many faces of self-control or behavior modification changes its focus. In R.B. Stuart (Ed.), *Behavioral self-management* (pp. 1–48). New York: Brunner/Mazel.

self-destruction (continuum of): Addicts show high death rates, shorter than average life expectancies, and greater than normal incidences of sudden deaths. Addicts view death as more positive and potent than pain and are more likely to express a wish for it than do other psychiatric patients. Family members state that they would rather see the addict dead than lost to people outside the family. There seems to be a contract within these families in which the addict's part is to die or come close to death. The addict becomes the martyr who sacrifices himself at the family's behest. The addict's behavior may be viewed as part of an unresolved family mourning process.

Source: Shanton, M.D., Todd, T.C., & Associates. (1982). *The family therapy of drug abuse and addiction.* New York: Guilford Press.

self-differentiation: The process of becoming a clearly defined individual with well-defined ego boundaries. A self-differentiated person is a mature person who is a contained emotional unit. Once differentiated, the person can be emotionally close to family members and other people without fusing into a new emotional oneness.

Example: Although the 20-year-old son still resides with his parents while attending a local college, he is able to assert himself emotionally, financially, and socially in an independent way with his parents.

Source: Bowen, M. (1976). Theory and practice in psychotherapy. In P. Guerin (Ed.), *Family therapy.* New York: Gardner Press.

self-disclosure: The process of revealing personal information, particularly of an intimate nature, such as revelations of past-life material, current feelings, moments of happiness and pride, sexual urges, fears, weaknesses, feelings of inadequacy and personal goals, and wishes and plans.

Example: After 11 years of marriage his wife revealed some of her childhood fears that helped him understand why she would not walk around her own home or outside of her home without wearing makeup. She had never told these feelings to anyone.

Source: Journard, S.M. (1964). *The transparent self: Self-disclosure and well-being.* Princeton: Van Nostrand.

sensate focus: In therapy with sexually dysfunctional couples, an emphasis on each partner giving pleasure to the other and on "thinking and feeling" sensuously, without direct physical approach to the pelvic area or intrusion upon the experience by the demand for either partner's end-point release. Sensate focus I involves a nongenital massage, while sensate focus II includes genital stimulation.

Source: Masters, W., & Johnson, V. (1970). *Human sexual inadequacy.* Boston: Little, Brown.

separateness and connectedness: Separateness and connectedness are issues that underlie a family's life. The process of attempting to achieve a satisfactory pattern of separateness and connectedness is basic to the family's functioning. "As each member of a family develops his own personality, adapts to changes through the life cycle, seeks gratification and, generally, creates an individual life space, he is also involved in more or less binding ties with other family members, ties which he endeavors to create and ties which the other members endeavor to create with him."

Source: Hess, R., & Handel, G. (1959). *Family worlds.* Chicago: University of Chicago Press.

separation anxiety: Traumatic tension resulting from time apart from the parent, particularly the mother or the "mother substitute." The separation poses a threat or creates a fear or neurotic belief that loss or abandonment will occur. As a developing biological and a social organism, the child normally sees separation as a process rather than an event.

However, in the case of a premature removal of the child from the biological mother—e.g., through death, chronic illness, desertion, emotional inadequacy, or temporary admission to a hospital—separation anxiety can develop.
Source: Bowlby, J. (1951). Maternal care and child health. *World Health Organization.* New York: Columbia University Press.
Quoted: Allen, F.H. (1955). Mother-child separation-process-event. In G. Caplan (Ed.), *Emotional problems of early childhood.* New York: Basic Books.

separation counseling: Crisis intervention counseling using a time-limited approach that deals specifically with the immediate crisis of family separation. The purpose is to help separating individuals understand their relationship, to resolve their conflicts, to decide whether their future relationship will be together or apart, and to grow through the separation process. A structured separation is a model for distressed families with children. In such cases, the children are presented with parental behavior that displays honesty, choice, and respect as primary values. The damage caused by the suddenness and emotional uproar common to most divorce situations is thereby mitigated. The children have the time and an open interpersonal situation in which to adapt to the major change in their lives.
Source: Toomin, M.K. (1975). Structured separation for couples in conflict. In A.S. Gurman & D.G. Rice (Eds.), *Couples in conflict* (pp. 353–362). New York: Jason Aronson.

separation response: The total experience stemming from a marital separation. The first response is a shock reaction, particularly when the separation is sudden and unexpected. The most frequent expressions of this shock reaction are denial and somatic disorder. The shock reaction is generally followed by an 8-to-12-week affective cycle. The first phase of this cycle is characterized by a 4-to-6-week period of either depression and withdrawal or euphoria and activity. In the following 4 to 6 weeks, those who have been depressed and withdrawn usually begin to feel more open and become more active. They seldom go as "high" as those who were initially euphoric. On the other hand, those who have at first been euphoric and active tend to withdraw and become somewhat depressed. Again, the "low" tends to be less intense than that experienced by those who were initially depressed. In both groups, the counterreaction gradually shifts and stabilizes at an intermediate affective and activity level.

Example: John has difficulty living alone and moves in with the first woman he dates after separating from his wife.
Source: Toomin, M.K. (1975). Structured separation for couples in conflict. In A.S. Gurman and D.G. Rice (Eds.), *Couples in conflict* (pp. 353–362). New York: Jason Aronson.

separation structure: The structure of personal and family relationships developed by a separating couple. The separating partners are asked to make a three-month commitment to explore themselves and the relationship. During this time both see the therapist individually and conjointly. They are asked not to live in the same house, not to see a lawyer, and not to make any permanent financial, property, or child custody arrangements. The children remain in their own home, with whichever parent is best able to care for them. Their lives are disrupted as little as possible. It is important that they maintain contact with such environmental supports as friends and school. As the partners communicate with each other, they realistically assess their needs and resolve practical issues. They are both free to initiate and end social contacts, as they wish and for whatever reason. They may have sex together only if both want it. Freedom to explore other relationships is encouraged on the theory that such exploration maximizes choice. A variety of social, emotional, and sexual encounters gives each a more realistic view of self interacting with others. These contacts serve to eliminate "If-it-weren't-for-you" games. The process of seeing each other only by choice requires that they examine themselves and each other often to decide whether or not they want to be together and if so when, or how to reject each other. In this process of repeatedly accepting and rejecting, each has an extraordinary opportunity to learn to be honest with the other in communicating love, appreciation and need—as well as hurt, fear, and anger—in a responsible way.
Source: Toomin, M.K. (1975). Structured separation for couples in conflict. In A.S. Gurman and D.G. Rice (Eds.), *Couples in conflict* (pp. 353–362). New York: Jason Aronson.

sequence: A repeating cycle of linked behaviors. A sequence is often analyzed as a linear event, in that each step in the cycle is followed by another. But since the final step in the progression is always the occasion to return to the beginning of the cycle, a sequence in fact describes a circular and repetitive unfolding of linked behaviors. A behavior-exchange sequence involves the transformation of psychological content into observable behaviors that are exchanged across subsystem boundaries. Content events occurring totally within a subsystem are usually unobservable and can only be inferred. When, however, these events result in interpersonal contact, the behaviors occur in sequence, among the subsystems, and these exchanges may be observed.

Example: A brother and his older sister engage in a sequence of fights that helps the mother to stay firmly allied with her daughter and estranged from her husband. The larger systems goal—the maintenance of strict subunit boundaries between men and women—is well-served by the repetitive fights. The sequence of fight activity is used by the family to achieve that larger systems goal.

Source: Umbarger, C.C. (1984). *Structural family therapy.* New York: Grune & Stratton.

sequential process: A process in which the therapist resolves an issue with part of the family before continuing with the whole or another part of the family on the same or another matter.

Example: A couple enters therapy for help with a teenage daughter. The couple is also in the midst of a marital crisis. The therapist recommends that they either separate or work on their relationship before trying to deal with their daughter's problem.

Source: Aponte, H., & Van Deusen, J. (1981). Structural family therapy. In A. Gurman & D. Kniskern (Eds.), *Handbook of family therapy* (pp. 310–360). New York: Brunner/Mazel.

serial monogamy: A succession of monogamous relationships of varying duration that is terminated by mutual agreement and/or divorce. Also referred to as progressive monogamy.

Source: Constantine, L., & Constantine, J. (1971). Group and multilateral marriage: Dysfunctional notes, glossary, and annotated bibliography. *Family Process, 10,* 157–176.

sex role adoption: Acting out the behavior characteristics of one sex or the other.

Source: Lynn, D. (1969). *Parental and sex role identification: A theoretical formulation.* Berkeley, Calif.: McCutchan.

sex role identification: Internalization of aspects of the role appropriate to a given sex and of the unconscious reactions characteristic of that role.

Source: Lynn, D. (1969). *Parental and sex role identification: A theoretical formulation.* Berkeley, Calif.: McCutchan.

sex role preference: A desire to adopt behavior associated with one sex or the other.

Source: Lynn, D. (1969). *Parental and sex role identification: A theoretical formulation.* Berkeley, Calif.: McCutchan.

sex therapist: A therapist who uses dynamic psychotherapeutic principles, marital counseling, and behavioral methods in the treatment of specific sexual problems. A sex therapist needs an understanding of psychopathology and the dynamics of marital interaction, as well as clinical skills in both individual and conjoint therapy. The sex therapist must also understand male/female sexuality and the dynamics of marital discord and should have extensive knowledge of learning theory and the theory and practice of dynamic psychotherapy. Standards for practice and certification are provided by the American Association of Sex Educators, Counselors, and Therapists.

Source: LoPiccolo, J. (1978). The professionalization of sex therapy: Issues and problems. In J. LoPiccolo and L. LoPiccolo (Eds.), *Handbook of sex therapy* (pp. 511–526). New York: Plenum Press.

sex therapy: A type of therapy, focused on the resolution of sexual problems, that (1) emphasizes the mutual responsibility of the couple for the sexual dysfunction, (2) stresses information and education in treatment, (3) is concerned with attitudinal change and performance anxiety, (4) increases communication skills and the effectiveness of sexual techniques, (5) prescribes changes in behavior, and (6) frees individuals from destructive life styles and sex roles. Sex therapy also recognizes the pervasive interaction between sexual dysfunction and the marital relationship.

Source: Kaplan, H. (1981). *The new sex therapy.* New York: Brunner/Mazel.

sexual anesthesia: A disorder in which a female "feels nothing" from sexual stimulation or penile intromission. Sexual anesthesia is not considered a true sexual dysfunction but rather a symptom of neurosis.

Source: Kaplan, H. (1974). *The new sex therapy.* New York: Brunner/Mazel.

sexual dysfunction: Cognitive, affective, and/or behavioral problems that prevent an individual or couple from engaging in and/or enjoying satisfactory intercourse and orgasm. A sexual dysfunction is distinguished from a sexual variation, in which an individual may successfully engage in intercourse in an unconventional way or with an unconventional object choice.

Source: LoPiccolo, J. (1978). The professionalization of sex therapy: Issues and problems. In J. LoPiccolo & L. LoPiccolo (Eds.), *Handbook of sex therapy* (pp. 511–526). New York: Plenum Press.

sexual identity: The perception of oneself as basically male or female.
Source: Glock, R., & Kessler, D. (1974). *Marital and family therapy.* New York: Grune & Stratton.

sexual scapegoating: A situation set up by one partner in which, because of fear of exposure of one's own sexual inadequacy, the other partner is blamed for an unsatisfactory sex life. Usually the blaming partner makes only hurried, halfway attempts to improve the sexual situation.
Example: An inorgasmic woman blames her husband for her problems, but she refuses to allow him to engage in extended foreplay with her.
Source: Kaplan, H. (1974). *The new sex therapy.* New York: Brunner/Mazel.

sexual task: An exercise used as a therapeutic tool to shift a couple's objective away from the achievement of a response to the giving and receiving of pleasure. When the goal has been achieved, sexual exercises designed to relieve specific problems are prescribed.
Source: Masters, W., & Johnson, V. (1970). *Human sexual inadequacy.* Boston: Little, Brown.

shadow reality: Integrated alternative realities not now in the relationship reality but at times available to those in the relationship. Shadow realities include unacceptable and threatening information and interpretations that fit the relationship and could undermine the negotiated relationship reality. Jung used the term *shadow* to describe a well-organized part of the individual's unconscious that can be either dangerous or valuable. Jung's analysis indicates that this individual shadow cannot be avoided; it is always there. To have a marital reality necessitates having a shadow reality. A couple cannot, for example, function as a "good" couple without putting out of sight aspects of their "bad" couplehood, or vice versa.
Example: A couple whose marriage reality includes a belief (reflecting societal standards and images of what relationships should be) that they are open with each other still retain "in the shadows" their awareness of withholding and the ways in which they are not open (the feelings, events, and beliefs that each keeps from the other).

Source: Rosenblatt, P.C., & Wright, S.E. (1984). Shadow realities in close relationships. *American Journal of Family Therapy, 12*(2), 45–54.

shaping: The process of reinforcing smaller approximations to the target behavior.
Example: A young retarded boy must wear glasses. He is initially reinforced for just wearing the frames, then the frames and lenses during selected reinforcing activities, and finally for longer and longer periods.
Source: Bandura, A. (1969). *Principles of behavior modification.* New York: Holt, Rinehart, & Winston.

shared meaning: A situation in which the message being sent coincides with the message being received. The sender sends the message briefly and clearly, and the receiver rephrases the message in different words and feeds it back to the sender. The sender can then confirm the message or clarify it.
Example: The husband conveyed to his wife that he wanted to be more than a sexual athlete to please her and his wife responded that she will be more attentive to his need to give and receive affection and tenderness in their lovemaking. The husband expressed his appreciation to his wife for her interest in trying to be more understanding to his needs for sexual intimacy.
Source: Bernard, C., & Corrales, R. (1979). *The theory and technique of family therapy.* Springfield, Ill.: Charles C Thomas.

shift: The transition from a statement of one's personal, subjective view to a statement of an opposite position, without any of the necessary indicators to acknowledge ambivalence.
Example: A client is talking about wanting his wife to return to the marriage, but then begins to discuss the advantages he had when single. He seems unaware of the fact that he has shifted his stance.
Source: Beavers, W. (1977). *Psychotherapy and growth: A family systems perspective.* New York: Brunner/Mazel.

sibling functioning position: A characteristic of people who are born into the same sibling position in different families and grow up with many personality characteristics in common.
Example: The middle child in a family is often more similar to another middle child in another family in the neighborhood than to older and younger siblings raised in the same family.
Source: Toman, W. (1976). *Family constellation* (3rd ed.). New York: Springer-Verlag.

sibling position profile: A technique in which a diagram of siblings is made to provide insight into why a certain child has been chosen to present the undesirable behavioral symptom for the whole family. The profile includes the birth order and sex of all children.
Source: Bowen, M. (1971). The use of family theory in clinical practice. In J. Haley (Ed.), *Changing families* (pp. 159–192). New York: Grune & Stratton.

sibling rivalry: The jealous desire of a child to usurp a sibling's place in the affection and attention of one or both parents. The overt characteristics of sibling rivalry take many forms, from a direct attack on a brother or sister to withdrawal or regressive behavior.
Source: Smart, M., & Smart, R. (1953). *An introduction to family relationships*. Philadelphia: Saunders.
Quoted: Schaefer, C., & Millman, H. (1977). *Therapies for children*. San Francisco: Jossey-Bass.

sibling subsystem: The grouping of children in a family in which they interact as peers, negotiating issues of competition, defeat, accommodation, cooperation, and protection.
Sources: Bank, S., & Kahn, M. (1982). *The sibling bond*. New York: Basic Books; Lamb, M., & Sutton-Smith, B. (Eds.). (1982). *Sibling relationship*. Hillsdale, New York: Lawrence Erlbaum Associates.

side-taking: A structural technique to support a particular subsystem in the family. The therapist may side with the mother against the father, or vice versa, or may side with nonverbal, reticent children against the parents, in an effort to help the family members verbalize and share thoughts, perceptions, and feelings.
Source: Minuchin, S. (1974). *Families and family therapy*. Cambridge, Mass.: Harvard University Press.

significant others: Nonrelated people who have an impact on the individuals in treatment—although not necessarily the same type of emotional impact and influence that the natural family unit has.
Source: Glick, I., & Kessler, D. (1974). *Marital and family therapy*. New York: Grune & Stratton.

silencing strategies: Maneuvers designed to punish a person for some transgression by isolating the person in silence in order to induce compliance or conformity at the public level and to possess the victim as an object for needed projection of feelings of being bad or inanimate.
Example: A wife asks her husband to spend more time with her. He responds by becoming silent, and then attempts to change the subject by criticizing her for always being busy.
Source: Zuk, G. (1971). *Family therapy*. New York: Behavioral Publications.

silent treatment: A maneuver in which family members agree not to speak to the victim as punishment for violation of a code.
Source: Zuk, G. (1971). *Family therapy*. New York: Behavioral Publications.

SIMFAM: A game-playing situation adapted by Straus and Tallman to elicit family interaction data. Family triads are asked to discover the rules of the SIMFAM game by playing it and then analyzing what they did correctly or incorrectly, as signaled by the lights. The interaction generated by the game's tasks can be analyzed by different types of coding systems.
Source: Aldous, T., Condon, T., Hill, R., Straus, M., & Talman, I. (1971). *Family problem solving*. Hinsdale, Ill.: Dryclere Press.

simplicity-speaks-the-truth rule: The injunction that self-statements should be made directly, openly, and honestly, free of any verbal excess. Manipulations that maneuver the listener into expressing the reaction desired by the speaker—regardless of the message's true impact—should be avoided.
Example: The therapist avoids such statements as, "You're going to like what I tell you," "Don't worry, but. . . ," "You haven't heard this yet, but. . ."
Source: Wierenberg, G.I., & Calero, H.H. (1973). *Meta-talk: Guide to hidden meanings on conversations*. New York: Simon & Schuster.
Quoted: Baruth, L.G., & Huber, C.H. (1984). *An introduction to marital theory and therapy*. Monterey, Calif.: Brooks/Cole.

simulated family: Members of an audience who role play family members as a training technique.
Source: Satir, V. (1967). *Conjoint family therapy*. Palo Alto, Calif.: Science and Behavior Books.

simultaneous bilateral identity delineation: The process of relating to both good and bad objects at the same time. The need to assign dichotomous roles of goodness and badness to others is based on a frame of reference of good and bad archetypes.
Source: Boszormenyi-Nagy, I. (1965). A theory of relationships: Experience and transaction. In

I. Boszormenyi-Nagy & J. Framo (Eds.), *Intensive family therapy: Theoretical and practical aspects* (pp. 33–86). New York: Harper & Row.

single parent: Someone who raises a child or children alone, without the presence of a substitute second parent that would be provided by a new spouse. This situation may be the result of marital separation, widowhood, parenthood without marriage, or, less frequently, adoption of a child by an unmarried individual or informal adoption of a child by a child's grandparent, older sibling, or other relative. Married men and women whose partners are away indefinitely in the armed forces, are working in another community, or are hospitalized with a chronic illness may also function as single parents, even though they may not identify themselves as such.
Source: Weiss, R.S. (1977). *Going it alone.* New York: Basic Books.

situational idiosyncracies: Events in particular geographic or social milieus that impinge on the family.
Example: Repairing the city drainage system requires digging up the streets in such a way that the children have no place to play, the parents have no place to park, and the inconvenience results in increased family tensions and frustration.
Source: Bernard, C., & Corrales, R. (1979). *The theory and technique of family therapy.* Springfield, Ill.: Charles C Thomas.

skewed family: A psychopathological family situation in which one parent is strong and the other is weak. The situation imposed by the psychopathologically dominant mate is accepted or shared by the other mate without any attempt to change it. The serious psychopathology of the dominant marital partner is indeed supported by the spouse, resulting in the distorted ideation being accepted in the family (folie á famille). There is considerable masking of conflict, creating an unreal atmosphere that does not help the child to trust self-perceptions and self-judgments or to learn social adaptive skills.
Source: Lidz, T., Fleck, S., & Cornelison, D. (1965). *Schizophrenia and the family.* New York: International Universities Press.

skewed marriage: A marital relationship in which one member is strong, overfunctioning, and therefore dominant and the other member is weak, underfunctioning, and generally submissive. A skewed marriage may also be one in which there is a schism, a failure to achieve mutuality, and in which, as a result, the children have difficulty in maintaining their own identity (the children need same-sex family members with whom to identify and opposite-sex members who are seen as desirable). In either of these marital structures, the environment is characterized by irrationality and the lack of a logical, rational basis for communication. In both contexts, the children cannot make sense of their environments and thus of their own identities.
Example: The father is a physician and a workaholic. The son decides that he does not want that kind of slaving and thus evolves pathologically in his professional choice or escalates to a failure in medical school.
Source: Lidz, T., Fleck, S., & Cornelison, A. (1965). *Schizophrenia and the family.* New York: International Universities Press.
Quoted: Barnard, C.P., & Corrales, R.G. (1979). *The theory and technique of family therapy.* Springfield, Ill.: Charles C Thomas.

skill-training program: Educational training or enrichment for couples and families, alone or in groups, that facilitates functioning but does not attempt to change structure therapeutically. Existing skill-training programs include systemic training for effective parenting and teaching couples how to fight nondestructively. A skill-training program encompasses issues facing couples or families before marriage, during marriage (as in marriage encounters), in parenting, in the family, and during divorce.
Source: L'Abate, L., & Rupp, G. (1981). *Enrichment: Skill training for family life.* Washington, D.C.: University Press of America.

social genes: Qualities of intimacy and separateness at various levels in a family. In a healthy family, a wide range of intimacy and separateness levels are found. These levels can be moved without inducing panic in the family. The size of the family "space bubble" and that of each individual's space bubble is determined by the experiences and historical perspective the family members have inherited via their social genes. Neither of the social genes of intimacy and separateness in the family can increase without an increase in the other; one can only be as close as one can be separate, and one can only be as separate as one can be close. Dependency and autonomy are similarly linked.
Source: Grinker, R.R. (1971). Biomedical education on a system. *Archives of General Psychiatry, 24,* 291–297.

Quoted: Keith, D.V., & Whitaker, C.A. (1982). Experiential/symbolic family therapy. In A.M. Horne & M.M. Ohlsen (Eds.), *Family counseling and therapy* (pp. 43–74). Itasca, Ill.: F.E. Peacock Publishers.

social influence: Influence that family members use to move each other, or to avoid being moved themselves, in certain directions. Social influence may take the form of (1) "private dependent power . . . the use of certain personalized dimensions implicit in the parent-child relationship to justify one's position or to demand a change in another's behavior"; (2) "information giving . . . the use of facts or opinions designed to provide a rational basis for behavior change in the listener"; or (3) "information seeking," which includes both "requests for information or permission" and "seeking explanations, opinions, or feelings."
Source: Goldstein, M., Judd, L., Rodnick, E., Alkire, A., & Gould, E. (1968). A method for studying social influence and coping patterns within families of disturbed adolescents. *Journal of Nervous and Mental Disease, 147,* 231–251.

social learning: A result of teaching people how to relate interpersonally. Social learning is learning that takes place within a social environment as a person observes, reacts to, and interacts with other people. In short, it is education in human relations. Within a social matrix, children learn ways of behaving (behavior patterns) by receiving support for some actions and punishment for others. The result of this selective social reinforcement is the behavior that we characteristically exhibit—our personalities.
Source: Horne, A.M. (1982). Counseling families—Social learning family therapy. In A.M. Horne & M.M. Ohlsen (Eds.), *Family counseling and therapy* (pp. 360–388). Itasca, Ill.: F.E. Peacock Publisher.

social learning approach: An assembly of several social learning models, most importantly, those based on operant learning, social exchange, general systems, and attribution theories. In this approach, the emphasis is on observational assessment methods, behavioral specifics, and the interplay of data, theory, and clinical application. Its basic tenets are readily translatable into treatment modalities and techniques that can be tested empirically. The treatment approach attempts to provide an environment in which effective learning may occur. Behavioral alternatives are expanded and new options are presented, so that families and couples may remedy deficits and develop new skills for dealing with the problems of living in close human relationships. The treatment occurs in a systematic teaching-modeling program that emphasizes learning procedures.
Source: Jacobson, N.S., & Margolin, G. (1979). *Marital therapy: Strategies based on social learning and behavior exchange principles.* New York: Brunner/Mazel.

social network: A societal pattern in which each individual is linked to several others by social bonds that partly reinforce and partly conflict with one another; the orderliness or disorderliness of social life results from the constraints these bonds impose on the actions of individuals.
Source: Collins, A.H., & Pancoast, D.L. (1976). *Natural helping network: A strategy for prevention.* Washington, D.C.: National Association of Social Workers.

social reinforcement: Verbal and nonverbal means of giving attention and recognition. Social reinforcement is the most important source of motivation for human behavior.
Example: Smiling and saying, "Good, you're using your fork," reinforces a child's eating behavior.
Source: Lieberman, R. (1972). Behavioral approaches to family and couple therapy. In G. Erickson & T. Hogan (Eds.), *Family therapy: An introduction to theory and technique* (pp. 120–137). Belmont, Calif.: Wadsworth.

social role: The adaptational unit of personality in action. The social role is a bridge between the intrapsychic and social life. It has semipermeable boundaries in that it permits a limited penetration in both directions, that is, between the environment and the self.
Source: Ackerman, N. (1958). *The psychodynamics of family life.* New York: Basic Books.
Quoted: Foley, V. (1974). *An introduction to family therapy.* New York: Grune & Stratton.

social work: One of the helping professions whose distinctive clinical or casework features has been its historic concern with the family as well as the specialists of social group work and community organization. The primary emphasis of study has been multi-person unit(s). Social workers have been involved in family problems since the inception of the profession. The development of family theories and practice models had to await the entrance of psychiatrists, however, which occurred in the late 1950s.

Example: At the local child guidance clinic in the 1960s, the social worker met with the parents and siblings, the psychologist conducted child psychological testing, and the psychiatrist treated the child individually.
Source: Sherman, S.N. (1981). A social work frame for family therapy. In E.R. Tolson & W.J. Reid (Eds.), *Models of family treatment* (pp. 7–32). New York: Columbia University Press.

societal emotional process: A process in which the forces tending toward individuality on the one hand and togetherness on the other operate to counterbalance each other on a societal level in a manner similar to that which exists in individual families.
Source: Kerr, M. (1981). Family systems theory and therapy. In A. Gurman & D. Kniskern (Eds.), *Handbook of family therapy* (pp. 226–266). New York: Brunner/Mazel.

sociogram: A graphic representation of the configuration of members of a group, indicating their sociometric relationship to each other.
Source: Moreno, J. (1953). *Who shall survive? Foundations of sociometry, group psychotherapy and sociodrama.* New York: Beacon House.
Quoted: Dodson, L., & Kurpius, D. (1977). *Family counseling: A systems approach.* Muncie, Ind.: Accelerated Development.

sociometry: A method for measuring the patterns of an individual's feeling interaction with other members of a group. The patterns are depicted on a sociometric map that consists of lines of preferred relationships between individuals. From such maps, one can determine the central figure, cliques, isolates, etc. in a group.
Source: Moreno, J. (1953). *Who shall survive? Foundations of sociometry, group psychotherapy, and sociodrama.* New York: Beacon House.
Quoted: Corsini, R.J. (1966). *Roleplaying in psychotherapy: A manual.* Chicago: Aldine.

sole custody: The most common type of custodial arrangement in which one parent has custody and the other has visitation privileges. The parent with whom the child lives makes most of the decisions regarding the child's life, although usually both parents participate in major decisions regarding education, religious training, and vacations. Usually, a fairly specific schedule of visitation is included in the separation agreement and divorce decree. Ideally, however, this schedule should serve mainly as a guideline for parents who are flexible enough to agree to alter it as conditions warrant. Such flexibility requires a certain degree of cooperation between the parents. The traditional visitation schedule is basically unnatural, because it cannot take into consideration the unpredictability of life situations or the vicissitudes and desires of all the individuals involved. Ideally, the sole custodial arrangement blends into a joint custodial pattern.
Source: Gardner, R.A. (1982). *Family evaluation in child custody litigation.* Cresskill, N.J.: Creative Therapeutics.

sorkc: A behavioral assessment procedure that focuses on the stimulus (S), the state of the organism (O), the target response (R), and the nature and contingency of the consequences (KC).
Example: When a boy throws temper tantrums to get a cookie, S is the sight of the cookie jar, O is the child's hunger or boredom, R is the tantrums, and KC is the parent giving in to the tantrums.
Source: Kanfer, F., & Phillips, J. (1970). *Learning foundations of behavior therapy.* New York: John Wiley & Sons.
Quoted: Nichols, M. (1984). *Family therapy: Concepts and methods.* New York: Gardner Press.

sororal polygyny: A marital relationship in which several sisters are cowives.
Source: Zelditch, M. (1964). Cross-cultural analyses of family structure. In H.T. Christensen (ed.), *Handbook of marriage and the family* (pp. 462–500). Chicago: Rand McNally.

specificity: The focus of a therapist or family member who directs statements to a specific family member, e.g., by looking directly at the member, by using the member's name, by answering the member's question, or by referring directly to the member's immediately preceding statement.
Source: O'Connor, W., & Stachawiak, J. (1971). Patterns of interaction in families with high adjusted, low adjusted, and mentally retarded members. *Family Process, 10,* 229–241.
Quoted: Riskin, M., & Faunce, E. (1972). An evaluative review of family interaction research. *Family Process, 11,* 365–455.

spectator role: A role assumed involuntarily by members of a sexually dysfunctional marital unit in which they become psychologically trapped into observing the physical aspects of the sexual exchange rather than involved in relaxing, enjoying the sensual stimulation, and becoming physiologically involved in the experience.
Source: Masters, W., & Johnson, V. (1970). *Human sexual inadequacy.* Boston: Little, Brown.

spectator therapy: Treatment based on vicarious reinforcement and modeling. By watching others

(in role-playing or therapy), the spectator is able to benefit by the experience. Treatment in which a person observes the behavior of another person, e.g., in a role-playing situation or audience effect of identification.
Source: Corsini, R.J. (1966). *Roleplaying in psychotherapy: A manual.* Chicago: Aldine.

split: The experience of opposition, alienation, or estrangement. A split usually occurs between the members or subsystems of a family. It is the opposite of alignment or coalition.
Example: A daughter feels hostile toward her mother and splits off from other family members. She actually opposes what her mother expects of her.
Source: Wynne, L. (1961). The study of intrafamilial alignments and splits in exploratory family therapy. In N. Ackerman, F. Beatman, & S. Sherman (eds.), *Exploring the base for family therapy* (pp. 95–115). New York: Family Service Association of America.

split custody: A custody arrangement in which the children are divided between the two parents. One or more children live permanently with the mother, and one or more live with the father. Most experts agree with the arguments for attempting to keep the children together. In this way, the children can provide support for one another and develop a sense of family continuity, in spite of the parental breakup.
Source: Gardner, R.A. (1982). *Family evaluation in child custody litigation.* Cresskill, N.J.: Creative Therapeutics.

split double bind: A situation in which the expectations of one parent with respect to a child conflict with the expectations of the other parent. The child who loves each parent equally is unable to satisfy one without frustrating the other.
Example: One parent expects an adolescent child to stay at home and never go out. The other parent expects age-appropriate behavior. Whatever the child does frustrates one of the parents.
Source: Ferreira, A. (1960). The double bind and delinquent behavior. *Archives of General Psychiatry, 3,* 359–367.

split loyalty: A situation in which the parents set up conflicting claims so that a child can offer loyalty only to one parent, at the cost of the child's loyalty to the other parent.
Example: A son chooses to support his mother's position in the postdivorce war because he resides

with her. His father whom he loves more, is only a "week-end visitor."
Source: Stierlin, H. (1974). *Separating parents and adolescents.* New York: Quadrangle; Boszormenyi-Nagy, I., & Ulrich, D. (1981). Contextual family therapy. In A. Gurman & D. Kniskern (Eds.), *Handbook of family therapy* (pp. 159–186). New York: Brunner/Mazel.

spontaneous agreement: The agreement of two or more family members on the same choice(s), as indicated in their answers on the Unrevealed Differences Questionnaire.
Source: Ferreira, A., & Winter, W. (1965). Family interaction and decision making. *Archives of General Psychiatry, 13,* 214–223.
Quoted: Riskin, M., & Faunce, E. (1972). An evaluative review of family interaction research. *Family Process, 11,* 365–455.

spontaneous recovery: The processes that lead to recovery in untreated controls.
Example: The husband and wife had finally made the decision to enter marital therapy, agreeing that they were ready and receptive to making changes as individuals as well as in their relationship. The family psychologist they chose was going on vacation during the summer, so they decided to begin couple therapy in the fall. Upon the psychologist's return, they realized that they were getting along better, their relationship had become more stable, and they were satisfied with how they were feeling about themselves.
Source: Bergin, A.E. (1967). Some implications of psychotherapy research for therapeutic practice. *International Journal of Psychiatry, 3,* 136–150.
Quoted: Levant, R.F. (1984). *Family therapy: A comprehensive overview.* Englewood Cliffs, N.J.: Prentice-Hall.

spouse-aided therapy: Therapy that involves the patient's spouse as a coagent of change. This approach is based on the recognition of marital problems that contribute to the creation and/or continuation of persisting psychological problems.
Example: A man seeks therapy because of depression. He wants individual therapy because he feels that most of his problems are internal, based on his extreme deprivation and abuse as a child. It is apparent, however, that there are numerous other problems in his marriage, e.g., his wife blames him for his lack of willpower in overcoming his depression.
Source: Hafner, R. (1981). Spouse-aided therapy in psychiatry: An introduction. *Australian and New Zealand Journal of Psychiatry, 15,* 329–337.

Quoted: Badenoch, A., Fisher, J., Hafner, J., & Swift, H. (1984). Predicting the outcome of spouse-aided therapy for persisting psychiatric disorders. *American Journal of Family Therapy,* *12*(1), 59–72.

squeeze technique: A technique employed by the female to deter premature ejaculation in the male. The women places her thumb on the frenulum (located on the ventral surface) and her first and second fingers on the superior (dorsal) surface of the penis in a position immediately adjacent to one another on either side of the coronal ridge. Pressure is then applied by squeezing the thumb and first two fingers together for an elapsed time of three to four seconds.
Source: Masters, W., & Johnson, V. (1970). *Human sexual inadequacy.* Boston: Little, Brown.

stable coalition: A coalition in which the child is allied to one of the parents, most commonly the mother. Such a coalition may exist in cases of spouse conflict. The excluded parent either keeps asking for the child's loyalties with no result, or gives up relating to the child and steps out of the situation.
Example: When the mother "bad-mouths" her exhusband, the son and daughter go along with their mother's assertions. When the father is critical of his exwife, the children resent his comments and defend their mother.
Source: Minuchin, S. (1974). *Families and family therapy.* Cambridge, Mass.: Harvard University Press.
Quoted: Aponte, H.W., & Van Deusen, J. (1981). Structural family therapy. In A. Gurman & D. Kniskern (Eds.), *Handbook of family therapy* (pp. 310–360). New York: Brunner/Mazel.

stable-unsatisfactory marriage: A marriage characterized by a couple profile described as the "sparetime battlers" or the "pawnbrokers." This profile determines the design of the therapeutic intervention. Other couple profiles are the stable-satisfactory, a marriage that is stable and provides a mutually supportive environment, with two subgroups, the "heavenly twins" and the "collaborative geniuses;" the unstable-unsatisfactory, characterized by the "weary wranglers" and the "psychosomatic avoiders;" and the unstable-satisfactory, characterized by the "gruesome twosome" and the "paranoid predators."
Example: "Spare-time battlers" usually do not seek professional help because they fight and get enough out of the family aspects of the marriage to

keep them going, and they are less apt to have problems with sex.
Source: Lederer, W., & Jackson, D.D. (1968). *Mirages of marriage.* New York: Norton.

stability: The least change in unit structure over time, i.e., in the patterns of "who-speaks-to-whom" or in the way coalitions in the family are organized.
Example: The son misbehaves, the father reprimands the son, the mother chastises the father, the fathers defends his action, and the mother is exasperated with him.
Source: Haley, J. (1963). *Strategy of psychotherapy.* New York: Grune & Stratton.

staging: The division of a therapeutic intervention into separate, self-contained units, which are in turn arranged in some sort of logical progression.
Example: In staging the complete entire treatment plan, the therapist begins with the entire family and then moves to progressively smaller family units. Or, in staging a single intervention, the therapist asks some central family members first to sit next to each other and then to begin a dialogue without interruptions from the other family members.
Source: Umbarger, C.C. (1984). *Structural family therapy.* New York: Grune & Stratton.

stagnation: A condition produced by ethically invalid attempts to solve life's problems, without awareness of what one's basic life interests might be. It represents a selfish attempt to live in the world.
Example: A father provides his family with an income, but refuses to invest anything else in the family because he feels he has fulfilled his responsibilities to it.
Source: Boszormenyi-Nagy, R., & Spark, G. (1973). *Invisible loyalties.* New York: Harper & Row.
Quoted: Boszormenyi-Nagy, I., & Ulrich, D. (1981). Contextual family therapy. In A. Gurman & D. Kniskern (Eds.), *Handbook of family therapy* (pp. 159–186). New York: Brunner/Mazel.

statement rule: The rule that, whenever possible, self-expressions should be in the form of statements rather than questions.
Example: A woman who feels ambivalent about going to a party says, "Do you really want to go out tonight?" rather than, "I'm not sure I want to go out."
Source: Stuart, R.B. (1980). *Helping couples change: A social learning approach to marital therapy.* New York: Guilford.

Quoted: Baruth, L.G., & Huber, C.H. (1984). *An introduction to marital theory and therapy.* Monterey, Calif.: Brooks/Cole.

staying with negative feelings: A therapeutic process in which specially structured interactions are employed to expose the patient to personal feelings and aspects that were previously avoided. Patients are placed in anxiety-producing situations that they previously managed to avoid and in which they are forced to stay with their negative feelings.
Example: A woman denies her sexual feelings because they are equated with sin. In an exercise, she is forced to experience herself sensually and sexually.
Source: Kaplan, H. (1974). *The new sex therapy.* New York: Brunner/Mazel.

stepfamily: (1) A family in which children live with a remarried parent and a stepparent; (2) a family in which children from a previous marriage visit with their remarried parent and stepparent; or (3) a family in which the couple is not married and children from a previous marriage either live with or visit the couple.
Source: Visher, E., & Visher, J. (1979). *Stepfamilies: A guide to working with stepparents and stepchildren.* New York: Brunner/Mazel.

step-function: A change in calibration. A step-function has a stabilizing effect in that it recalibrates the system and makes it more adaptive.
Example: Psychosis in the family represents a sharp change that recalibrates the system.
Source: Watzlawick, P., Beavin, J.H., & Jackson, D.D. (1967). *Pragmatics of human communication.* New York: Norton.

stereotyping: A strategy that isolates an offending person by caricaturing certain of that person's physical or mental traits, or the process whereby a characteristic is generalized to a whole population.
Example: A husband who works with computers is accused of being a computer when he does not respond to his wife in the way she expects, or all workaholics are poor husbands.
Source: Zuk, G. (1971). *Family therapy.* New York: Behavioral Publications.

stimulus control strategies: Strategies in which spouses are instructed to bring their problem-solving attempts under control at particular times and in particular settings, such as during "administrative time." Specifically, regular times are scheduled during the week, such as after dinner with coffee, when the spouses can engage in problem-solving discussions.

Source: Weiss, R., Hops, H., & Patterson, G. (1973). A framework for conceptualizing marital conflict: A technology for attaining it, some data for evaluating it. In L. Hamerlynck, L. Handy, & E. Mash (Eds.), *Behavior change: Methodology, concepts, and practice* (pp. 309–342). Champaign, Ill.: Research Press.

stop-start technique: A treatment devised by Semans for premature ejaculation. The female extravaginally stimulates her partner's penis to erection until the sensation premonitory to ejaculation is experienced. The stimulation is then interrupted until the sensation has disappeared. Penile stimulation is resumed until the premonitory sensation returns, and then it is again discontinued. The amount of time involved is variable, designed to increase the length of time between stops and starts.
Source: Semans, J. (1956). Premature ejaculation: A new approach. *Southern Medical Journal, 49,* 353–361.
Quoted: Kaplan, H. (1974). *The new sex therapy.* New York: Brunner/Mazel.

strategic family therapy: Therapy in which the clinician actively designs interventions to fit a problem. Three specific strategic therapeutic approaches are:

1. *Haley's approach.* This approach blends Minuchin's structural work with formal ideas of communication theory. Although Haley strives for a clear generational hierarchy, he describes his diagnostic and intervention work in terms of communication rather than "structural engineering." He focuses on the presenting problem (e.g., symptomatic behavior) and tries to see what communicative function the problem has in the sequence of family events that embody it. The task is then to change the sequence, which, if effectively done, will change the outcome (e.g., alleviation of the symptomatic behavior).

2. *Mental Research Institute (MRI) communicational approach.* If one eliminated the parts of Haley's work related to structural family therapy, one would come close to the MRI communication approach. The MRI approach attends strictly to a "chess-game" approach to solving problems. Thus, the context of the problem is first perceived and then altered. A change is metaphorically tagged as a "second-order change" when the target of change is the system and not just the symptom. This

approach gives particular attention to the therapeutic paradox and the use of therapeutic language that addresses the right (nonrational) hemisphere of the brain. The work of Bateson and Erickson has signficantly influenced the MRI orientation.

3. *The strategic group approach.* Selvini Palazzoli's strategic group model in the treatment of schizophrenic transaction is based on a blending of the work of Bateson, Haley, and Watzlawick. At the heart of this approach is a paradoxical relabeling maneuver called "positive connotation" in which the family's homeostatic, yet dysfunctional, organizational pattern is respected. The injunction not to change, paradoxically, gives the family freedom to change. The strategic group approach uses a wide variety of other paradoxical maneuvers, including family rituals, to achieve the desired end.

Source: Olson, D.H., Russell, C.S., & Sprenkle, D.H. (1980). Marital and family therapy: A decade review. *Journal of Marriage and the Family, 42,* 973–993.

structural balance theory: A theory that postulates that triads in a family attempt to balance themselves, i.e., when all three relationships are positive or when two form a stable alliance against the third. *Source:* Hoffman, L. (1981). *Foundations of family therapy.* New York: Basic Books.

structural family therapy: A form of therapy developed by Salvador Minuchin that focuses on changing the communication, functioning, and power structures of the family so as to alter symptomatic behavior in the identified patient. A change in family interaction is considered to bring about changes in the individual behavior of family members. The focus is ahistoric, i.e., in the "here and now," with the therapist playing an active role, e.g., in monitoring communication or even rearranging the seating to change the structure and functioning of the family. For instance, the marital and parental subsystems are given clear boundaries to protect the privacy of the spouses and the parents respectively. The focus is on the realignment of the structural relationships within the family, on a change of rules that will allow the system to maximize its potential for conflict resolution and individual growth. *Example:* The mother and daughter are acting like siblings. The therapist puts the mother in charge of the daughter's activities for the week.

Sources: Minuchin, S. (1974). *Families and family therapy.* Cambridge, Mass.: Harvard University Press; Levant, R. (1984). *Family therapy.* New York: Harper & Row.

structural insufficiency: A lack of the structural resources in a family or other social system that are needed to meet the functional demands of the system. *Example:* A single-parent mother living in the slums with several children lacks the financial, social, and emotional resources to rear her children. *Source:* Aponte, H., & Van Deusen, J. (1981). Structural family therapy. In A. Gurman & D. Kniskern (Eds.), *Handbook of family therapy* (pp. 310–360). New York: Brunner/Mazel.

structural intervention: In structural family therapy, an attempt to change the organization of a family system. A structural intervention is frequently aimed at delineating or creating subsystem boundaries, shifting power systems, or redefining family coalitions or alliances. *Example:* The therapist gives the parents a task to do at home that excludes the children, such as leaving home suddenly. Normally, the children would be involved in the parental system. The task is designed to establish a boundary between the parents and the children. For example, the children are not to disturb the parents in the mornings before a certain time. *Source:* L'Abate, L., Baggett, M.S., & Anderson J.S. (1983). Linear and circular interventions with families of children with school related problems. In B.F. Okun (Ed.), *Family therapy with school related problems.* Rockville, Md.: Aspen Systems.

structuralism: A theoretical perspective that sees social behavior and cultural products as a communicative code. Not only verbal and nonverbal activity, but the entire range of what humans produce culturally is in a communication code context. The codes are rule-governed; the rules define the formation and transformation of the relationships of the elements in the code in a given system. The rules of formation and transformation are related to fundamental cognitive characteristics and capabilities of the human organism. Structuralism assumes that these rules can be represented by a relatively general, abstract, and, in some degree, formal calculus. That is, the rules may be formalized for the system. *Source:* Cromwell, R.E., & Olsen, D.H. (1975). *Power in families.* New York: Halsted Press.

structure: The interactional patterns that arrange or organize a family's component subsystems into relatively constant relationships. These constant relationships endure through time, but are less enduring than the continuous activity of the superordinate, total system. That is, the system, as an entity, continues through the family's entire lifetime, while various structures, or organizational arrangements of the components, shift and change from time to time. Structures are seen in the relatively stable subsystems, alliances, and hierarchies that characterize a family's organizational map. Structures may also be thought of as slow processes of long duration. The expression of a process over time gives that process the status of a structure.
Example: The mother and son repeatedly, over time, join forces against the father's effort to direct a decision. This represents a mother-son coalitional structure. If this arrangement does not persist over time, it may be viewed as a transitional process in the evolving movement of family life, not as an enduring structure.
Source: Umbarger, C.C. (1984). *Structural family therapy.* New York: Grune & Stratton.

structured family interview: A series of interactional tasks that involve either the whole family or various subgroups of the family. The structured family interview was developed at the Mental Research Institute both as a clinical interview technique and as a family research tool.
Source: Watzlawick, P. (1966). A structured family interview. *Family Process, 5,* 256–271.

structured interview technique: A technique that focuses on a family disorder through such tasks as identifying the main problem, planning something together, and discussing the meaning of a proverb. The technique has the advantage of shortening the time needed to gain information necessary for unveiling the family system.
Source: Watzlawick, P. (1972). A structured family interview. In G. Erickson & T. Hogan (Eds.), *Family therapy: An introduction to theory and technique* (pp.265–278). Belmont, Calif.: Wadsworth.

structured mediation: A process in which a husband and wife agree to reach a divorce settlement based on marital mediation rules. Nonstructured mediation is conducted without advance agreement on the rules of procedure and the guidelines to be followed by the parties and the mediator. The advantages of structured mediation are that:

- The issues to be decided are clearly defined.
- The issues are limited to those whose resolution is needed for reaching settlement.
- Procedural methods are established for collecting and examining factual information.
- All options for the settlement of each issue are systematically examined.
- Options are selected within socially acceptable guidelines.
- The consequences likely to follow selection of each option are examined.
- Uninterrupted time is regularly allocated for working toward resolution.
- Impasses are promptly resolved by arbitration.

Source: Coogler, O.J. (1978). *Structured mediation in divorce settlement.* Lexington, Mass.: Lexington Books.

structured sexual experiences: The integrated use of systematically structured sexual experiences with conjoint therapeutic sessions. Structured sexual experiences are the main innovation and distinctive feature of sex therapy.
Example: The wife informs her husband each time he touches her in a way that pleases her; otherwise, she says nothing. Or, a therapist directs a couple to engage in bodily massage for 30 minutes, 15 minutes each, without touching the genital areas. Coitus is not permitted. This experience is designed for establishing a sensual bond between the couple.
Source: LoPiccolo, J. (1978). Direct treatment of sexual dysfunction. In J. LoPiccolo & L. LoPiccolo (Eds.), *Handbook of sex therapy* (pp. 1–18). New York: Plenum Press.

subconscious wisdom: Imagining a problem as if it were being revealed through a crystal ball, a TV series, or a dream. This is a technique used in diagnostic sex hypnotherapy technique.
Source: Araoz, D. (1982). *Hypnosis and sex therapy.* New York: Brunner/Mazel.

subgroups: A subset of a larger group. Breaking into small subgroups and then reassembling can help focus resistances and provide new possibilities for moving in different directions.
Source: Alger, I. (1976). Multiple couple therapy. In P. Guerin (Ed.), *Family therapy* (pp. 364–387). New York: Gardner Press.

subject/object: A code designed by Mishler and Waxler to classify the subjects and objects of all acts in terms of whether they refer to someone within or outside the interacting family group.

Source: Mishler, E., & Waxler, N. (1968). *Interaction in families: An experimental study of family processes and schizophrenia*. New York: John Wiley & Sons.

subsystem: An element or functional component that is itself a system but that also plays a specialized role in the operation of a larger system. A subsystem is the totality of all structures in a particular living system that carry out a particular process. At least three types of subsystems can be identified as parts of an open system; an input subsystem, a conversion or operating subsystem, and an output system. Family systems are differentiated by generation, sex, interest, or function such as the dyads of husband/wife, mother/father, mother/child, or child/child. An individual can belong to a number of subsystems.
Example: A child and his dog (the family pet) are subsystems of the family.
Source: Sauber, S.R. (1983). *The human services delivery system*. New York: Columbia University Press.

superego binding: A type of binding created through the exploitation of loyalty. The parents attempt to instill repressive breakaway guilt. They convey, overtly or covertly, that they have totally sacrificed themselves for their children and that they can live only through them. The children typically become hospitalized as psychiatric patients, remaining targets of their parents' intrusive and ambivalent concern.
Source: Stierlin, H. (1974). *Separating parents and adolescents*. New York: Quadrangle.

superperson: One who expects to manage a career, home, and family with complete ease. Such a person expects to have a perfect job, a perfect marriage, and a perfect house and to be in perfect control of the children.
Example: A woman feeds her children and husband a nutritional breakfast, goes off to her $35,000-a-year job, spends an hour of quality time after school with her children, feeds the family a healthy, well-balanced meal, cleans the house, and spends time with her husband, talking and loving, before they go to sleep.
Source: McCubbin, H.I., & Figley, C.R. (1983). *Stress and the family: Coping with normative transitions* (Vol. 1). New York: Brunner/Mazel.

support: Positive emotional involvement among family members.
Source: Bales, R. (1950). *Interaction process analysis: A method for the study of small groups*. Cambridge, Mass.: Addison-Wesley Press.

Quoted: Riskin, M., & Faunce, E. (1972). An evaluative review of family interaction research. *Family Process, 11*, 365–455.

suprasystem: A higher-level system in which other systems play subsystem roles. A living system may be analyzed in terms of its components or subsystems, or it may be viewed as part of a larger system. The suprasystem of an individual is the group of which that individual is a member.
Example: Family therapy is a subsystem of the suprasystem of psychotherapy; it is at the same time the suprasystem of the subsystem of multiple family group therapy.
Source: Sauber, S.R. (1983). *The human services delivery system*. New York: Columbia University Press.

surrogate partners: A sexual partner provided by the therapist when a patient does not have an available partner. For a fee, the surrogate partner participates in prescribed sexual tasks during the treatment.
Source: Kaplan, H. (1974). *The new sex therapy*. New York: Brunner/Mazel.

symbiosis: A psychological state in which the involvement of two or more individuals is so intense that their boundaries become blurred. The individuals respond as one. Schizophrenia has been conceptualized as an unresolved symbiotic attachment between the child and his mother. The attachment is initiated by the emotional immaturity of the mother, who uses the child to fulfill her own emotional needs.
Example: A mother feels guilty because, while she covertly does things to block the child's development, she simultaneously tries to force the child to achievement. The child, once entangled, tries to perpetuate the symbiosis along with an opposite effort to grow up. The father passively permits himself to be excluded from the intense twosome and marries his business and other outside interests.
Source: Bowen, M. (1978). *Family therapy in clinical practice*. New York: Jason Aronson.
Quoted: L'Abate, L. (1976). *Understanding and helping the individual in the family*. New York: Grune & Stratton.

symbiotic involvement: A family situation in which the boundaries between two or more individuals are blurred or fused. This is characteristic of very disturbed families.
Example: In one family a mother and patient were highly symbiotic. One ego could function as that of the other. These two members accurately knew the other's thoughts, feelings, and fantasies. If the

mother was physically ill or emotionally stressed, the patient would reflect the same problems. There were even examples of the patient's psychosis acting out the mother's unconscious.
Source: Epstein, N., & Bishop, D. (1981). Problem-centered systems therapy of the family. In A. Gurman & D. Kniskern (Eds.), *Handbook of family therapy*. New York: Brunner/Mazel.

symbolic interaction theory: A theory that assumes that valid principles of human behavior can be derived from the study of social interaction, defined as a form of communication characteristic of human social life, involving either language or symbolic gestures. The theory assumes that these principles cannot be derived or inferred from the study of nonhuman forms.
Source: Stryker, S. (1964). The interactional and situational approaches. In H. Christensen (Ed.), *Handbook of marriage and the family* (pp. 125–170). Chicago: Rand McNally.

symbolic-experiential family therapy: A form of family therapy, developed by Carl A. Whitaker, that considers change as coming primarily from experiential learning and self-evaluation. Insight into genetic factors is not considered necessary to change; however, interactional insights related to the "here and now" of treatment are valued. Cotherapy is encouraged, since it provides an additional model or "metaexperience" for the family. Interpretations are most valuable when they are metaphorical and made symbolically about family relationships—using humor, teasing, fantasy, or free association to challenge the family's method of resolving stressful situations. For example, Whitaker uses "acting crazy" as a therapeutic tool, utilizing irrelevant phrases or free associative fantasy during the session. This is seen to work in the same way as regression in the service of the ego, i.e., it is controllable and reversible. In the process, the family is forced to assume the "sane" component. The therapist serves as an example, giving the patient or the family permission to remain crazy under controlled circumstances. Whitaker also stresses the importance of the therapist being inconsistent—of being a change agent. This undermines the rigid style of functioning of the family and prevents the therapist from following a technique mechanically.
Sources: Keith, D.V., & Whitaker, C.A. (1982). Experiential symbolic family therapy. In A.M. Horne & M.M. Ohlsen (Eds.), *Family counseling and therapy* (pp. 43–74). Itasca, Ill.: F.E. Peacock Publishers; Neil, J.F., & Knis-

kern, D.P. (1982). (Eds.). *From psyche to system: The evolving therapy of Carl Whitaker*. New York: Guilford Press.
Quoted: Pinney, E.L., & Slipp, S. (1983). *Glossary of group and family therapy*. New York: Brunner/Mazel.

symmetrical escalation: Runaway competitiveness to remain on at least an equal footing with a partner. The partners go through an escalating pattern of frustration until they eventually stop from sheer physical or emotional exhaustion.
Source: Watzlawick, P., Beavin, J.H., & Jackson, D.D. (1967). *Pragmatics of human communication*. New York: Norton.

symmetrical relationship: A relationship based on equality or sameness. Statements indicating this type of relationship are either balanced (A: "I like bowling;" B: "I like golf.") or competitive (A: "I have a new bike;" B: "So what, I have a new camera.") A symmetrical marital relationship is one in which the spouses continually need to state to each other behaviorally, "I am as good as you are." Differences are minimized, role definitions are similar, and problems seem to stem from competition.
Source: Watzlawick, P., Beavin, J.H., & Jackson, D.D. (1967). *Pragmatics of human communication*. New York: Norton.

symmetrical schizmogenesis: An interaction characterized by a tendency for its participants to remain even with one another, no matter how casual or intense the competition.
Example: When members of one group begin to boast, the members of the other group reply with boasting, thereby setting up a vicious circle.
Source: Bateson, G. (1958). *Naven* (2nd ed.). Stanford, Calif.: Stanford University Press.
Quoted: Watzlawick, P., Beavin, J.H., & Jackson, D.D. (1967). *Pragmatics of human communication*. New York: Norton.

symptom: A behavior that signals dysfunction in an individual or family. While psychodynamic and systems theories argue that a symptom indicates wider circles of pathology, family theory argues that the symptom is a focus of both intervention and treatment of the interpersonal context in which it is embedded.
Example: Whenever the husband returns home, he complains of headaches that begin when he greets his wife.
Source: Umbarger, C.C. (1984). *Structural family therapy*. New York: Grune & Stratton.

symptom bearer: A family member who, by malfunctioning in the community, the school, and/or at home, signals pain in the family.
Example: The seven-year-old daughter keeps complaining to the school nurse that her stomach is upset every morning following a parental fight at home.
Source: Dodson, L., & Kurpius, D. (1977). *Family counseling: A systems approach.* Muncie, Ind.: Accelerated Development.

symptom exchange: A relationship in which the two parties experience the same problem but their defenses against it are opposite. The one who resents the problem gets vicarious satisfaction from the one who expresses it. The danger in oneself is dealt with by dealing with it in another.
Example: Two individuals have a problem centered in sexuality. One acts out sexually while the other acts inhibited and accuses the first person of being immoral. The inhibited person vicariously enjoys the acting-out behavior of the other person and deals with personal feelings through the other's misconduct.
Source: Framo, J. (1965). Systematic research on family dynamics. In I. Boszormenyi-Nagy & J. Framo (Eds.), *Intensive family therapy: Theoretical and practical aspects* (pp. 407–463). New York: Harper & Row.

symptom focusing: A restructuring technique, developed by Minuchin, to approach change directly through the symptom by exaggerating, deemphasizing, relabeling, or moving to a new symptom.
Example: A man who has withdrawn from his family by sitting at home in the corner is told to do more of the same on a prescribed basis.
Sources: Aponte, H., & Van Deusen, J. (1981). Structural family therapy. In A. Gurman & D. Kniskern (Eds.), *Handbook of family therapy* (pp. 310–360). New York: Brunner/Mazel; Minuchin, S. (1974). *Families and family therapy.* Cambridge: Harvard University Press.

symptom-oriented treatment: An approach to treatment in which the therapist focuses on the presenting problem or symptom rather than searching for underlying causes and psychodynamic processes. This approach is in sharp contrast to psychoanalytic and psychodynamic therapies and is more related to behavioral approaches. However, the family therapist realizes the symptoms may represent a problem in the system, not just an isolated individual.

Source: Nichols, M. (1984). *Family therapy: Concepts and methods.* New York: Gardner Press.

synchronizing: A mechanism through which a family develops and maintains a program for regulating the family's total use of time, including the ways in which its members clock and orient their movements. Synchronizing is the temporal equivalent of the spatial mechanism of centering. It includes the creation and execution of temporal guidelines, much as centering includes the creation and execution of spatial guidelines. For example, How do we spend our time so we can get the maximal amount of what we want out of life? Which targets are we going to devote our time to pursuing? How much time do we want to spend together? How do we manage to spend the time together we think we want to spend together?
Example: The oldest son in the family notices that his father seems grumpy every morning, and he passes this information on to his mother. That evening she approaches her husband and asks him whether he thinks he is working too hard.
Source: Kantor, D., & Lehr, W. (1975). *Inside the family.* San Francisco: Jossey-Bass.

syntax: The way in which information is transmitted, e.g., means of encoding; channels of communication; the capacity, variability, noise, and redundancy inherent in the communicational transmitting system; and the patterns of speech over time. In marriages, syntax refers to such qualities as who-to-whom speech, the percentage of speaking time, the parsimony of speech, and the ratio of information to noise.
Source: Steinglass, P. (1978). Marriage from a systems theory perspective. In T. Paolino & B. McCrady (Eds.), *Marriage and marital therapy* (pp. 298–365). New York: Brunner/Mazel.

system: A system is a set of interrelated variables and a family is a system of interrelated individuals. "The totality of elements in interaction with each other." General systems theory is a body of organized theoretical constructs that can be used to discuss general relationships in the empirical world. In a system, the focus is upon the relationship between elements rather than on the elements themselves. General systems theory was introduced into family therapy by the Palo Alto group (Bateson, Jackson, etc.) as a way of relating the interaction of the family and the individual and of determining how the homeostasis of the family system is maintained through negative feedback loops (morphostasis).

Sources: von Bertalanffy, L. (1968). *General systems theory.* New York: Braziller; Sauber, S.R. (1983). *The human services delivery system.* New York: Columbia University Press.

system conflict: In structured family therapy, conflict that develops from the competing needs of the components of the family system.

Example: A depressed father with an alienated wife desires emotional support from his adolescent son, who in time wants more distance from the family. Each individual is trying to meet a different need, which conflicts with those of the other members.

Sources: Aponte, H., & Van Deusen, J. (1981). Structural family therapy. In A. Gurman & D. Kniskern (Eds.), *Handbook of family therapy* (pp. 310–360). New York: Brunner/Mazel; Minuchin, S., Rosman, B.L., & Baker, L. (1978). *Psychosomatic families: Anorexia nervosa in context.* Cambridge: Harvard University Press.

system purist: A therapist who seeks to establish control with the family by perceiving the ways in which the family tries to influence the therapist to accept a relationship that, in effect, is an extension of the family system and would maintain its homeostasis. Once this is perceived by the therapist, the rules of the therapeutic relationship are so arranged as to make it impossible.

Source: Watzlawick, P., Beavin, J.H., & Jackson, D.D. (1967). *Pragmatics of human communication.* New York: Norton.

Quoted: Skynner, A. (1976). *Systems of family and marital psychotherapy.* New York: Brunner/Mazel.

system recomposition: A restructuring technique that addresses structural change by adding to or taking away systems from those systems that are involved in the creation or maintenance of the problem.

Example: A mother and son have problems because of the exclusiveness of their relationship. Adding a spouse and thereby a father to the household enriches the family structure and takes some of the pressure off of the mother-son system.

Source: Minuchin, J., & Fishman, H.C. (1981). *Family therapy techniques.* Cambridge: Harvard University Press.

system suction: Maneuvering by the family to entice the therapist to join the family system in such a way as to limit the therapist's objectivity and helpfulness. System suction is a way a family resists change.

Example: The parents of an adolescent son see him as bad. The parents want the therapist to see the son as bad too in order to fix only the son. They resist the idea that they too need help.

Source: Rabkin, R. (1970). *Inner and outer space.* New York: Norton.

Quoted: Riskin, M., & Faunce, E. (1972). An evaluative review of family interaction research. *Family Process, 11,* 365–455.

systematic desensitization: A process by which an individual's incompatible behavior is conditioned to inhibit neurotic anxiety through a system of progressive muscle relaxation paired with a graded exposure to anxiety-eliciting cues.

Source: Wolpe, J. (1969). *The practice of behavior therapy.* New York: Pergamon Press.

Quoted: LeBow, M. (1972). Behavior modification for the family. In G.Erickson & T. Hogan (Eds.), *Family therapy: An introduction to theory and technique* (pp. 347–376). Belmont, Calif.: Wadsworth.

systematic training for effective parenting: A parent education program, designed and developed by Dinkmeyer and McKay, that is based on the democratic principles of child-rearing of Alfred Adler and Rudolph Driekurs. Emphasis is placed on ''encouragement'' (acting positively rather than negatively) and ''responsibility'' as learned from the consequences of one's own behavior. This program has received international recognition and is currently the most popular parenting program in use in the United States.

Source: Dinkmeyer, D., & McKay, G.D. (1976). *Systematic training for effective parenting.* Circle Pines, Minn.: American Guidance Service.

systemic intensity: Intense emotional behavior, often resulting from a systemic void and reflecting boundary dysfunction. Systemic intensity has been described as the ''crowded elevator'' syndrome. When emotional intensity in a subsystem exceeds a tolerable level, distancing behavior results in the form of seapage, escape, or symptomatology.

Example: People in a crowded elevator do not look at each other. Instead, they look for ways of reclaiming their personal space through some form of distancing behavior.

Source: Hoffman, L. (1981). *Foundations of family therapy.* New York: Basic Books.

systemic rocking: The dynamic reaction of a subsystem to an increase in tension, with no available outlet for the tension. Once a subsystem begins to rock, a stabilizer enters the subsystem with the objective of restoring equilibrium. Systemic rocking, operating in the presentation of acting out, most often reflects a lack of tension outlet or lack of resolution in the marital subsystem, with the acting-out child functioning as the stabilizer. In most therapy with disturbed children, it can be assumed that, if the parents could conceal their marital difficulties, the child would not be expressing the problems.

Example: A child with a problem stabilizes a marital dyad.

Source: Haley, J. (1976). *Problem-solving therapy.* San Francisco: Jossey-Bass.

systemic void: The systemic condition that results from the absence, obstruction, or inadequate functioning of a subsystem, with a consequent effect on the members of interrelated subsystems and overall systemic functioning. The notion of "void" or "emptiness" has often been noted in the literature with reference to illness and death and to the intrapsychic or internal system of individuals who are experiencing emotional pain.

Example: Children are used to fill an emptiness in the lives of the parents who have lost their own parents or who, by choice or by failure, do not participate in the nondomestic sphere of life. Clinically, this emerges as the child-focused family, in which the child becomes the replacement for an unrealized achievement, for a "place in the world," or for a family member who is dead or out of contact (cutoff).

Source: Bowen, M. (1978). *Family therapy in clinical practice.* New York: Jason Aronson.

Quoted: Bradt, J.O. (1980). The family with young children. In E.A. Carter & M. McGoldrick (Eds.), *The family life cycle* (pp. 121–146). New York: Gardner Press.

systems orientation: In family therapy, a focus on comprehending the sources of leverage and power in the immediate field of action. A systems orientation explains change in terms of positive and negative feedback rather than in terms of linear, cause-effect sequences.

Source: Zuk, G. (1971). *Family therapy.* New York: Behavioral Publications.

systems theory: A theory that, when applied to families, delineates the interrelatedness of the family members to each other. Systems therapists believe that change in one family member necessitate change(s) in other members. Family systems psychotherapy is oriented to structural interventions even though it deals with individual processes.

Source: Bowen, M. (1972). The use of theory in clinical practice. In J. Haley (Ed.), *Changing families* (pp. 159–192). New York: Grune & Stratton.

Quoted: Hansen, J.C., & L'Abate, L. (1982). *Approaches to family therapy.* New York: Macmillan.

systems wholeness: The tendency of a system, its elements and the interrelationship of its parts to take on the character of the system's gestalt.

Example: A family is much more than the sum of its members' individual personalities; it is, in a sense, a totality, having an inner life and existence of its own.

Source: Bowen, M. (1971). The use of family theory in clinical practice. In J. Haley (Ed.), *Changing families* (pp. 159–192). New York: Grune & Stratton.

T

tactfulness: A personal approach that involves being sincere and open in communication, showing respect for the other person's feelings and taking care not to hurt that person unnecessarily. Tactfulness involves sincerity and implied trust.

Source: Wahlroos, S. (1974). *Family communication.* New York: Macmillan.

task accomplishment: The interplay of forces affecting the outcome of critical transition points in a process. Task accomplishment is a product of factors antecedent to the situation in which the tasks arise.

Example: In a marriage, the way the partners accomplish the tasks presented to them on their honeymoon (e.g., developing a competence to participate in an appropriate sexual relationship and developing a competence to live in close association with one another) is related to the couple's potential for growth or disturbance.

Sources: Rapoport, R., & Rapoport, R. (1964). New light on the honeymoon. *Human Relations, 17,* 33–56; Stuart, R.B. (1980). *Helping couples change: A social learning approach to marital therapy.* New York: Guilford Press.

task-centered family therapy: A short-term, structured, problem-solving practice model. Specific target problems are identified, and a plan is set with a defined number of sessions during a specified period of time. Tasks are described as individual, reciprocal, or shared, and conversation or enjoyable activity tasks.

Example: Mother and son agreed to the task objective of increased independence by being together less and respecting self-made decisions. The operational tasks called for specific action such as not stating where the son was going and what time he would return home.

Source: Reid, W.J. (1981). Family treatment within a task-centered framework. In E.R. Tolson & W.J. Reid (Eds.), *Models of family treatment* (pp. 306–331). New York: Columbia University Press.

task setting: In structural family therapy, the assignment to family members to carry out among themselves an operation within prescribed transactional parameters.

Example: The therapist asks that the father be totally responsible for his son's behavior in order to break up a pattern of overinvolvement between the mother and the son.

Source: Aponte, H., & Van Deusen, J. (1981). Structural family therapy. In A. Gurman & D. Kniskern (Eds.), *Handbook of family therapy* (pp. 310–360). New York: Brunner/Mazel.

TAT: A projective technique (Thematic Apperception Test—TAT) that has been adapted for use in eliciting family interaction data. Two or more family members are asked to make up a story about a TAT card or a series of TAT cards. The cards usually depict scenes that are commonly described as "family" scenes.

Source: Walsh, F. (Ed.). (1982). *Normal family processes.* New York: Guilford Press.

TEAM: Trust (T), expectation (E), attitudes (A), and motivation (M). The elements in the acronym (introduced by Araoz) are those that make hypnosis possible in sex hypnotherapy.

Source: Araoz, D. (1982). *Hypnosis and sex therapy.* New York: Brunner/Mazel.

teasing technique: A sex therapy technique in which the female stimulates the male to erection, then stops and resumes stimulation after the penis has returned to a flaccid state.

Source: Masters, W., & Johnson, V. (1970). *Human sexual inadequacy.* Boston: Little, Brown.

temporal compatibility: Being on acceptably similar wavelengths regarding short- and long-term goals. Temporal compatibility is a component of stability/instability.

Example: A couple agrees on the timing and spacing in having children.

Source: Lederer, W., & Jackson, D. (1968). *The mirages of marriage.* New York: Norton.

Quoted: Bodin. A. (1981). The interactional view: Family therapy approaches of the M.R.I. In A. Gurman & D. Kniskern (Eds.), *Handbook of family therapy* (pp. 267–309). New York: Brunner/Mazel.

tension: A state produced by problematic events, transitions, and related hardships. When tension is not overcome, stress or distress emerges. Family stress is produced by an actual or perceived imbalance between demand (e.g., challenge, threat) and capability (e.g., resources, coping) in the family's functioning. Family distress is a negative state produced by a family's defining the demands—resources imbalance as unpleasant. In contrast, stress may be construed as a positive state that results from the family's defining the demands—resources imbalance as desirable, as a challenge family members enjoy.

Example: The husband's overcommitment to work to make financial ends meet has contributed to family imbalance and marital tension between the spouses. The tension is reduced when the wife returns to work and the husband has more time to be with his wife and children.

Source: McCubbin, H.I., & Figley, C.R. (Eds.). (1983). *Stress and the family: Coping with normative transitions* (Vol. 1). New York: Brunner/Mazel.

tertiary locus: In structural family therapy, the passive environment of a problem. The tertiary locus is part of the context in which the problem occurs, but it is only incidental to the problem.

Example: A couple with a son fights chronically. The son manages not to get caught up in the fighting. However, he is an onlooker and, hence, part of the problem's passive environment.

Source: Aponte, H., & Van Deusen, J. (1981). Structural family therapy. In A. Gurman & D. Kniskern (Eds.), *Handbook of family therapy* (pp. 310–360). New York: Brunner/Mazel.

theoretical-therapeutic system: A system in which theory determines therapy, and in which observations from therapy can in turn modify the theory.

Source: Bowen, M. (1969). The use of family theory in clinical practice. In B. Ard & C. Ard (Eds.), *Handbook of marriage counseling* (pp. 139–168). Palo Alto, Calif.: Science and Behavior Books.

therapeutic contract: A contract used by a family therapist to broaden the focus of the problem to include family interactions, in addition to the identified patient and other family members, as targets of change.
Source: Barker, P. (1981). *Basic family therapy.* Baltimore: University Park Press.

therapeutic paradox: A therapeutic situation in which the psychotherapist (1) sets up a benevolent framework in which change is to take place, (2) permits or encourages the client to continue with an unchanged behavior, and (3) provides an ordeal that will continue as long as the client continues with the unchanged behavior. Typically it takes the form of "prescribing the symptom."
Source: Haley, J. (1963). *Strategies of psychotherapy.* New York: Grune & Stratton.

therapist-family fit: The similarity of the therapist's race, ethnic background, social class, and value system with those of the family. It is hypothesized that the greater the therapist-family fit, the more likely that mutual understanding and sensitivity will ensue.
Source: Glick, I., & Kessler, D. (1980). *Marital and family therapy* (2nd ed.). New York: Grune & Stratton.

therapy team: A team comprising a male and a female cotherapist, each trained to treat the problems of sexual and family dysfunction.
Source: Masters, W., & Johnson, V. (1970). *Human sexual inadequacy.* Boston: Little, Brown.

threat to adaptive defenses: Threats that arise when partners in a dysfunctional marriage inadvertently fail to support each other's defenses against anxiety. The partners' self-esteem is so low that each seeks only self-relief and hence does not notice the anxiety of the other.
Example: A husband whose self-esteem has been lowered due to a setback at work fails to notice his wife's increased anxiety level over problems with one of their children.
Source: Blinder, M., & Kirschenbaum, M. (1969). The technique of married couple group therapy. In B. Ard & C. Ard (Eds.), *Handbook of marriage counseling* (pp. 233–246). Palo Alto, Calif.: Science and Behavior Books.

three generation hypothesis: The hypothesis that schizophrenia is the result of an intergenerational process. It asserts that the grandparents' combined immaturities were acquired by the one child who was most attached to the mother. When this child marries a spouse with an equal degree of imma-

turity, and when the same process repeats itself in the third generation, it results in one child (the patient) with a high degree of immaturity, with the other siblings more mature.
Source: Bowen, M. (1960). A family concept of schizophrenia. In D. Jackson (Ed.), *The etiology of schizophrenia* (pp. 346–372). New York: Basic Books.

tickling the defenses: The use of surprise to keep from arousing unmanageable defensiveness in the family during a therapeutic session. A technique to expose dramatic discrepancies between family members self-justifying rationalizations and other nonverbal attitudes.
Source: Ackerman, N.W. (1966). *Treating the troubled family.* New York: Basic Books.
Quoted: Levant, R.F. (1984). *Family therapy: A comprehensive overview.* Englewood Cliffs, N.J.: Prentice-Hall.

time distortion: A sex hypnotherapy technique used to treat women who climax too soon or with too little pleasure. The client is taught to distort time in order to lengthen the sexual experience.
Source: Araoz, D. (1982). *Hypnosis and sex therapy.* New York: Brunner/Mazel.

timebinding: The condition in which each generation of humans starts, at least potentially, where the previous generation left off.
Source: Korzybski, A. (1933). *Science and sanity.* Lancaster, Pa.: International Non-Aristotelian Library.
Quoted: Lewis, J., Beavers, W.R., Gossett, J.T., & Phillips, V.A. (1976). *No single thread.* New York: Brunner/Mazel.

time-out: Removal of a person from a reinforcing environment for a brief time (isolation) or having the person physically remain in the situation but with a complete cessation of reinforcement.
Example: When the siblings were arguing and asking for mother's side-taking, she went into the bathroom.
Sources: Reese, R. (1966). *The analysis of human operant behavior.* Dubuque, Iowa: William C. Brown; Green, D.R., Budd, K., Johnson, M., Larg, S., Pinkston, E., & Rudd, S. (1976). Training parents to modify problem child behaviors. In E.J. Marsh, L.C. Handy, & L.A. Hamerlynck (Eds.), *Behavior modification approach to parenting* (pp. 3–18). New York: Brunner/Mazel.

time squeeze: Family member(s) demanding a response or solution in advance of the optimal therapeutic time frame. When the time frame is compromised, the therapeutic or mediation efforts can be sabotaged.

Example: A spouse stated: ''I want your decision right now, so I can sell the house and get a loan, accept a new job offer, move out of the house and find a rental.'' The other spouse froze. The spouse was pushing to get things settled because of pain suffered in the divorce.

Source: Saposnek, D.T. (1983). *Mediating child custody disputes.* San Francisco: Jossey-Bass.

timing and pacing: A procedure by which the therapist checks the client's view before taking a firm stance. Throughout treatment, the therapist takes small steps and evaluates how each step is received before proceeding.

Example: The therapist does not believe history-taking is important, but the client feels it is essential. Before making a firm statement about the role of history or skipping history-taking altogether, the therapist assesses the client's view so that the therapeutic process can move forward without causing a rift in the relationship.

Source: Fisch, R., Weakland, J., & Segal, L. (1982). *The tactics of change.* San Francisco: Jossey-Bass.

topic continuity: A category of Riskin and Faunce's Topic Scale which measures whether or not family members stay on the same topic as that of the immediately preceding speech.

Source: Riskin, M., & Faunce, E. (1972). An evaluative review of family interaction research. *Family Process, 11,* 365–455.

tracking: A procedure by which the therapist helps the family elaborate the details of behavioral routes so that a coherent picture emerges of the particular complaint. Tracking the content of family life promotes such elaboration. Tracking also involves a therapeutic possibility, namely, that the extended inquiry into facets of family life will subtly guide the family to a new and expanded version of reality, thereby taking the focus off of the index patient.

Example: The mother complains that her oldest daughter hates being a child and wants to be a teenager and work in a store in the neighborhood. The mother says, ''She should enjoy being a child as the best time in her life.'' The therapist asks the 9-year-old to describe what her responsibilities are around the house, including the ways in which she is supposed to take care of her younger sister.

Source: Umbarger, C.C. (1984). *Structural family therapy.* New York: Grune & Stratton.

trading of dissociations: An interlocking network of perceptions about others based on dissociations about oneself. Each person projects the totality of a particular quality or feeling onto another family member and, in exchange, allows the other member to project unacceptable qualities onto the first person.

Example: In a family, all the members have dissociated into unawareness their hostile feeling toward the others, but each is keenly perceptive of that same feeling in the other members.

Source: Wynne, L. (1965). Some indications and contraindications for exploratory family therapy. In I. Boszormenyi-Nagy & J. Framo (Eds.), *Intensive family therapy: Theoretical and practical aspects* (pp. 289–322). New York: Harper & Row.

transaction: The unit of social intercourse when two people contact each other. Complementary transactions occur when we address an ego state in another person, and the response is from the same ego state. As long as transactions are complementary, communication can continue indefinitely, with the response of each person serving as the stimulus for the next transaction. When transactions are crossed, communication stops or the subject changes. The most common crossed transactions involve a child-to-parent response or a parent-to-child response.

Source: Spiegel, J. (1971). *Transactions.* New York: Science House.

Quoted: Erskine, R.G. (1982). Transactional analysis and family therapy. In A.M. Horne, & M.M. Ohlsen (Eds.), *Family counseling and therapy* (pp. 245–275). Itasca, Ill.: F.E. Peacock Publishers.

transactional analysis: Analysis based on a theory of personality that focuses on communication. Each personality is viewed as being composed of ego states: parent, child, adult. Each ego state organizes external and internal stimuli in a specific way, resulting in uniquely different communication. The analysis of the transactional patterns provides a tool to understand and to change the interpersonal and intrapersonal dynamics that may be blocking effective communication.

The tendency of a person to favor a particular ego state as a basis for communication is determined in part by the life script, a plan decided upon in childhood as a way to fit into the family. It is formulated out of what the child hears, experiences, and perceives as possible options.

Transactional analysis provides family members with a cognitive understanding of the dynamics of family scripts, of the functions of personality, and of transactional patterns. The counseling methodology encourages each person to take responsibility for self, consistent with the person's developmental age, to express the emotions that are often held back or are ineffectively communicated, and to focus on specific behavioral changes that can improve family life.

Sources: Erskine, R.G. (1982). Transactional analysis and family therapy. In A.M. Horne & M.M. Ohlsen (Eds.), *Family counseling and therapy* (245–275). Itasca, Ill.: F.E. Peacock Publishers; Berne, E. (1961). *Transactional analysis in psychotherapy*. New York: Glove Press.

transactional patterns of enacting: Scenarios that a therapist deliberately creates so that conflicts and other family problems can be acted out, rather than just described, in the family session. In essence, the task of the therapist is to help the family members demonstrate in the "here and now" how they deal with life situations.

Example: In the session, the therapist requests the family to act out an argument over how their son is disciplined.

Source: Minuchin, S. (1974). *Families and family therapy*. Cambridge, Mass.: Harvard University Press.

Quoted: Gerson, M., & Barsky, M. (1979). For the new family therapist: A glossary of terms. *American Journal of Family Therapy, 7*, 15–30.

transactional thought disorder: The chaotic communication that frequently occurs in schizophrenic families. In such families, each person's statements, apart from the transactional context, may appear sufficiently normal so that one would not ordinarily question the rationality of specific, isolated statements. However, the overall transactional sequence is bizarre, disjointed, and fragmented. Even if the parents are psychotic to some degree, the overall transactional disorder in these families often exceeds the severity of the individual parental disorder. Transactional thought disorder is referred to by Wynne as "collective cognitive chaos."

Source: Wynne, L., & Singer, M. (1963). Thought disorder and family relations of schizophrenics. I. A research strategy. *Archives of General Psychiatry, 9*, 191–198.

Quoted: Wynne, L. (1965). Some indication and contraindications for exploratory family therapy. In

I. Boszormenyi-Nagy & J. Framo (Eds.), *Intensive family therapy: Theoretical and practical aspects* (pp. 289–322). New York: Harper & Row.

transfer of blame: A defense against accepting responsibility for one's behavior. The transfer can be achieved by (1) qualifying a behavior as not having been done or as not done in a particular way, (2) indicating that it is someone else's fault, or (3) accepting the blame but claiming that one has been falsely accused.

Source: Haley, J. (1972). The family of the schizophrenic. In G. Erickson & T. Hogan (Eds.), *Family therapy: An introduction to theory and technique* (pp. 51–75). Belmont, Calif.: Wadsworth.

transference: A psychoanalytic term for distorted emotional reactions to present relationships based on unresolved family situations. Family relationships themselves are embedded in a transference context, and the family therapist can enter the ongoing transference relationship system rather than having to recreate it in the privacy of an exclusive therapist-patient work relationship.

Example: Marital conflict may be viewed as the result of mutual projection by each partner of early internalized objects, and thus may become the battleground for past conflicts. The therapist must be aware of each spouse's transference projection onto the partner as well as onto the therapist.

Source: Boszormenyi-Nagy, I. (1972). Loyalty implications of the transference model in psychotherapy. *Archives of General Psychiatry, 27*, 374–380.

Quoted: Nichols, M. (1984). *Family therapy: Concepts and methods*. New York: Gardner Press.

transference distortions: In family therapy, a behavioral pattern in which members of the family not only react to the therapist as a grandparent, parent, or sibling, but also respond in accordance with one another without being aware of their postinfantile relationships. This situation creates a very complex array of transferences.

Source: Framo, J. (1965). Rationale and technique of intensive family therapy. In I. Boszormenyi-Nagy & J. Framo (Eds.), *Intensive family therapy: Theoretical and practical aspects* (pp. 143–212). New York: Harper & Row.

transference neurosis: A neurosis that occurs when a patient reacts in the treatment relationship a panorama of neurotic conflicts, including many that are rooted in the patient's childhood experience. The cumulative transference reactions become so pervasive as to make therapy and the therapist the central concerns in the patient's life.

Source: Weiner, I. (1975). *Principles of psychotherapy.* New York: John Wiley & Sons.

Quoted: Gurman, A. (1978). Contemporary marital therapies. In T. Paolino & B. McCrady (Eds.), *Marriage and marital therapy* (pp. 445–566). New York: Brunner/Mazel.

transpersonal unconscious: The unconscious involved in cross-communication between one person and another, without the involvement of the conscious of either person.

Example: An adolescent daughter sexually acts out her mother's unconscious wishes to be sexually free.

Source: Freud, S. (1957). The unconscious. In J. Strachey (Ed.), *The standard edition of the complete psychological works of Sigmund Freud,* (Vol. 14, pp. 166–204). London: Hogarth Press.

Quoted: Framo, J. (1965). Systematic research on family dynamics. In I. Boszormenyi-Nagy & J. Framo (Eds.), *Intensive family therapy: Theoretical and practical aspects* (pp. 407–462). New York: Harper & Row.

triad: A group of three family members, frequently viewed as inherently unstable as a unit.

Source: Bowen, M. (1978). *Family theory in clinical practice.* New York: Jason Aronson.

triadic model: A model that assumes that psychological problems are the result of multiperson interactions. Thus, the system must be the target of intervention.

Example: Johnny shoplifts because his father covertly encourages him to defy his mother.

Source: Nichols, M. (1984). *Family therapy: Concepts and methods.* New York: Gardner Press.

triadic one: In the schizophrenic family, the child who functions as a stabilizer for the parents, converting the unstable father/mother ego mass into a more stable triad.

Source: Bowen, M. (1960). The family concept of schizophrenia. In D. Jackson (Ed.), *The etiology of schizophrenia* (pp. 346–372). New York: Basic Books.

Quoted: Bowen, M. (1965). Family psychotherapy with schizophrenia in the hospital and in private practice. In I. Boszormenyi-Nagy & J. Framo (Eds.), *Intensive family therapy: Theoretical and practical aspects* (pp. 213–245). New York: Harper & Row.

triadic-based technique: In family therapy, the use of mediation and side-taking judiciously to break up

and replace pathogenic relating. The technique is composed of a series of negotiations in which the therapist and the family vie for control. The therapist is not only a releaser, but also a fashioner, of change.

Source: Zuk, G. (1971). *Family therapy.* New York: Behavioral Publications.

trial marriage: A premarital relationship established with the avowed aim of eventual legal marital union. It is usually restricted to adult partners without plans for the birth or nurturance of children.

Source: Bowman, H. (1974). *Marriage for moderns.* New York: McGraw-Hill.

triangle: A three-person subsystem that is the molecule of an emotional system. This term is contrasted with triad, which has come to have fixed connotations. The triangle has definite relationship patterns that predictably repeat in periods of calm and stress. In periods of calm, the triangle is made up of a comfortably close twosome and a less comfortable outsider. The twosome works to preserve the togetherness. In stress, each works to get the outside position to escape tension in the twosome. The outside position is the most comfortable and desired one.

Example: In a father-mother-child triangle, tensions exist between the parents. The father gains the outside position—regarded as passive, weak and distant—leaving the conflict between the mother and the child. The mother—regarded as aggressive and domineering—wins over the child, who moves another step toward chronic functional impairment. Thus, the family projection process unfolds.

Source: Bowen, M. (1978). *Family theory in clinical practice.* New York: Jason Aronson.

triangles, interlocking: A way in which members of a family fit together in interlocking relationships. The therapist must consider all the triangles and how they interlock before attempting to differentiate or, in Bowen's words ''de-triangulate,'' the family in the therapeutic process.

Source: Bowen, M. (1966). The use of family theory in clinical practice. *Clinical Psychology, 7,* 347–374.

Quoted: Hoffman, L. (1981). *Foundations of family therapy.* New York: Basic Books.

triangulation: (1) A situation in which the parents, who are in conflict, ask for the child's loyalties, making it impossible for the child to get close to one of them without betraying the other. (2) The process by which a dyadic emotional system encompasses a

third system member for the purpose of maintaining or reestablishing homeostatic balance.
Example: A 12-year-old son depends on and protects his mother against his father during and after the divorce.
Source: Bowen, M. (1971). The use of family theory in clinical practice. In J. Haley (Ed.), *Changing families* (pp. 159–193). New York: Grune & Stratton.

true statements: In sex hypnotherapy, statements that treat negative sexual processing. Some clients have accepted untrue statements about sex. Clients are asked to formulate true statements, before being placed in a hypnotic state. Then, in the hypnotic state, they are asked to imagine that an important authority figure is lecturing and directing the same statements to them. This technique is used to treat negative sexual processing.
Source: Araoz, D. (1982). *Hypnosis and sex therapy.* New York: Brunner/Mazel.

two-question rule: The rule that the asker should always have a second question, seeking amplification of the answer to the first question. This avoids the possibility that the answer will be used by the asker for an immediate attack on the answerer. It also conveys the asker's interest in the answerer's response.
Source: Baruth, L.G., & Huber, C.H. (1984). *An introduction to marital theory and therapy.* Monterey, Calif.: Brooks/Cole.

U

unbalancing: A technique used to change the hierarchical relationship of the members of a system. Family members are encouraged to experiment with differing and expanded roles and functions. This experience may provide new understanding and new perspective to the family and its relationships. The therapist forms a coalition and supports one family member or subsystem at the expense of the others. The therapist usually joins with an underdog in the hierarchy, thus ignoring the family's preexisting patterns. This often prevents the family from noticing and responding to cues given by the upper part of the hierarchy, and the affiliated member begins to respond in daring and

unfamiliar ways, highlighting possibilities that were previously ignored.
Source: Minuchin, S., & Fishman, H. (1981). *Family therapy techniques.* Cambridge, Mass.: Harvard University Press.

unclarity: The situation when the content and tonal aspects of a speech do not fit with each other, i.e., are incongruent and/or are unintelligible to the observer.
Source: Riskin, M., & Faunce, E. (1972). An evaluative review of family interaction research. *Family Process, 11,* 365–455.

unconscious collusion: Acting collusively on an unconscious level in order reciprocally to serve another's needs. In some problem families, two or more members may have narcissistically regressive attitudes that are complementary with one another. These complementarities are collusive in that they may contribute to an endless postponement of growth or of the resolution of mourning among the participants.
Example: The parents constantly fight over their son's problems and overtly agree on a way of solving the problem. However, they want to retain him in the symptom-bearer role at the unconscious level, which results in the parents sabotaging their own efforts.
Source: Boszormenyi-Nagy, I. (1965). Intensive family therapy as process. In I. Boszormenyi-Nagy & J. Framo (Eds.), *Intensive family therapy: Theoretical and practical aspects* (pp. 87–142). New York: Harper & Row.

unconscious interpersonal conflict: Conflict resulting from incompletely experiencing a forbidden desire to relate in a certain way to oneself and others.
Example: The parents feel inhibited about expressing themselves sexually. Their daughter begins to act out sexually. The parents cannot relate to her behavior in an appropriate way because part of them receives vicarious gratification from her behavior while the other part of them finds the behavior abhorrent.
Source: Esterson, A. (1970). *The leaves of spring.* London: Tavistock.

underdog fallacy: The fallacy that a younger or weaker child is less skillful than an older child in getting someone else into trouble.
Source: Wahlroos, S. (1974). *Family communication.* New York: Macmillan.

underorganization: A deficiency in the degree of constancy differentiation and flexibility of the structural organization of the family system. This is accompanied by a lack of organizational continuity in the family.

Example: A mother is the controlling force in her family. When she is absent, the family becomes chaotic, due to the lack of other structures and supports to keep it working.

Source: Aponte, H. (1976). Underorganization in the poor family. In P. Guerin (Ed.), *Family therapy* (pp. 432–448). New York: Gardner Press.

undifferentiated ego mass: The fused cluster of egos of individual family members with a common ego boundary. The ego fusion is most intense in the least mature families. In a family with a schizophrenic member, the fusion between father, mother, and child approaches maximum intensity. Theoretically, the fusion is present to some degree in all families, but least so in those in which the family members have attained relatively complete emotional maturity. Clinically, the undifferentiated family ego mass is considered equivalent to a single ego.

Source: Hall, C.M. (1981). *The Bowen family therapy and its uses.* New York: Aronson.

unfreezing (and refreezing): In the quasi-stationary social equilibrium of individuals, groups, and families, first something must be shaken up to unsettle accustomed beliefs and behaviors. Only then will the person or family member be prepared to accept change. Examples include Minuchin's promotion of crisis in family lunch sessions, Paul's use of cross-confrontations, and Papp's family choreography. Based upon field theory, people occupy "life spaces," experience varying degrees of "tension," and are driven by fluctuating amounts of "energy" in pursuit of a variety of "needs" whose salience at the moment provides the "valence" for movement among certain "vectors."

Source: Lewin, K. (1951). *Field theory in social science.* New York: Harper & Row.

Quoted: Nichols, M. (1984). *Family therapy: Concepts and methods.* New York: Gardner Press.

unit of analysis: The part of interaction that is coded and analyzed. The unit of analysis varies greatly among researchers.

Source: Mishler, E., & Waxler, N. (1968). *Interaction in families: An experimental study of family processes and schizophrenia.* New York: John Wiley & Sons.

unitization: The process of breaking down an individual's speech into the smallest meaningful units that can be coded, i.e., subject, verb, and object.

Source: Bales, R. (1950). *Interaction process analysis: A method for the study of small groups.* Cambridge, Mass.: Addison-Wesley.

unrelatedness: The situation in which nothing a family member does, is, or becomes matters to anyone in the family. Thus, detachment and separateness occur.

Source: Framo, J. (1965). Rationale and techniques of intensive family therapy. In I. Boszormenyi-Nagy & J. Framo (Eds.), *Intensive family therapy: Theoretical and practical aspects* (pp. 143–213). New York: Harper & Row.

unrevealed differences questionnaire: A questionnaire based on Strodtbeck's revealed differences technique in which family members are asked to indicate their personal preferences on seven items by choosing the three choices they like best and the three they like least out of a list of ten possible choices for each item. After the family members have each made their choices in private, the family is brought together and asked to come to a joint decision on the three choices the whole family likes best and the three choices the whole family likes least. What each individual privately chose is not revealed to the whole family.

Source: Ferreira, A., & Winter, W. (1965). Family interaction and decision making. *Archives of General Psychiatry, 13,* 214–223.

Quoted: Riskin, M., & Faunce, E. (1972). An evaluative review of family interaction research. *Family Process, 11,* 365–455.

untensing: A sex hypnotherapy technique used to treat female vasocongestive dysfunction. The technique emphasizes the health forces within the body. The woman relaxes herself and her pelvic area and then explores all her sexual parts in her imagination.

Source: Araoz, D. (1982). *Hypnosis and sex therapy.* New York: Brunner/Mazel.

use of self: The therapist's feeling response to the family members. This is a basic cue to the therapist in interaction with the family. Knowing oneself and one's own family system provides a safeguard to assist the therapist in responding to the family rather than to a projection of the therapist's own personal conflicts.

Source: Bowen, M. (1976). Theory in the practice of psychotherapy. In P.J. Guerin (Ed.), *Family therapy: Theory and practice* (pp. 72–90). New York: Gardner Press.

utopia syndrome: Extremism in the solving of human problems. This syndrome, cited by Watzlawick, seems to occur most frequently as a result of the belief that one has found the ultimate, all-embracing answer. It may take three forms: (1) blame of oneself for the inability to attain the unattainable, (2) devotion to an endless quest and hence experience of fulfillment as a loss, and (3) self-righteous mission to encourage or embrace one's own answers.
Source: Watzlawick, P. (1977). The utopia syndrome. In P. Watzlawick & J. Weakland (Eds.), *The interactional view: Studies at the Mental Research Institute, Palo Alto, 1965–1974.* New York: Norton.

V

vaginal photoplethysmograph: A tampon-like acrylic tube that uses a photocell and light source to measure blood volume and pressure pulse changes in the vagina.
Source: Heiman, J. (1978). Uses of psychophysiology in assessment and treatment of sexual dysfunction. In J. LoPiccolo & L. LoPiccolo (Eds.), *Handbook of sex therapy* (pp. 123–136). New York: Plenum Press.

vaginismus: A sexual dysfunction that makes coitus difficult or impossible. The outer part of the vaginal outlet involuntarily closes, making attempts at penetration painful, if not impossible.
Source: Masters, W., & Johnson, V. (1970). *Human sexual inadequacy.* Boston: Little, Brown.

value orientation discrepancy: A situation in which the values of one partner conflict with the values of the other.
Example: The husband values most his free time; his wife values most her extra part-time job in order to bring in more money for the family.
Source: Spiegel, J. (1971). *Transactions.* New York: Science House.
Quoted: Foley, V. (1974). *An introduction to family therapy.* New York: Grune & Stratton.

values: Worth or merit of an idea or item that gives meaning to life and explains why family members make specific selections from alternative courses of action. Values are inclusive, deeply internalized, personal feelings about behavior and expectations of life that direct action. Since values cannot be seen, they must be recognized in behavior; freedom, love, honesty, prestige, and leisure are intangibles. Values can be verbalized and held at the conscious level (explicit) or held subconsciously and recognized only in behavior (implicit). Intrinsic values are desirable for their own sake, whereas instrumental values are important means of achieving higher level values. Patterns of attitudes, beliefs, interests, activities, and goals are reflections of values called value indicators.
Source: Nickell, P., Rice, A.S., & Picker, S.P. (1976). *Management in family living.* New York: John Wiley.

vasocongestion: The reflex dilation of penile and circumvaginal blood vessels in response to sexual stimuli, causing the genitals to become engorged and distended with blood. This produces erection in the male and lubrication and swelling of the female genitals.
Source: Kaplan, H. (1981). *The new sex therapy.* New York: Brunner/Mazel.

vasocongestive dysfunction: Inadequate physiological arousal of the sexual system. In the male, vasocongestion dysfunction (VCD) refers to the lack of an erection; in the female it refers to little or no vaginal lubrication.
Source: Jehu, D. (1979). *Sexual dysfunctions.* New York: John Wiley & Sons.

vector relations: Synchrony in being able to handle marital change by heading toward a collaborative relationship rather than taking a collision course. Vector relations are components of stability/instability.
Source: Lederer, W., & Jackson, D. (1968). *The mirages of marriage.* New York: Norton.

vector therapy: A form of family therapy, based upon K. Lewin's "field," whose aim is the readjustment of the pattern of emotional forces within the life space to bring improvement to individual family members. Vector therapy involves (1) a change in the magnitude of the emotional forces, (2) a change in the direction of emotional force with no change in magnitude, (3) a change in the length of time during which the emotional force operates, and (4) a change in the quality of the emotional force when one force replaces another.
Source: Howells, J. (1975). *Principles of family psychiatry.* New York: Brunner/Mazel.

vertical bookkeeping: A one-way system of relationships that does not provide for reciprocation.

Example: The parents provide a positive and conducive environment without allowing for the opportunity of repayment, and the child becomes a debtor. The child's indebtedness prevents him from committing himself to other relationships because of his feelings of disloyalty to his family. As an adult, he becomes oversolicitous of his own children as a way of ridding himself of the debt.
Source: Boszormenyi-Nagy, I., & Spark, G. (1973). *Invisible loyalities.* New York: Harper & Row.

victim-victimizer couple: A couple in a marital relationship in which one partner blames and the other accepts the blaming.
Example: A wife blames her husband for being lazy, while he simply says he is what he is and she is what she is.
Source: Sluzki, C. (1978). Marital therapy from a systems perspective. In T. Paolino & B. McCrady (Eds.), *Marriage and marital therapy* (pp. 366–394). New York: Brunner/Mazel.

videotape/audiotape playback: Devices used in therapy sessions to help family members become more self-aware and correct distortions in their communications. Such playback also reveals nonverbal aspects of the communications. The technique may be used in treatment, for diagnosis, for therapist self-monitoring, or for training.
Source: Alger, I. (1976). Integrating immediate video playback in family therapy. In P. Guerin (Ed.), *Family therapy* (pp. 530–548). New York: Gardner Press.

violation of function boundaries: Inappropriate intrusion of family members into functions that are in the domains of other members.
Example: A child tries to decide where the parents should live, and thereby crosses over a boundary into the parents' decision area.
Source: Minuchin, S. (1974). *Families and family therapy.* Cambridge, Mass.: Harvard University Press.
Quoted: Aponte, G., & Van Deusen, J. (1981). Structural family therapy. In A. Gurman & D. Kniskern (Eds.), *Handbook of family therapy* (pp. 310–360). New York: Brunner/Mazel.

violent behavior: Acts that involve great force and are capable of and intended to injure, damage, or destroy. The study of domestic violence includes rape, incest, child molestation, gang warfare, victimization, aggressive behavior within institutions, and other crimes. Aggressive behaviors become family norms and are distributed across all of the interacting family members for intervention planning. Physical violence occurs at home between family members more often than it occurs between any other individuals or in any other setting except for wars and riots.
Source: Stuart, P.B. (1981). Violence in perspective. In R.B. Stuart (Ed.), *Violent behavior: Social learning approaches to prediction, management, and treatment* (pp. 3–30). New York: Brunner/Mazel.

vital marriage: A marriage in which the partners are able to work together and find their relationship intensity satisfying.
Source: Glick, I., & Kessler, D. (1080). *Marital and family therapy* (2nd ed.). New York: Grune & Stratton.

voice technique: A technique in which the individual is encouraged to talk about a feeling in order to get emotional distance from it. A discrepancy may be produced between the feeling and the words used to describe it. An opportunity is thus provided for experiencing the feelings as they happen. This technique is especially effective when a discrepancy exists between the content of what one says and one's body messages.
Example: As a woman talks about the loss of a relationship, she begins to shed some tears, but she says that it is better that the relationship is ended. She does not appear to be in touch with her sadness. Using the voice technique, the therapist asks her to give her tears a voice so that she can experience the feelings associated with the event.
Source: Dodson, L., & Kurpius, D. (1977). *Family counseling: A systems approach.* Muncie, Ind.: Accelerated Development.

volume of communication: The median number of statements made during an interview by the individual family members and by the whole family.
Source: Lennard, H., & Bernstein, A. (1969). *Patterns in human interaction.* San Francisco: Jossey-Bass.

walking on eggs: Using the other person's sensitivities as an excuse for not being open and sincere. The term connotes contempt for the other person's feelings.

Example: A woman avoids bringing up problems she has with her husband because she believes that, if she does, he will severely criticize her.
Source: Wahlroos, S. (1974). *Family communication.* New York: Macmillan.

weak executive functioning: A condition in which parents lack the leverage required to direct their children.
Example: The parents in a family believe they have no way to control what time their son comes home at night. They do not know how to execute their roles as parental figures.
Source: Aponte, H., & Van Deusen, J. (1981). Structural family therapy. In A. Gurman & D. Kniskern (Eds.), *Handbook of family therapy* (pp. 310–360). New York: Brunner/Mazel.

weekend family marathon: An arrangement in which the family unit comes together for extended periods of time, with facilitators or leaders conducting a variety of intensive encounters.
Source: Bosco, A. (1977). *Marriage encounter: Rediscovery of love.* St. Meinrad, Ind.: Abby Press.
Quoted: L'Abate, L. (1981). Skill training programs for couples and families. In A. Gurman & D. Kniskern (Eds.), *Handbook of family therapy* (pp. 631–661). New York: Brunner/Mazel.

whom spoken to: A variable denoting the target of the speech in family interaction research.
Source: Mishler, E., & Waxler, N. (1968). *Interaction in families: An experimental study of family processes and schizophrenia.* New York: John Wiley & Sons.
Quoted: Riskin, M., & Faunce, E. (1972). An evaluative review of family interaction research. *Family Process, 11,* 365–455.

who-speaks: A variable indicating the number of times each family member speaks in family interaction research. It is usually involved in the analysis of the variables of dominance, control, and power.
Source: Lennard, H., & Bernstein, A. (1969). *Patterns in human interaction.* San Francisco: Jossey-Bass.
Quoted: Riskin, M., & Faunce, E. (1972). An evaluative review of family interaction research. *Family Process, 11,* 365–455.

who-speaks-to-whom: A pattern of interpersonal communication analyzed in family interaction research.
Source: Mishler, E., & Waxler, N. (1962). *Interaction in families: An experimental study of family processes and schizophrenia.* New York: John Wiley & Sons.

Quoted: Riskin, M., & Faunce, E. (1972). An evaluative review of family interaction research. *Family Process, 11,* 365–455.

withdrawal of positive reinforcement: A behavioral therapy technique in which a pleasant event is removed, denied, or terminated, contingent on the emission of undesirable behavior. Its major effect is to decelerate the behavior it follows.
Example: When a child is disobedient, swimming in the backyard pool is denied for that day.
Source: Patterson, G.P. (1971). *Families: Application of social learning theory to family life.* Champaign, Ill.: Research Press.

Y

yielding: A definite acceptance of an attitude or desired behavioral change, a noncommittal response, or an inability to respond.
Source: Goldstein, M., Judd, L., Rodnick, E., Alkire, A., & Gould, E. (1968). A method for studying social influence and coping patterns within families of disturbed adolescents. *Journal of Nervous and Mental Disease, 147,* 233–251.

yo-yo syndrome: A relationship in which a child is pulled toward the parents when they need the child and is pushed away or ignored when the child's own needs come to the fore. Outright parental rejection is never expressed, however; the child is simply teased with love that is never quite delivered or sustained.
Source: Framo, J. (1965). Rationale and techniques of intensive family therapy. In I. Boszormenyi-Nagy & J. Framo (Eds.), *Intensive family therapy: Theoretical and practical aspects* (pp. 143–212). New York: Harper & Row.

Z

zero-sum game: In marital conflicts, both the "winner" and the "loser" of any game are losers because the conflict issues are seldom resolved and the relationship becomes less unified and more individuated. The "win-lose trap" seeks gain at the other's expense. When the loser does not accept defeat (commonplace in marital disagreements), the victory is only an illusion, safe for a time, but sure to be overthrown. This concept has been expressed as a ''one-winner'' as opposed to a ''two-winner'' tactic. The former is based on the incorrect assumption that marriage is a zero-sum game; the latter is based on the more accurate assumption that marriage is the essential non-zero-sum game. The issue must be resolved ''equitably'' rather than intending to ''win the battle.''

Example: The couple argued about the wife cooking dinner for the husband's friend. Although she was going to have to work a full day, she complied under pressure to prepare dinner at home, as opposed to her preference to dine out. Following that dinner, she politely excused herself, explaining to her guest that she was tired from a long day at the office; she kindly asked her husband to clean up the dishes. The couple may have brought in Chinese food in order to entertain at home (husband's preference or win) and avoid all cooking and cleaning (wife's preference or win).

Source: Patterson, G.P. (1971). *Families: Application of social learning theory to family life.* Champaign, Ill.: Research Press.

Professional Organizations and Publications

Mental health professionals have access to professional associations, such as the American Psychological Association, the American Psychiatric Association, the National Association of Social Workers, the American Association for Counseling and Development, and the Division of Psychiatric Mental Health Nursing Practice of the American Nurses Association.

These associations require certain educational and training backgrounds, and a level of current professional functioning. The associations are involved in the credentialing process, including accreditation and designation of educational programs and, in some cases, nonstatutory certification of individuals. In addition, the associations are usually active in promoting statutory certification and licensure. The associations are involved in setting standards for professional behavior, particularly ethical behavior, and all these associations have codes of ethics. Continued membership in each association requires a commitment to its code. Ethical violations are dealt with by select committees, which generally try to educate the professional and remedy the situation, rather than punish the individual.

Marital and family therapists can turn, in addition, to several specialized professional associations. The largest by membership and reputation is the American Association of Marriage and Family Therapy (AAMFT).

Founded in 1942 as the American Association of Marriage Counselors, and for many years representing the specific discipline of marriage counseling, this organization has recently become recognized as the primary affiliation for family therapists. An interdisciplinary group of leaders established the organization, including Dr. Robert Latou Dickinson, one of America's most distinguished gynecologists; Dr. Ernest R. Groves, a pioneer in family life education; psychiatrist Robert Laidlaw; Dr. Emily Mudd, a social worker and for many years director of the Marriage Council of Philadelphia; and Lester Dearborn, long-time counselor in Boston. Later, the group was joined by Dr. Alfred Kinsey, whose research was strongly supported and greatly assisted by a number of AAMFT members.

AAMFT has authority to accredit graduate programs and training centers, and has been active in pursuing state certification and licensure for marriage and family therapists. In addition, it offers credentials of its own for those who meet certain qualifications of a clinical member, fellow, and approved supervisor.

The AAMFT recently has published a draft version of its ethical code (AAMFT, 1982), which includes eight principles: responsibility to clients, competence, integrity, confidentiality, professional responsibility, professional development, research responsibility, and social responsibility. AAMFT publishes the *Journal of Marital and Family Therapy*, whose current editor is Dr. Alan S. Gurman and whose former editor was Dr. Florence W. Kaslow. Its association newsletter, the *Family Therapy News*, is edited by Dr.

Sources: Levant, R.F. (1984). *Family therapy: A comprehensive overview.* Englewood Cliffs, N.J.: Prentice-Hall; Nichols, M. (1984). *Family therapy concepts and methods.* New York: Gardner; Williamson, D.S. (1982). AAMFT & AFTA epilogue, *Family Therapy News, 13*(3), 2.

William J. Hiebert. Association information is available at its headquarters located at: 1717 K Street, N.W., Suite 407, Washington, D.C. 20006. Sidney Johnson is the executive director.

For psychologists who are also marriage and family therapists, there is the Academy of Family Psychology, formerly the Academy of Psychologists in Marital, Sex, & Family Therapy issues. Founded in 1958, the organization recognizes that training in professional psychology does not always provide adequate preparation in marital and family therapy. The organization sets professional standards and conducts continuing education programs. The Academy of Family Psychology is soon to become the Division of Family Psychology in the American Psychological Association. The Association newsletter, *The Relationship,* is edited by Dr. Robert Wellman, and it is professionally associated with the interdisciplinary *American Journal of Family Therapy,* published by Brunner/Mazel. Dr. Daniel L. Araoz was the founder of the *Journal* in 1973, originally called the *Journal of Family Counseling,* and Dr. S. Richard Sauber has served as editor of the *Journal* since 1976. Association information may be obtained by writing to Dr. Anthony J. Vilhotti, executive director, at 246 Virginia Avenue, Fort Lee, New Jersey 07024.

Since 1980, the Academy has sponsored the American Board of Family Psychology (ABFamP). ABFamP is a diplomate board designed to assess and recognize qualified psychologists with advanced competence in the specialized areas of psychotherapy primarily involving marital and family therapy. Although the Board is autonomous, it continues its affiliation with the Academy. The Board was founded under the leadership of Dr. Araoz, who served as its first president. Diplomates are awarded in marital and family therapy and, marital and sex therapy. The Board publishes a newsletter entitled *The Family Psychologist.* Information regarding the Board may be obtained from Dr. Don-David Lusterman, executive director, 856 McKinley Street, Baldwin, New York 11510.

Another important organization is the American Family Therapy Association (AFTA). Founded in 1978 and representing the interests of systemic family therapists as distinct from psychodynamic marriage counselors, AFTA has been viewed by some as a rival organization to AAMFT. A joint liaison committee was established between the two organizations, which met for a year from spring 1981. Through the process, the respective roles of the two organizations was clarified, with AAMFT retaining credentialing responsibilities. AFTA was founded under the leadership of

Dr. Murray Bowen, following a discussion of the Editorial Board of *Family Process* (edited by Dr. Donald Bloch) in 1977. Its first officers were Dr. Murray Bowen, president; Dr. Gerald Berenson, executive vice president; Dr. John Spiegel, vice president; Dr. James Framo, secretary; and Dr. Geraldine Spark, treasurer.

Association objectives include:

1. Advancing family therapy as a science, which regards the entire family as a unit of study;
2. Promoting research and professional education in family therapy and allied fields;
3. Making information about family therapy available to practitioners in other fields of knowledge and to the public;
4. Fostering cooperation among those concerned with medical, psychological, social, legal, and other aspects of the family and those involved in the science and practice of family therapy.

Members of AFTA often are identified as family therapy teachers and researchers, as well as practitioners. Requirements for membership include serving as a teacher of family therapy for at least five years and making important contributions to the field. Its headquarters are located at 2550 M Street, N.W., Suite 275, Washington, D.C. 20037. The executive director is Susan Watson and the *AFTA Newsletter* is edited by Dr. Peter Kinney.

The National Council on Family Relations (NCFR) is concerned with a wide variety of issues affecting the family, from basic research and theory to political action. The Council has sections on family therapy, and on education and enrichment. NCFR sponsors several of the primary journals in the field of family studies, including the *Journal of Marriage and the Family,* the *Journal of Family Issues, Family Relations* and the *Journal of Family History.* Its headquarters are located at 1219 University Avenue, S.E., Minneapolis, Minnesota 55414.

The American Association of Sex Educators, Counselors, and Therapists (AASECT) was founded in 1967 and provides nonstatutory certification for sex educators, counselors, and therapists. AASECT is recognized as the only national interdisciplinary interest group whose charter and central purpose are training, education, and research in sex education and therapy. Standards of training and competency for certification were established in 1972 for sex educators, in 1973 for sex therapists, and in 1977 for sex counselors. AASECT offers publications, tapes, and educational materials for interested professionals. The

Journal of Sex Education and Therapy is the official publication of AASECT. The Association also maintains a national registry of certified health service providers in specialties such as sex education, sex counseling, and sex therapy. Its central office is located at 11 Dupont Circle,N.W., Suite 220, Washington, D.C. 20036.

There are still other family oriented, interdisciplinary organizations offering a variety of opportunities for professionals to become involved with research, education, and therapy. These groups include:

American Orthopsychiatric Association
1775 Broadway
New York, New York 10019

Washington Coalition of Family Organizations
Cardinal Station
Washington, D.C. 20064

Academy of Family Mediators
P.O. Box 246
Claremont, California 91711

National Academy of Counselors and Family
Therapists
(formerly the National Alliance for Family Life, Inc.)

5885 Warner Avenue
Huntington Beach, California 92649

National Family Life Education Network
1700 Mission Street, Suite 203
P.O. Box 8506
Santa Cruz, California 95061–8506

Family Services Association of America
44 E. 23rd Street
New York, New York 10010

Family Resource Coalition
230 N. Michigan Avenue, Suite 1625
Chicago, Illinois 60601

Association of Sexologists
1523 Franklin Street
San Francisco, California 94109

Sex Information and Education Council of the
United States
84 Fifth Avenue
New York, New York 10011

The Society for the Scientific Study of Sex
P.O. Box 29795
Philadelphia, Pennsylvania 19117

About the Authors

S. RICHARD SAUBER, Ph.D., is Associate Professor of Clinical Psychology in the Department of Psychiatry at Columbia University. He has served as Editor-in-Chief of the *American Journal of Family Therapy* for the past eight years, as well as serving on numerous other editorial boards. Dr. Sauber has published many books. His most recent is *The Human Services Delivery System*, published by Columbia University Press in 1983.

LUCIANO L'ABATE, Ph.D., is Professor of Psychology and Director of the Family Study Center at the Georgia State University in Atlanta. He serves on numerous family therapy editorial boards, and has written many books in the family therapy field. His most recent work is *Family Psychology: Theory, Therapy and Training*, published by University Press of America in 1983.

GERALD R. WEEKS, Ph.D., is Director of Training with the Marriage Council of Philadelphia and the Division of Family Study in the Department of Psychiatry at the University of Pennsylvania School of Medicine. He is the senior author of *Paradoxical Psychotherapy: Theory and Practice with Individuals, Couples, and Families*, published by Brunner/Mazel in 1982. He is also the editor of *Promoting Change through Paradox Therapy*, published by Dow Jones-Irwin in 1984.